绪论 —— 桥文化33则，介绍有关桥梁事宜，包括一些国外桥梁和3位世界杰出的桥梁专家，是本书一个楔子，用以引导出本书而开拓读者视野。因编者病甚，只英译了标题。

我国桥梁建设和其他建设一样，突飞猛进，发展异常迅速。近些年来，编者也参与了若干座大桥撰写英文向国外报导，以宣传我国建设成就，有的被外国朋友译成其他文字发表。2009年4月，对南京长江四桥建设的英文报导，被译成其他文字发表。在这些文章中编者署名均在最后，这是希望将中青年同志推向国际交流第一线。

在编者编写本书时，得到学校领导和出版社的支持，并作为"国庆60周年献礼"著作，编者深感荣幸。

在书中引用了我国专家、院士在国际有关学报上发表的英文论文。由于全书文字的统一，不得不有所改动和删节，敬请鉴谅。对他们赠我工程照片为本书增光，编者谨表示衷心感谢。

对赠我照片和资料的高级工程师和专家（包括台湾朋友和旅美华人朋友）表示深深的谢意。很多朋友寄赠在不同角度、时间（包括施工）拍摄的系列照片，它们确实美不胜收，不忍舍弃，尽多引用，以供有关科技工作者参考。

本书多取材于《中国桥梁》（Bridges in China），并对编排亦多参照，对该书的作者们表示崇高的敬意和衷心的感谢。

最后还要提到的是，承东南大学结构试验中心邰扣霞工程师几乎为打印全稿，并为发信，发电（电话、邮件）请求支援照片和查找资料，辛苦备尝，编者不胜感谢。

在选择介绍桥梁时，由于知识的局限，主要根据较熟悉的和资料易于获得者，也考虑桥的类型。挂一漏万，敬希读者和专家为指出并惠赠资料和彩色照片，再版时当补入，谢谢！

编者英文水平低下，虽作了最大努力，英译中定多错舛（包括中、英文不一致），敬希指出而必更正。

编者2006年底即患前列腺癌，2007年初住院100天治疗，2009年3月，正值整理图片关键时刻，又因药物引起肝功能指标过高而不得不住院20天，心急如焚，但仍完成了前言中文，因不敢片刻忘记献礼大事。

编者平时每天上下午强忍痛楚，各工作1.5~2小时。临撰前言时，深感惴惴，虑贻"自不量力"之讥。歉甚。

86老人、癌症患者丁大钧在重病中
于东南大学2009年4月10日

（签名系病前多年所留书）

FORWARD

Introduction — Bridge Culture includes 33 sections for introducing the things relative to bridges, involving some bridges in foreign countries and 3 outstanding bridge experts in the world, is a prologue to lead out this book and to widen the vision field of readers. Owing to serious illness, only the topics of section are translated into English.

The bridge construction is the same as the other construction, advances by leaps and bounds and develops extremely rapidly. In recent years, the Editor takes part in composing English articles to report in foreign countries for publicizing the construction achievements in this country, some have been translated into the other languages to be published, such as, in 2009, the English article on the 4th Nanjing Bridges over Yangtze River has been translated into the other language to be published. In these articles, the signature of the Editor is always placed at the end, he hopes to push our young and middle-aged persons to the 1st line of international exchange.

As the Editor composes this book, he has obtained the supports from the relative leaders at Southeast University and from SE Press, and this book has been selected as one Greeting Writing for "60 Anniversary of the Founding of the People's Republic of China", the Editor treasures deeply this honour.

In this book, the Editor has cited the English articles of experts and academicians published in relative international journals, because the characters used the entire book should be united, the Editor have to change, do hope to excuse him. For the engineering photos given by friends to the Editor to add luster to this book, he expresses his heartfelt gratitude to them.

To the senior Engrs. and experts (including the friend in Taiwan and the Chinese person residing in USA) who gave the Editor photos and materials he expresses deep thanks. Many friends post a series of photos taken at different angle and time (including construction), certainly, they are so beautiful that one simply can not take them all in. The Editor cites in this book as possible in order to be referred by the relative technical workers.

In this book, many materials are drawn from "Bridges in China", the composing and printing are also referred to that book, to the Editors of "Bridge book", the Editor offers his highest consideration.

Finally, the Editor thanks Ms. Tai Kouxia, the Engr. of Structural Test Center, she typewrites almost the entire draft of this book, and sends letters, tel. and e-mails to ask support for photos and find materials for this book, she sustains much toil, the Editor should say many thanks to her.

As selecting bridges to be introduced, because of the limitation of knowledge, the Editor considers those familiar, the materials easy to be obtained, also considers the bridge types, the list is far from being complete, do hope the readers to point out and to grant the Editor material and coloured photos, the new bridge must be added. Thanks.

The English level of the Editor is very low, though he makes greatest efforts, the mistakes(including that Chinese & English are not consistent) must be many yet, please point out, those must be corrected.

The Editor has suffered prostate cancer since the end of 2006. At the beginning of 2007, he was in hospital for 100 days to cure. In the March of 2009, the index liver function is too high due to medicines, the Editor has to be in hospitalized for 20 days, during the key time for arranging photos, the Editor is burned with impatience, he dare not forget the important thing of offering gift for a moment, so finishes the Chinese Forward in hospital.

At before noon and afternoon, the Editor makes an effort to tolerate pain to compose this book for 1.5~2 hours. During composing the forward, the Editor fells deeply being anxious and fearful, fears to have the ridicule for overestimate his ability (to compose this book), please excuse him.

86-year aged old man, cancer sufferer Ding Dajun in
serious sickness, at Southeast University, April 10, 2009

Ding Dajun

(written before many years)

目录

CONTENTS

早见于记载的为晋太康三年（282年）建造的洛阳七里涧旅人桥（石拱桥）。现保存完好的我国最早石砌拱桥为河北赵县安济桥，又名赵州桥②（图1-1）大约在隋开皇十一年至开皇十九年（591—599年）由李春建造，净跨37.02m，矢高7.23m，宽约10m。拱上
复锐其前，以分水势，遂开今日"分水金刚墙"（桥墩迎水面带尖端）之先例。后来国内外不少桥墩采用这种先进构造。现存福建泉州石桥安平桥（图1-2）始建于南宋绍兴八年（1138年），原有361个桥墩，总长2 500m，为中国古长桥记录。后由泥砂淤积，
79—1368年）、明（1368—1644年）41座和清（1644—1911年）550座。现存最早的石拱桥光相桥始建于东晋年间（317—419年），传王羲之于桥头题扇而又称题扇桥，桥头立存石碑，编者曾为该桥及石碑拍照；又唐昭宗乾宁年间（894—897）的霸王桥
但在桥上而不是在桥洞内，未构成立交条件。编者已撰文"绍兴八字桥与立交桥"，刊于《中国勘察设计》（月刊），2004（3），pp.26-27，予以澄清。在八字桥南的广陵桥（图2-2），为七折石拱桥，桥南北各设16级和20级石台阶，分别长25.30m和26.30
00m、147.00m和154.00m，在此短短437.00m内就有4座宋桥，可见此处局部古桥分布密度之大[2]。经罗关洲同志考证、量测和分析对比，表明新昌县明迎仙桥（图2-3）（l=14.70m，f=7.10m，明成化年间（1465—1486年）编纂的绍兴县志中已纪录了此桥
bitation of Bridges Completed on Yangtze River and Its Branches 至今，在长江及其支流上已建成了40多座大桥，其丰富的结构和造型，构成了一幅波澜壮阔的桥梁展览图，这其中有很多座都是世界纪录。例如：荆州大桥中简支的预应力混凝土梁桥，南京长江
非云见2，海上游龙逐浪寻3。电讯频传来画片，友朋惠赠报长文4。写成惊感难全述，伟业宏图世未闻。4.九类桥世界纪录前若干位Some Places in the Front of Worldwide Records in 9 Kinds of Bridges 在表4-1～表4-9中列出9类桥世界纪录前若干位，供
因为国外一直认为1961年国际石拱桥纪录为德国于1903—1904年建成的Syratal Plauen石拱桥（图5-2）"tal"在德文中为山谷、峡谷、河谷，"Plauen"为萨克森的小镇。该桥基本为实腹式的，桥冠截面厚1.5m，拱座厚3.4m，系德国朋友Dr. -Ing Klaus St
作者（等）照相和彩色工程照片，1999、2000年承为印4文。仍由原出版社承印。6. 钢管混凝土拱桥Arch Bridges Constructed of Concrete-Filled Steel Tube 钢管混凝土拱桥是用钢管混凝土构成的。当跨度不大时可为单管，如我国江苏无锡新安北桥、泰州
tube(CFST),在俄文中称 с т а л е т р у б о б е т о н，在德文中称stahlrohrbeton, 在法文中称tube replies en beton，在日文中称钢管コンクリート，钢管混凝土拱桥在国际采用亦较普遍，但跨度都不太大，印度不采用钢管混凝土建桥和建造高层建筑，但E
管受力则要小得多。8. 独塔无背索斜拉桥Single-Pylon Cable-Stayed Bridges without Backstays 世界第一座独塔无背索的斜拉桥Marian（图8-1）[22]，坐落于捷克首都布拉格之北大约100km处乌斯季（ú st í ），跨越易北河(Elbe River)上游拉贝河①。Marian
拉瓦（Santiago Calatrava）设计，位于西班牙塞维利亚（Sevilla）的阿拉米罗桥（图8-2）为无背索独塔斜拉桥[23]，两市分别位于西班牙之东北和西南。我国2000年在哈尔滨太阳岛设计建造了一座斜独塔无背索斜拉桥（图8-3），跨度为140m＋60m[24]，200
的。但我国沿海地区许多城市为软土地基，采用这种有推力的斜靠式拱桥，从经济上和技术上都不是合适的。我国首座大跨度斜靠式拱桥为上海昆山市玉峰大桥，总体布置图如图9-1所示。主桥跨径110m，主拱圈矢跨比为1/5.5，斜拱在拱圈平面内的矢跨比为1/5.4
受拱的推力，而在房屋建设中，还可以将大厅拱屋盖推力传至两侧屋的横向（钢或钢筋混凝土）刚架或横墙。今因玉峰桥需建造曲线形（平面内）人行观景台，即必需建造斜靠拱桥，则承受主桥拱推力的拉杆只需按斜拱建造前的荷载设计，在斜靠桥建造后的主桥推
紧后，陆续建造了多座双曲石拱三叉和四叉桥，在表11-1中示出5座四叉桥，最大跨度达20m，该表系公司前董事长苏松源教授赐文，附此致谢。从1969—1985年在无锡县共建造了三叉双曲拱桥7座，四叉（又称十字）双曲拱桥多座，一桥跨四岸。在表10-1中列
cky分段预制斜拉桥（图11-1）方案，曲线跨度长约400m，中心角45°[5]。为避免设置若干个须承受很大水平地震作用的桥墩（桥墩高约106m），如果设计成直线桥，则两端40°陡壁边坡将须开凿接引隧道，斜拉的弧形桥使接引隧道开凿量减至最少，而利用陡壁
教授(编者曾邀他来东南大学访问过)联系访问，但未约好时间，届时他因遇到宗教节日而未能实现，故编者只在布市住了两夜即飞经芬兰回国。林老赐赠的Bulletin[26]中，示出1958年他协同华盛顿参议员、美国参议院商务委员会主席Warren Maynuson公开提出建
已通过连接阿拉斯加和西伯利亚海洋来联系世界各大洲，将成为沟通东西方政治文化的纽带[27]。这一设计虽未实现，但这种富于改革的精神值得介绍学习。林老在1991年在IABSE学报SEI创刊号发表对直布罗陀海峡桥方案之一，他采用的航道最短，但水深很大，
学报（Journal, Concrete Materials以及CI）发表State-of-the-Arts of Application and Research, Concrete (No.12, 1991, pp56-60) 林老看到很高兴，当即航空寄来一本，编者于12月22日即收到，样本则于次年4月才收到（余后来在CI发表多篇文章，关于
1图5-138示出编者在东京拍摄的一梁桥，支柱则偏于一侧，整个梁则支于从柱挑出的悬臂上，柱及其基础的设计将很不经济，但在交通拥挤之东京已是何等不易。现在国内外在市区道路和公路线上，往往采取单柱支承的，以争取桥下的交通空间。图12-1示1991
即获回复，获益匪浅，颇为感念。2000年2月1日惊接莱氏计闻，急复信致唁并作七律诗致哀悼，见拙诗集《惜分阴》pp. 11-13，谨录于此，以志纪念，并作短序于前。惊闻世界著名预应力混凝土和桥梁权威学者、德国Fritz Leonhardt 教授噩耗（公生于1909年，
切余撰《混凝土结构发展》一书（中国建筑工业出版社约稿）需述及据我国报刊和专著上所载1978年建成跨度为270m的阿根廷－巴拉圭界河上预应力混凝土刚构桥，如果属实，应为当时该类桥的世界纪录。但交通部设计院老友史尔毅教授级高工见告，在《大英百科
为弟子，指出上两句意为"后继有人"。公复函大为赞赏。接计闻急致唁函，并告以将作诗悼念。觉绝句不足以记述交往经历，决定作律诗，疾构思第二日成初稿，几经更易，定稿如下，诗曰：忘年交过廿年期，互赠书文总及时。彩照传神真馨铄，嘉言惠贶足深思。
格桥，芜湖长江大桥系公铁两用桥，即属于矮塔斜拉桥，这是因为桥头现有列车编车场，因此桥位已定，而附近有一机场，故采用矮塔斜拉桥。我国曾将这种斜拉桥又称为部分斜拉桥(partially cable-stayed bridge)，其含义为：在结构性能上，斜拉索仅仅分担部分
当中支点梁高相同时，部分斜拉桥的跨度可较连续梁大1倍以上；②对大跨度梁而言，相同跨度的部分斜拉梁较连续梁经济。与斜拉桥相比有如下优点：①塔高较矮，塔身结构简单，施工方便；②斜拉索应力变化幅度小，可采用较高的应力，一般情况下斜拉索
作栏杆，桥面铺有纵横两层木板。铁链由扁环扣联而成，扁环内径3cm，外径9cm，长17~20cm，每根铁链平均890个扁环。铁链在两端固定的方法是在石砌的桥台内，开有宽2m、长5m、深6m的落井4个，近井底部埋有生铁铸的直径20cm铁地龙桩（水平向），
建成的这种桥（1992年编者访问瑞士洛桑工业大学时，Klinger博士为编者放映了30多张该桥的幻灯片，但无工程照片），跨径达216.4m，悬垂达14.75m（承受度带传送机）。从上可见应力板带桥亦与中国竹索桥和铁链桥构造相似，虽亦属柔性（索）桥，但由
分别为1.41 m3、61.1kg和141.2kg，可见淘金桥设计较为经济。但是这种桥的锚固似没有美国桥锚固在邻跨中的自然可靠（岩石可能风化）。15. 世界最高混凝土桥墩The Highest Concrete Pier in the World 世界最高混凝土也是最高桥墩，当属法国Millau大桥
3.0m的紧急车道。4.45m宽中间保留带为锚固拱排的、中心间距为12.5m的斜拉索，而在桥面两侧设有保护的半透风的屏蔽。桥在平面内微曲，曲率半径为20 000m。Millau桥采用推进法（launch）施工，第一次钢桥面推进是在2003年2月进行的，总共需进行18次
气缸，总的，在推进最后阶段，从南坡有5280t推力，而从北坡则有2 400t推力。该桥两边推进在2004年5月合龙，由于这一背景，在下一月由钢应用技术办公室（Office Technique pour L' Utilisation）支持在Millau镇举行了一次为期3天的钢桥国际会议，参加者
）其形式为建筑师和工程师紧密合作所作出的很好的设计。4块板具有固定的尺寸，另4块每段则略有变化，包括其方向。Millau 桥为单索面斜拉桥，主梁为钢箱梁，截面高度4.20m，桥面宽27.75m，每向有两条各宽3.5m的车道，其一为快车道，一为慢车道。
0m，超过提早4个月于2005年8月建成的希腊桥（2 252m），成为世界当时最长的斜拉桥。在编写Millau桥时，承英国朋友、Bd&e主编Ms. Helena Russell及时用电子邮件寄来参考文献，在此表示衷心的感谢。16. 世界最长的桥The Longest Bridge in the World
）成型，通过箱内的纵向体外索、千罐、就位、后张拼装。高架桥全长都建筑在原有行车速度为80km/h的第34号高速公路上空，桥下净空高14m，上部高架桥施工，不得影响下部道路的正常行驶。规定工期很紧，仅为3.5年，于2000年1月建成。该桥采用离心混凝
预加应力分两次完成，每次施加50%。梁跨最大为44.4m，一般为42m。D2、D3（图16-4）均为单室箱形截面，分别用于2车道和3车道匝道桥面，以及交叉平台和收费平台桥面。在一些区段，即在收费平台处和匝道交汇处（merging area）主线路需加宽，这
钢筋混凝土地面。建场投资，不包括地价、设备、运输车辆大约为2 300万美元。预制厂设施包括木工、机械、焊接、后张管道、钢筋加工、预应力筋加工等车间和搅拌站，以及试验室、办公、生活等设施。从平整场地到开始构件生产大约用了9个月时间。预制厂执
Pa，然后对箱梁块体顶板施加50%的横向预力，以便拆除模板，移动到匹配浇筑的位置。这种箱形梁的截面比较轻巧单薄，要做到尺寸准确，可以进行纵向匹配拼装，对混凝土的配比、养护、运输和预加应力等各个阶段，都需要高技术与严格控制。本工程是设计
之比应在0.2左右，照上可以达到这一要求。梁高自边墩的2m到主塔墩的5m，再由主塔墩的5m曲线变化到海河中部的2m。桥塔采用斜塔形式，立面上有两高两矮四座桥塔，两座高塔（主塔）为桥的主要承重结构，两座矮塔（辅塔）的设置起到减小桥梁的支承跨度
公路桥かつしかハープ（Katsushika Harp Bridge），为一座S形曲线独柱双塔不对称的斜拉桥（图18-1），支承间距为40.5m＋134m＋220m＋60.5m。塔高不同，高塔墩P37为钢筋混凝土的，高49.0m，直径24.0m，低塔墩为41.0m，钢管的，高31.0m共89根（
la的Barqueta拱桥（图18-4），它常被称为弦弓型桥（string-bow-typed bridge）[31]。中承式拱桥拱肋也有外倾的，其造型独特，折射出桥梁建筑风格的时代性，如法国某市的这种桥具有一定的代表性。这种桥一般不设风撑，因这将破坏其造型美，且风撑长，
7°。该桥北塔墩采用3个特大吨位的盆式球型钢支座，其中间一个承重量达13 000t。荷兰鹿特丹Erasmus独塔斜拉桥为带有倾向短跨的折线形[15]。（2）四斜柱桥塔希腊Rion-Antirion（两城市）桥（图18-7）位于帕特雷市，横跨隔断希腊大陆与其最大的伯罗
）（Eine Brü cke mit Druckspannbewehrü ng-Konstruktion）[36]这种桥是编者的德国朋友Prof. Dr. Hans Reiffenstuhl于20世纪80年代为奥地利ALM桥设计建造的，该桥系单箱截面，跨中截面高度为2.5m=1/30.4，箱形竖壁宽度为6.0m；支承处截面高度为
改变了截面的应力分布，最后的应力图形将如图19-3(b)所示。这将提高梁的抗裂荷载和减小跨中挠度，因而截面高度可减小。双预应力桥与同跨径桥相比，混凝土用量虽可略有节省，但用钢量明显增多，总造价约提高47%左右，其最大优越性是可使建筑高度减小，
必要时可调整预应力或撤换预应力筋。我国在桥梁中第一次采用体外预应力的是汕头海湾预应力混凝土悬索桥，而在房建中是在石家庄东方购物中心12层裙楼8层大厅18m大梁中第一次采用体外预应力筋。1984年秋编者参加在匈牙利首都布达佩斯（Budapest）
梁桥，跨度为17m和15m。预弯梁制作分为3个阶值：首先使用将工字钢制成（无应力状态）向上弯的梁；然后加载（1/4点集载）后使平直，在工字钢下翼缘浇混凝土，待其达到设计强度后卸载，钢梁的回弹使混凝土获得预压应力，梁向上拱，但拱度较工字钢原拱
×4.0m，下端为1.5m×1.5m，均为栓焊带肋的箱形结构。该桥于1982年建成[39]。邯长线浊漳河桥，是我国第一座预应力混凝土斜腿刚构铁路桥（图22-3），主跨82m。梁体和腿部均为单室箱形截面。该桥于1981年9月建成[39]。23. 刚架拱桥Rigid-Framed A
工放大而成），在此斜拉索用桁架上弦代替，下承式斜拉桥桁架T-构桥。福州西郊洪塘桥即是这种构造的桥，跨度分布为：16m+27m+4×30m+60m+ 120m+60m+31×40m+8×25m，主跨为：60m+120m+60m，由4片预应力混凝土斜拉式桁架T-构组成，其作
缝，每一排架顶部只有一个支承代替两个，跨度连续性提供材料的较有效利用。丁汉山教授设计了我国第一座福建省福州市岩头口不互通整体闭合环形结构（图25-1），于1987年建成，该桥于1991年6月获福建省科技进步奖。混凝土环形桥的内直径为40m，外直径
的挠度。为了调整拱跨不向下位移，在II号拱拱冠截面断开处，设置混凝土块，在两三年后移去，代之以液压千斤顶，用以调整拱的中心线，以消除在一段时间后的变形。假定对中心线并不产生显著变化，则不至影响交通安全。另一方面，因为结合在拱内的设备（管线
人行桥，故没有这种必要，是不为也，非不能也。编者作为当时南京土建学会理事长，曾代表学会邀请已故中国科学院学部委员、同济大学校长李国豪前辈来南京在东南大学土木学院讲课，他非常欣赏瑞士Gunter桥（图27-1），并放映幻灯片。李老在国际上曾获得
时，知Gunter桥距洛桑约300km，较远，故不便劳动主人送去参观，但该桥梁博士Klinger曾为编者放映建成后板带的幻灯片，其上未经描绘的多道裂缝已清晰可见。1988年，经过修葺后，桥板带面整洁光鲜，在日光下熠熠生辉，更为大桥增加了魅力（图27-2）
原因，建成一边跨为斜拉的，如我国香港青马大桥和西堠门大桥，后者主跨为1 650m，位居世界第二，但非双塔三跨。在建的二者，一为南京长江四桥，另一为韩国Gwangyang桥，跨度357.5m+1545m+357.5m，计划2012年建成。编者于2008年元月7日作诗：
100年的混凝土。30. 大桥基础Foundation of Bridges 大直径管柱基础是介于桩基和沉井基础之间的结构形式，它既有沉井刚度大的特点，又有可预制管节在工地直接拼装成桩的方便，用振动打桩机并在管柱内射水吸泥下沉，使能加快速度和便于在管柱内吸出土
sure）工艺提高桩承载力的方法已有40多年历史。端压桩自1961年在修建委内瑞拉Maracaibo斜拉桥（1962年建成，5个主跨都为235cm，两端跨为160m，一般认为该桥是第一座现代化混凝土斜拉桥）时，对该桥首次采用压力灌浆桩。我国自1983年北京市建筑
ge 桥梁事故原因有多种，但多由质量原因引起，这可能是：①因偷工减料而造成"豆腐渣工程"；②因赶工引起；③使用过程中管理监控不严等原因引起；④设计问题；⑤其他。桥梁事故不仅造成很大的损失，也导致人员伤亡。①典型的"豆腐渣"工程——我国重庆
建成后拱脚常年浸泡水中，因裂缝原因，可能还因混凝土保护层不密实而导致钢筋锈蚀，于2004年某月早晨突然倒塌。④美国华盛顿州塔科马峡谷桥。该桥建于1940年，主跨长853m，加劲钢板梁的高跨比小至1：79。通车后不久表明增大柔度是"走得太远了"，
最后的振荡中，风速为56~67km/h，并不是最大的，而远低于桥设计抵抗的最大风速，但是当进行风作用下的结构分析时，仅考虑静压力时该桥完全是安全的。没有进行有关在板梁尖角处形成的脉冲风涡流的动力研究，因而所选择具有极大柔度的设计，后来证明它
计划于2008年竣工，但于2007年9月26日上午，一座距离地面约30m的脚手架突然倒塌，砸向刚浇注的混凝土桥段上，导致三段桥面连锁倒塌，至少149人伤亡，其中至少有52人死亡。b．舟山大陆上宁波一镇海连岛工程中有5座大桥，其中第四座为主桥——西堠
Induced Vibrations of Inclinced Cables in Cable-Stayed Bridge 1986年Y. Hikami于Meikonishi桥上首次发现了风雨激振现象（在干燥气候下稳定的拉索，在风和雨共同作用下将产生大振荡）以来，国内外对此进行了大量研究，并进行了试验室模拟试验后建
32-1a），这种阻尼器由智能材料（磁流变体）制造，能够调节阻尼器输入电压来获得可变阻尼，实现半主动控制，可使全桥每个拉索都取得理想的减振效果。试验表明，该阻尼器使拉索体系模态阻尼比增大3~6倍（磁流变体由液体变为固体）。根据实地风雨振的实
等。这些问题可能归答于建设速度过快、设计规范不完善以及经济高速度增长下交通量的增加等原因。在发达国家交通基础设施建设高峰30~50年后出现的养护维修高峰在我国可能提早到来，因此对新建大跨度桥梁设置健康监测系统具有重要意义。桥梁结构健康监
"混凝土结构长期观测国际学术讨论会"（International Symposium on Long-Term Observation）会上编者斯洛伐克朋友T. Javor博士（已于2003年逝世）报告了他撰写的"Long-Term Observation of PC Bridges"，在其中报告了对12座预应力混凝土桥
数据对分析计算影响较大，要求测试精度最高；以一节段梁的架设为一个施工周期，钢梁栓接、湿接头浇筑、桥面板混凝土强度达到设计强度要求后前移桥面吊机、张拉斜拉索作为一个标准控制阶段，进行各种数据测试。① 索力控制与调整拉索索力的大小准确与否，
高程对比表"，分析后可看出主线形是否在控制范围内，梁段间是否平顺。如超过范围，则配合索力分析，通过适当调整索力来调整主梁线形，要求误差不超过1cm。结构环境和条件不同，施工监控的实施方案也各异，需根据具体情况，研究制订切实可行的方案。1.
属寓言，且时间较晚[1]。渭河上、中、下三桥，其中中桥建于秦始皇在统一后（公元前221年—公元前210年），为68跨梁桥，用750根木柱建造67个桥墩，每墩11或12根柱，桥宽达13.8m；另二渭桥建于西汉，唐徐坚《初学记》中有"汉作灞桥，以石为梁"[1]。插
中国土木工程学会代表在桥前举行碑的揭幕仪式，以作纪念。后发现河南小商河桥于隋开皇四年（584年）建造，在漯河市小商河上，桥长约21m，跨度约11m，宽约6.5m，基本完好待修，这样该桥将早于赵州桥7~15年[2]-[4]。唐武后时，李昭德重修利涉桥，叠石
分溉巨豹。2. 绍兴古桥文化Culture of Antique Bridge in Shaoxing 我国古桥分布区域很广，但浙江省绍兴市（辖绍兴县、新昌县、嵊州市、诸暨市和上虞市）最为集中，尤以市区为最。现全绍兴市共存古桥604座，其中宋代（960—1279年）及以前13座，元（1
工字形的，乃至3个八字形的。在八字桥基石上镌有"宝祐丙辰年第二个冬日吉日刻"字样，按宝祐为南宋理宗年号之一，丙辰年应为1256年，即八字桥应建于1256年之前[6]。有谓该桥为立交桥之始，但根据编者实地考察，虽沿其东端南北落坡石台阶上有纤道，但
绩桥之南代两座宋桥，其北向南是东双桥（半圆形石拱桥）和纺车桥（石梁桥）。编者在绍兴的实地考察和学习过程中得到获国家津贴的古桥专家罗关洲经济师的热情帮助与指导，附此，谨表示衷心的感谢，他还应编者要求，为量出四桥间距离顺次为137.00m，1
"绍兴古桥文化"。绍兴古石桥申报中国非物质文化遗产已获批准，名称为《绍兴石桥营造技艺非物质文化遗产》，载于国务院2008（19）号文件，2009年争取申报《世界非物质文化遗产》。编者为此亦与有荣矣。3.长江及其支流上建成桥梁展览Exhabitation of B
用桥*，重庆石板坡连续刚架桥*①[18]，江苏润扬悬索桥[15]，苏通斜拉桥*[19]等。有"*"号的为或曾为世界纪录。编者曾撰长文"我国拱桥与索桥建设新进展"载于参考文献[15]，后又作诗（新韵）一首:多少长虹新纪录，刷新往往仍华人。空中拉索排云见2，海
=100m(1978);⑨山西晋城丹河桥，l=105m(1982);⑩湖南凤凰县乌巢河桥，l=120m(1991)。芬兰朋友J.Virola工程师（他研究世界桥梁史，编有7种世界最长桥的表，随时调整，均见赠），见之对编者来电说，此10座桥，任何一座都是世界纪录[1]，因为国外一直
，至20世纪30年代后期改为Beton und Stahlbetonbau。Beton und Stahlbetonbau由德、奥轮流主编（因奥地利母语亦系德语）。从1999年开始，由维也纳土壤培育学院土木系Dr. - tech-phil. Prof. Konrad Bergmeister主编，增加篇幅达1/3，加印作者（等
月建成通车的湖北三峡下牢溪上承式肋拱桥，采用Φ1000×10~12mm钢管，其中距约为1.5m。跨度在100m以上的拱桥，往往采用3肢或4肢，用缀杆（桁片）焊联组成桁式截面则成混合式结构，见图6-1。钢管混凝土在英文中称concrete-filled steel tube(CFST
计算也基本如此，说明混凝土受力是主要的[21]：表7-1 巫山桥主拱圈一根钢管混凝土内力计算成果表(kN)组合I：恒+汽+人；组合II：恒+汽+人+温度影响。可见将巫山桥和丫髻沙桥列入钢拱桥，的确是不妥当的，因为拱肋中混凝土受力是主要的，而钢管受力则要小
构的一个稳定部分。该桥由于地理位置要求而设计成斜塔无背索桥。文献称世界上最大的斜塔无背索桥为西班牙巴塞罗那（Barcelona）阿拉米罗(Alamillo)独塔斜拉桥，其长跨为200m,编者未查到此桥（有谓未曾建造），但知由西班牙著名建筑师卡拉特拉瓦（San
quely Depending Trustless Arch Bridge 世界第一座斜靠式拱桥是于1987年由西班牙建筑师Santiago Calatrava 成功设计的。该桥直立式主拱为双铰，其水平推力直接传至主梁，形成拱梁组合结构。其斜拱则为无铰拱，水平推力直接传至地基，是有推力的。但我
且管内不灌注混凝土。主拱系梁采用钢箱截面，斜拱系杆采用预应力钢绞线，桥面系采用钢-混凝土叠合梁[25]。一般结构以最直接的传力途径为最好。故拱结构传力途径有直接将荷载传向地基，过去的石拱桥都是这样，即成重力式基础，或用拉（钢）杆承受拱的推力
英国建造第三座这种桥。以上系编者朋友、《英国桥梁设计与工程》（季刊）（Bridge, Design and Engineering, Bd&e）主编Ms. Helene Russell见告，附此致谢。但有时需建造四叉桥。无锡桥梁工程公司于1965年将前苏联双曲砖拱屋盖构造移植于桥梁后，陆续
晋祠系北宋仁宗天圣年间（1023—1032年）建造，和张择端《清明上河图》中虹桥一样，如无工程实例，是难想象出的。11. 因地制宜设计桥梁Design of Bridge with Local Conditions 典型的例子是T.Y. Lin International设计的Ruck-A-Chucky分段预制斜拉
布鲁塞尔西北部约50km处的根特（与布市有铁道联系）学习，在根特大学Mannel预应力实验室获硕士学位①。1992年10月编者曾访问（讲学）欧洲五国（希腊、奥地利、意大利、瑞士、比利时）(在意四校、瑞士两校、余一校)讲课。编者曾与该校一教授(编者曾邀他

图1-3 江东桥
Fig.1-3 Jiangdong Bridge

图1-1 赵州桥
Fig.1-1 Zhaozhou Bridge

图1-2(b)

图1-2 安平桥（承王安生教授惠赠）(a)
Fig.1-2 Anping Bridge (courtesy of Prof. Wang Ansheng) (a)

1. 中国古桥

1. Ancient and Antique[①] Bridges in China

　　我国新石器时代仰韶文化（约在公元前5 000—公元前3 000年）的原始人聚居的重要遗址——西安半坡遗址中，在四周挖掘成宽3~4m、深5~6m的梯形大围沟，以防野兽入侵，人则通过单根树干做成的独木桥通行，这可能是最原始的桥梁。

　　至迟在战国时期（公元前475年—公元前210年），我国已正式开始建桥。战国前期智伯家臣豫让以漆涂身，吞炭使哑，暗伏桥下谋刺赵襄子为智伯复仇（赵、韩、魏灭智伯于公元前453年，赵襄子卒于公元前425年，刺赵事当在这段时间的后期），而《庄子》（庄子生活在约公元前369年—公元前286年）"盗跖"篇中，尾生抱桥柱事乃属寓言，且时间较晚[1]。

　　渭河上、中、下三桥，其中中桥建于秦始皇统一后（公元前221年—公元前210年），为68跨梁桥，用750根木柱建造67个桥墩，每墩11或12根柱，桥宽达13.8m；另二渭桥建于西汉，唐徐坚《初学记》中有"汉作灞桥，以石为梁"[1]。

　　拱桥最早见于记载的为晋太康三年（282年）建造的洛阳七里涧旅人桥（石拱桥）。现保存完好的我国最早石砌拱桥为河北赵县安济桥，又名赵州桥[②]（图1-1），大约在隋开皇十一年至开皇十九年（591—599年）由李春建造，净跨37.02m，矢高7.23m，宽约10m。拱上开洞，既可节约材料，又可减轻洪水期的水压力，保证桥的功能。赵州桥无论在材料使用、结构受力、艺术造型和经济上都达到极高的成就，是世界上最早的敞肩式拱桥（open spandrel arch bridge），它早于欧洲同类桥约1 000年。1991年该桥被美国土木工程师学会(ASCE)选为世界第12个土木工程里程碑，这对弘扬我国民族文化有深远意义。ASCE代表与中国土木工程学会代表在桥前举行碑的揭幕仪式，以作纪念。后发现河南小商河桥于隋开皇四年（584年）建造，在漯河市小商河上，桥长约21m，跨度约11m，宽约6.5m，基本完好待修，这样该桥将早于赵州桥7~15年[2]-[4]。

　　唐武后时，李昭德重修利涉桥，叠石代柱，复锐其前，以分水势，遂开今日"分水金刚墙"（桥墩迎水面带尖端）之先例。后来国内外不少桥墩采用这种先进构造。现存福建泉州石桥安平桥（图1-2）始建于南宋绍兴八年（1138年），原有361个桥墩，总长2 500m，为中国古长桥记录。后由泥沙淤积，淹没桥墩，墩数降至331个，桥长减至2 070m，在这2 070m范围内，桥身下已变成农田。又福建漳州江东桥（图1-3）[1][5]，于南宋嘉熙元年（1237年）由木梁改为石梁，计有15跨，每跨3片石梁，石梁现存5跨，其中最大石梁长23.7m，宽1.7m，高1.9m，重达2 000kN。这样巨大的石梁，在当时没有重型起重设备的条件下，其采运、安装等工作都应是十分艰巨的。

① "Ancient"和"Antique"都表示古代的，但前者的含义为实物已不存在，而后者则仍存在。

② 丁大钧. 墙体改革与可持续发展（附工程彩照30幅）. 北京：机械工业出版社，2005：248

图2-1 绍兴八字桥（承屠剑虹工程师惠赠）
Fig.2-1 Bazi Bridge (courtesy of Engr. Tu Jianhong)

图2-3 明代迎仙桥（承罗关洲专家惠赠）
Fig.2-3 Yingxian Bridge (courtesy of Expert Luo Guanzhou)

2. 绍兴古桥文化

2. Culture of Antique Bridge in Shaoxing

我国古桥分布区域很广，但浙江省绍兴市（辖绍兴县、新昌县、嵊州市、诸暨市和上虞市）最为集中，尤以市区为最。现全绍兴市共存古桥604座，其中宋代（960—1279年）及以前13座，元（1279—1368年）、明（1368—1644年）41座和清（1644—1911年）550座。现存最早的石拱桥光相桥则始建于东晋年间（317—419年），传王羲之于桥头题扇而又称题扇桥，桥头立存石碑，编者曾为该桥及石碑拍照；又唐昭宗乾宁年间（894—897年）的霸王桥，为五折石拱桥。后又陆续发现古石桥，总计绍兴地区共有古石桥约近千座。桥型是多样的，有梁桥、拱桥、折线拱桥，拱桥有半圆拱、浅拱、高拱和椭圆形拱，折线拱有三折、五折和七折，无偶数折，否则拱顶推力很难处理[6]。

绍兴最著名的石桥八字桥（图2-1）为石梁桥，因桥南北落坡石台阶在平面上形成两个相向的"八"字形而得名，此外在平面上有成Y形的、工字形的，乃至3个八字形的。在八字桥基石上镌有"宝祐丙辰年第二个冬日吉日刻"字样，按宝祐为南宋理宗年号之一，丙辰年应为1256年，即八字桥应建于1256年之前[6]。有谓该桥为立交桥之始，但据编者实地考察，虽沿其东端南北落坡石台阶上有纤道，但在桥上而不是在桥洞内，未构成立交条件。编者已撰文"绍兴八字桥与立交桥"，刊于《中国勘察设计》（月刊），2004（3），pp.26-27，予以澄清。

在八字桥南的广陵桥（图2-2），为七折石拱桥，桥南北各设16级和20级石台阶，分别长25.30m和26.30m，桥跨径6.25m。该桥在南宋宁宗嘉泰年间（1201—1204年）之前建造，明清时重修过，于此可见，我国在800年前已知用折线形代替圆形以简化拱桥施工，又一次证明我国古代建设石拱桥技术的先进。在广宁桥桥孔下各设纤道，即将桥基石挑出约70cm，供纤夫拉纤时行走，也可供人行走，是中国，也可能是世界立交桥的雏形，该桥是浙江省文物保护单位[7]。在广陵桥之南还有两座宋桥，自北向南是东双桥（半圆形石拱桥）和纺车桥（石梁桥）。编者在绍兴的实地考察和学习过程中得到获国家津贴的古桥专家罗关洲经济师的热情帮助与指导，附此，谨表示衷心的感谢，他还应编者要求，为量出四桥间距离顺次为137.00m、147.00m和154.00m，在此短短437.00m内就有4座宋桥，可见此处局部古桥分布密度之大[2]。

经罗关洲同志考证、量测和分析对比，表明新昌县明迎仙桥（图2-3）（l=14.70m，f=7.10m，明成化年间（1465—1486年）编纂的绍兴县志中已记录了此桥）和清嵊州玉成桥（l=12.00m，f=4.80m，清道光二十四年——1844年建）轴线均为倒悬链线，即我国是世界上采用倒悬链线拱桥最早的国家，后罗同志又发现了几座倒悬链线拱桥。表2-1示（由罗关洲同志）量测的迎仙桥轴线[8]。

图2-2 绍兴广陵桥（编者自拍摄）
Fig.2-2 Shaoxing Guangning Bridge (taken by the Editor)

表2-1 量测的迎仙桥轴线

距拱座截面距离	拱座0	1	2	3	4	5
截面位置	1.0 000	0.7 785	0.5 951	0.4 507	0.3 349	0.2 428

6	7	8	9	10	11	拱冠12
0.1 700	0.1 133	0.0 701	0.0 384	0.0 163	0.0 041	0.0 000

为了申报世界文化遗产，编者专为著文在国内进行宣传，并撰（英）文在法国国际权威刊物Travaux上发表。

图2-4示编者应罗专家之约书写的"绍兴古桥文化"。

绍兴古石桥申报中国非物质文化遗产已获批准，名称为《绍兴石桥营造技艺非物质文化遗产》，载于国务院2008（19）号文件，2009年争取申报《世界非物质文化遗产》。编者为此亦与有荣矣。

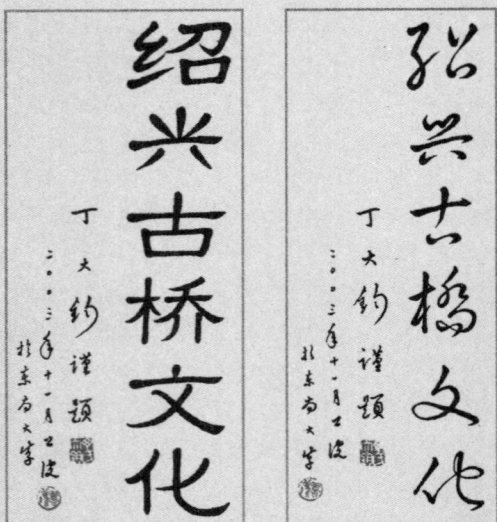

图2-4 编者书法（见《惜分阴续集》p.14）
Fig.2-4 Calligraphy by the Editor (see "the continuation of poem collection Xifenyin" p.14)

3. 长江及其支流上建成桥梁展览

3. Exhabitation of Bridges Completed on Yangtze River and Its Branches

至今, 在长江及其支流上已建成了40多座大桥, 其丰富的结构和造型, 构成了一幅波澜壮阔的桥梁展览图, 这其中有很多座都是世界纪录. 例如: 荆州大桥中简支的预应力混凝土梁桥, 南京长江二桥预应力混凝土连续梁桥[3][9], 简支的武汉钢桁架桥和南京钢桁架桥, 连续的九江钢桁架桥, 上承式四川万县钢筋混凝土拱桥*[3][10]-[12], 中承式重庆巫山钢管混凝土拱桥*[13], 下承式钢管混凝土武汉三桥*[14], 上海卢浦中承式钢箱拱桥*[15], 重庆朝天门中承式钢桁架拱桥*[16], 带斜拉索的湘江四桥*, 三承重架武汉天兴洲公铁两用桥*[17], 三承重架南京大胜关重型公铁两用桥*, 重庆石板坡连续刚架桥*①[18], 江苏润扬悬索桥[15], 苏通斜拉桥*[19]等。有 "*" 号的为或曾为世界纪录。

编者曾撰长文 "我国拱桥与索桥建设新进展" 载于参考文献[15], 后又作诗 (新韵) 一首:

多少长虹新纪录,　刷新往往仍华人。
空中拉索排云见②,　海上游龙逐浪寻③。
电讯频传求画片,　友朋惠赠撰长文④。
写成惊感难全述,　伟业宏图世未闻。

①在此之前湖北黄石连续刚架桥为此类桥之世界纪录。
②指香港昂船洲斜拉桥 (预计2008年建成通车) 和江苏苏通斜拉桥 (预计2009年建成通车, 已提前于2008年5月通车), 跨长分别为1 018m和1 088m, 桥塔分别高290m和304m, 都是世界新记录。
③指杭州湾大桥, 全长36km, 长度为世界跨海桥之最, 平面呈S形, 宛如海上游龙。
④向中外朋友索取工程彩照, 不论识与不识, 均承惠赠, 电子邮件, 传送无虚日, 至 "箱" 装满而发不进, 电告知后删去一些始获通。

4. 九类桥世界纪录前若干位

4. Some Places in the Front of Worldwide Records in 9 Kinds of Bridges

在表4-1~表4-9中列出9类桥世界纪录前若干位，供参考。

表4-1 钢箱/板梁桥（*l*≥240m，截至2005年6月）

No.	桥名	较大跨(m)	桥址	国家	建成年份	备注
1	Costa de Silva瓜纳巴拉桥	300	里约热内卢	巴西	1934	
2	Neckarta1号桥	263	Weitingen	德国	1978	主跨用下边索加劲
3	萨瓦河[①]1号桥	261	贝尔格莱德	前南斯拉夫	1956	
4	Vitona3号桥	260	Espirito Sante	巴西	1989	
5	Zoo桥	259	科隆	德国	1966	
6	萨瓦河2号桥	250	贝尔格莱德	前南斯拉夫	1970	跨度在斜撑底部量测
7	Kaita桥	250	广岛	日本	1991	
8	Nanihaya (Shivinaski)	250	大阪	日本	1994	
9	Auckland海港桥(Widening)	244	Auckland	新西兰	1969	
10	横跨东京湾桥	240	川崎—Kawasaki	日本	1997	

①萨瓦（Save）河为多瑙河支流。

表4-8 独塔斜拉桥（$l_{lar} \geq 303\text{m}$，截至2006年10月）

No.	桥名	较大跨(m)	桥址	国家	建成年份	备注
1	鄂毕河桥	408	西伯利亚, Khanty-Mansiyd	俄罗斯	2000	钢
2	伏尔加河（中游）桥	407	乌里扬诺夫斯克	俄罗斯		钢
3	莱茵河桥	368	杜塞尔多夫	德国	1979	钢
4	高（雄）屏（东）桥	330	台湾高雄	中国	2000	钢（较大跨），PC（较小跨）
5	恰尔纳里Karnali河桥	325	Chisapani Camp	尼泊尔	1993	钢
6	莱茵河桥	319	杜塞尔多夫	德国	1969	钢
7	Dangava河桥	312	里加	拉脱维亚	1981	钢
8	海河桥	310	天津	中国	2002	钢
9	Frierfjorden海峡桥	305	Brevik-Stathelle	挪威	1996	混凝土
10	Dubrovacka河桥	304	Dubrovnik	克罗地亚	2002	钢-混凝土组合
11	多瑙河桥	303	Bratislava	斯洛伐克	1972	钢

表4-9 悬索桥（$l_{lar} \geqslant 124m$，截至2006年10月）

No.	桥名	较大跨(m)	桥址	国家	建成年份	备注
1	明石海峡桥	1 991	神户 — Naruto	日本	1998	
2	西堠门大桥	1 650	舟山群岛	中国	2008	
3	大带东桥	1 624	Eorsor	丹麦	1998	
4	润扬长江大桥	1 490	江苏镇江 — 扬州	中国	2005	
5	亨伯尔桥	1 410	赫尔	英国	1981	
6	江阴长江大桥	1 385	江苏江阴	中国	1999	
7	青马大桥	1 377	香港	中国	1997	公铁两用
8	Hardanger	1 310	Vallavik-Bu	挪威	2010	
9	韦拉扎诺	1 298	纽约	美国	1964	
10	金门大桥	1 280	旧金山	美国	1937	
11	阳逻大桥	1 280	武汉	中国	2007	
12	Hoga Husten	1 210	Tramfors	瑞典	1997	

图5-1 云南长虹桥（承范立础院士惠赠）
*Fig.5-1 Yunnan Changhong Bridge
(courtesy of Academician Fan Lichu)*

图5-2 德国Syra峡谷桥（承德国挚友Klaus Stiglat博士惠赠）
*Fig.5-2 German Syratal Bridge (courtesy of best friend German
Dr. –Ing. Klaus Stiglat)*

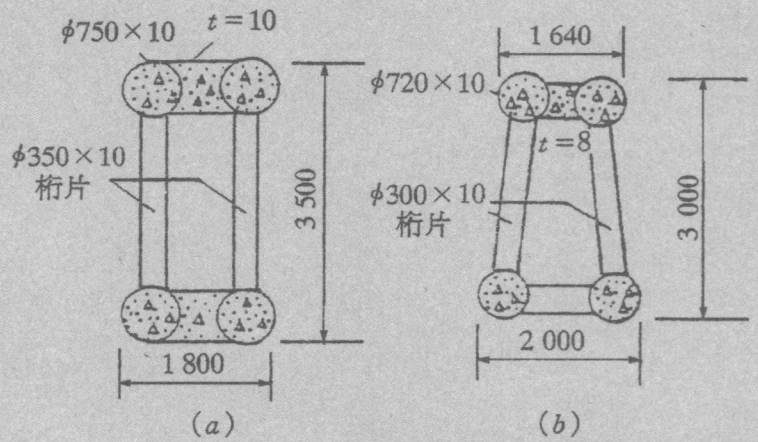

图6-1 钢管混凝土拱桥拱肋构造
*Fig.6-1 Arch rib construction of concrete-
filled of steel tube*

表4-7 斜拉桥（*l*≥602m，截至2006年1月）

No.	桥名	较大跨(m)	桥址	国家	建成年份	备注
1	苏通大桥	1 088	江苏南通	中国	2009	主桥：钢；混凝土桥塔高304m
2	昂船洲大桥	1 018	香港	中国	2008	主跨：钢，侧跨：混凝土
3	多多拉桥	890	Onomichi-Imabari	日本	1999	主跨、侧跨：钢，两端：预应力混凝土
4	诺曼底桥	856	勒阿弗尔	法国	1995	主跨中部624m：钢，其余两边各116m及侧跨：混凝土
5	Incheon黄海桥	800	Incheon-Songdo	韩国	2009	钢
6	上海 — 崇明岛斜拉桥	730	上海	中国	2008	钢
7	南京三桥	648	江苏南京	中国	2005	钢
8	南京二桥	628	江苏南京	中国	2001	钢
9	金塘桥	620	金塘岛—宁波市	中国	2008	钢
10	白沙洲桥	618	湖北武汉	中国	2000	主跨：钢，侧跨：钢混凝土组合
11	青州大桥	605	福建福州	中国	2003	钢混凝土组合
12	杨浦大桥	602	上海市	中国	1993	钢混凝土组合

表4-2 钢桁架梁桥（l≥400m，截至1998年）

No.	桥名	较大跨(m)	桥址	国家	建成年份	备注
1	魁北克桥	549	魁北克市	加拿大	1917	铁路桥
2	福斯湾桥	521	爱丁堡市	英国	1890	铁路桥
3	港大桥	510	大阪市	日本	1974	是现代化的跨度最大的公路纵桁架桥
4	Commodore Berry桥	501	切斯特市, PA	美国	1974	
5	大新奥尔良①1号桥	480	新奥尔良市, LA	美国	1958	
6	大新奥尔良①2号桥	480	新奥尔良市, LA	美国	1988	
7	豪拉桥	457	加尔各答	印度	1943	
8	Veteram Memorial	445	Gramenay, LA	美国	1995	
9	Transbay	427	旧金山，CA	美国	1936	
10	Ikitsaki	400	长崎	日本	1991	

① Greater New Orleans, Greater：此处表示包括郊区。

表4-3 预应力混凝土箱梁刚构桥（主跨/≥250m，截至2006年10月）

No.	桥名	较大跨(m)	桥址	国家	建成年份	备注
1	石板坡桥	330	重庆市	中国	2006	新桥，原桥改造2007年建成
2	Stolma海峡桥	301	Austervoll	挪威	1998	
3	Raft海峡桥	298	Lofoten	挪威	1998	
4	Sundoy	298	Leir海峡	挪威	2003	
5	辅航道桥	270	广东省	中国	1997	2003年12月量测挠度达22cm
6	苏通桥辅航道桥	268	苏州—南通	中国	2009	140m+268m+140m
7	红河大桥	265	云南省	中国	1997	5跨
8	门道桥	260	Brisbane	澳大利亚	1986	
9	Varodd	260	Kristiansand海峡	挪威	1994	
10	鱼洞长江大桥	2×260	重庆市	中国	2007	145m+2×260m+155m，公路和城市轻轨
11	泸州桥	252	四川省	中国	2000	
12	Schottwien桥	250	Semmering	奥地利	1989	
13	S. Joao	250	波尔图	葡萄牙	1991	
14	Skye	250	Skye岛	英国	1995	
15	Confederation	250	Nanada	加拿大	1997	43跨
16	黄花园嘉陵江大桥	3×250	重庆市	中国	1999	137.16m+3×250m+137.16m
17	黄石桥	3×245	湖北黄石	中国	1995	162.5m+3×245m+162.5m

表4-6 钢拱桥（l≥380m，截至2006年5月16日）

No.	桥名	较大跨(m)	桥址	国家	建成年份	备注
1	朝天门桥	552	重庆市	中国	2008	钢桁架
2	卢浦桥	550	上海市	中国	2003	钢板焊箱
3	新河海峡桥	518	Fayetteville, WV	美国	1997	钢桁架
4	Bayomnne桥	504	纽约，NY	美国	1931	
5	悉尼港桥	503	悉尼	澳大利亚	1932	钢桁架
6	Chenab桥	461	Katra	印度	2008	
7	菜园坝桥	420	重庆市	中国	2005	钢管混凝土
8	Fremont桥	283	Portlane, OR	美国	1973	
9	Numata River海峡桥	380	Hiroshima	日本	2007	

表4-5　钢管混凝土拱桥（l≥235m，截至2006年10月）（由张佐安高工和陈保春教授补充）

No.	桥名	较大跨(m)	桥址	国家	建成年份	备注
1	巫山长江大桥	460	重庆市巫山县	中国	2005	中承式
2	支井河桥	430	湖北恩思	中国	2008	中承式
3	湘江四桥	388（净）	湖南湘潭	中国	2007	中承式
4	茅草街大桥	368	湖南南县	中国	2005	中承式，斜拉拱桥
5	丫髻沙大桥	360	广东广州市	中国	2000	中承式
6	永和大桥	349.5	广西南宁	中国	2005	中承式
7	太平湖大桥	336	安徽黄山	中国	2004	中承式
8	南浦大桥	308	浙江淳安	中国		下承式
9	梅溪河大桥	288	重庆市奉节县	中国	2001	上承式
10	汉江三桥	280	湖北武汉	中国	2000	下承式
11	水道大桥	280	广东东莞	中国	2006	中承式
12	三岸邕江大桥	270	广西邕宁	中国	1999	中承式
13	三门口北门大桥	270	浙江象山	中国	2006	中承式
14	三门口中间大桥	270	浙江象山	中国	2003	中承式
15	宜昌长江铁路大桥[1]	2×275	湖北宜昌	中国	2007	下承式，铁路
16	金沙江戎州大桥	260	四川宜宾	中国	1998	中承式
17	千岛湖1号桥	252	浙江千岛湖	中国		
18	青干河大桥	248	湖北秭归	中国	2004	中承式
19	三门	245	浙江三门	中国	2002	中承式
20	汉江五桥	240	湖北武汉	中国	2000	中承式
21	落脚河大桥	240	贵州	中国	2001	中承式
22	钢瓦门大桥	238	浙江	中国	1998	中承式
23	北盘江大桥	236	贵州	中国	2001	上承式，铁路
24	京杭运河大桥	235	江苏徐州	中国	2002	上承式，铁路

[1]这是在宜昌（湖北省）—万州（重庆市）线上宜昌一侧的大
桥，为连续刚构和柔性钢管混凝土拱构，刚构跨度（中心）为
130m+2×275m+130m，而拱计算跨则为264m。

表4-4 混凝土拱桥 (*l*≥270m, 截至2006年3月16日)

No.	桥名	较大跨(m)	桥址	国家	建成年份	备注
1	万县长江大桥	420	四川万县	中国	1997	上承式
2	KRK-1（东跨）	390	KRK岛	克罗地亚	1980	上承式
3	江界河桥	330	贵州瓮安县	中国	1995	上承式
4	胡佛坝旁道桥①	323	博尔德市, NV	美国	2008	
5	邕宁邕江桥	312	广西邕宁	中国	1996	中承式
6	格莱兹维尔桥	305	悉尼	澳大利亚	1964	上承式
7	Amizade桥②	290	Foz do Iguacu/Cirdad Eteste	巴西/巴拉圭	1964	
8	Infante Don Hanrique桥	280	波尔图	葡萄牙	2003	
9	布罗克蓝斯Bloukrans桥	272	Natures谷	南非	1983	
10	Arrabida桥	270	波尔图	葡萄牙	1963	上承式

①Hoover Dam Bypass, 胡佛坝为混凝土重力拱坝, 建于美国科罗拉多
（Coroado）河下游上, 位于内华达(Nevada)州和亚利桑那（Arizona）
州博耳德（Boulder）市, NV,
②在参考文献[20]中为巴拉那—约基（Parana-Jiki）桥。

5. 1991年前建成的10座敞肩式石拱桥

5. 10 Spandrel Stone Arch Bridges Completed before 1991

①云南长虹桥（图5-1），主跨/=112.5m(1961)；②广西红渡桥，/=100m(1965)；③四川酉阳龚滩桥，/=100m(1965)；④四川富顺沱江桥，/=111m(1968)；⑤湖南浒湾桥，/=105m(1971)；⑥四川江津游渡桥，/=100m(1972)；⑦四川九溪沟桥，/=110m(1972)；⑧广西龙武桥，/=100m(1978)；⑨山西晋城丹河桥，/=105m(1982)；⑩湖南凤凰县乌巢河桥，/=120m(1991)。芬兰朋友J.Virola工程师（他研究世界桥梁史，编有7种世界最长桥的表，随时调整，均见赠），见之对编者来电说，此10座桥，任何一座都是世界纪录[1]，因为国外一直认为1961年国际石拱桥纪录为德国于1903—1904年建成的Syratal Plauen石拱桥（图5-2）"tal"在德文中为山谷、峡谷、河谷，"Plauen"为萨克森的小镇。该桥基本为实腹式的，桥冠截面厚1.5m，拱座厚3.4m，系德国朋友Dr.-Ing Klaus Stiglat [他担任24年（1975—1998年）德文Beton und Stahlbetonbau 学报（国际权威学报）主编，从Bauzeitung (建设报) July 17, 1904] 为复印寄赠，因年久模糊，个别处经编者略为加工[1]。1901年德国工程师Friedrich （英文作Fredrick）von Empeiger出版一本有关小册子，1903年他和德国出版社Ernst & Sohn（1851年创始于柏林）合作创立新学报Beton und Eisen，至20世纪30年代后期改为Beton und Stahlbetonbau。Beton und Stahlbetonbau由德、奥轮流主编（因奥地利母语亦系德语）。从1999年开始，由维也纳土壤培育学院土木系Dr.-tech-phil. Prof. Konrad Bergmeister主编，增加篇幅达1/3，加印作者（等）照相和彩色工程照片，1999、2000年承为印4文。仍由原出版社承印。

6. 钢管混凝土拱桥

6. Arch Bridges Constructed of Concrete-Filled Steel Tube

钢管混凝土拱桥是用钢管混凝土构成的。当跨度不大时可为单管，如我国江苏无锡新安北桥、泰州引江桥和浙江义乌篁圆桥，它们的跨度分别为60m、70m和80m,均采用800mm单管，厚度分别为16mm、16mm和18mm。国外有采用大直径单管的，如日本松岛跨度为126m的上承式拱桥，采用直径为1.8m的钢管。

跨度较大的拱桥可用双管（竖立）并用钢板焊联成封闭形，于空腔中也填混凝土构成哑铃形，作为拱肋，用这种形式建成的拱桥跨度有达160m的，如1990年11月建成通车的湖北三峡下牢溪上承式肋拱桥，采用ϕ1000×10-12mm钢管，其中距约为1.5m。

跨度在100m以上的拱桥，往往采用3肢或4肢，用缀杆（桁片）焊联组成桁式截面则成混合式结构，见图6-1。

钢管混凝土在英文中称concrete-filled steel tube(CFST),在俄文中称сталетрубобетон，在德文中称stahlrohrbeton，在法文中称tube replies en beton，在日文中称钢管コンクリート，钢管混凝土拱桥在国际采用亦较普遍，但跨度都不太大，印度不采用钢管混凝土建桥和建造高层建筑，但印度混凝土学报(The Indian Concrete, Journal)为了向印度读者介绍这种建筑材料，友好地发表了我们3篇有关论文①。

我国CFST拱桥的建设规模和技术水平在国际上是居前列的。

①Qiu Hongxing, Ding Dajun. Concrete tall buildings in China. The Indian Concrete Journal. 2005(11): 11-15; Ding Dajun. Concrete bridges constructed in China. The Indian Concrete Journal. 2006(3): 11-19及参考文献[21]

图8-1 捷克无背索独塔斜拉桥（承斯洛伐克朋友Prof. Dr. Ivan Balaz惠赠）
Fig.8-1 Czech single-pylon cable-stayed bridge without backstays (courtesy of Prof. Dr. Ivan Balaz)

图8-2 西班牙塞维利亚独塔无背索桥（承瑞士老友洛桑工业大学退休教授、前FIP主席Prof. R. Walther惠赠）
Fig.8-2 Single-pylon cable-stayed bridge without backstays, completed in Sevilla (courtesy of old friend, retired Prof.R.Walther of Lausame Tech.Univ. the President of former FIP)

图8-3 哈尔滨太阳岛上无背索独塔斜拉桥（承章曾焕高工惠赠）
Fig.8-3 Single-pylon cable-stayed bridge without backstays on Sun Island (courtesy of Senior Engr. Zhang Cenghuan)

7. 巫山桥内力分布

7. Distribution of Internal Forces in Wushan Bridge

巫山桥上、下弦杆内力N分传给钢管N_s和混凝土N_c的计算成果，见表7-1，表内数据表明$N_c>N_s$（属弹性阶段），按塑性理论计算也基本如此，说明混凝土受力是主要的[21]：

表7-1 巫山桥主拱圈一根钢管混凝土内力计算成果表(kN)

截面	截面	组合I		组合II	
		钢管内力(N_s)	混凝土内力(N_c)	钢管内力(N_s)	混凝土内力(N_c)
拱脚	上弦	7 065	30 760	7 147	30 278
	下弦	10 034	29 666	10 021	32 229
1/8L	上弦	6 191	19 209	6 092	18 692
	下弦	9 233	26 792	9 212	27 988
1/4L	上弦	6 382	22 118	6 273	20 002
	下弦	6 519	27 931	6 194	25 681
3/8L	上弦	6 690	24 410	6 611	25 439
	下弦	6 633	19 792	6 599	18 926
拱顶	上弦	7 008	25 592	7 019	26 981
	下弦	4 557	16 033	4 399	16 304

注：资料由四川公路规划勘查设计研究院牟廷敏高级工程师根据测量的应变换算提供，附此谨致谢忱。

组合I：恒+汽+人；　　组合II：恒+汽+人+温度影响。

可见将巫山桥和丫髻沙桥列入钢拱桥，的确是不妥当的，因为拱肋中混凝土受力是主要的，而钢管受力则要小得多。

8. 独塔无背索斜拉桥

8. Single-Pylon Cable-Stayed Bridges without Backstays

①易北河在英文中称"Elbe"，在捷克语中称"Lab"，但非为中文文献中谓易北河上游称拉贝的，"Ústí nad Labern, nad"为英语"over"，即跨易北河上游，"Ústi"英语为"estuary"，即港湾，实际上Marian市并无港湾。该桥于1998年6月30日开放。以上均由编者的斯洛伐克朋友、布拉迪斯拉发工业大学Ivam Balaz教授赐告，附此致谢。

②9.25m+37.7m+27.05m，见：中国土木工程学会桥梁及结构工程分会. 第17届全国桥梁学术会议论文集（下册）. 北京：人民交通出版社，2006：113

世界第一座独塔无背索的斜拉桥Marian（图8-1）[22]，坐落于捷克首都布拉格之北大约100km处乌斯季(Ústí)，跨越易北河(Elbe River)上游拉贝河①。Marian市约10万人口，沿河两岸分布，仅有一座公路桥连接河两岸。桥的设计基本概念是减轻左岸玛利安峭壁（Marian Cliff）和主斜拉跨重量，而将所有结构重量移至右岸。这要求首先设置斜拉塔；其次要求避免采用背索以便尽量使右岸桥头空敞，而不妨碍此处原有的道路网。该桥为斜(倾向短跨)独塔斜拉桥，主跨长123.3m，短跨55.5m，采用钢结构以减轻重量；其三是将短跨作为结构的一个稳定部分。该桥由于地理位置要求而设计成斜塔无背索桥。文献称世界上最大的斜塔无背索桥为西班牙巴塞罗那（Barcelona）阿拉米罗(Alamillo)独塔斜拉桥，其长跨为200m，编者未查到此桥（有谓未曾建造），但知由西班牙著名建筑师卡拉特拉瓦（Santiago Calatrava）设计，位于西班牙塞维利亚（Sevilla）的阿拉米罗桥（图8-2）为无背索独塔斜拉桥[23]，两市分别位于西班牙之东北和西南。

我国2000年在哈尔滨太阳岛设计建造了一座斜独塔无背索斜拉桥（图8-3），跨度为140m+60m[24]，2008年2月又在苏州石湖建造了另一座跨度为100m+50m[15]，两者都为钢结构。另西安白庙路桥亦系斜塔无背索桥，但尺度较小②。

以上几座桥中，唯Marian无背索斜拉桥的设计是充分考虑地理位置并作为标志性结构，在工程师与建筑师的紧密合作下再考虑建筑美学作出的，其余均为考虑建筑景观而设计建造的，显然这对发展旅游业是很有益的。

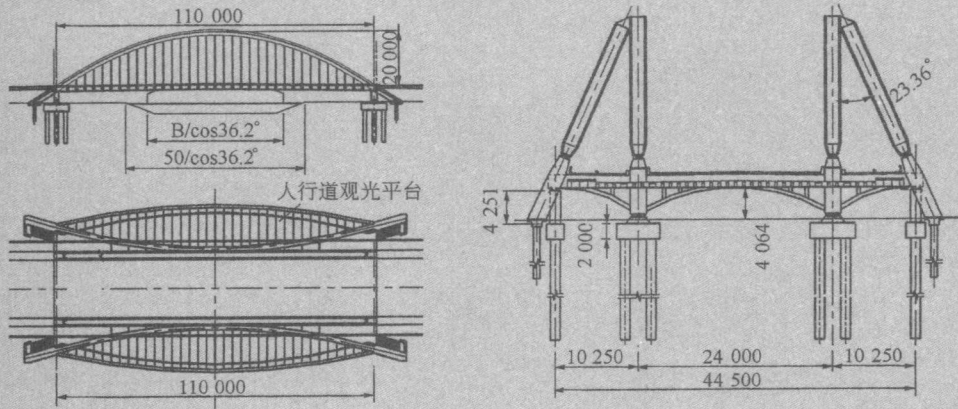

图9-1 玉峰大桥总体布置图

Fig.9-1 General Arrangement Drawing of Yufeng Bridge

表10-1 三叉和四叉桥

桥型	位置	桥名	跨度(m)	宽度(m)	t (cm)	砖厚加5mm厚混凝土
三叉双曲拱桥	前洲镇	北圩桥	半跨10	3	60	16.5cm+5cm加厚混凝土
	玉祈镇	民主桥	半跨10	4	60	16.5cm+5cm加厚混凝土
	查桥镇	谈村桥	半跨10	3	60	16.5cm+5cm加厚混凝土
四叉双曲拱桥	前洲镇	中圩桥	半跨24	3	65	16.5cm+5cm加厚混凝土
	东湖塘镇	五星桥	半跨24	4	65	16.5cm+5cm加厚混凝土

注：半跨指跨中交接处至拱座距离，t指拱顶混凝土面至拱座竖向高度。

图10-2 五星桥（承苏松源教授级高工惠赠）

Fig.10-2 Wuxing Bridge (courtesy of Senior Engr. Prof. Su Songyuan)

9. 无推力斜靠式拱桥

9. Obliquely Depending Trustless Arch Bridge

世界第一座斜靠式拱桥是于1987年由西班牙建筑师Santiago Calatrava 成功设计的。该桥直立式主拱为双铰，其水平推力直接传至主梁，形成拱梁组合结构。其斜拱则为无铰拱，水平推力直接传至地基，是有推力的。但我国沿海地区许多城市为软土地基，采用这种有推力的斜靠式拱桥，从经济上和技术上都不是合适的。

我国首座大跨度斜靠式拱桥为上海昆山市玉峰大桥，总体布置图如图9-1所示。主桥跨径110m，主拱圈矢跨比为1/5.5，斜拱在拱圈平面内的矢跨比为1/5.4，两拱圈轴线均采用二次抛物线。因为弧形观景平台的存在，桥面宽度从主墩处的48.0m，变化到跨中处的60.9m，其中机动车道宽21m，主拱与斜拱间共设13道一字形横撑，吊杆间距均为3m。主拱肋采用钢管混凝土，截面形式为等边三角形，由3根ϕ20cm小钢管和1根ϕ110cm的大钢管及钢连接板和系板焊接构成，大钢管内灌注混凝土。斜拱肋截面采用形式同主拱肋，但管内不灌注混凝土。主拱系梁采用钢箱截面，斜拱系杆采用预应力钢绞线，桥面系采用钢-混凝土叠合梁[25]。一般结构以最直接的传力途径为最好。故拱结构传力途径有直接将荷载传向地基，过去的石拱桥都是这样，即成重力式基础，或用拉（钢）杆承受拱的推力，而在房屋建设中，还可以将大厅拱屋盖推力传至两侧屋的横向（钢或钢筋混凝土）刚架或横墙。

今因玉峰桥需建造曲线形（平面内）人行观景台，即必需建造斜靠拱桥，则承受主桥拱推力的拉杆只需按斜桥建造前的荷载设计，在斜靠桥建造后的主桥推力将由斜靠桥承受，使成空间受力体系。

对这种桥未见有经济指标分析，在此介绍，聊备一格。

10. 三叉桥和四叉桥

10. 3-Pronged And 4-Pronged Bridges

在由编者主编的《土木工程概论》（中国建筑工业出版社，2003年）图4-94中，示出2001年在英国用玻璃纤维加强聚合物GRP建造的三叉桥，它跨越Ribble和Calder 两条河的交叉口，整个GRP模板用直升机起吊。这是英国建造第三座这种桥。以上系编者朋友、《英国桥梁设计与工程》（季刊）（Bridge, Design and Engineering, Bd&e）主编Ms. Helene Russell见告，附此致谢。但有时需建造四叉桥。

无锡桥梁工程公司于1965年将前苏联双曲砖拱屋盖构造移植于桥梁后，陆续建造了多座双曲石拱三叉和四叉桥，在表11-1中示出5座四叉桥，最大跨度达20m，该表系公司前董事长苏松源教授赐文，附此致谢。

从1969—1985年在无锡县共建造了三叉双曲拱桥7座，四叉（又称十字）双曲拱桥多座，一桥跨四岸。在表10-1中列出5座桥。

图10-1、图10-2分别示三叉北圩桥和四叉五星桥。

此材料均由老友，江苏省无锡路桥工程总公司前董事长苏松源教授级高工惠赠，附此表示感谢。

编者2003年9月在太原参加第13届全国现代结构研讨会，与会代表偕游晋祠，作长诗十韵中有"鱼沼飞梁双向桥跨水，结构新颖如斯之早世无伦"（见拙诗词《惜分阴》续集，p.54）。桥系木制，即四叉桥，跨度约10m，晋祠系北宋仁宗天圣年间（1023—1032年）建造，和张择端《清明上河图》中虹桥一样，如无工程实例，是难想象出的。

图10-1 北圩桥（承苏松源教授级高工惠赠）
Fig.10-1 Beiwei Bridge (courtesy of Senior Engr. Prof. Su Songyuan)

图11-1 Ruck-A-Chucky桥
（承T. Y. Lin International惠赠）
Fig.11-1 Ruck-A-Chucky Bridge
(courtesy of T. Y. Lin International)

图11-2 有V形墩的我国桂林雉山漓江刚架桥
（承项海帆院士惠赠）
Fig.11-2 Zhishan Lijiang Rigid Frame
Bridge with V-shaped Piers (courtesy of
Academician Xiang Haifan)

11. 因地制宜设计桥梁

典型的例子是T.Y. Lin International设计的Ruck-A-Chucky分段预制斜拉桥（图11-1）方案，曲线跨度长约400m，中心角45° [5]。

为避免设置若干个须承受很大水平地震作用的桥墩（桥墩高约106m），如果设计成直线桥，则两端40°陡壁边坡将须开凿接引隧道，斜拉的弧形桥使接引隧道开凿量减至最少，而利用陡壁斜拉全跨，分散的斜拉钢索构成曲面，刚度很大，使桥在风荷载和地震作用下保持稳定，同时，可以抵消曲桥在自重和垂直荷载作用下全部或部分的双向弯曲应力。以上材料是Prof. T. Y. Lin（林同炎教授，年长编者11岁）前辈赐赠的Engineering Bulletin，T.Y. Lin International中所介绍的。由于种种原因，此桥迄今未建造。

林老一生荣获很多名誉博士称号。早年曾在比利时首都布鲁塞尔西北部约50km处的根特（与布市有铁道联系）学习,在根特大学Mannel预应力实验室获硕士学位①。1992年10月编者曾访问（讲学）欧洲五国（希腊、奥地利、意大利、瑞士、比利时）(在意四校、瑞士两校、余一校)讲课。编者曾与该校一教授(编者曾邀他来东南大学访问过)联系访问，但未约好时间，届时他因遇到宗教节日而未能实现，故编者只在布市住了两夜即飞经芬兰回国。

林老赐赠的Bulletin[26]中，示出1958年他协同华盛顿参议员、美国参议院商务委员会主席Warren Maynuson公开提出建造跨过白令海峡的大桥，以促进美国和苏联人民间的贸易和了解。10年后，林老组织了国际和平大桥公司（International Peace Bridge, Inc.），该公司作为一项慷慨合作曾经美国财政部批准。按照林老规划，提出建设220座斜拉桥，其中一孔为了通航，跨度取为1 800ft（548.8m），余均为1 200ft（365.9m）(图11-2)，桥为高40ft（12.2m）的箱形截面，分3层，上层为双车道公路，系敞开式的，双车道铁路及管线分别设在高度40ft及14ft（4.27m）箱形截面内。桥的支座设在双曲线空心混凝土筒体上，筒体则支承在岩石上。估计上部结构用25.5万m³轻混凝土，下部结构用420万m³重混凝土。这是一项宏伟的计划，它通过连接阿拉斯加和西伯利亚海岸来联系世界各大洲，将成为沟通东西方政治文化的纽带[27]。这一设计虽未实现，但这种富于改革的精神值得介绍学习。

林老在1991年在IABSE学报SEI创刊号发表对直布罗陀海峡桥方案之一，他采取的航道最短，但水深很大，建议用2座5 000m悬索-斜拉组合桥，而丹麦COWI公司的方案水深较浅，航道较长，故采用2 000~3 000m的多座悬索桥方案。当论文印出单印本后，林老立即赐赠给编者，COWI方案刊登于该公司资料。

T.Y. Lin International在20世纪60年代中设计美国加利福尼亚州Hegenberger桥时采用了V形桥以减小计算跨度，因而获得较大的经济效益，现在世界上已建有多座V形墩大桥，我国1988年建成的桂林雉山漓江刚架桥（图11-2），主跨95m，40m挂梁，V形墩上口20m,节约是明显的。

编者于1991年在美国Concrete International上 (ACI出版有3种国际学报，即混凝土结构学报Journal, Concrete Structures和混凝土材料学报（Journal, Concrete Materials以及CI）发表State-of-the-Arts of Application and Research, Concrete (No.12, 1991, pp56-60) 林老看到很高兴，当即航空寄来一本，编者于12月22日即收到，样本则于次年4月才收到（余后来在CI发表多篇文章，关系较好，样本收到即较快），足见林老对后辈的关怀。

2002年5月林老接受东南大学名誉教授的邀请来南京，编者曾与数位同事去金陵饭店探望，奉赠于2000年中国建筑工业出版社出版的拙编《现代混凝土结构学》（1 047pp，计160万字），已签好上下款，见面后即告知，告别时他仍要求签名，同时林老行走虽没要人搀扶，但走碎步，其健康状况颇令人担忧，而同行的师母高玉珮太夫人年相若，则步伐矫健，身体硬朗，果2004年8月传来林老噩耗，不禁泪倾。

①网上"结构人物"谓1993年获美国加州柏克利大学硕士学位。

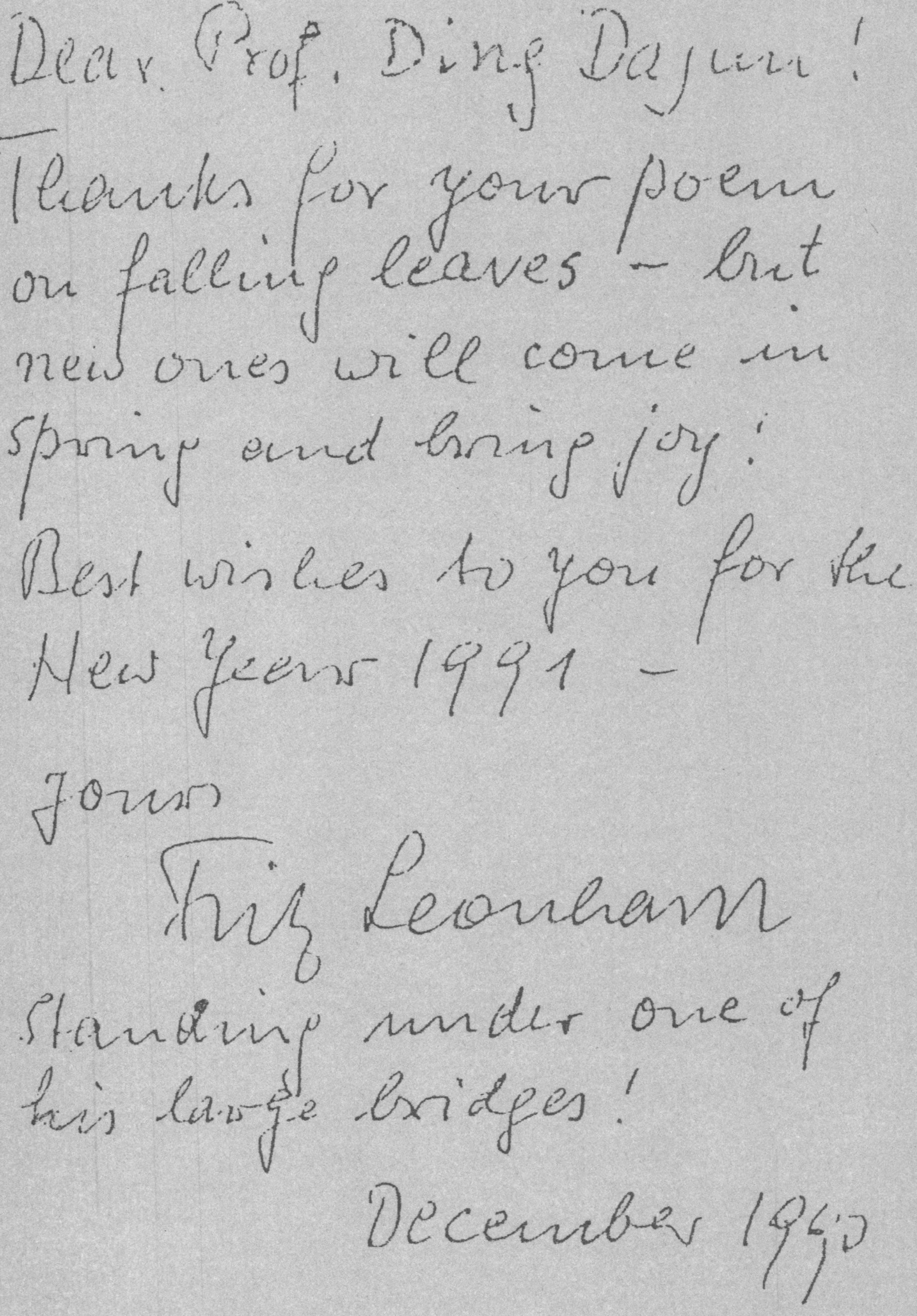

Dear. Prof, Ding Dajun!

Thanks for your poem on falling leaves — but new ones will come in spring and bring joy!
Best wishes to you for the New Year 1991 —

Yours

Fritz Leonhardt

Standing under one of his large bridges!

December 1990

图12-2 莱氏在照片背面题字的复印件照片
Dear Prof. Ding Dajun!
Thanks for your poem on falling leaves — but new will come in spring and being joy!
Best wishes to you for the New Year 1991.
Yours Fritz Leonhardt
Standing under one of his large bridge!
December 1990

12. 单柱桥

12. Bridge Supported on Single Columns

在市区内为争取交通空间，往往采取单柱支承的桥，在拙编《土木工程总论》（中国建筑工业出版社）1997，p.151图5-138示出编者在东京拍摄的一梁桥，支柱则偏于一侧，整个梁则支于从柱挑出的悬臂上，柱及其基础的设计将很不经济，但在交通拥挤之东京已是何等不易。

现在国内外在市区道路和公路线上，往往采取单柱支承的桥，以争取桥下的交通空间。图12-1示1991年已故前辈德国预应力混凝土专家Fritz Leonhardt 教授（1909—1999.12.30）（以下称"莱氏"）赠编者的照片。

他立于他设计的PC单柱桥前。后询来东南大学讲课的德国朋友莱氏弟子Prof. H. W. Reinhardt 承告知此桥跨度约为220m。莱氏在照片背面题字复印，照片如图12-2所示。在图下方将题字打出，以便于读者阅读。

编者结识莱氏系在1979年5月参加国际桥协（IABSE）在哥本哈根召开、由编者挚友丹麦技术大学Prof. M. P. Nielson (1935.1.6 —)主持的"混凝土塑性"(Plasticity of Concrete)国际会议上有幸认识莱氏而成为忘年交。因他较余年长14岁，故来往函电编者都尊他为前辈，请教问题和问候信件，很快即获回复，获益匪浅，颇为感念。

2000年2月1日惊接莱氏讣闻，急复信致唁并作七律诗致哀悼，见拙诗集《惜分阴》pp. 11-13，谨录于此，以志纪念，并作短序于前。

惊闻世界著名预应力混凝土和桥梁权威学者、德国Fritz Leonhardt 教授噩耗（公生于1909年，于1999年12月30日逝世），曷胜哀悼。谨成七律，仅叙私交，不及其他，因莱氏在土木工程界的建树为世人所熟知，无须述及。但个人交往不为人知，乃作短序，2000年2月3日。

自1979年与公结识，逾20年矣，其间互赠著作（书和论文）多次。1990年莱氏赠我个人照片，背景为其设计并建成的大桥，桥墩特别高，我回报以1987年9月应Prof. H. Kupfer、Prof .E. Grasser 和Dr. K. Müller 邀请在慕尼黑工业大学讲课之照片。在编者主持1989年3月南京土木建筑学会等举办的"高层建筑国际会议"前曾与莱氏联系，他来函希望中国朋友对兴建过多高层建筑应持谨慎态度，指出某些国家的大城市深受高层之"害"。90年代初余撰《混凝土结构发展》一书（中国建筑工业出版社约稿）需述及据我国报刊和专著上所载1978年建成跨度为270m的阿根廷-巴拉圭界河上预应力混凝土刚构桥，如果属实，应为当时该类桥的世界纪录。但交通部设计院老友史尔毅教授级高工见告，在《大英百科全书》中亦未见记载此桥。在拙编中提与不提，颇为难。估计该桥是当时提出的一个方案，因函询莱氏，迅速获复，亦认为可能系方案，建议向阿根廷桥梁专家Prof. Dr. Pablo M. Micheli询问，并为具函介绍。承米氏寄来1985年建成的该界河桥详细资料，因航运要求设计建造了主跨为330m的预应力混凝土斜拉桥，当时该桥仍为公铁两用预应力混凝土斜拉桥的世界纪录。1999年11月下旬，拙诗词集《耕余诗词》印出后曾用平信寄公一册，孰意书在邮递中公溘焉长逝而未邀青及，深悔当时未寄航空信。吁嗟何及！犹记曾以拙画菊花图作年卡寄赠，图中题诗有"行看春色好，桃李满园芳"句。对外英译并注明中国将桃李比喻为弟子，指出上两句意为"后继有人"。公复函大为赞赏。接讣闻急致唁函，并告以将作诗悼念。觉绝句不足以记述交往经历，决定作律诗，疾构思第二日成初稿，几经更易，定稿如下，诗曰：

忘年交过廿年期，互赠书文总及时。
彩照传神真矍铄，嘉言惠贶足深思。
桥型更改疑终释，诗著滞邮恨寄迟。
古喻阐明承谬许，忍悲疾撰忆公辞。

图12-1 已故前辈Prof. Fritz Leonhardt 赠编者照片

Fig.12-1 Photo of the died Senior Prof. Fritz Leonhardt sent to the Editor

图14-1 美国Sacramento应力板带桥
Fig.14-1 Stressed ribbon bridge in Sacramento, USA

图14-2 美国Rio Cololado倒桁架桥
Fig.14-2 Inverted truss bridge in Rio Cololado, USA

13. 矮塔斜拉桥

13. Cable-Stayed Bridge with Low Pylon or Extradosed Cable-Stayed Bridge

这种桥是法国Jacques Mathivat 教授于1988年提出的新结构体系[28]，采用两个参数界定[29]，即矮塔斜拉桥特征参数α与相应模式下斜拉索对索力的影响度δ_T，α考虑塔高（与斜拉索长度有关），拉索截面方程和主梁抗弯刚度对矮塔斜拉桥斜拉索的作用效果等影响因素，给出计算公式，$\delta_T = Tv, as / pl$（pl—总荷载），Tv、as为相应模式下拉索的垂直分力，当$\alpha \leq$（40°~50°），δ_T一般不超过25%，可认为是矮塔斜拉桥。矮塔斜拉桥适宜用于铁路桥，芜湖长江大桥系公铁两用桥，即属于矮塔斜拉桥，这是因为桥头现有列车编车场，因此桥位已定，而附近有一机场，故采用矮塔斜拉桥。

我国曾将这种斜拉桥又称为部分斜拉桥(partially cable-stayed bridge)，其含义为：在结构性能上，斜拉索仅仅分担部分荷载，还有相当部分荷载由梁的受弯受压来承受，"部分斜拉"即源于斜拉索的斜拉程度。部分斜拉桥的适用跨度在100~300m之间，如主梁采用钢和混凝土组合结构，跨度有望突破400m[30]。部分斜拉桥具有一些特点：①主边跨的比例α接近于连续梁（漳州备战大桥80.8m+132m+80.8m）；②塔高较矮，拉索倾角较小，拉索为主梁提供较大的轴向力；③主梁刚度大；④斜拉索较为集中，通常布置在边跨中及1/3中垮附近；⑤斜拉索在塔上多以索鞍形式通过；⑥主梁的施工方法更接近于梁式桥。

部分斜拉桥是介于连续梁和斜拉桥之间的半柔性桥梁，因而兼有两者的优点，与连续梁比较有如下优点：①跨越能力较连续梁大。当中支点梁高相同时，部分斜拉桥的跨度可较连续梁大1倍以上；②对大跨度梁而言，相同跨度的部分斜拉梁较连续梁经济。与斜拉桥相比有如下优点：①塔高较矮，塔身结构简单，施工方便；②斜拉索应力变化幅度小，可采用较高的应力，一般情况下斜拉桥拉索的应力为标准强度的0.4~0.45，而部分斜拉桥可用至0.5~0.6，从而减少钢材用量；③主梁抗压刚度大，可采用梁式桥施工方法，而毋须像斜拉桥那样采用大型牵索挂篮，极大地方便了施工；④整体刚度大，变形小，尤其适用于荷载大，标准高的铁路桥梁。

部分斜拉桥因为具有以上的特点，经济、美观、刚度大、施工方便，其发展具有很大的潜力，因此是有很大的发展前景的。

14. 应力板带桥和分段倒桁架桥

14. Stressed Ribbon Bridge and Inverted Segmental Truss Bridge

（1）清康熙四十四年（1705年）始建的四川泸定县大渡河桥，该桥为世界著名的单跨铁链桥，跨长103m，宽约2.8m，用9根铁链作底索，每边2根铁链作栏杆，桥面铺有纵横两层木板。铁链由扁环扣联而成，扁环内径3cm，外径9cm，长17~20cm，每根铁链平均890个扁环。铁链在两端固定的方法是在石砌的桥台内，开有宽2m、长5m、深6m的落井4个，近井底部埋有生铁铸的直径20cm铁地龙桩（水平向），西桥台8根，东桥台7根；另有同样直径、长4m的铁锚桩一根，地龙桩埋置在桥台的深度估计有7m多，埋入部分四周用灰浆块石胶固，锚桩横于7或8根地龙桩之下。铁链一端在西岸固定，另一端铁链围绕在东岸2个直径约5.6m圆木棍上，棍上挖有很多交叉洞眼，用木棒插入，扳动木棒以拉紧铁链。

前西德V. Finsterwalder应用预应力混凝土技术建造成应力板带桥，与上述柔性铁链桥结构相似，特别是锚固方法与铁索桥相似。由（略）

图15-1 Millau桥工程照片（承Dipl. Ing. Eberhard Pelke惠赠）
Fig.15-1 Engineering photos of Millau Bridge (courtesy of Dipl. Ing. Eberhard Pelke)

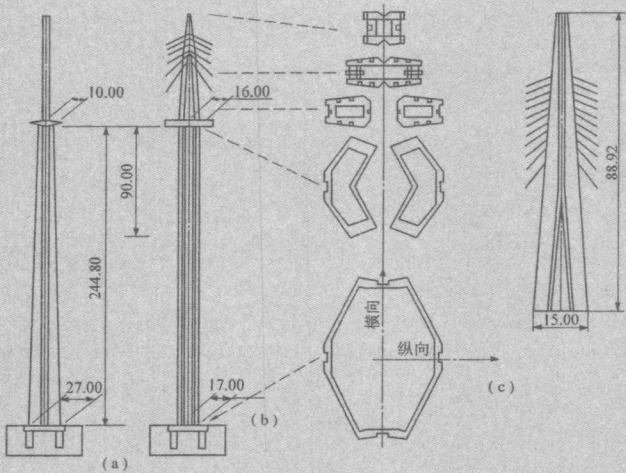

图15-3 Millau 桥墩截面
Fig.15-3 Section of Millau bridge pier

图15-2 Millau桥在建造中的桥塔（承Dipl. Ing. Andreas Tausend, PERI公司惠赠）
Fig.15-2 Pylon of Construction Millau Bridge under construction (courtesy of Dipl. Ing. Adnreas Tausand, Co. PERI)

向下垂的（在侧视图中）而锚固在桥座和基土或岩石内的预应力混凝土板或肋构成，一般用于人行桥或管道桥。现在世界上已建成这种桥若干座，跨径最大的为在瑞士Holderbank-Wildegg水泥厂建成的这种桥（1992年编者访问瑞士洛桑工业大学时，Klinger博士为编者放映了30多张该桥的幻灯片，但无工程照片），跨径达216.4m，悬垂达14.75m（承受皮带传送机）。从上可见应力板带桥亦与中国竹索桥和铁链桥构造相似，虽亦属柔性（索）桥，但由于系预应力混凝土索板，在柔性程度上，与中国古索桥是大大不同的[31]。图14-1为美国Sacramento河上人行应力板带桥，其净跨度为127.4m（总长137.42m）。

（2）分段倒桁架桥　由T. Y. Lin International设计在美国Rio Colorado于1972年建成跨度为148m的分段倒桁架桥，全桥跨过200m宽峡谷（图14-2）。我国1989年在湖南建成淘金桥，跨度70m，锚固于两岸岩石中，相似于应力板带桥的锚固。这种桥跨度结构由倒板带加劲，其承载力和刚度较应力板带桥大大提高，故可行驶汽车。淘金桥每平方米混凝土、非预应力和预应力钢筋用量分别为0.96m³、20.6kg和88.1kg，相似的日本赤峰桥（1977），材料用料分别为1.41 m³、61.1kg和141.2kg，可见淘金桥设计较为经济。但是这种桥的锚固似没有美国桥锚固在邻跨中的自然可靠（岩石可能风化）。

15. 世界最高混凝土桥墩

15. The Highest Concrete Pier in the World

世界最高混凝土也是最高桥墩，当属法国Millau大桥（图15-1）[12]，桥长2 460m，宽度达32m的大桥将米洛（Millau）山谷和西南部的塔恩（Tarn）河谷连接起来。桥塔总高达343m。塔恩河谷上方桥面高达270m。整桥的最高桥墩高度达到破纪录的245m。该桥有一个36 000t重的钢制桥面，相当于5个艾菲尔铁塔的重量。

大桥由7个钢筋混凝土桥塔组成（图15-2），墩到上部结构的高度在78~245m之间，用爬模建造，分为两个箱形"腿"，其顶上建造87m高钢塔，7个有特色的A-形桥塔将在桥面上升起，它们支承单索面钢索，沿钢箱梁结构中心线锚固。桥面总长度为2 775m（两端各有一段桥面），在车行方向将是一宽3.5m的快车道，一宽同为3.5m的卡车慢车道和一宽3.0m的紧急车道。4.45m宽中间保留带为锚固并排的、中心间距为12.5m的斜拉索，而在桥面两侧设有保护的半透风的屏蔽。桥在平面内微曲，曲率半径为20 000m。

Millau桥采用推进法（launch）施工，第一次钢桥面推进是在2003年2月进行的，总共需进行18次推进。7个混凝土桥墩和7个临时钢支墩的每个用Enerpac高液压推进设施装备以移动36 000t的钢桥面，这项重量相当5于个艾菲尔铁塔。液压体系设计从两端推动27.3m宽桥面至7个混凝土桥墩上。混凝土桥墩用高强混凝土C60建造，而结构其余混凝土构件则采用C35，桥面和桥塔采用的钢为S355和S460。在推进过程中桥面结构由永久桥墩之间的7个临时钢支墩支承，而推进的桥面段用伸缩式液压体系提升，每一体系包括提升能力为250t的提升汽缸。它提升桥面离开桥墩支承结构，每个汽缸有2个或4个滑动装置，每个装有2个60t汽缸，每次推进桥面最大进程为600mm。推进过程中用2个滑拽装置启动，每个有2个120t汽缸，总的，在推进最后阶段，从南坡有5 280t推力，而从北坡则有2 400t推力。

该桥两边推进在2004年5月合龙，由于这一背景，在下一月由钢应用技术办公室（Office Technique pour L'Utilisation）支持在Millau镇举行了一次为期3天的钢桥国际会议，参加者有来自世界各地的工程师、建筑师和桥梁专家数百名。引导报告者之一为Foster & Partners

图16-2 主线路柱和上部结构
Fig.16-2 Column on mainline and superstructure

27.20m

2.60m

7.00m

6.31m

1.80m

16.00m

18.60m

7.89m

1.00 5.00 1.00

7.00m

27.20m

4.75m   8.85m   2.60m   8.85m   4.75m

0.20m

0.45m

0.25m

0.20m

7.00m

预制斜撑

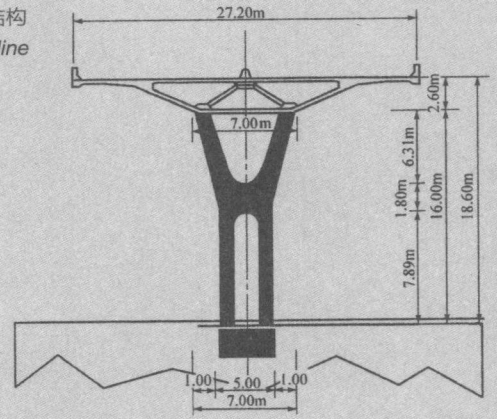

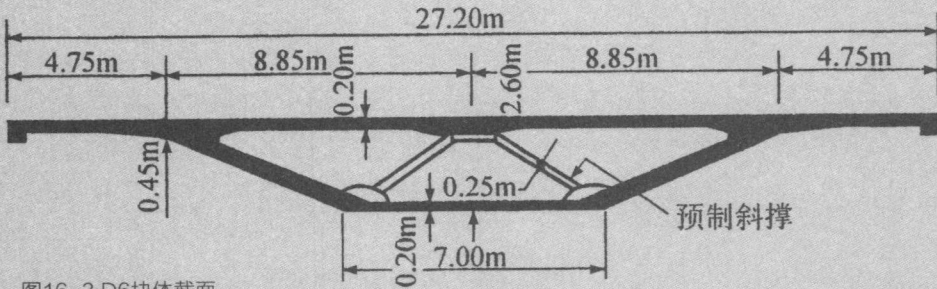

图16-3 D6块体截面
Fig.16-3 Cross section of block D6

图16-4 D2/D3块体截面
Fig.16-4 Cross section of blocks D2/D3

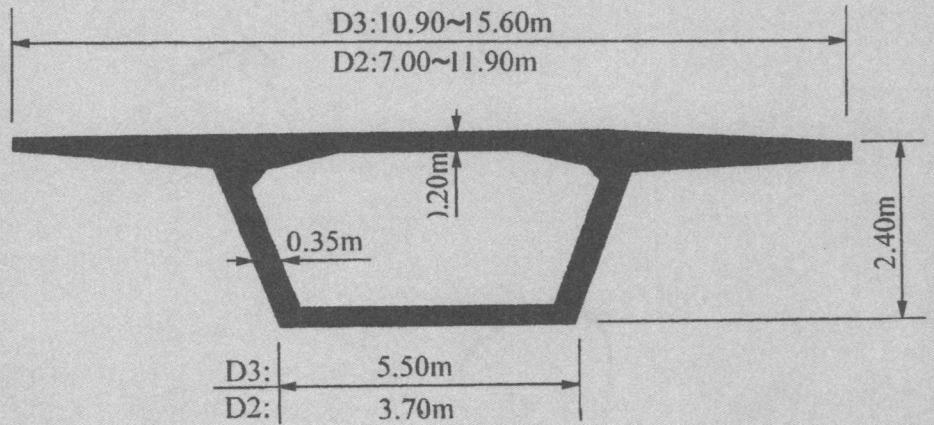

D3:10.90~15.60m

D2:7.00~11.90m

0.20m

0.35m

2.40m

D3:   5.50m

D2:   3.70m

图16-5 门架外形
Fig.16-5 External form of portal frame

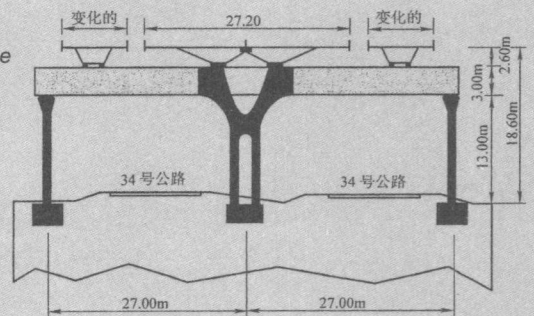

变化的   27.20   变化的

2.60m

3.00m

18.60m

13.00m

34号公路   34号公路

27.00m   27.00m

的Alistair Lenczer，Millau桥的建筑师说，他需要提出一个工程师与建筑师在设计这一结构时很好合作实例。回顾历史，他说，铁、随后是钢的发展为桥梁设计开阔了广阔的领域，特别是能采用"金银丝饰品"（filigree）结构。较早的例子，如巴黎艺术桥（the Pont des Arts in Paris）可以很好地表明轻型设计与传统的石桥设计具有强烈的对比。

38m高塔腿由两个刚性金属箱梁组成，其上则有49m高的桅杆，上面大部分锚固斜拉索，塔的总高为87m，其顶部为17m，并非为结构需要而单纯为了美学。桥墩截面为变化的（图15-3），其形式为建筑师和工程师紧密合作所作出的很好的设计。4块板具有固定的尺寸，另4块每段则略有变化，包括其方向。

Millau 桥为单索面斜拉桥，主梁为钢箱梁，截面高度4.20m，桥面宽27.75m，每向有两条各宽3.5m的车道，其一为快车道，一为慢车道。同时两侧各有一条宽3m的紧急车道，中间突出4.45m以布置并列的斜拉索。箱梁除按传统装配外，另加风筛（wind screen）以限制作用在高架桥上的风速至地上引桥风速值，防止车辆上桥时因风导致桥梁摇摆；安装风嘴（fairing）是希望空气动力气流和美学质量，协调包括伸出桥面外的风嘴，桥的总宽为32.05m。

因为该桥总长几乎有2.5km，旅行者将有足够的时间观赏峡谷景物，同时也欣赏他们驰驶其上的、造型雅致的结构，可使驾驶者感觉良好，心旷神怡。

Millau桥按计划于2005年12月建成通车，它的2号塔塔高345m，为世界最高的桥塔（只有在意大利墨西拿海峡385m桥塔建成后才退居第2位），而桥的长度2 460m，超过提早4个月于2005年8月建成的希腊桥（2 252m），成为世界当时最长的斜拉桥。

在编写Millau桥时，承英国朋友、Bd&e主编Ms. Helena Russell及时用电子邮件寄来参考文献，在此表示衷心的感谢。

16. 世界最长的桥

16. The Longest Bridge in the World

世界最长的桥原为美国彭洽特伦湖桥（Pontchartrain Lake）1、2 号桥，俱长38.4km，现在已为2000年1月，在泰国曼谷建成的长55km的Bang Na高速公路（BNE）高架桥代替而成为新的世界最长桥纪录（图16-1），获得进入《吉尼斯纪录大全》（Guinness book of Records）。该工程的预制预应力混凝土高架桥总长度为55km，宽27.2m，外加40km匝道(ramp)，连同交叉平台(interchange)和收费平台(tool plazas)，桥面总面积达190万m²，是环绕曼谷市的主要交通干线，对泰国东南部的发展具有重大影响。设计方案采用预制箱形截面块体、逐孔建造的后张混凝土箱形梁。箱梁块体用匹配浇筑（match-cast）成型，通过箱内的纵向体外索、干缝、就位、后张拼装。高架桥全长都建筑在原有行车速度为80km/h的第34号高速公路上空，桥下净空高14m，上部高架桥施工，不得影响下部道路的正常行驶。规定工期很紧，仅为3.5年，于2000年1月建成。

该桥采用离心混凝土桩基，桩的直径为800mm，壁厚120mm，长一般为30m，由两节焊成，桥墩为预制混凝土H形双柱框架，高16m（图16-2）。箱梁块体主要有D2、D3和D6 三种截面，比较轻巧纤细，都已经具有实际应用经验。

D6（图16-3）用于主要线路，其截面尺寸为宽27.2m、高2.6m、块长2.55m，每块重约85t。D6采用单室（仅有2块斜腹板）箱形截面，中间顶板跨度虽大到17.7m，由于箱内有2根斜撑，顶板厚度可以做得很薄。箱梁的纵向拼装用22根后张束，其中20根放置在箱内混凝土体外，其余2根设置在箱梁斜腹板混凝土内。箱梁块体的横向预应力束一部分设

图16-1 BNE高架桥工程照片（承陆勇博士请泰国研究生Mr. Noppom Saelem拍摄惠赠）

Fig.16-1 Engineering photo of BNE Viaduct (courtesy of Dr. Lu Yong to ask a Thailand postgraduate Mr. Noppom Saelem for taking this picture)

图17-1 吉兆桥灯光夜景效果图（承曹诚高工惠赠）
Fig.17-1 Effect picture lamplight of Jizhao Bridge in night scene (courtesy of Senior Engr. Cao Cheng)

图17-2 吉兆桥日景效果图（承曹诚高工惠赠）
Fig.17-2 Effect picture of Jizhao Bridge in the daytime (courtesy of Senior Engr. Cao Cheng)

置在顶板混凝土中，另一部分则放置在底板和斜腹板混凝土中，预加应力分两次完成，每次施加50%。梁跨最大为44.4m，一般为42m。

D2、D3（图16-4）均为单室箱形截面，分别用于2车道和3车道匝道桥面，以及交叉平台和收费平台桥面。

在一些区段，即在收费平台处和匝道交汇处（merging area）主线路需加宽，这必须将上部结构设置在门架梁(portal beam) 上，因为34号高速公路的截面必须保持（图16-5），因此需加设总数为180道门架。门架梁刚性固结在主线路门架柱上，而在两端则与外侧柱铰接。最大跨度为27m。梁用匹配浇筑形成具有竖向腹板、体外后张的箱形结构，门架柱有相同的H形柱，但具有和门架梁相同截面的挑腿，必须提供现场浇筑的节点以调节挑腿和先匹配浇筑的截段。

为供应工程应用的全部预制构件，建造了一个规模庞大的邦波(Bang Bo)露天预制场，位置选择在主干线29km以北3.5km处。场地位于沿河河岸的沼泽区，占地总面积650 000m²，由于重型构件生产和运输的需要，整个生产区采用带桩基的现浇钢筋混凝土地面。建场投资，不包括地价、设备、运输车辆大约为2 300万美元。预制厂设施包括木工、机械、焊接、后张管道、钢筋加工、预应力筋加工等车间和搅拌站，以及试验室、办公、生活等设施。从平整场地到开始构件生产大约用了9个月时间。预制厂规模及预制构件产量都是全世界最大的。

预制厂一共要生产40 000件箱梁块体和30 000件其他钢筋混凝土构件，如桥墩、离心桩、路障与匝道工字梁等，预制混凝土总量为1 100 000m³。每月大约生产箱梁块体1 800件，构件堆放场地考虑储存7个星期的产品，占地面积260 000m²。预制厂两端各设一个搅拌站，用3m³竖筒式搅拌机，产量为100m³/h。用25台搅拌车和皮带运输机将混凝土直接倒入模板。混凝土振捣同时用附着式和插入式两种振动器。箱梁混凝土强度规定为55MPa，混凝土初始塌落度为200mm，泌水率要求为0，以防止新鲜混凝土离淅。为加速匹配浇筑，要求用早强配合比，混凝土10h强度应达到20MPa，然后对箱梁块体顶板施加50%的横向预加力，以便拆除模板，移动到匹配浇筑的位置。

这种箱形梁的截面比较轻巧单薄，要做到尺寸准确，可以进行纵向匹配拼装，对混凝土的配比、养护、运输和预加应力等各个阶段，都需要高技术与严格控制。本工程是设计、施工总承包的交钥匙工程，由泰国公司与德国、美国公司组成的合资公司总承包。

17. 吉兆桥

17. Jizhao Bridge

吉兆桥是天津市跨越海河的一座斜拉桥，其夜景灯光效果图示于图17-1，日景效果图示于图17-2。它融合了建筑艺术与结构为一体的新的概念设计。采用四塔柱稀索斜拉。从柳林风景区海河河畔看该桥的整个景观将会非常壮观。

吉兆桥是一座具有划时代建筑风格的桥，桥梁的基本形态好像一个放射的字母"W"，桥的背面成曲线形，体现设计的动态感觉。由于海河两岸景观方案的亲水平台间净距约200m，为实现桥梁墩柱完全不侵入海河，确定主跨跨径为192m，边跨采用40m，从桥梁美学观点考虑，边跨与主跨之比应在0.2左右，照上可以达到这一要求。梁高自边墩的2m到主塔墩的5m，再由主塔墩的5m曲线变化到海河中部的2m。

桥塔采用斜塔形式，立面上有两高两矮四座桥塔，两座高塔（主塔）为桥的主要承重结构，两座矮塔（辅塔）的设置起到减小桥梁的支承跨度、减小主梁内力的作用。四座塔横桥向均位于行车道中间，通过桥塔散开的空间索，分别吊在桥面的中间和两侧支承着桥梁的荷载。

因为吉兆桥在海河上的位置尚未最后确定，故该桥尚未建造。

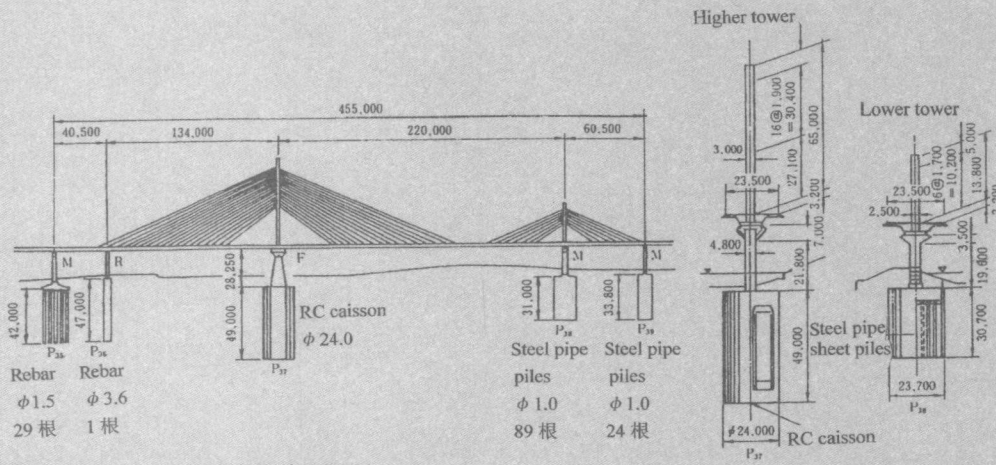

Higher tower
Lower tower

455.000

40.500 134.000 220.000 60.500

16@1.900 = 30.400
65.000
3.000
27.100
23.500
3.200
4.800
7.000 3.200
21.800

16@1.700 = 10.200
13.800 5.000
23.500
2.500
3.500 3.200
119.600

M R F M M

42.000 47.000 28.250 49.000

RC caisson φ24.0

31.000 33.800

P38 P39
P37

Steel pipe piles φ1.0 89根
Steel pipe piles φ1.0 24根

Rebar φ1.5 29根
Rebar φ3.6 1根

Steel pipe sheet piles

49.000

30.700

23.700

φ24.000
RC caisson
P37
P38

图18-2 S形曲线斜拉桥总图（线条图）
Fig.18-2 General configuration of S-curved cable-stayed bridge

图18-3 Sereleryany Bar桥
Fig.18-3 Sereleryany Bar Bridge

图18-1 日本S形曲线斜拉桥
（承川崎重工惠赠）
Fig.18-1 Japanese S-shaped cable-stayed Bridge (courtesy of Kawasagi Heavy Inelustriec)

图18-4 西班牙Barqueta拱桥
Fig.18-4 Barqueta arch bridge

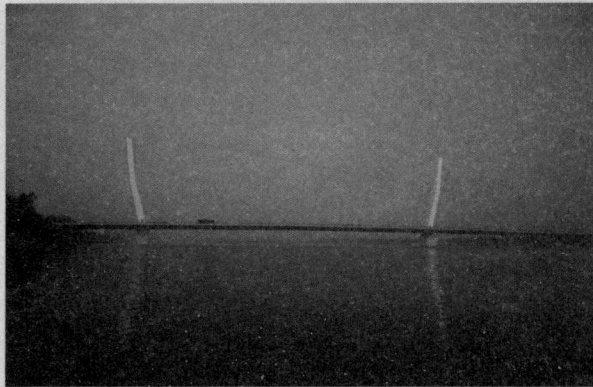

图18-6 有折线型桥塔的沈阳富民桥（承李帼昌教授惠赠）
Fig.18-6 Shenyang Fumin Bridge with broken-line-shaped pylon (courtesy of Prof. Li Guochang)

18. 异形桥及异形桥塔

18. Special Bridges and Special Pylons

1. 异形桥可能多种多样的，在此处介绍了3种异行桥

(1) 斜桥（Shew Bridge）当道路与河流斜交时，往往建造斜桥，这时桥轴线与河岸斜交。斜桥跨度一般不大。如果改变道路走向，反较费事。瑞士洛桑工业大学一博士的学位论文即系研究斜桥（细石混凝土配筋板桥），并进行缩小比例的模型试验。当编者1992年访问该校时，承将全文见赠，惜未能找出。

(2) 日本京都高速公路桥かっしかハ-プ（Katsushika Harp Bridge），为一座S形曲线独柱双塔不对称的斜拉桥（图18-1），支承间距为40.5m+134m+220m+60.5m。塔高不同，高塔墩P$_{37}$为钢筋混凝土的，高49.0m，直径24.0m，低塔墩为41.0m，钢管的，高31.0m共89根（图18-2）。由于在曲线上，斜拉索亦成曲面。

(3) 法国著名结构工程师Eugene Freyssinet获得靠近俄罗斯莫斯科Sereleryany Bar桥造型的合同，并提供和安装为统一不寻常的结构的72根斜拉索，该桥为具有跨度410m的钢拱，其矢高为102m，它是从Sereleryany Bar（银木，Silver Woods）至莫斯科立面。建设的桥设计成包含一餐厅建于拱冠之下若干米距离处，用支于钢拱的梁支承，并用在拱平面外的成曲面的斜拉索固定（图18-3）[33]。

一般拱桥两肋为平行竖立，但有时为了造型，或为了改善抗风支撑的稳定性，将其向内斜置，常称为提篮桥。真正的提篮桥是将两拱肋向中心线并为一道中心肋，如西班牙历史城市Sevilla的Barqueta拱桥（图18-4），它常被称为弦弓型桥（string-bow-typed bridge）[31]。

中承式拱桥拱肋也有外倾的，其造型独特，折射出桥梁建筑风格的时代性，如法国某市的这种桥具有一定的代表性。这种桥一般不设风撑，因这将破坏其造型美，且风撑长，其稳定性也不利。常州某桥要求跨越70m运河和40m道路，方案采用两跨拱塔斜拉桥（图18-5）[34]。设计以常规钢管拱和斜拉桥的结构手段，创造出独特的新颖结构。全桥设置两根向外倾斜的钢管拱圈作索塔，在两拱圈间以及拱圈与主梁之间，使用了5片扭曲的空间索面支承桥面，又对拱塔起到稳定作用。

也有3拱肋的拱桥，如上海五尺沟三拱肋钢管混凝土简支系杆拱桥，它位于上海南汇芦潮港，与东海大桥相连，桥总宽37.8m，计算跨度100m，矢高50m。

2. 异形桥塔

（1）折线型桥塔 沈阳浑河富民桥系单索面折线型双斜塔预应力混凝土斜拉桥（图18-6），主跨242m，折线型斜塔高67.5m，其上下部倾角分别为15°、7°。该桥北塔墩采用3个特大吨位的盆式球型钢支座，其中间一个承重量达13 000t。

荷兰鹿特丹Erasmus独塔斜拉桥为带有倾向短跨的折线形[15]。

（2）四斜柱桥塔 希腊Rion-Antirion（两城市）桥（图18-7）位于帕特雷市，横跨隔断希腊大陆与其最大的伯罗奔尼撒半岛的科林西亚湾，是希腊西部新干线和欧洲运输网的一部分。该桥为5跨连续斜拉桥，采用漂浮体系，在主桥两端采用纵向可摆动的钢排架。主桥跨径为286m+3×560m+286m=2 252m，两岸引桥分别为392m（Rion一侧）和239m（Antirion一侧），原计划于2005年12月建成，它总长短于法国全长为2 460m的Millau桥，它按计划于2005年12月建成通车，但希腊桥则提前于2005年8月建成通车，在这4个月内，希腊桥为世界上第一长斜拉桥。

希腊桥桥塔为4斜柱至顶上合而为一的特异造型，见图18-7[35]。

图18-5 拱塔斜拉桥
Fig.18-5 Cable-stayed bridge with arch pylons

图18-7 希腊Rion-Antirion桥桥塔（及基础）示意图（承周世忠教授级高工惠赠）
Fig.18-7 Sketch of the pylon (and foundation) of Greek Rion-Antirion (courtesy of Senior Engr. Prof. Zhou Shizhong)

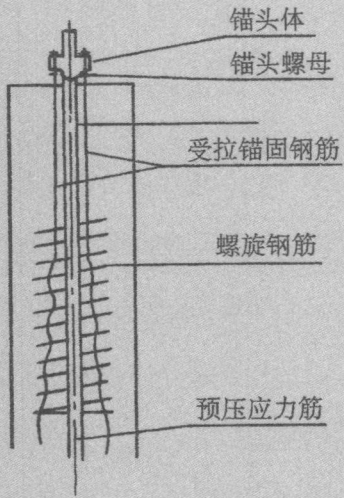

图19-2 预压钢筋的构造
Fig.19-2 Construction of prestressed compressive bar

锚头体
锚头螺母
受拉锚固钢筋
螺旋钢筋
预压应力筋

图19-1 双预应力桥（承Prof. Hans Reinffenstuhl惠赠）
Fig.19-1 Bi-prestressed Bridge (courtesy of Prof. Hans Reinffenstuhl)

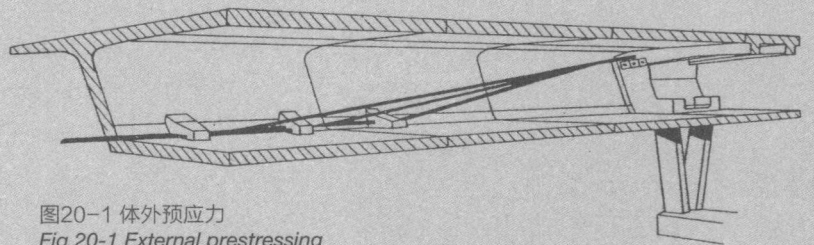

图20-1 体外预应力
Fig.20-1 External prestressing

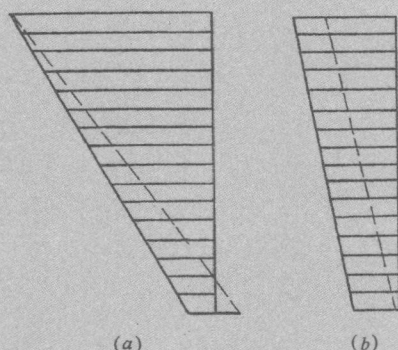

图19-3 双预应力图形(a), (b)

Fig.19-3 Bi-prestressing diagrams (a), (b)

19. 双预应力桥

19. Bi-Prestressed Bridge

　　编者在书中介绍的德文原文称"有压应力配筋构造的桥"（图19-1）（Eine Brücke mit Druckspannbewehrüng-Konstruktion）[36]这种桥是编者的德国朋友Prof. Dr. Hans Reiffenstuhl于20世纪80年代为奥地利ALM桥设计建造的，该桥系单箱截面,跨中截面高度为2.5m=1/30.4，箱形竖壁宽度为6.0m；支承处截面高度为2.3m，竖壁宽度为2.6m，即在梁端，箱形成为封闭的，总宽6.0m，但留有0.8m×1.2m的洞口，即这时梁腹宽为（6-0.8）/2=2.6m。梁内受拉预应力筋共用80束，每束12根的钢绞线，而在梁的顶部，采用96根 ϕ 36高强粗钢筋，钢筋用量分别为56.486t及59.82t。每根预压钢筋是通过其端部的锚头体将它和埋设在梁端内，末端做成波纹状的受拉锚固钢筋连接起使传递拉力（受压预应力筋受压后在套管内将伸长顶使锚固钢筋受拉，因而使梁上部受拉）。预压钢筋的构造见图19-2。

　　当只有受拉预应力钢筋时，梁在使用荷载下的应力图形如图19-3(a)所示。当加设受压预应力钢筋时，由这项预应力钢筋使梁顶受拉，梁底受压，改变了截面的应力分布，最后的应力图形将如图19-3(b)所示。这将提高梁的抗裂荷载和减小跨中挠度，因而截面高度可减小。

　　双预应力桥与同跨径桥相比，混凝土用量虽可略有节省，但用钢量明显增多，总造价约提高47%左右，其最大优越性是可使建筑高度减小，尤其适用于城市多层立交工程和高架桥工程中。这种桥在国外是专利的。尽管如此，采用大量受压预应力筋（用量且超过受拉预应力筋）来提高截面刚度是否合理，还值得进一步探讨。

　　1992年9月编者访问维也纳工业大学时，曾访问过Hans Reiffenstuhl教授，承告知至当时在欧洲也只建造一座这种桥，但后来在日本则建造了10多座双预应力梁桥，最大跨度达65.66m。我国也建造了2座，同济大学并进行了有关试验，后在东南大学也进行过4根双预应力混凝土梁的实验研究。

20. 体外预应力

20. External Prestressing

　　在大截面构件中国外首先采用体外预应力（图20-1），这样可方便地监测预应力筋的工作性能，如锈蚀情况等，必要时可调整预应力或撤换预应力筋。我国在桥梁中第一次采用体外预应力的是汕头海湾预应力混凝土悬索桥，而在房建中是在石家庄东方购物中心12层裙楼8层大厅18m大梁中第一次采用体外预应力筋。

　　1984年秋编者参加在匈牙利首都布达佩斯（Budapest）（该市实为二市：布达和佩斯由多瑙河分开）参加ACI-RILEM长期观测国际会议时由捷克（当时捷克和斯洛伐克尚合并在一起）老友T. Javor博士、Bratislava（分治后为斯洛伐克首都）工业大学副教授（2004年逝世，英年早逝，惜哉，悲夫！）率领部分与会者至捷克参观旅游。当时曾进入一大桥混凝土梁参观，该桥采用体外预应力筋，对该大桥曾进行振动及变形等观察，观测是在大型汽车内进行，几乎几天读数。在会议论文集中列示有27年的变形曲线[37]。

图22-1 安康斜腿桥（承项海帆院士惠赠）
Fig.22-1 Ankang Bridge with inclined leg (courtesy of Academician Xiang Haifan)

图22-3 浊漳河桥（承范立础院士惠赠）
Fig.22-3 Zhuozhanghe Bridge (courtesy of Academician Fan Lichu)

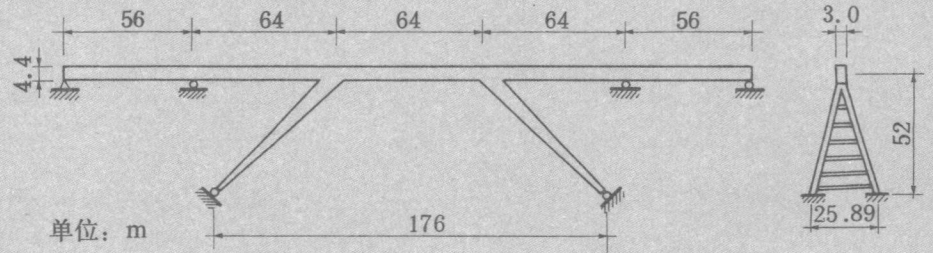

图22-2 安康桥尺寸图
Fig.22-2 Dimensions of Ankang Bridge

图23-1 江西永平铜矿桥（承范立础院士惠赠）
Fig.23-1 Jiangxi Yangping Bridge at copper mine (courtesy of Academician Fan Lichu)

21. 预弯梁

21. Preflex Beam

预弯梁是第二次世界大战后由比利时工程师提出的，接着有所推广。我国于1989年和1991年分别在湖南和河南建造了两座预弯预应力混凝土梁桥，跨度为17m和15m。

预弯梁制作分为3个阶值：首先使用将工字钢制成（无应力状态）向上弯的梁；然后加载（1/4点集载）后使平直，在工字钢下翼缘浇混凝土，待其达到设计强度后卸载，钢梁的回弹使混凝土获得预压应力，梁向上拱，但拱度较工字钢原拱度小很多；最后浇上翼缘和腹板混凝土，即构成预弯预应力混凝土梁。这种预应力梁不需张拉设备和锚具设备，也省去后张法中的管道，如在现场施工，浇混凝土时不需设立模架，具有一定的经济效益。

90年代中，重庆交通学院提出采用混凝土梁代替工字钢，采用横向张拉设在钢筋混凝土梁体外适当处的预应力钢筋代替横向加载使预应力梁钢筋受拉，降低了对张拉设备的要求。对这一设想进行了30m的工程试点[38]。

22. 斜腿桥

22. Bridge with Inclined Leg

我国最大的斜腿刚构桥为陕西省安康县跨汉江的铁路桥（图22-1），其尺寸示于图22-2。主跨长（斜腿铰间距离）为176m。主梁截面为3m × 4.4m，斜腿截面上端为1.5m × 4.0m，下端为1.5m × 1.5m，均为栓焊带肋的箱形结构。该桥于1982年建成[39]。

邯长线浊漳河桥，是我国第一座预应力混凝土斜腿刚构铁路桥（图22-3），主跨82m。梁体和腿部均为单室箱形截面。该桥于1981年9月建成[39]。

23. 刚架拱桥

23. Rigid-Framed Arch Bridge

这种拱桥主要受力构件为主拱肋、上纵梁及其间的斜撑，适用于中小跨径拱桥。图23-1示江西省永平铜矿中于1984年建成的刚架拱桥，主跨67m，其中设一斜撑，撑梁整结成一体，使拱成为刚度很大刚架拱桥。在江苏于1985-1988年陆续建成国内最大的金城、金匮和下甸三座跨度同为100m、国内最大的刚架拱桥，前二桥分别设3和2斜撑，拱为等截面，而下甸桥不设撑，撑身上部加厚成变截面，桥上建筑采用23m预应力混凝土简支梁以过渡，仍成刚度很大的刚架拱桥[39]。

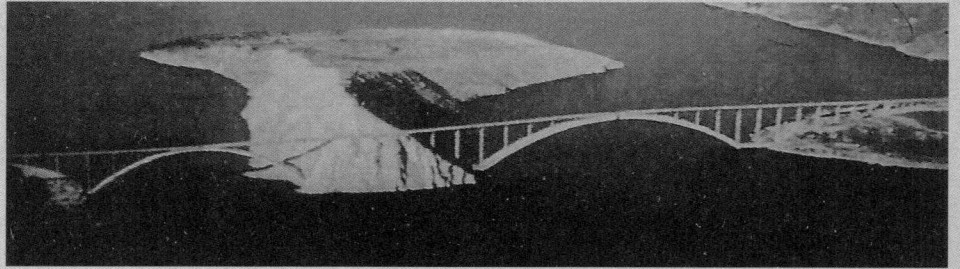

图26-1 KRK拱桥（承高级工程师Ms. Michaeln Zamolo[1]惠赠）
Fig.26-1 KRK Arch Bridge (courtesy of Senior Engr. Ms. Michaeln Zamolo)

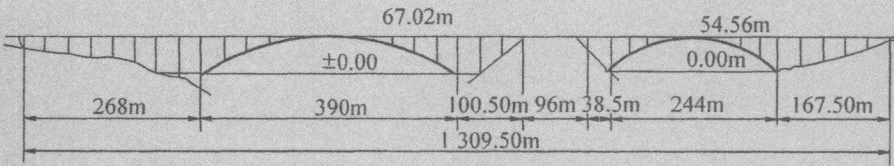

图26-2 KRK桥纵向布置
Fig.26-2 Longitudinal Arrangement of KRK Bridge

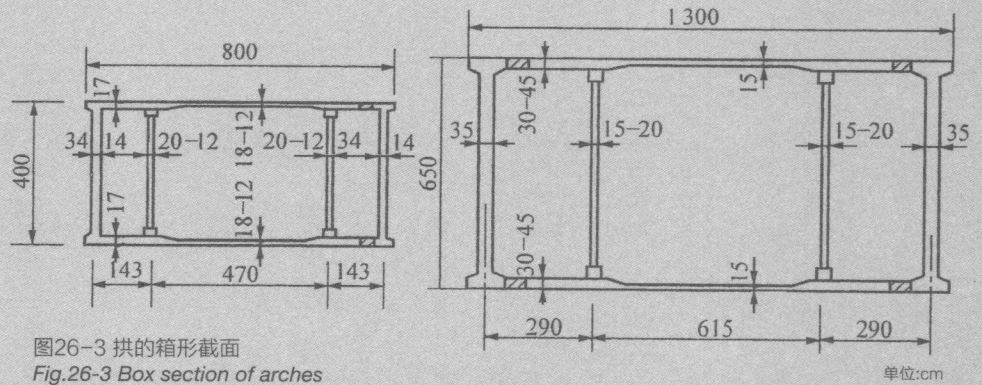

图26-3 拱的箱形截面
Fig.26-3 Box section of arches

单位:cm

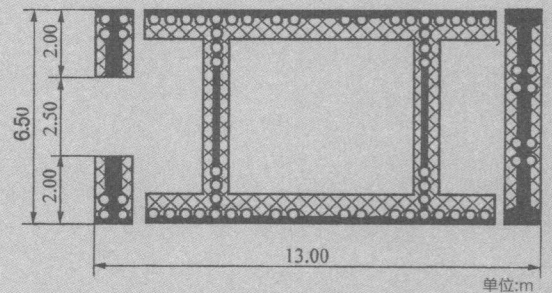

图26-4 长拱内拱冠干斤顶的位置
Fig.26-4 Arrangement of jacks at the crown in long arch

单位:m

图24-1 斜拉桁架T-构桥
Fig.24-1 Inclined-tensioned trussed T-rigid frame bridge

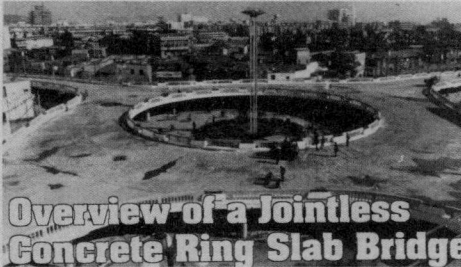

图25-1 岩头口不互通立交桥
Fig.25-1 Yantoukou Jointless Concrete Ring Slab Bridge

①Senior Engineer Ms.Michaeln Zamolo 是编者1984年9月在匈牙利布达佩斯RILEM-ACI召开的混凝土结构长期观察学术讨论会上结识的，后常有通讯联系，图26-1照片也是她寄来惠赠的。

24. 斜拉式桁架

24. Inclined-Tensioned Trussed T-Rigid Frame Bridge

　　我国还曾建造一座 T-构斜拉桥（图24-1）（从参考文献[39]经编者加工放大而成），在此斜拉索用桁架上弦代替，下承式斜拉桥桁梁T-构桥。福州西郊洪塘桥即是这种构造的桥，跨度分布为：16m+27m+4×30m+60m+ 120m+60m+31×40m+8×25m，主跨为：60m+120m+60m，由4片预应力混凝土斜拉式桁架T-构组成，其特点为以刚性的预应力混凝土拉杆（桁架上弦杆）代替斜拉桥的柔性钢索，克服了斜拉桥主索需防护和养护的缺点。T构之间以剪力铰相连，两端以拉压支座支承在桥墩上。桁架总高度18m。每跨由两榀桁架及横梁、T形纵梁和桁架顶横系梁组成。上弦杆截面为矩形，在桁顶两节点间为变截面，采用56ϕ5预应力钢丝束，下弦杆为挖空的T形截面。该桥于1990年12月建成[5]。

25. 无铰混凝土环形板桥

25. Jointless Concrete Ring Slab Bridge

　　虽然无梁板和箱梁环形结构是较普通用于中国城市圆弧形立交桥的设计，但采用无铰整体闭合环作主要结构并不普遍。圆形立交设计为一整体闭合环较铰结构具有几项优点。没有需维修的膨胀缝，每一排架顶部只有一个支承代替两个，跨度连续性提供材料的较有效利用。丁汉山教授设计了我国第一座福建省福州市岩头口不互通整体闭合环形结构（图25-1），于1987年建成，该桥于1991年6月获福建省科技进步奖。

　　混凝土环形桥的内直径为40m，外直径68m，上部结构用橡胶盆式支座支承在15个双柱排架上，沿环向柱间较长和较短距离分别为15.25m和7.05m。闭合环板沿环向的厚度为常数，沿横截面方向，每个排架柱间为0.6m；环板从排架柱边各挑出3.0m，厚度横向变化到悬臂边缘的0.2m；柱直径为1.0m[40]。

26. 关于KRK拱桥

26. On KRK Arch Bridge

　　1980年6月，在前南斯拉夫、现克罗地亚首都萨格列布附近的KRK岛上建成连接大陆的桥（图26-1）[41]，桥的纵向布置如图26-2所示，长跨390m，用混凝土C50建造，短跨244m，用C45混凝土建造。箱形截面如图26-3所示。箱形截面外形尺寸沿整个拱考虑混凝土收缩和徐变将使拱轴随时间而缩短，这将引起拱的挠度。为了调整拱跨不向下位移，在II号拱拱冠截面断开处，设置混凝土块，在两三年后移去，代之以液压千斤顶，用以调整拱的中心线，以消除在一段时间后的变形。假定对中心线并不产生显著变化，则不至影响交通安全。另一方面，因为结合在拱内的设备（管线等）要求调整。拱的变形对管线的应力状态将有直接的影响。

　　在较后的一些时间，在施工完成后决定在两拱冠截面内设置千斤顶，使可能对中心线"连续"调整，这对所考虑的结构更为合适。图26-4示II号拱内液压千斤顶的布置（30只在上面，32只在下面）。在I号拱内千斤顶的数目大大减少（分别为8只和10只）。

　　对II号拱第一次调整从1982年4月24日开始进行，桥被抬高63mm；第二次调整从1982年4月至1983年5月后进行。

图27-1 瑞士Gunter桥（承瑞士朋友Prof. R. Walther惠赠）
Fig.27-1 Swiss Gunter (courtesy of Swiss friend Prof. R. Walther)

图27-2 1988年经修葺后的Gunter板拉桥
（承编者好友德国Dr.-Ing.Klaus Stiglat惠赠）
Fig.27-1 Gunter slab-tensioned bridge repaired in 1988
(courtesy of good friend German Dr. -Ing. Klaus Stiglat)

图28-1 南京长江四桥
（承章登精教授级高工惠赠）
Fig.28-1 The 4th Nanjing Bridge (courtesy
of Senior Engr. Prof. Zhang Dengjing)

27. 国际桥梁及结构工程协会年度大会奖

27. Yearly Prize from IABSE

①IABSE的全称为International Association for Bridge and Structural Engineering（国际桥梁及结构工程协会，简称"国际桥协"）

对混凝土桥，除应力板带桥（Stressed ribbon bridge）外，其余各种型式的桥都曾建造过。因应力板带桥刚度很小，只能作为人行桥，故没有这种必要，是不为也，非不能也。编者作为当时南京土建学会理事长，曾代表学会邀请已故中国科学院学部委员、同济大学校长李国豪前辈来南京在东南大学土木学院讲课，他非常欣赏瑞士Gunter桥（图27-1），并放映幻灯片。李老在国际上曾获得1998年国际桥梁协会（IABSE）①颁发的协会年度大奖（每年一人），中国迄今仅他一人获此殊荣。2005年获得者则为编者好友、印度的R.C.Alimchandani博士。瑞士Gunter桥（图27-2）的优美造型，该桥为预应力混凝土刚性板拉桥，即斜拉索包在预应力混凝土板带内，它建造在深谷中，跨度为127m+174m+127m，桥塔很高，且在曲线上，故造型飘逸潇洒。该桥于1980年建造，而第一座这种类型桥是日本于1979年建成的小本川桥，其跨度为46m+85m+46m，其造型远不如Gunter桥优美。我国1985年10月建成的湖南马迹塘桥跨度更小，为30.7m+60m+30.7m。编者1992年秋访问瑞士洛桑工业大学（法语区）时，知Gunter桥距洛桑约300km，较远，故不便劳动主人送去参观，但该校桥梁博士Klinger曾为编者放映建成后板带的幻灯片，其上未经描绘的多道裂缝已清晰可见。1988年，经过修葺后，桥板带面整洁光鲜，在日光下熠熠生辉，更为大桥增加了魅力（图27-2）。

28. 南京长江四桥

28. The 4th Nanjing Yangtze River Bridge

南京长江四桥（图28-1）已于2008年1月6日奠基。它建于距南京长江二桥上游约10km处，为双塔三跨悬索桥，跨度分布为409m+1 418 m+364m，主跨1 418 m。大桥两岸锚碇基础是一个立方体，非常巨大，如江北锚碇的平面尺寸即达69 m×58m，埋入地下近52.8m，浇筑一个锚碇基础所需混凝土近1.8万m^3，重量超过40万t。大桥侧跨端距锚碇分别为166m和119m。大桥主缆共分127股，由高强钢丝组成，直径达76.7cm。桥面为双向6车道，核批建设工期为5年。

据知世界现有双塔三跨悬索桥只有日本明石海峡桥和丹麦大海带桥，其余大跨悬索桥由于种种原因，建成一边跨为斜拉的，如我国香港青马大桥和西堠门大桥，后者主跨为1 650m，位居世界第二，但非双塔三跨。在建的二者，一为南京长江四桥，另一为韩国Gwangyang桥，跨度357.5m+1545m+357.5m，计划2012年建成。

编者于2008年元月7日作诗：

大桥公铁昔时建，先后二三桥建成。

高速京申铁路线，过江选址建康城。

巨龙大胜关前渡，三幅双虹水上生。

今日四桥新建设，桥型各异世堪惊。

(a)

(b)

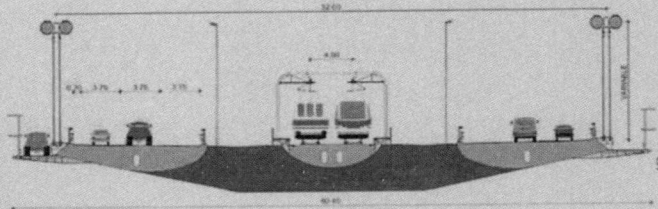

(c)

图29-1墨西拿海峡桥（承大桥建设指挥部惠赠）
(a) 纵向示意图；(b) 纵向效果图；(c) 横向效果图
Fig.29-1 Messina Strait Bridge (courtesy of the Headquarters of bridge construction)
(a) longitudinal sketch, (b) longitudinal effect picture, (c) transverse effect picture

图29-2 90年代意大利友人所赠大桥桥面模型照片
Fig.29-2 Photo of bridge deck model presented by Italian friend in the 90' of last century

29. 待建的意大利墨西拿海峡桥

29. Italian Messina Strait Bridge to be Constructed

意大利墨西拿海峡（Messina Strait）桥，主跨达3 300m（图29-1）桥塔高385m，高于我国苏通大桥高304m的塔柱，也高于现世界最高法国米洛（Millau）桥345m塔柱。 计划于2007底开始兴建。图29-2示20世纪90年代中期，国际预应力学会（FIB）意大利朋友Prof. Mancini Giuseppe所赠大桥模型照片，桥面中间为双向电车轨道，两侧各为三汽车车道，承见告对该桥水下结构将研究耐久性为100年的混凝土。

30. 大桥基础

30. Foundation of Bridges

大直径管柱基础是介于桩基和沉井基础之间的结构形式，它既有沉井刚度大的特点，又有可预制管节在工地直接拼装成桩的方便，用振动打桩机并在管柱内射水吸泥下沉，使能加快速度和便于在管柱内吸出土塞，打进和直接支承在较好的持力层上。但管柱本身系薄壳结构，轮廓尺寸较大，自重又限制其强度不耐重锤锤击。当遇到厚黏土层或覆盖层很深时，强迫下沉将较困难。

空气幕管柱基础箱基本原理和空气幕沉井一样，从预先埋设在管壁内四周的气管中压入高压空气，通过设在管壁上的喷气孔（气龛，在管柱下方1.5m范围内不设气龛）喷出，并沿管壁外表面上升逸出地面，从而在管壁周围形成松动的含有气体支承的液化土层，这一含气土层围绕管柱外壁如同帷幕一样，减小了土层对管壁的侧向摩擦力而利于管壁下沉，故称空气幕管柱[42]。

泥浆护壁灌注桩桩端后压浆技术采用桩端压力注浆（Base grouting under pressure）工艺提高桩承载力的方法已有40多年历史。端压桩自1961年在修建委内瑞拉Maracaibo斜拉桥（1962年建成，5个主跨都为235cm，两端跨为160m，一般认为该桥是第一座现代化混凝土斜拉桥）时，对该桥首次采用压力灌浆桩。我国自1983年北京市建筑研究所研究开发了预留注浆空腔方式的桩端压力注浆桩后，1987年又开发在桩底设活动式隔离钢板的预留注浆空腔方式的桩端压力注浆桩，1988年徐州市第二建筑设计院在国内首先研制开发出泥浆护壁灌注桩的预留注浆通道方式的桩端压力注浆技术。进入20世纪90年代，桩端压力注浆技术在国内得到蓬勃发展，具体表现在：①注浆形式多种，国内已有20多种装置；②注浆的工艺水平得到较大提高和完善，承载力大为提高；③有的单位创新工艺操作及质量控制发表的文章已逾百篇；④推广应用于工民建深基础中；⑤国内还开发了柱侧压力注浆工艺，桩端、桩侧联合注浆工艺（称后压浆桩）[43]。

31. 大桥事故

31. Events of Bridge

桥梁事故原因有多种，但多由质量原因引起，这可能是：①因偷工减料而造成"豆腐渣工程"；②因赶工引起；③使用过程中管理监控不严等原因引起；④设计问题；⑤其他。

桥梁事故不仅造成很大的损失，也导致人员伤亡。

图31-3 美国塔科马桥的振荡和塌落 （a）振荡（承丹麦好友N. J. Gimsing惠赠）[1]
Fig.31-3 Oscillation and Collapse of American Tacoma Bridge (a) oscillation (courtesy of Danish good friend N. J. Gimsing)[1]

图31-3 （b）塌落（承芬兰朋友Juhani Virola惠赠）[2]
Fig.31-3 (b) collapse (courtesy of Finnish friend Engr. Juhani Virola)[2]

图31-1 彩虹桥断裂的钢管混凝土
Fig.31-1 Broken concrete-filled steel tube in Coloured-Rainbow Bridge

图31-2 金沙江桥（承老友史尔毅教授级高工惠赠）
Fig.31-2 Jinshajiang Bridge (courtesy of old friend Senior Engr. Prof. Shi Eryi)

①典型的"豆腐渣"工程 —— 我国重庆綦江大桥（又称彩虹桥），净跨120m，是一座用钢管混凝土建造的中承式拱桥，于1999年1月4日晚6时50分突然塌落，造成40人死亡，多人受伤的严重后果。调查表明，该工程有多项质量问题，图31-1示断裂的钢管混凝土。在綦江桥上游约40m处重建新桥，长160m，主桥跨度为130m，宽7.5m，于2000年12月18日建成，质量优良。在原桥头竖立"警示碑"，碑上镌刻1999年1月4日原彩虹桥垮塌的惨痛教训和40名遇难者姓名等[1]。

②湖南凤凰县沱江大桥，因某种原因而赶工，造成倒塌，后果严重。

③ 我国金沙江大桥（图31-2），系中承式钢筋混凝土拱桥，1989年建成通车，曾是中承式钢筋混凝土拱桥的世界纪录，建成后拱脚常年浸泡水中，因裂缝原因，可能还因混凝土保护层不密实而导致钢筋锈蚀，于2004年某月早晨突然倒塌。

④美国华盛顿州塔科马峡谷桥。该桥建于1940年，主跨长853m，加劲钢板梁的高跨比小至1：79。通车后不久表明增大柔度是"走得太远了"，因为桥在风中显出振荡的迹象；在建成后的前4个月内，振荡是竖向的，不包含截面的旋转，而且在达到幅值为1.5m往往即衰减下去。继续使用几个月后，随着某些防止加劲梁和跨中主索间相互位移的稳定索断裂，振荡形式突然改变为扭转运动，这时在跨中的两段主跨反对称振荡成节点。扭转运动愈来愈剧烈致使在四分点处的桥面倾斜成+45°~-45°。在大约1h由空气动力的负阻尼引起的剧烈自激振荡后，在套承处一些吊杆开始疲劳断裂，桥的大部分跌落。在桥发生振荡过程中一摄影记者恰经过该桥而拍摄下这一难得的振荡电影，惜所携胶带不足未能拍全最后过程。图31-3示塔科马桥在振荡中和塌落的情况。

在塔科马桥最后的振荡中，风速为56~67km/h，并不是最大的，而远低于桥设计抵抗的最大风速，但是当进行风作用下的结构分析时，仅考虑静压力时该桥完全是安全的。没有进行有关在板梁尖角处形成的脉冲风涡流的动力研究，因而所选择具有极大柔度的设计，后来证明它发生了由空气动力作用引起的失稳。

在塔科马桥灾害后，空气动力学的研究成为所有悬索桥设计过程的一个重要部分。对已建成的悬索桥也要研究是否会出现动力作用下的失稳。第二次世界大战后重建塔科马峡谷桥，结构体系做了明显的改变，很大程度地提高了抵抗风的自激振荡能力。这些改变是将2.4m高的钢板梁改为10m高的桁架，宽度由11.9m增至18.3m，并将不同的减振设施砌入桥内。建成后看，对满足合理的安全度而言，新桥尺寸似过大了。

⑤桥梁事故有可能在多种意外情况下发生，现列举两例说明：a.越南芹苴大桥位于芹苴市，跨后江，全长16km，是越南湄公河三角洲最长的桥，于2004年9月动工兴建，计划于2008年竣工，但于2007年9月26日上午，一座距离地面约30m的脚手架突然倒塌，砸向刚浇注的混凝土桥段上，导致三段桥面连锁倒塌，至少149人伤亡，其中至少有52人死亡。b.舟山大陆上宁波—镇海连岛工程中有5座大桥，其中第四座为主桥——西堠门悬索桥，是世界第二长悬索桥，主跨1 650m，第五座为金塘桥，其东通航孔为122m＋216m＋122m预应力混凝土连续钢拱桥；主通航孔为（77＋218）m＋620m＋（218＋77）m钢箱梁、双塔、双索面斜拉桥，两通航孔为87m＋156m＋77m预应力混凝土连续梁桥，外通航孔为60座预应力混凝土连续梁桥。2008年3月27日凌晨，一艘货船撞上外通航孔，使桥面断裂并塌落，两块重达3 000t的钢筋混凝土砸在了货轮的驾驶座舱上。4名高级船员，包括船长、大副和二副失踪。桥墩局部失损。舟山大陆连岛工程是继我国已建成杭州湾跨海大桥和东海跨海大桥，第三长的跨海大桥。

①见Niel. J. Gimsing. Cable Supported Bridges. Cencept and Desing, 2nd Edition. New York: Join Wiley & Sons Ltd., 1988: 461
②见Juhani Virola. Stora broar I varlden (in Swedish, notable bridges in the world). Vag-Och Vattenbyggaren (Road and Water Construction), 1996(6): 14-22

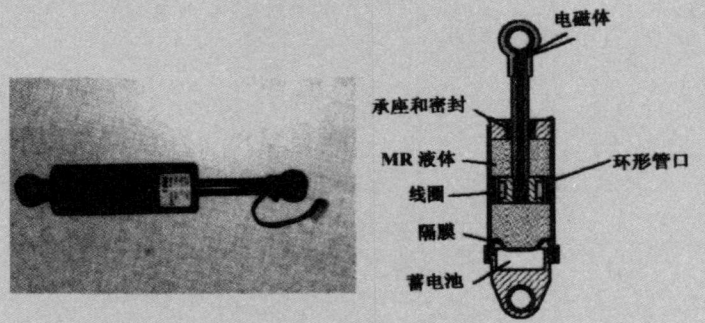

电磁体
承座和密封
MR 液体
线圈
隔膜
蓄电池
环形管口

图32-1 洞庭湖大桥抗风雨振（承陈政清教授惠赠）
(a) 磁流变阻尼器
Fig.32-1 Dongting Lake Bridge against Wind-Rain Induced Vibrations (courtesy of Prof. Chen Zhengqing)
(a) MR damper

图32-1(b) 装上磁流变阻尼器的桥索
Fig.32-1(b) cables installed with MR damper

32. 斜拉桥斜拉索风雨振动

32. Wind-Rain Induced Vibrations of Inclined Cables in Cable-Stayed Bridge

1986年Y. Hikami于Meikonishi桥上首次发现了风雨激振现象（在干燥气候下稳定的拉索，在风和雨共同作用下将产生大振荡）以来，国内外对此进行了大量研究，并进行了试验室模拟试验后建立了索的单自由度风雨激励模型。

洞庭湖大桥是一座三塔斜拉桥，主桥跨度为130m+310m+310m+130m，位于洞庭湖与长江接口处，此处风雨共振时间长，满足发生风雨振的诸多条件。该桥自2000年12月建成通车至2001年5月约半年时间内，发生多次严重风雨振。2001年4月9和10日，在8级大风和中等降雨条件下，洞庭湖大桥发生极严重的风雨振，最大振幅超过40cm，拉索振动还激起桥面振动并撞击桥面的钢护筒发生巨大的惊人响声，如不及时采取措施，后果将十分严重。为此湖南大学陈政清教授研究在桥索（外径达119mm）上安装美制RD-1 000型智能磁流变阻尼器（Magnetorheological, MR damper）（图32-1），这种阻尼器由智能材料（磁流变体）制造，能够调节阻尼器输入电压来获得可变阻尼，实现半主动控制，可使全桥每个拉索都取得理想的减振效果。试验表明，该阻尼器使拉索体系模态阻尼比增大3~6倍（磁流变体由液体变为固体）。根据实地风雨振的实测资料表明加速度响应降低20-30倍，为大桥全桥（共安装312只）采用磁流变阻尼器提供了科学依据[15]。

斜拉桥斜拉索振动机理较为复杂，振动形式较多，除风雨振外，有时还需考虑Karman涡致振动（karman vortes induced vibration），尾流驰振（wake galloping）。

33. 大跨度桥梁结构健康监测

33. Health Monitoring of Bridges with Large-Span

近20多年，特别是近10多年来我国（包括香港和台湾地区）已建成了100多座大跨度桥梁，而目前这些桥梁中有些上部结构已发现损伤和功能方面已显出一些问题，例如斜拉索或预应力索中钢丝腐蚀和断裂、混凝土构件开裂或非结构（如路面、伸缩缝、污水管）的退化破坏等。这些问题可能归咎于建设速度过快、设计规范不完善以及经济高速增长下交通量的增加等原因。在发达国家交通基础设施建设高峰30~50年后出现的养护维修高峰在我国可能提早到来，因此对新建大跨度桥梁设置健康监测系统具有重要意义。

桥梁结构健康监测一般具有以下功能：利用先进的传感技术，自动实施监测[①]：①环境条件和对桥梁的物理及几何状态；②结构状态并对结构的异常反应做出紧急警报；③评估结构的静力和动力安全性、耐久性和使用性，并对结构异常进行识别，为结构的维护管理决策提供依据。对环境监测应用风速仪、温度传感器、温、湿度计、气压计、动态地坪摄像机等，应变传感器、位移传感器、水平仪、倾斜仪、GPS全球定位系统、伸长仪、加速度传感器、地震检波仪等。对各类大桥如拱桥、连续刚构桥、斜拉桥都进行了监测，如对卢浦大桥（拱）、东营大桥（连续刚构桥，主跨/=200m），苏通大桥和润扬大桥监测中，东南大学也参加了部分工作。

①编者在1984年9月17-20日在匈牙利参加RILEM-ACI召开的国际会议，参会者都被安排至捷克旅游并参观了PC箱梁桥（在箱内体外配筋——参观者进入箱内可直立行走）。进行长期有线观测（对环境及结构物），因系有线，故在桥旁停放一辆汽车，量测仪器置于车厢内，工作者在箱内工作，该桥自20世纪50年代即作纪录，故有20多年的挠度纪录，并发表过。

"混凝土结构长期观测国际学术讨论会"（International Symposium on Long-Term Observation）会上编者斯洛伐克朋友T. Javor博士（已于2003年逝世）报告了他撰写的"Long-Term Observation of PC Bridges"，在其中报告了对12座预应力混凝土桥在交通下从1960—1984年进行了10~24年（有达27年的）的静力性能观测。

我国已进行利用公路现有的SDH通信网络为传输媒介，实现桥梁集群监测系统的远程通信，从而实现同时对不同位置的多座桥梁的运行状态进行远程在线监测的研究[46]。这一系统的传输带宽远远高于PSTN传输方式，传输距离和可靠性也高于无线传输方式，并节约额外重复建设远程传输网络的费用，因而是一种较有前景的远程通信方式。

桥梁在施工中也应进行监控，其目的有三：① 使结构在建成时达到设计所希望的几何形状；② 结构在建成时达到合理的内力状态；③ 保证在施工期间结构的安全。如对斜拉桥，在各种测试数据中，线型和索力测试数据对分析计算影响较大，要求测试精度最高；以一节段梁的架设为一个施工周期，钢梁栓接、湿接头浇筑、桥面板混凝土强度达到设计强度要求后前移桥面吊机、张拉斜拉索作为一个标准控制阶段，进行各种数据测试。① 索力控制与调整拉索索力的大小准确与否，不仅影响到桥的线形而且关系到安装过程中整个结构的安全，必需严格控制。对每一个施工周期的控制阶段（挂拉完一对索），要求测量悬臂端前5对索的索力，与计算值比较，如有差歧，立即对其分析，根据分析结构对索力进行调整，保证当前张拉索索力偏差控制在5%左右，尽量避免误差积累。对关键工序，如边跨和中跨合龙等关键工序时要求对全桥索力进行量测，及时了解整个结构的受力状态，与理论值比较，编制"全桥索力一览表"，了解每个节点实际与理论的偏差，如较大，可通过"平差洞索"予以调整。② 线形控制与调整，对每一标准控制阶段，要求测试出5个预制节段前端的高程，然后与计算值比较，制作"高程对比表"，分析后可看出主线形是否在控制范围内，梁段间是否平顺。如超过范围，则配合索力分析，通过适当调整索力来调整主梁线形，要求误差不超过1cm。结构环境和条件不同，施工监控的实施方案也各异，需根据具体情况，研究制订切实可行的方案。

参考文献

REFERENCES

1.丁大钧，蒋永生. 土木工程概论. 第3版. 北京：中国建工出版社，2003：410 *Ding Dajun, Jiang Yongsheng. Introduction to Civil Engineering (3rd Edition). Beijing: China Building & Architecture Press, 2003: 410*

2.丁大钧主编. 砌体结构. 第3版. 北京：中国建筑工业出版社，2004：253 *Ding Dajun, Editor-in-Chief. Masonry Structures (3rd Edition). Beijing: China Building & Architecture Press, 2004: 253*

3.丁大钧. 中国古桥与现代化桥. 土木工程学报，1993，26（4）：69–76 *Ding Dajun. Chinese antique and modern bridges. Civil Engineering Journal. 1993. 26(4): 69-76*

4.*Ding Dajun. Ancient and Modern Chinese Bridges. Structural Engineering International, IABSE, 1994(1): 41-43*

5.丁大钧. 现代混凝土结构学. 北京：中国建筑工业出版社，2000：1047 *Ding Dajun. A Science of Modern Concrete Structures. Beijing: China Building & Architecture Press, 2000: 1047*

6.屠剑虹. 绍兴古桥. 杭州：中国美术学院出版社，2001 *Tu Jianhong. Antique Bridges in Shaoxing Region. Hangzhou: China Arts College Press, 2001*

7.*Luo Guanzhou, Ding Dajun, Juhani Virola. The existing earliest overpass and catenary stone arch bridges. RIA. 2004(6): 62-63*

8.*Luo Guanzhou, Tu Jianhong, Ding Dajun. Existing antique stone bridges in Zhejiang Province, China. Travaux, Ponts, N°814, Dec, 2000: 76-86*

9.*Ye Jianshu, Liu Shilin, Feng Yunchen, Ding Dajun (written by Ding). Nanjing Second Yangtze River Bridge. Concrete International. July, 2004: 80-82 (translated by Italian friend into Italian language "Compless infrastrutturale sullo Yangtze" to be published in "L'insudtria Italiana del Cemento. April, 2002: 318-321)*

10.*Ding Dajun, Juhani Virola. Long-span concrete arch and stone arch bridges. RIA. 1996(6): 26-28*

11.*Ding Dajun, Liu Yongfu. Erfolge des Bogen bruckenbaus in China. Bautechnik. 78 Jehragang. Jan. 2001, S. 63-66*

12.丁大钧. 高性能混凝土及其在工程中的应用（附工程彩照约110幅）. 北京：机械工业出版社，2007：274 *Ding Dajun. High Performance Concrete and Its Applications (attached with 110 coloured engineering photos or so). Beijing: China Machine Press, 2006: 274*

13.*Zhang Zuo'an, Liu Shilin, Ding Dajun. Wushan Arch Bridge. The 1ˢᵗ worldwide longest arch constructed of concrete-filled steel tube. Travaux, International. 2006(6): 75-76*

14. *Ding Dajun. Development of Concrete-Filled Tubular Arch Bridges, China. Structural Engineering International, Journal of IABSE. 2001. 11(4): 265-267*

15. 丁大钧. 中国大陆拱桥和索桥建设的新进展. 中国台湾土木水利学会会刊，2004. 31（4）：56—66 *Ding Dajun. New Advance of The Construction of Arch Bridges and Cable Supported Bridges in Mainland China. Proceedings of Civil and Hydraulic Engineering Society. Taiwan, China, 2004. 31(4): 56-67*

16. *Duan Xuewei, Juhani Virola, Ding Dajun. The Chaotianmen Bridge. RIA. 2007(1): 60-67 (Finnish translation published in "Tierakennsumestari", 2007(1): 46-49)*

17. *Ding Dajun, Ivan Balaz. Tianxingzhou bridge with the span of 504m—the world's record in the category of dual-purpose cable-stayed bridges (in Czech). KONSTRUKCE. 2006(1): 60-62*

18. *Ding Dajun, Juhani Virola. The Shibanpo Bridge—Longest-span concrete rigid frame bridge. RIA. 2006(2): 64-66*

19. *Ding Hanshan, Juhani Virola, Ding Dajun. The Suzhou-Nantong Bridge—worldwide longest-span cable-stayed bridge. RIA. 2006(3): 49-54*

20. 陈宝国. 钢管混凝土拱桥发展综述. 桥梁建设，2003(3)：29—33 *Chen Baoguo. Summarization of the development of concrete-filled tubular arch bridges. Bridge Construction. 2000(3): 29-33*

21. *Tai Kouxia, Zhang Zuo'an, Ding Dajun. Construction of concrete-filled steel tube arch bridges in China. The Indian Concrete Journal. 2007. 81(11): 41-47*

22. *Milan Kominek. The Marian Bridge. Czech Republic. SEI, Journal of IABSE. 1998. 8(4): 283-284*

23. *Towers for Cable-Stayed Bridges: An Introduction. SEI, Journal of IABSE. 1998. 8(4): 248*

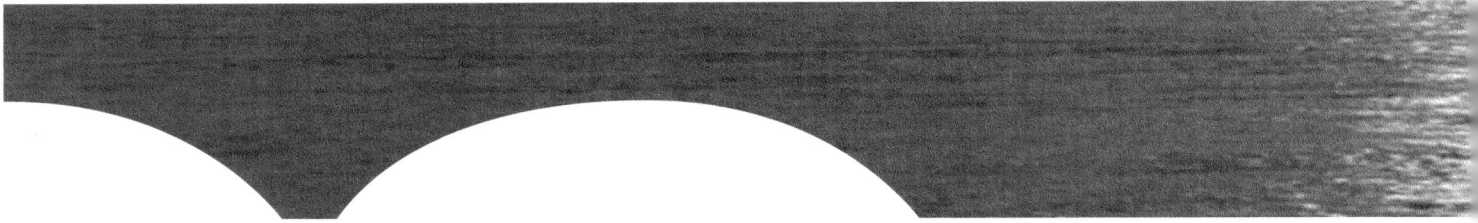

钱塘江二桥

钱塘江大桥（或称一桥）为双层钢桁架公铁两用桥，在茅以升前辈主持下于1937年国难前夕建成，当时总工程师为罗英前辈。

钱塘江二桥（图1）[1]为公铁并列的箱梁桥（图2）[1]，正桥梁跨布置公铁均为45m+65m+14×80m+65m+45m共18孔一联预应力混凝土连续箱形梁桥，共长1 340m，在铁路桥方面是世界最长、不设中间缝的混凝土连续梁。

支承布置

在整个连续梁的中点——9号墩上设置固定支座，在其左、右相邻的8、10号墩上设置半固定支座，目的在于分散一部分地震作用，其余各墩为活动支座。每个墩上设置两个支座，一侧为多向活动支座，另一侧为纵向活动支座。各跨桥支座承载力为7 000kN，20 000kN，30 000kN，铁路桥支座7 000kN，20 000kN，25 000kN，为盆式橡胶支座。固定支座为抗震型的，要求能够承受20%垂直力的水平力。

正桥公路箱梁的截面型式：支点处梁高5.1m，跨中梁高2.4m，下缘呈曲线形。采用单箱单室截面，箱梁顶宽20m，斜腹板1：3，底宽支点处6.6m渐变至跨中8.45m，顶板每边伸出腹板5.24m，腹板、底板、顶板的厚度分别为600~400mm，600~300mm，330mm。在支点及跨中设横隔板（图3）。

正桥铁路箱梁截面型式：采用单箱单室，支点处梁高5.5m，跨中梁高2.8m，梁下缘与公路桥有相同的曲线形，箱梁顶宽11.4m，底宽6.3m，直腹板，腹板、底板、顶板厚度分别为600~480mm；1 000~650mm；480~350mm。在支点及跨中设横隔板。

预应力体系

箱梁采用三向预应力，纵向采用ϕ15钢绞线，强度为1 500MPa，锚具XM及QM-7、9、12；横向（顶板）采用ϕ5高强钢丝束，24丝弗氏锚，强度为1 600MPa；竖向（腹板）采用IV级冷拉粗钢筋ϕ25，用金属波纹管成孔；混凝土采用C50级。

公路面板按A类部分预应力构件设计，目的在于改善结构性能及减少钢丝用量。

1

The 2nd Qiantangjiang Bridge

Qiangtangjiang Bridge (or called the 1st Qiantangjiang Bridge) is a double-decked steel truss bi-purpose bridge for highway and railway, was directed by the Senior Mao Yisheng to be completed on the eve of national calamity in 1937, the Chief Engr. Was the Senior Luo Ying.

The 2nd Qiantangjiang Bridge (Fig.1)[1] is a parallel but separate highway-railway bi-purposed box bridge (Fig.2)[1], the main span arrangement of these 2 bridges is: 45m+65m+14×80m+65m+45m, 18 spans in a unit of PC continuous box girder, the total length is 1 340m, in railway bridge, it is the worldwide longest continuous concrete girder without setting middle joint.

Support layout

At the middle point of whole continuous girder—on pier No.9, the fixed support is set, on the adjacent left and right piers No.8, No.10, the semi-fixed supports are set, it aims at dispersing a part of earthquake-effect, the others are movable supports. On every pier, 2 supports are set, on one side, it is movable one in multi-directions and the other is a movable only in the longitudinal. The carrying bearing capacities of supports in every span are 7 000kN, 20 000kN, 30 000kN, those of railway bridge are 7 000kN, 20 000kN, 25 000kN, basin-typed rubble supports are adopted. The fixed supports are aseismic and required to be able to bear the horizontal force of 20% vertical one.

The section form of the box girder in the main highway bridge: the girder depth at support is 5.1m, that in span center 2.4m, the bottom edge appears to be curvilinear. A single-box and single-cell section is adopted, the top width of box girder is 20m, the web is inclined with slope of 1:3, the bottom width: at support is 6.6m and gradually various to 8.45m at span center, the top slab extends 5.24m from web on each side, the thicknesses of web, bottom and top slabs are respectively 600~400mm; 600~300mm; 330mm. At supported and span center, there are set the diaphragms (Fig.3).

For the box girder in the main railway bridge, the single-box and single-cell section form is adopted, the girder depth at support is 5.5m that at span center is 2.8m, the bottom edge has the same curve as that in highway bridge, the top width of box girder is 11.4m, bottom width 6.3m, the web is vertical. The thicknesses of web, bottom and top slabs are respectively 600~480mm; 1 000~650mm; 480~350mm. At support and span center, there are set the diaphragms.

Prestressing system

For the box girder, 3-dimensional prestressing, in the longitudinal ϕ15 strands are adopted, their strength is 1 500MPa, anchorage devices XM and QM-7, 9, 12 are used; in the transverse (top slab) the highstrength steel tendons ϕ5 are adopted, 24-thread Freyssinet anchorages with strength of 1 600MPa are used; in the vertical cold tensioning grade IV thick bars ϕ25 are used. For making conduit, the metal corrugated pipes are used. Concrete C50 was adopted.

2

图1 钱塘江二桥（远景）
Fig.1 The 2nd Qiantangjiang Bridge (distant view)

图2 钱塘江二桥 —— 公铁两用桥
*Fig.2 The 2nd Qiantangjiang Bridge —
highway-railway bi-purpose bridge*

伸缩装置

正桥与引桥连接处根据计算伸缩总量达506mm。公路部分引进国内制造的承力式橡胶钢材组合型伸缩缝；铁路部分设计特殊的过渡梁及研制伸缩量为600mm的60kg级伸缩轨。

正桥基础

正桥公、铁路各18个桥墩，完全分开，上下游对齐。其中仅一个固定墩（9号），每墩用9φ2.2m钻孔桩，其他各墩采用12～14φ1.5m钻孔桩（图3），钻孔桩均钻入砾石土层。

引桥上部结构

铁路为跨度32m预应力混凝土连续箱形梁。北岸引桥共25孔另加一孔12m梁，分为3联，南岸引桥22孔，亦分为三联，每联在中部设一对固定支座，其余各墩均设活动支座。支座均采用盆式橡胶支座。箱梁为等高、单箱单室截面，梁高2.2m，底宽4.5m。采用顶推法施工，顶宽在顶推时为7.9m，就位后加宽至11.4m。顶推时预应力体系采用IV级冷拉粗钢筋φ32，轧制螺纹。梁体就位后张拉φ15钢绞线，XM及QM-12锚具，强度为1 600MPa。

公路引桥南岸设7孔，北岸14孔。上部结构跨度32m、等高预应力混凝土箱梁，梁高1.8m，梁体上、下行分为独立体系，每个梁体单箱单室，顶宽10m，底宽4.6m，采用鹰架法就地灌注，预应力体系用φ15钢绞线和XM及QM锚具。

引桥基础均用φ1.0m钻孔桩，桩长约40m，桩底均深入砾石土内。公路墩子上、下行车道间分开。

总工程量

铁路桥全长2 861.40m；公路桥全长1 792.8m。全桥混凝土19.5万m³，钢材1.89万t。

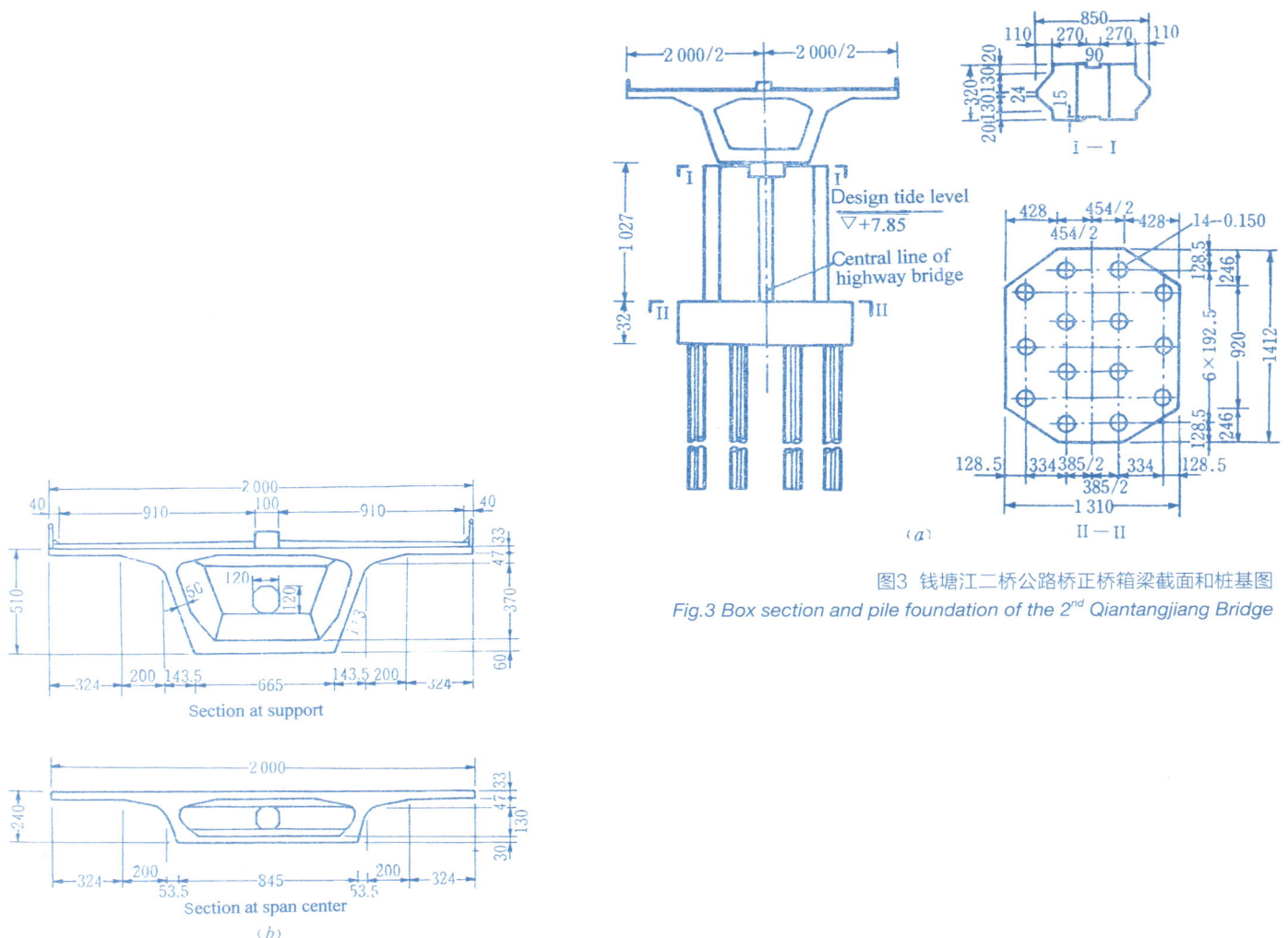

图3 钱塘江二桥公路桥正桥箱梁截面和桩基图
Fig.3 Box section and pile foundation of the 2nd Qiantangjiang Bridge

The highway deck was designed following partially prestressing members of kind A, it aimed at improving the structural behaviour and decreasing the consumption of wires.

Expansion device

At the connection of main bridge and approach, following calculation the sum of expansion and contraction reaches 506mm. In highway bridge, the bearing composite rubber expansion joint made in China is applied; for railway bridge, a transitional girder designed specially and the expansion and contraction rail of grade 60kg developed with the sum 600mm of expansion and contraction are adopted.

Foundation of the main bridge

In both of highway bridge and railway bridge, there are respectively 18 piers fully separated with pier to pier on upper and lower reaches. There is only a fixed pier (No.9), under each of which, $9\phi2.2$m bored piles are set, under the others $12\sim14\phi1.5$m bored piles adopted (Fig.3), all the bored piles were driven into gravel stratum.

Superstructures of approach

Railway approaches are 32m-span PC continuous box girders. On the north bank, there are 25 spans with a 12m-span girder to be divided into 3 units, on the south bank, there are 22 spans to be also divided into 3 units. At the center of every unit, a pair of fixed supports is set, on the other piers, the movable supports are set. On all supports the basin-type rubber bearings are adopted. The box girder section is constant-depth, single-box and single-cell, girder depth is 2.2m, bottom width 4.5m. The bridge was constructed by launching method, the top width was 7.9m during launching, it was widened to 11.4m after being in place. During launching the prestressing system adopted cold-tensioning IV–grade thick bars $\phi32$ with rolled thread. After the girder was in place, $\phi15$-strands were prestressed anchorages XM and QM-12 were used, their strength is 1 600MPa.

For the approaches in highway bridge, there are set 7 span on south bank, 14 spans on north bank. The superstructures are 32m-span PC box girders with constant depth of 1.8m, the upper-lower run bridges are separate systems, each bridge body is single-box and single-cell with top width of 10m and bottom width of 4.6m, the box girders were cast in site on centering, the prestressing system of $\phi15$ strand and XM and Q-12 anchorages was used.

All the foundations of approaches adopt $\phi1.0$m bored piles with length of 40m or so, the points of which were driven into gravel soil. The lanes on piers of highway bridge are separated in upper-lower run.

The total quantities

The total length of railway bridge is 2 861.40m, that of highway bridge 1 792.8m. The concrete used in whole bridge is 195 000m³ and steel 18 900t.

参考文献

1.丁大钧. 高性能混凝土及其在工程中的应用. 北京：机械工业出版社，2007：274
2.丁大钧. 混凝土结构发展. 北京：中国建筑工业出版社，1994：277

REFERENCES

1.Ding Dajun. High Performance Concrete and its Applications in Engineering. Beijing: China Machine Press, 2007: 274
2.Ding Dajun. Development of Concrete Structures. Beijing: China Building & Architecture Press, 1994: 277

STONE ARCH BRIDGES

石拱桥

乌巢河石拱桥

　　我国从1961年建成跨度为112.5m的云南长虹桥后，至1991年，陆续建成跨度为100m和大于100m的敞肩式石拱桥10座（详见绪论6），其中最大的湖南乌巢河石拱桥 l=120m（图1），为双肋式，肋厚1.6m，肋宽冠处为2.5m，拱座处为4.6m。该桥不仅跨度比安济桥大至3.24倍，且为现代化的公路桥。它造型空灵轻巧，设计颇具匠心，而作为其设计者的老工程师（较编者年长）设计多座桥梁，但却非正规大学毕业者，可见实践出真知。

　　乌巢河石拱桥位于湖南省凤凰县沱江源头的乌巢河峡谷的县道上。大桥全长241m，因地制宜，就地取材，建成主跨120m的双肋石拱桥，桥宽为8m。腹拱9孔13m，南岸引桥3孔13m，北岸引桥1孔15m。主拱圈由2条分离式矩形石肋和8条钢筋混凝土横系梁组成。图2示乌巢河石拱桥的纵横截面。拱轴线为m=1.543悬链线，拱矢度1/5，拱肋采用20MPa细石混凝土和100kPa块石砌成。

　　该桥于1991年建成通车，它刊载于《吉尼斯世界纪录大全》（1996年版p.96）

2

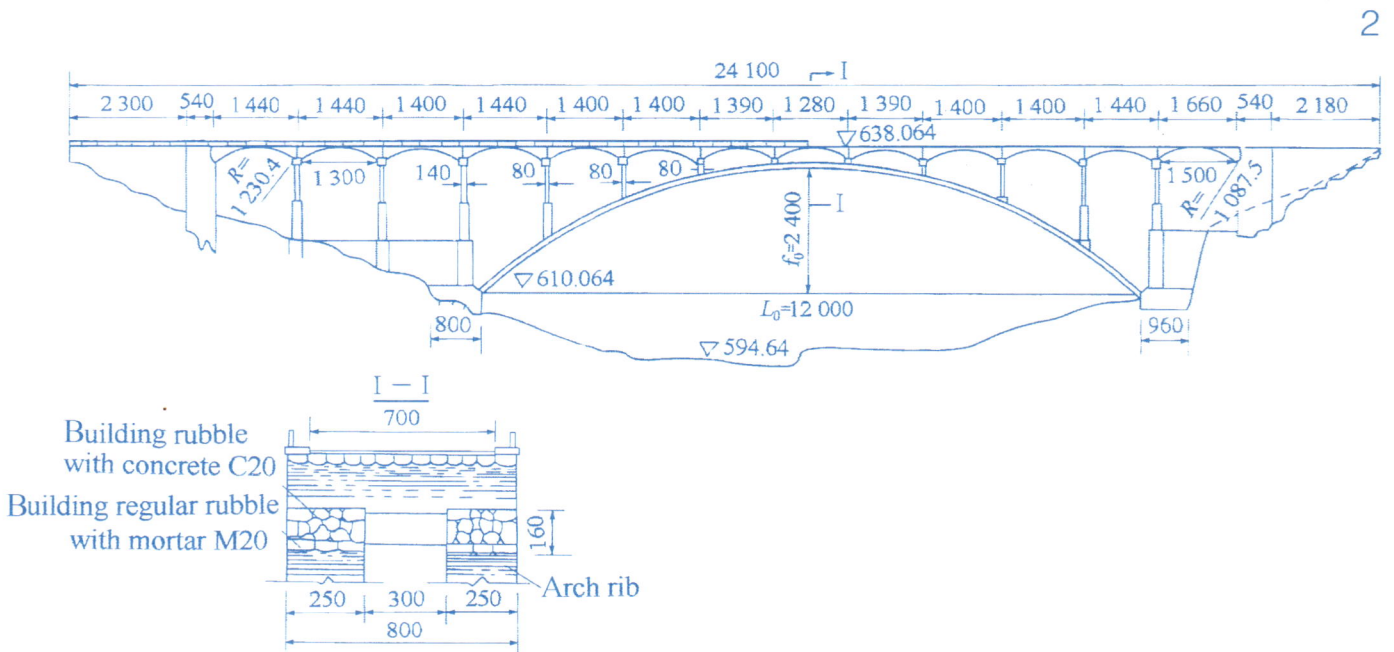

Wuchaohe Stone Arch Bridge

After the Changhong (Long Rainbow) Bridge with span of 112.5m had been completed in 1961 in Yunnan Province, up to 1991 in China there were completed 10 open spandrel arch bridges with spans of 100m or larger than 100m (see Introduction 6), among which the largest Hunan Wuchaohe stone arch bridge (Fig.1) is a double-ribbed one with span of 120m, rib thickness of 1.6m and varied widths of rib: 2.5m at crown and 4.6m at springing. This bridge is not only with span being 3.24 times of that of Anji Bridge, but is also a modern highway one. Its modeling is empty, efficient and light, the design shows ingenuity, the designer, an old Engr. (is older than the Editor) has designed many bridges, but did not graduate from a formal university, it can be seen that the genuine knowledge comes from practice.

Wuchaohe Stone Arch Bridge is located on the county road along Wuchaohe Gorge of the source of Tuo River in Fenghuang County, Hunan Province. The total length of this bridge is 241m, considering local conditions and using local materials, a double-rib stone arch bridge was complete with a main span of 120m, bridge width is 8m. There are 9 spandrel arches, every 13m, approaches on south bank are 3 span 13m, that on north bank is a span 15m. The main arch rings are constituted of 2 separate rectangular stone ribs and 8 reinforced concrete transverse tie beams. Fig.2 shows the longitudinal and cross section of Wuchaohe Stone Arch Bridge. The arch axis is a catenary with $m=1.543$, and rise span ratio is 1/5. The arch ribs are constructed of 100kPa stone block with 20MPa fine stone concrete.

This bridge was completed and opened in 1991, it is included in the "Guinness Book of Worldwide Records" on p.96 of 1996 edition.

图1 乌巢河石拱桥（承吴刚博士惠赠）
Fig.1 Wuchaohe Stone Arch Bridge (courtesy of Dr. Wu Gang)

图2 纵横截面
Fig.2 Longitudinal and cross section

参考文献

1.李国豪主任编委，项海帆主编. 中国桥梁. 上海：同济大学出版社；香港：建筑与城市出版社有限公司，1993：269

REFERENCES

1.Chainman Li Guohao, Editor-in-Chief Xiang Haifan. Bridge in China. Shanghai: Tongji University Press; HK: A&U Publication Ltd., 1993: 269

新丹河石拱桥

新丹河石拱桥（图1）位于山西晋城至河南焦作的高速公路上，跨过丹河，为多跨空腹变截面石板拱桥，于2001年建成。因原晋城丹河石拱桥，*l*=105m，1982年建成，故编者特加一"新"字以示与其区别。新丹河桥跨度分布为2×30m（晋城一侧）+146m+5×30m（焦作一侧）（图2），桥面宽度24.8m，桥梁高度80.6m。据早期所知，拟建的主桥跨度考虑采取154m，因为误传丹麦建有150m跨石拱桥，在那个年代，人们总希望为了祖国光荣而创造世界纪录，后知丹麦150m跨拱桥为用混凝土建造的，因为国外不曾建造过跨度超过90m石拱桥，如德国Syratal-Plauen桥，也考虑无此必要，所以最后决定主桥跨度为146m。它迄今仍居世界石拱桥之首位，将石拱桥建造技术推向一个新的高度，这也是编者加"新"的另一深层意义。

对该桥曾进行1：10模型试验。新丹河桥为大跨度、高荷载石拱桥设计与施工提供了工程范例。专家组认为该桥课题研究成果达到国际领先水平。新丹河桥已被收入《吉尼斯世界纪录大全》。

1a

1b

New Danhe Stone Arch Bridge

New Danhe Stone Arch Bridge (Fig.1) lies on the express highway line from Jincheng, Shanxi Province to Jiaozuo City, Henan Province across Danhe, is a multi-span open spandrel stone slab arch bridge with varied sections, completed in 2001. Because the original Jincheng Danhe stone arch bridge has a span of 105m, completed in 1982, so the Editor added a Chinese character XIN, i.e., "new" in English for distinguishing from the original. The span distributions of new Danhe Bridge are 2×30m (on the side of Jincheng) + 146m + 5×30 (on the side of Jiaozuo) (Fig.2), the deck width is 24.8m, and bridge height 80.6m. As the Editor know in early time, a main span of 154m was intended to adopt, since it was understood by mistake that there was a 150m-span stone arch bridge in Denmark, in that years, people always wish to create worldwide record for the glory of their motherland, later they knew the 150m-span Danish arch bridge is constructed of concrete, since there not constructed a span over 90m stone arch bridge in foreign countries as German Syratal-Plauen Bridge, and consider also no need, so finally the span of main bridge is determined as 146m. Up to now, it occupies the 1st place in the world, and advances the technique of constructing stone arch bridge to a new level, it is another profound meaning of adding "new" by the Editor.

For New Danhe Bridge, a 1:10 model test has been conducted. This Bridge provides an engineering example for the design and construction of large-span and construction of large-span and high-loading stone arch bridges. The Group of experts consider that the research result of the problems in this bridge has reached the leading level. New Danhe Bridge has been included in the "Guinness Book of Worldwide Records".

图1 新丹河石拱桥（承西安中交第一勘察设计研究院惠赠）
(a) 前视；(b) 侧视
Fig.1 New Danhe stone arch bridge (courtesy of Xi'an Zhongjiao First Exploration and Design Research Institute) (a) front view, (b) side view

图2 新丹河桥纵截面
Fig.2 Longitudinal section of New Danhe Bridge

2

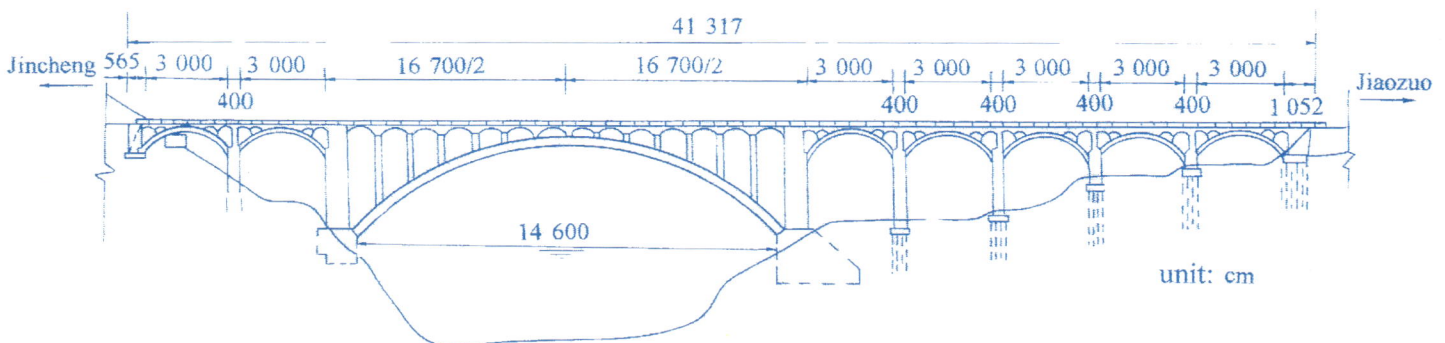

unit: cm

参考文献

1.中国第一公路勘察设计研究院. 丹河大桥 —— 世界最大跨石拱桥（画册），5页

REFERENCES

1.China 1st Highway Exploration Design & Research Institute. Danhe Bridge — stone arch bridge with largest span in the world (album), 5pp

REINFORCED CONCRETE ARCH BRIDGES

钢筋混凝土拱桥

万县长江上承式拱桥

　　万县长江公路大桥（图1）是国道318线（从上海经成都至拉萨）重要工程项目，是交通部重点工程。大桥位于重庆市万州区长江上游7km黄牛孔处，全长856.12m，主跨为上承式钢筋混凝土预应力箱型拱桥，跨度420m（图2a），双向4车道，桥面宽24m。它超过1980年建成的前南斯拉夫、现克罗地亚KRK拱桥中较大跨390m（参看绪论 —— 桥文化第26条）成为世界新纪录。虽然较2005年建成的重庆巫山拱桥主跨460m为小，但后者系钢管混凝土拱桥。万县大桥于1994年5月正式动工建造，于1997年6月建成。

　　万县大桥主跨轴线是悬链线，矢跨比为1/5，拱轴系数1.6，拱圈为单箱三室截面，箱高7.0m，宽16m，拱箱标准段顶、底板各厚0.4m，腹板厚0.3m；拱脚段顶、底板各厚0.8m，腹板厚0.6m，如图2b所示，图中小圆内数字为分成8个对称布置区段（仅写在图的右边），它们示混凝土浇筑顺序为自内向外，并自下而上地对称进行，每一区域从2拱座到拱冠形成一次浇筑合拢的混凝土带结硬后，将承受随后阶段浇筑的下一区域混凝土重量。每一拱带混凝土从拱座向跨中对称地分3节，每节分12段顺序浇筑。

　　拱上及引桥为相同孔跨贯通布置，共27孔，30.66m预应力T形梁，桥面连续。

　　拱圈采用钢管混凝土劲性骨架外包C60级高强混凝土复合结构，其中钢管混凝土劲性骨架先期是施工构架，在拱圈形成后它就成为拱圈内的劲性钢筋。

　　钢管混凝土劲性骨架由5片钢管桁架组成空间桁架，弦杆采用Φ351×16钢管，腹杆和连接系为角钢组合杆。空钢管骨架分36节段，整体在工厂制造，段重61t，段长13m，段间采用法兰盘螺栓接头，节段在工地以缆索吊机起吊运输，两岸斜拉扣挂悬拼，跨中合拢，成拱后压注高强混凝土形成钢管混凝土劲性骨架。图3示安装好的钢管骨架。待钢管骨架安装后，用C60混凝土由拱座至拱冠，泵压至管内。当管内混凝土强度达70%时在鹰架上浇筑箱形截面混凝土。

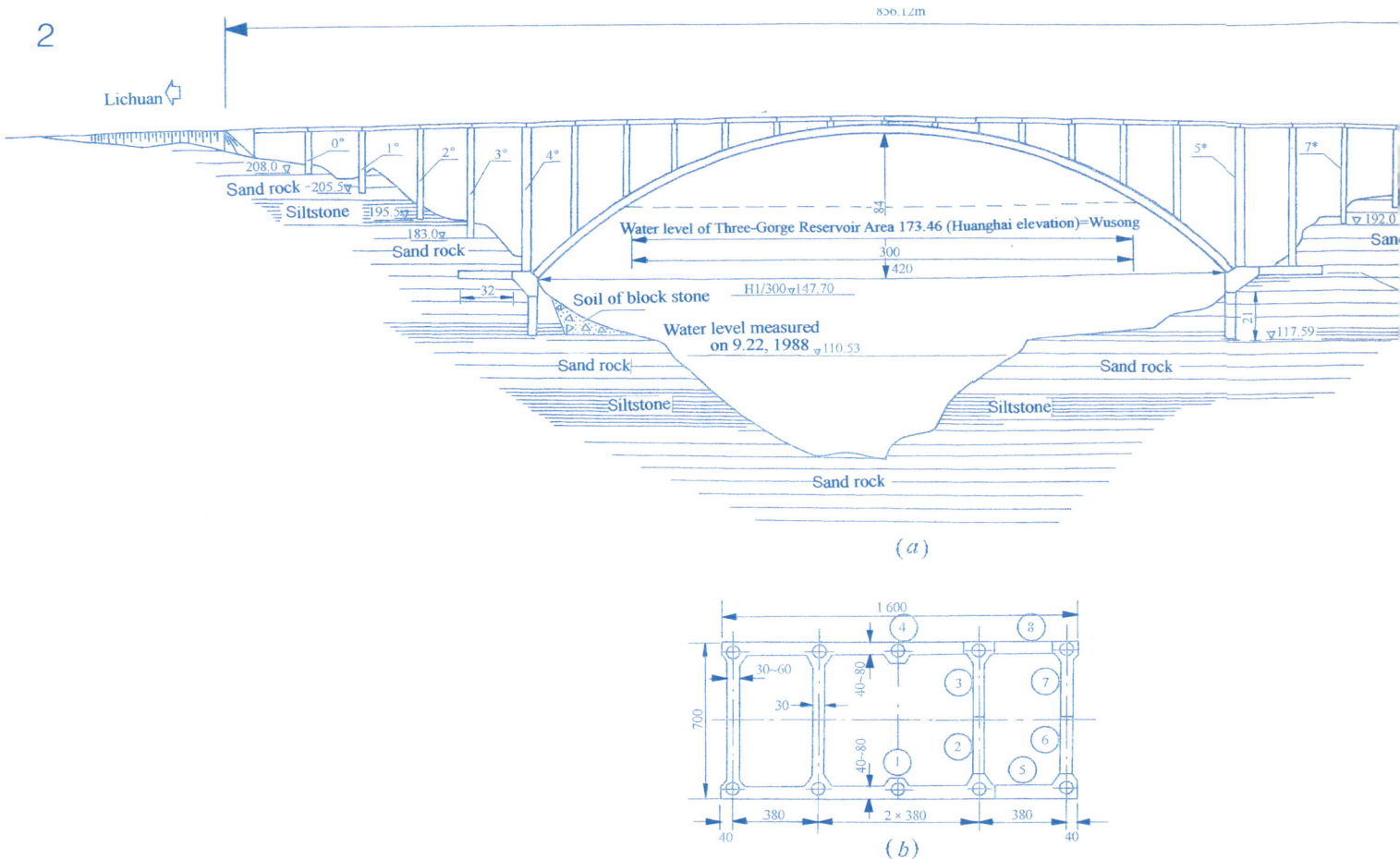

(a)

(b)

Wanxian Decked Arch Bridge over Yangtze River

Wanxian Yangtze River Highway Bridge (Fig.1) is an important engineering project of national highway line 318 (from Shanghai through Chengdu to Tibet), a major engineering of China Ministry of Communications. This bridge is located at Huangniukong, with distance of 7km on the upper reaches of Yangtze River in Wanzhou District, Chongqing City, its total length is 856.12m and the main span is a decked prestressed reinforced concrete box-typed arch bridge with length of 420m (Fig.2a) and 2-way 4 lanes to have width of 24m. This bridge exceeds the larger span of KRK with span length of 390m, completed in former Yugoslavia, recent Crodia in 1980 (see the 26th section of Introduction — Bridge Culture) and becomes a new interwide record of RC arch bridge. Though, the span of Wanxian Bridge is smaller than 460m, the span of Chongqing Wushan Bridge completed in 2005, yet the latter is constructed of concrete-filled steel tube. Wanxian Bridge started to construct formally in May 1994 and was completed in July 1997.

The axis of Wanxian Bridge is a catenary, the rise-span ratio is 1/5, the axis factor 1.6, the ring section of this bridge is a 3-cell single box, its depth is 7.0m, width 16m, the thickness of top and bottom slabs of standard segments is 0.4m respectively, that of web 0.3m; that of top and bottom slabs of springing segments is 0.8m respectively, that of web 0.6m, as shown in Fig.2b, the digits in the small circles in the figure (written only in the right) can be divided into 8 area segments with symmetrical arrangement they show that the sequence of casting concrete is conducted symmetrically from the internal, then outwards and from below, every area formed a concrete strip closed in a casting time from 2 springings to crown, after being hardened, it would undertake the weight in concrete next area cast in followed stage. Concrete is every arch strip was cast symmetrically following the sequence from springing towards span center divided into 3 segments, every of which was divided into 12 small segments.

For the arch and bridge approach, there are 27 spans of same length 30.66m T-typed PC beams through arrangement and continuous deck.

The arch ring is adopted by using the composite structure of concrete-filled steel tube (CFST) stiff frame enveloped with high-strength concrete C60, in the composite structure, the CFST frame was construction scaffold in early time, after the arch ring formed, the CFST frame would become the stiff reinforcements of arch ring.

The CFST stiff frame is a spatial truss constituted of 5 steel tube trusses, for chords members, the $\phi351\times16$ tubes are used, for web, members and connecting ties, the angle composites are used. The empty steel tube frame was fabricated integrity in factory by dividing in 36 segments with segment weight of 61t and length of 13m, the joint of segments was finished in site by using flange and connection bolts, and cable crane to hoist and transport, and to conduct hanging splice on 2 banks, through stays to close in span center, after the

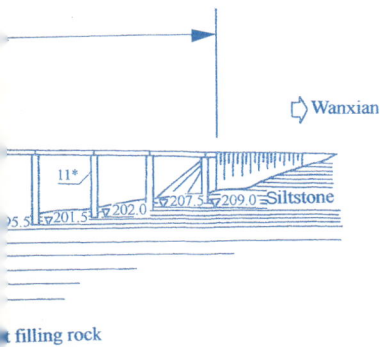

图2 万县大桥纵横截面
(a) 纵截面；(b) 横截面
Fig.2 Longitudinal and cross section of Wanxian Bridge
(a) longitudinal section, (b)cross section

图1 万县长江大桥〈承黄启宇教授级高工惠赠〉
Fig.1 Wanxian Yangtze River Bridge (courtesy of Senior Engr. Prof. Huang Qiyu)

在万县大桥中，曾在新技术应用与科技创新方面进行了多项研究，现举例如下。

根据有限元基本原理，提出了拱圈强度验算的非线性综合分析法，方法的正确性通过1／5节段模型试验所验证；根据有限元基本原理，建立了施工过程非线性稳定性分析方法，并通过1／10全桥模型试验验证；根据劲性骨架混凝土拱桥的特点，提出了两级控制的施工控制方法，使大跨混凝土拱桥的施工控制技术走向科学化；通过研究变截面空心薄壁杆几何特性、力学特性的变化规律，提出了变截面空心薄壁高立柱稳定计算的解析公式。

建成后的万县大桥还曾用载重卡车进行1 000t静动力试验。

3

图3 万县大桥的钢管混凝土骨架（承黄启宇教授级高工惠赠）
Fig.3 Steel tube concretes sketch in Wanxian Bridge (courtesy of Senior Engr. Prof. Huang Qiyu)

arch formed, high-strength concrete was injected to form CFST stiff frame. Fig.3 shows the completed steel tube frame. After the tube frame had been installed, the concrete C60 was pumped into tube from springing to crown. The concrete of box section was poured on scaffold after the strength of concrete in tube had been reached 70%.

In Wanxian Bridge, there were conducted many studies of new technique application and scientific and technology creation, some examples are given as follows.

In the field of design and calculation: according to the fundamental theory of finite element method (FEM), a nonlinear comprehensive analysis method for checking the strength of arch ring has been suggested, the exactness of this method has been checked through the experiment of 1/5 segment model; following the basic principle of FEM a nonlinear analysis method for stability in construction process was created and checked through the test of 1/10 whole bridge model; following characteristics of concrete arch bridge with stiff frame, a construction control method of 2 stages was suggested to make the construction control technique of large-span concrete arch bridge to become scientific; an analysis formula for stability calculation of high columns with hollow thin-walled variable cross section was proposed through studying the variable law of their geometric and mechanical characteristics.

After completion, statical and dynamical tests of 1 000t were conducted by using loaded truck.

参考文献

1.丁大钧. 现代混凝土结构学. 北京：中国建筑工业出版社，2000：1047

2.丁大钧. 高性能混凝土及其在工程中的应用. 北京：机械工业出版社. 2006：274

REFERENCES

1.Ding Dajun. Science of Modern Concrete Structures. Beijing: China Architecture & Building Press, 2000: 1047

2.Ding Dajun. High Performance Concrete and Its Applications in Engineering. Beijing: China Machine Press, 2006: 274

台湾碧潭无推力拱桥

　　台湾碧潭桥（图1a~c）长781.5m，位于台北市北部第二高速公路上，距台北市15km处。它实为两座靠近并接近平行的结构。它连接几座低位高架桥于一隧道，具有750m曲率半径和约1%的坡度。南北线各为3车道，桥面宽2×16.35m，桥面由预制预应力混凝土单箱组成；并配以Y型悬臂拱圈，形成主跨为160m及2×100m的独特无推力拱。结构图示于图2。所谓无推力并非拱肋内无推力，而是指拱肋支座交接处，其水平分力相交抵消不对支座产生影响，只由其垂直分力将竖向荷载传递于支座。引桥跨度分别为76.5m+85m和57m+72m+64m+67m。全桥以简洁明快的弧形曲线构成，与近水远山、蓝天白云相协调，颇具结构造型美。

　　该桥已于1994年建成通车。

1a

1b

1c

Taiwan Bitan Trust-less Arch Bridge

Taiwan Bitan Bridge (Fig.1a~c) with length of 781.5m is located at distance of 15km to Taipei City on the 2nd express highway in the north of this city, constitutes actually of 2 structures approximately parallel to each other. This bridge connects several low-level viaducts to a tunnel; has a curvature of 750m and a slop of 1%. In the north and south line, there are all 3 lanes, with deck width of 2×16.35m. The deck is constructed of precast PC single box with Y-shape cantilever arch rings to form a special thrust-less arch having main span of 160m and 2×100m. The structural sketch is shown in Fig.2. The so-called "trust-less" is not meant that there is no trust in arch rib, but is indicates the horizontal components in ribs at a joint do not produce influence on the support, only the vertical components transfer the vertical loads to the support. The spans of approach are respectively 76.5m+85m and 57m+72m+64m+67m. Whole bridge is constituted of succinct and sprightly arc-shaped curves, harmonizes well with waterfront and distant mountains and possesses beautiful structural modeling.

This bridge has been completed and opened in 1994.

图1 建成的台湾碧潭桥（承台湾大学陈振川教授惠赠）
(a), (b), (c)

Fig.1 Completed Taiwan Bitan Bridge (courtesy of Prof. Chen Zhenchuan at Taiwan University)
(a), (b), (c)

图2 结构图
Fig.2 Structural sketch

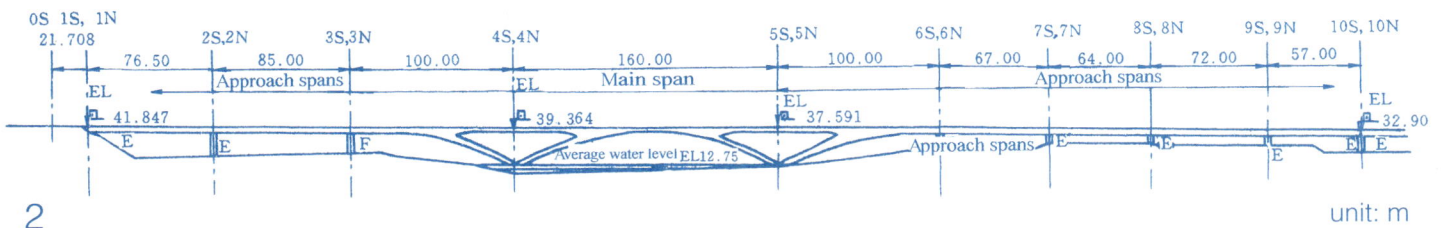

2

unit: m

REFERENCES

1. Knong M. Chang. The Bitan Bridge, Taiwan, China, Journal of IABSE, 1994. 11(4): 231-234

广西邕宁中承式钢筋混凝土拱桥

　　邕宁桥（图1）的两片拱肋为单室单箱截面，其尺寸在跨中为3.0m×5.0m（图2），截面高度变化至拱座处为6.8m。为了美观，箱肋宽度在桥面上为常数，在桥座附近25m范围内增大为4.0m；箱肋顶底板厚360mm，侧板厚320mm，采用 C50高强混凝土。箱形四角各设1根16Mnϕ402×12无缝钢管，在顶、底和侧面用4根角钢焊接联成桁架，并在顶底各采用2根160×100×8.5贯通的槽钢加强；在立面上，上下钢管用2L160×100×10不等边角钢通过节点板焊接成竖杆和斜杆，在顶、底面则用2L100×80×8焊成水平斜杆，2L160×100×10焊成水平直杆，这样便将4根钢管连成空间桁架。待钢管中高强混凝土C50结硬后以之为支架浇筑箱肋混凝土，在其中还采用了136ϕ12mm纵向钢筋。拱的矢高为52.0m，拱轴线为无铰悬链线。

　　在邕宁桥中采用4道X形撑（在桥下靠近两岸），2道K形撑和3道横梁，亦采用箱形截面，混凝土采用C50。

　　当钢管不浇筑在混凝土内而暴露在外时，则成钢管混凝土，而结构照上述埋设混凝土，仍称为钢筋混凝土，钢管即成配筋。

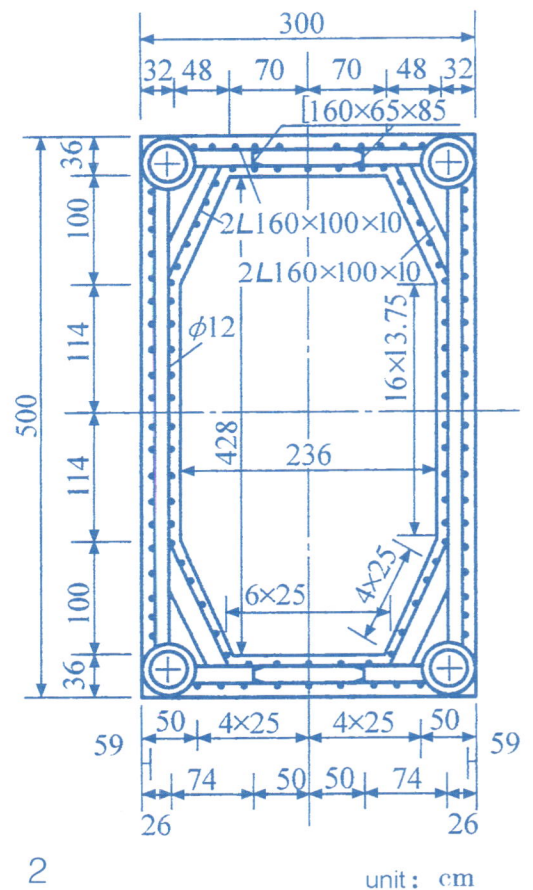

2

unit：cm

Guangxi Yongning Through-Deck Arch Bridge

In Yongning Bridge (Fig.1), the 2 arch ribs are single-cell and single-box section, the dimensions of which are 3.0m×5.0m at span center (Fig.2), but the section depth varies into 6.8m at springer. For the sake of aesthetic effect, the width of arch ribs is kept to be constant over deck, and increased into 4.0m in the segment about the spring within 25m; the thickness of top and bottom slabs is 360mm, that of side slabs 320mm, high-strength concrete C50 was used. In every corner of box, there is set a seamless tube 16Mnϕ402×12, in top, bottom and side slabs 4 angles were welded to connect into a truss and in the top and bottom slabs, 2 full-length channels 160×100×8.5 are set for strengthening; on the elevation, the upper and bottom tubes were welded by using 2 angles with unequal sides 2L160×100×10 into vertical and inclined members through gussets, on the upper and bottom sides 2L100×80×8 were welded into horizontal inclined members, 2L160×100×10 were welded into horizontal straight members, thus these 4 tubes were connected into a spatial truss. After the highstrength concrete C50 in tubes had hardened, using this truss as trestle poured the concrete of box rib, in which 136ϕ12mm longitudinal bars are adopted. The rise of arch is 52.0m, a hingeless catenary is adopted as the axis of arch.

In Yongning Bridge, 4 X-shape bracings (near 2 banks under bridge) are set, 2 K-bracings and 3 transverse beams are also adopted box sections, concrete C50.

When the tubes are not buried in concrete and exposed in air, this construction will become concrete-filled tube concrete and the structure constructed by being buried in concrete is still called RC, and the tubes are the rebars.

1

图1 邕宁桥（承王贵良教授惠赠）
Fig.1 Yongning Bridge (courtesy of Prof. Wang Guiliang)

图2 邕宁桥拱肋箱形截面构造
Fig.2 Yongning Bridge box section construction of arch rib

参考文献

1.丁大钧. 高性能混凝土及其在工程中的应用. 北京：机械工业出版社，2007：273

REFERENCES

1.Ding Dajun. High Performance Concrete and Its Applications in Engineering . Beijing: China Machine Press, 2007: 273

钱江四桥

钱塘江三桥为由双独塔斜拉桥和中间及两端以等高度连续梁连成整体，斜拉桥为等跨度，跨长各为168m，两侧连续梁跨度分别为80m+72m，中间为80m+72m+72m+80m，共12跨，全桥长1 280m。

钱江四桥（图1）位于杭州钱塘江上，距1937年建成的钱塘江大桥下游4.3km处的复兴地区南星桥附近，为双层钢管混凝土拱桥，跨度分布为2×45.75m（连续梁）+2×89m（副通航孔小拱）+196m（主通航孔大拱）+5×89m（小拱）+196m（大拱）+2×45.75m（连续梁）（图1上部）。小拱为上承和下承式，两大拱则为中承和下承式组合构成多跨双层桥（图1下部），拱肋采用单钢管φ1 700mm×22mm，管内灌注C50高强混凝土。对大拱桥面上拱肋间设5道风撑。上、下层桥面同宽，均为26.4m，上层为双向6车道，下层中间为地铁车道，两侧为公交专用道和人行道。桥的全长1 376m，颇具规模。大桥已于2005年10月10日通车。图2示建成的四桥。

钱江四桥的建成为钱塘江增添秀美，与遥遥相望的西子湖争奇斗艳，为杭州增添旅游景点，在春秋佳日，游客必将赏心悦目，充分获得放松，为工作增加活力。

钱江四桥立面布置见图3，跨中截面见图4，钢管及系梁截面分别见图5和图6。四桥采用了复杂的空间结构体系，由梁、杆、板等多种结构及钢管、钢劲性骨架、预应力钢筋、混凝土等多种材料组合而成，包括了钢构件、钢管混凝土构件、方钢管混凝土构件、钢骨架预应力混凝土构件、预应力混凝土构件等多种组合构件，是一种复杂的双层桥面系统。桥址处河床较深，涌潮及风浪影响较大，由于施工期通航等因素的要求，须采用无支架施工方法。全桥拱肋采用先吊装钢管拱肋，再灌注钢管混凝土的施工方法，系梁首先预架设钢劲性骨架，再立模现浇混凝土。因而，由于徐变收缩等因素影响，会使钢劲性骨架在施工过程中及成桥后承受幅度较大的内力变化，有可能使钢劲性骨架的应力变化超过其极限允许应力，而拱肋中由于徐变收缩影响，会使钢管拱肋与钢管混凝土之间内力重分布，钢管拱肋的轴力会大幅增加，所以，研究分析由于混凝土的徐变收缩引起的钢管拱肋、拱肋混凝土、系梁钢劲性骨架、分层浇筑的系梁混凝土的内力变化及其增长规律，有利于弄清结构不同材料之间的相互影响、相互作用及它们的性能、受力特点，对于整个桥梁施工及运营安全具有重要意义。

根据设计要求，在每一主跨必需设置4个大吨位支承，包括1个固定支承、2个在单向可动支承和1个在两向可动支承。每个支承设计承载力为65 000kN，抗滑摩擦系数不大于0.03，抗旋转摩擦系数不大于0.04，旋转角不小于0.0 116rad，抗震烈度为7级，设计水平承载力为4 200kN，顺桥向位移±120mm，横桥向位移±20mm。

1

The 4th Qianjiang Bridge

The 3rd Qianjiang Bridge is connected by two single-pylon cable-stayed bridges and continuous girders with equal depth into an integral, the span length of cable-stayed structures is equal 168m respectively, the spans of continuous girders at 2 ends are 80m+72m respectively, those in central span are 80m+72m+72m+80m, 12 spans in total with entire length of 1 280m.

The 4th Qianjiang Bridge (Fig.1) is located on Qiantangjiang (jiang means river in Chinese), near Nanxing Bridge in Fuxing area with a distance of 4.3km on the lower reaches from Qiantangjiang Bridge completed in 1937, is a double-deck arch bridge constructed of concrete-filled steel tube, the span distribution: 2×45.75m (continuous girder) +2×89m (smaller arch for auxiliary navigable span) +196m (larger arch for main navigable span) +5×89m (smaller arches) +196m (larger arch) +2×45.75m (continuous girder) (upper part of Fig.1). The smaller arches are upper- and lower-decked, the larger ones middle-through and lower-decked (lower part of Fig.1), they constitute multispan double-decked bridge, the arch ribs adopt single tube ϕ1700mm×22mm, into which the highstrength concrete C50 was poured. For the larger arches, over deck there are set 5 wind bracings. The widths of upper and lower decks are the same of 26.4m, on the upper deck there are 6 lanes in 2-way, on the lower, in the middle field, there are railways of metro, on both sides, special lanes and walkways. This bridge has total length of 1 376m, and a larger scale. Qianjiang Bridge has been opened on Oct.10, 2005. Fig.2 shows the completed 4th Qianjiang Bridge.

The completion of the 4th Qianjiang Bridge increases beautiful scene in Qiantangjiang, wins the beauty with the nice scene of West Lake standing at a distance adds the scenery point for Hangzhou tour, on the tourists will be sure to find scenery pleasing to both the eye and the mind so as to obtain full relaxation, then to increase vigour for working.

The elevation layout of Qianjiang Bridge is shown in Fig.3, its section at span center in Fig.4 and the section of tube rib and tie beam in Figs.5, 6, respectively. The 4th Bridge adopts a complicate spatially structural system, constituted of girder member slab structures and the materials of steel tube, stiff frame, prestressed bar, concrete etc. including steel member, concrete-filled steel tube member, concrete-filled square tube member, steel-frame PC member etc. of many composite members, is a complicate double-decked system. At the site of bridge, the river bed is deeper and the influences of surrying tide and wind-wave are more great, and the navigable requirements during construction, this bridge should be constructed by using the method without scaffold. The arch ribs of entire bridge adopted the construction method to hoist firstly the tube arch ribs, then to pour the concrete-filled steel tube, for the tie beams, the stiff steel frames were firstly erected, then erected formwork to pour concrete, hence, the stiff steel frames might sustain the variety of internal forces in larger field during construction and completion due

图1　钱江四桥在施工中（承陈光辉总工惠赠）
Fig.1 The 4th Qianjiang Bridge under construction
(courtesy of general Engr. Chen Guanghui)

图2 建成的钱江四桥（承赵林祥高工惠赠）
Fig.2 Completed the 4th Qianjiang Bridge (courtesy of Senior Engr. Zhao Linxiang)

图3 钱江四桥立面布置
Fig.3 Elevation layout of the 4th Qianjiang Bridge

图4 跨中截面
Fig.4 Section at span center

图5 钢管截面
Fig.5 Section of tube

图6 系梁截面
Fig.6 Section of tie beam

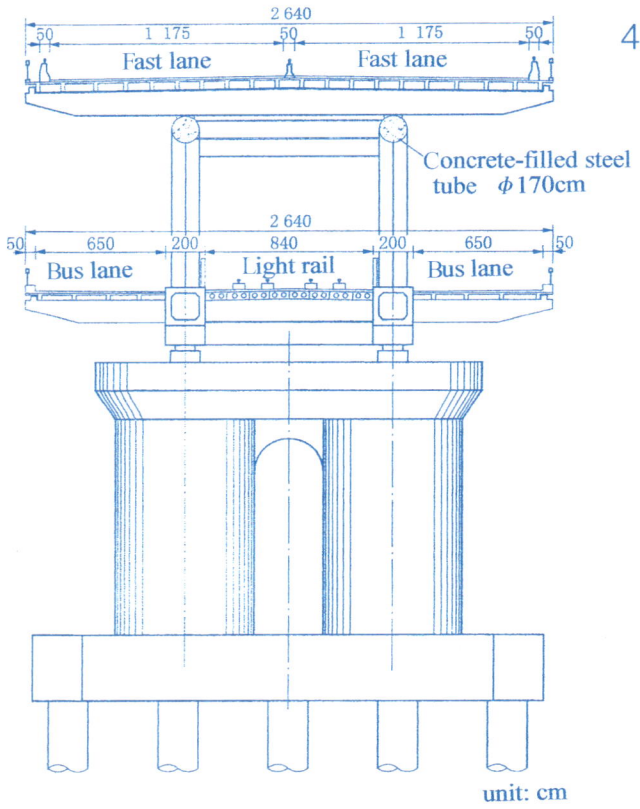

4

unit: cm

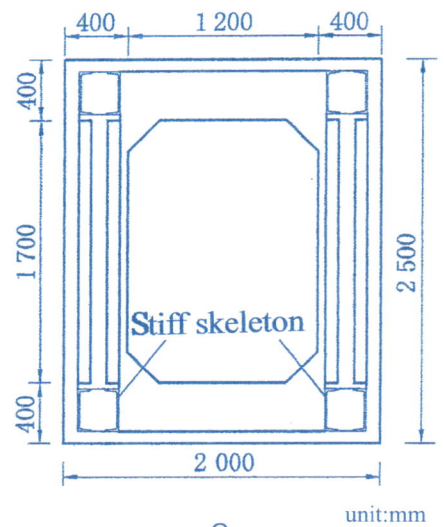

6

unit:mm

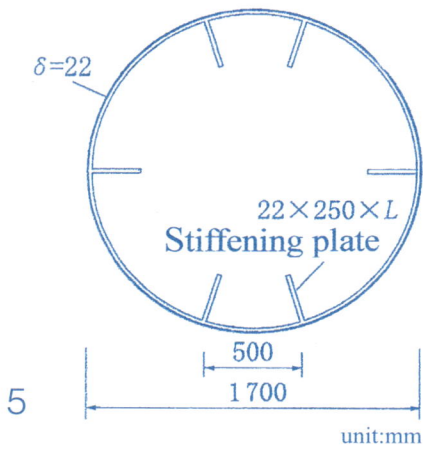

$\delta=22$

$22\times250\times L$

Stiffening plate

500

1700

unit:mm

5

to the influences of the factors of creep and shrinkage etc., there is the possibility that this variety exceeds the allowable stress of frame, there will occur the redistribution of internal forces between steel tube of arch ribs and concrete-filled due to creep and shrinkage in arch ribs, the axial forces of steel tube arch ribs might increase fleetly, so to study and analyse the variety and the increase law of internal forces in the steel tube arch ribs, in the concrete in ribs, in stiff steel frame of tie beams and in the tie beam concrete cast in layers due to the creep and shrinkage of concrete is favourable to understand the mutual influence and mutual action between different materials in a structure, and the behaviour and stressed characteristic of these materials, it has an important sense to the construction of entire bridge and the safe operation.

Following the design requirements, 4 supports with large tonnage must be set in every main span, including 1 fixed support, 2 supports movable in single direction and 1 support movable in two directions. The designed vertical bearing capacity of all every support is 65 000kN, the friction coefficient against slide is not larger than 0.03, and that against rotation not larger 0.04, the rotated angle not smaller 0.0 116 rad, the aseismic intensity 7 degree. Besides, designed horizontal bearing capacity is 4 200kN, the displacement along bridge: ±120mm, that across bridge ±20mm.

3

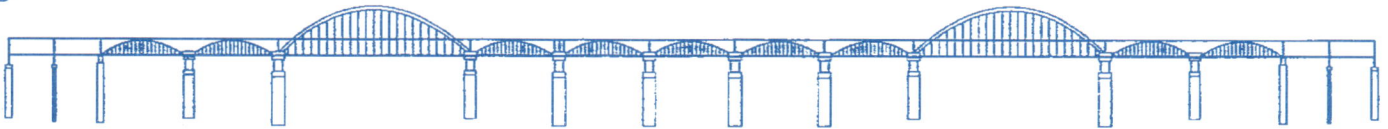

参考文献

1.邰扣霞，丁大钧. 大桥建设为城市景观添亮点. 中国勘察设计，2006（12）：30-32

2.俞菊虎，孙建渊，陈阶亮. 钱江四桥双层桥面钢−混凝土组合结构拱桥的时效分析. 桥梁建设，2003（6）：30-33

3.邢艳，等6人. 钱江四桥大吨位抗震球形支座技术研究. 桥梁建设，2003（5）：67-70

REFERENCES

1.Tai Kouxia, Ding Dajun. Bridge construction adds bright points for urban landscape. China Exploration Design. 2006(12): 30-32

2.Yu Juhu, Sun Jianyuan, Chen Jieliang. Analysis of Aging Effect of Steel-Concrete Composite Arch Spans of the 4th Qian(tang)jiang (River) Double-Deck Bridge, Bridge Construction. 2003(6): 30-33

3.Xing Yan, et al 6 persons. Research of Large Tonnage Seismic Isolation Spherical Bearings for the 4th Qian(tang)jiang (River) Bridge. Bridge Construction. 2003(5):67-70

贵州江界河桁架式组合拱桥

预应力混凝土桁梁组合拱桥是我国首创的一种新型拱桥，它除保持桁架拱桥结构用料省、造型轻巧美观、竖向刚度大等特点外，还具有桁梁的特性和可以采用悬臂法施工，施工阶段和使用阶段的受力趋于一致等优点。这种桥在施工阶段拱座和相邻跨或拱座与连接部分是连续的，能承受负弯矩，而将铰接点移至跨中距拱座一定节点处，在此节点，用两个竖杆在上面断开使下节点组成铰，因而中间拱即成为跨度小较多的"双铰拱"。

在建造330m跨的贵州江界河桁架组合拱桥（图1）[4]之前，从1981年开始，在我国已建成若干座跨度为75~160m的这类新型拱桥，取得丰富的经验。

江界河位于贵州瓮安县，跨越乌江中游峡谷，桥面高出常水位270m，边跨桁架顺着山坡分别为30m+25m+20m和30m+20m，桥的全长461m。桥的边跨布置特点是利用山坡岩石，使边跨的下弦杆与岩盘合一，斜拉杆的预应力粗钢筋锚固于岩盘内。桥面的净宽为9m+2×1.5m人行道，全宽13.4m。桥的矢跨比为1/6。

图2(a)、(b)分别示江界河桥的纵横截面，上下弦均为箱形截面，先预制两边室，而后吊装就位，加盖中间顶底板，组成3室箱形截面，室的中心宽度为2.2m+5.6m+2.2m，顶底板厚度分别为22cm和16cm；中间室顶底板均加腋。下弦截面构成与上弦基本相同，斜杆与竖杆均为分离箱组成，截面尺寸分别为1.4m×1.6m和1.2m×1.6m，箱厚12~16cm。

切开的节点在距拱座84m（图2a）处，即中间小拱的跨度减小为162m，中间74m长部分为实心截面。上弦杆和斜杆加预应力。在上弦杆内，采用冷拉Ⅳ级钢，直径32mm，在斜杆内采用24φ5高强钢丝束。该桥分段预制，从拱座向拱冠逐段悬拼。

江界河桥于1995年建成通车。该桥跨度迄今仍为世界纪录。

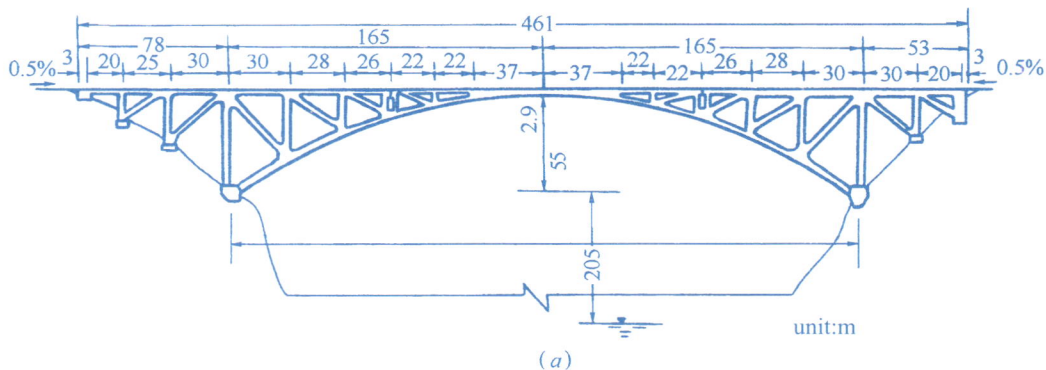

(a)

2

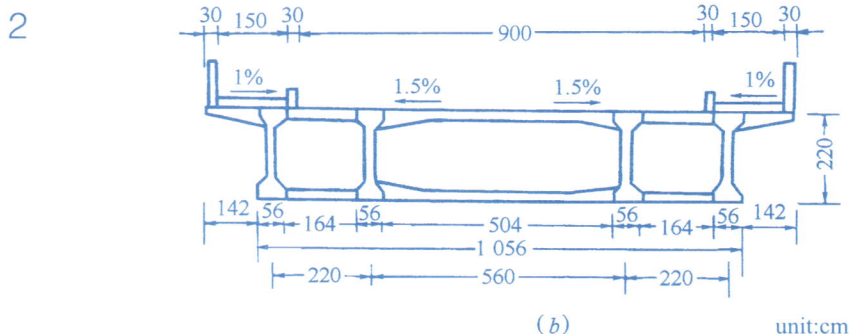

(b)   unit:cm

图1 江界河桁架组合拱桥（承1996年Bd&e惠赠）
*Fig.1 Jiangjiehe trussed combination arch bridge
(courtesy of Bd&e, 1996)*

图2 江界河纵横截面
(a)纵截面图；(b)上弦横截面图
*Fig.2 Longitudinal and cross sections of Jiangjiehe
(a) longitudinal section, (b) cross section*

1

参考文献

1.李国豪主任编委，项海帆主编. 中国桥梁.
上海：同济大学出版社；香港：建筑与城市出版
社有限公司，1993：269

2.丁大钧. 现代混凝土结构学. 北京：中国建筑工
业出版社，2000：1047

4.丁大钧. 高性能混凝土及其在工程中的应用.
北京：机械工业出版社，2007：276

REFERENCES

*1.Chairman Li Guohao, Editor-in-Chief Xiang
Haifan. Bridges in China. Shanghai: Tongji
University Press; HK: A & U Publication Ltd.,
1993: 269*

*2.Ding Dajun. Advance of Modern Concrete
Structures, Beijing: China Architecture & Building
Press, 2000: 1047*

*3.Ding Dajun. Recent long-span concrete bridges
in China. Journal of the Indian National Group of
IABSE. The Bridges and Structural Engineers. 1998.
28(1): 28-47*

*4.Ding Dajun. High Performance Concrete and
Its Applications in Engineering. Beijing: China
Machine Press, 2007: 276*

Guizhou Jiangjiehe Trussed Combination Arch Bridge

PC trussed combination arch bridge is created firstly in China and a new-typed arch bridge. Besides holding the characteristics of saving materials, to have light and nice modelling, to be possessed of great vertical stiffness, etc, there are also some advantages such as the special property of truss girder, being able to construct by cantilever method, being stressed to tend towards unison in construction stage and in service stage. In this typed bridge, the springing and adjacent span, or springing and connected part should be continuous in construction, namely can take negative moment to make hinge points to move to the panel joints with definite distances, at each of these joints, there are set 2 vertical members and to be cut on upper for making the lower joints to constitute hinges, hence the middle arch will become "2-hinge arch with much smaller span".

Before the construction of Guizhou Jiangjiehe Bridge with span of 330m span (Fig.1)[4], some this new-typed arch bridges with spans of 75~160m have been completed, rich experience is obtained.

Jiangjiehe Bridge is located on Weng'an County, Guizhou Province and spans over the george of middle reaches of Wujiang (jiang means river in Chinese), the deck is over constant water level by 270m, the trusses of side span are arranged along the slopes of mountain with spans respectively: 30m+25m+20m and 30m+20m, the total length of bridge is 461m. The arrangement characteristic of side span utilizes the rock on slope to make that as the lower chords, and the prestressed thick bars in inclined tension members are anchored in rock. The clear width of deck is 9m+2×1.5m (walkway) and the total width is 13.4m. Rise-span ratio of this bridge is 1/6.

Fig.2(a), (b) shows respectively the longitudinal and cross sections, the upper and lower chords have box sections, 2 side cells are prefabricated firstly and hoisted to position, then covered with the middle upper and lower slabs to constitute 3-cell box section, the central widths of cells are 2.2m+5.6m+2.2m, the thicknesses of upper and lower slabs are 22cm and 16cm respectively; both of the upper and low slabs of middle cell are haunched. The constitutions of the section of lower chord is the same as that of upper chord, both of the inclined and vertical members are constituted of separate boxes with section dimensions are 1.4m×1.6m and 1.2m×1.6m respectively, the wall thickness are 12~16cm.

The cut joint is at the point with a distance of 84m from springing (see Fig.2a), i.e., the span of the middle smaller arch is decreased to 162m, the central length of 74m has solid section. The upper chord members and the inclined ones are prestressed. In the upper chord members, cold-tensioned bars of IV grade steel with diameter of 32mm are adopted, in the inclined members, 24ϕ5 high-strength wire tendons are used. This bridge was precast in segments and spliced by cantilever method from springing to crown.

Jiangjiehe Bridge has been completed and opened in 1995, up to now, its span is still a worldwide record.

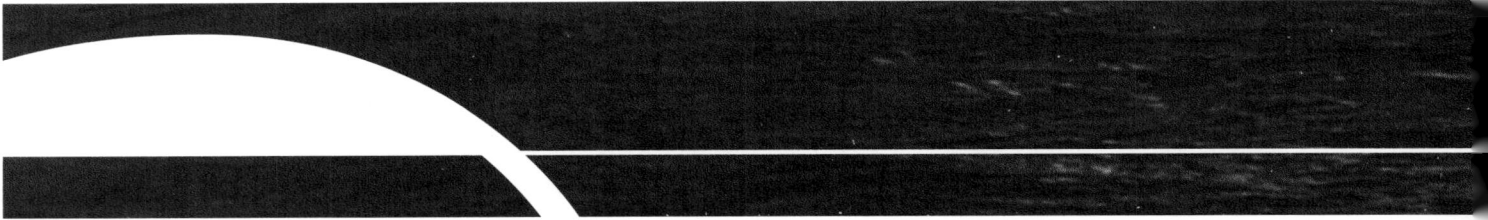

CONCRETE-FILLED STEEL TUBE ARCH BRIDGES
钢管混凝土拱桥

广西三岸邕江中承式拱桥

广西三岸邕江桥（图1）于1999年建成通车，它是南宁至北海高速公路上跨邕江的大桥，北起南宁三岸园艺场，南至邕宁县龙岗村，是用钢管混凝土组成桁架结构的中承式双肋拱桥，桥宽32.8m，跨度为270m，拱轴线为倒悬链线，矢跨比f/l=1/5。拱肋为等截面，上、下弦各采用$2\phi1\,020mm\times16mm$钢管，拱肋截面高度为5.6m，宽度为2.4m。弦杆主管及横联板腔内均填充C50高强混凝土，构成横哑铃状；竖腹杆和斜腹杆均为外径400mm、壁厚12mm的圆管，腹杆成对设置，分别与弦杆圆管直接连接。上、下弦杆主管和横联板均采用16Mn钢，主管采用螺旋焊接管，所有焊缝强度均应大于本材强度，吊杆由$61\phi7$镀锌高强钢丝组成，两端镦头锚，吊点顺桥向中距为10.0m，每个吊点设2根吊杆，以便今后更换。一组2根吊杆顺桥向间距为1.17m。当一根吊杆失效时，另一根在恒载下的安全系数为1.75。弦杆壁厚除拱脚以上21.5m内为14mm外，其余截面均为12mm。

全桥共采用8道横向联接系，在桥面与拱肋相交处设置两道预制钢筋混凝土肋间横系梁，与肋杆固接。

三岸桥建成时为当时中国、也是世界最长的中承式钢管混凝土拱桥，但第二年即被主跨为360m的广州丫髻沙桥所代替，可见中国钢管混凝土拱桥建设发展之快。

Guangxi San-an Yongjiang Through Deck Arch Bridge

Guangzhou San-an Yongjiang Bridge (Fig.1) was completed and opened in 1999, it is a half-through arch bridge with 2 ribs, constituted of concrete-filled steel tube in truss-typed structure over Yongjiang on the express highway from Nanning to Beihai, and starts from Nanning San-an horticulture yard in the north to Yongning County Longgang Village in the south, the width of bridge is 32.8m, the span is 270m, and the arch axis in the rise-span ratio f/l =1/5. The section of arch rib is constant, the upper and lower chords adopt $2\phi 1\,020mm\times16mm$ steel tubes, the depth of rib section is 5.6m, the width is 2.4m. Into the main tubes of chords and the cavity of transversely connecting plates, the high-strength concrete C50 was filled to constitute in a transverse dumbbell shape; the external diameters of circular tubes as vertical and diagonal web members are 400mm with wall thickness of 12mm and the web members are set in pairs, directly connected to the chord tubes respectively. The main tubes of upper and lower chords as well as the transversely connecting plates adopt 16Mn steel, the main tubes adopt spiral welded tubes and all the strengths of welded joints should be larger than those of the matrix materials. The hangers are constituted of $61\phi 7$ galvanized high-strength wires with forged head anchorages at 2 ends, the central spacings of hung points are 10.0m along bridge, at every hung point, 2 hangers are set so as to be replaced in the future. The spacing of 2 hangers in a group is 1.17m along bridge. When a hanger fails, the safety factor of the other is 1.75 under dead loads. Except that the wall thickness is 14mm in the field of 21.5m above springing, in the other sections, all are 12mm.

In whole bridge, there are 8 transverse connection system; at the intersection of deck and arch ribs, there are set 2 precast reinforced concrete transverse tie beams between ribs with fixed connection.

When San-an Bridge was completed, it was the longest half-through concrete-filled steel tube arch bridge (CFSTAB) in China, also in the world, but in next year, it was replaced by Guangzhou Yajisha Bridge with main span of 360m, it can be seen that the construction of CFSTAB in China is rapid.

1a

图1 三岸邕江桥（编者请当地照相馆为拍摄）
(a) 正视图；(b) 侧视图
Fig.1 San-an Yongjiang Bridge (the Editor asked the photo studio in the locality)
(a) front view, (b) side view

参考文献

1.丁大钧. 高性能混凝土及其在工程中的应用. 北京：机械工业出版社，2007：274

REFERENCES

1.Ding Dajun. High Performance Concrete and its Applications in Engineering. Beijing: China Machine Press, 2007: 274

广州丫髻沙钢管混凝土拱桥

1. 背景

在20世纪60年代，钢管混凝土（CFST）开始用于房屋建筑和北京地铁站台柱，而从1990—1992年开始广泛的研究，陆续颁布了三本规程CECS28-90、DLGJ99-91和DLGJ-S11-92，使这种材料在建筑和某些特种结构中得到广泛的应用。在20世纪90年代初，CFST应用于拱桥建设。当跨度不大时，例如$L \leq 80m$，可用单管，在浙江义乌80m跨元簧桥中，采用$\phi 800 \times 18mm$单管。当跨度略大时，采用2管连接成哑铃形；或$3\phi 600 \times 12mm$管用于100m跨。伊兰牡丹江桥在黑龙江省建成：采用3管，1管在顶部，2管在底部，以及在湖北建成的跨度$L=160m$的黄柏河桥和下牢溪桥中两者都是采用4管的；上下各用$2\phi 1000 \times 12mm$。此外广西三岸邕江桥，为中承式拱桥，$L=270m$，于1999年通车，在当时为这种桥的世界纪录。

广州丫髻沙桥，主跨$L=360m$，于2000年6月通车，代替三岸邕江桥而成为新的世界纪录，直至2005年跨度为460m的重庆巫山桥的建成。在丫髻沙桥中，我国首次采用6管，其细部将在下节给出。在拱桥中也可用另外方式采用钢管混凝土，即这时钢管混凝土用作加劲骨架，于其上悬挂模板，然后浇筑混凝土箱梁，例如在万州长江拱桥，其主跨$L=420m$，现仍为上承式钢筋混凝土拱桥的世界纪录，因为在这种情况，混凝土箱梁仍称钢筋混凝土结构，而钢管混凝土则视为混凝土中的劲性钢筋。

广州丫髻沙桥和万县长江大桥一样构造，不过为中承式拱桥，主跨$L=312m$，亦是中承式钢筋混凝土拱桥的世界纪录。

2. 丫髻沙拱桥

丫髻沙拱桥为一座跨过珠江、在广州市西南环高速公路上特大的钢管混凝土拱桥，其跨度分布为76m + 360m + 76 m。图1示丫髻沙桥立视图，它具有1中承式中跨和2上承式半跨侧跨。半跨为倒悬链线无铰拱，计算跨度$L=344m$，

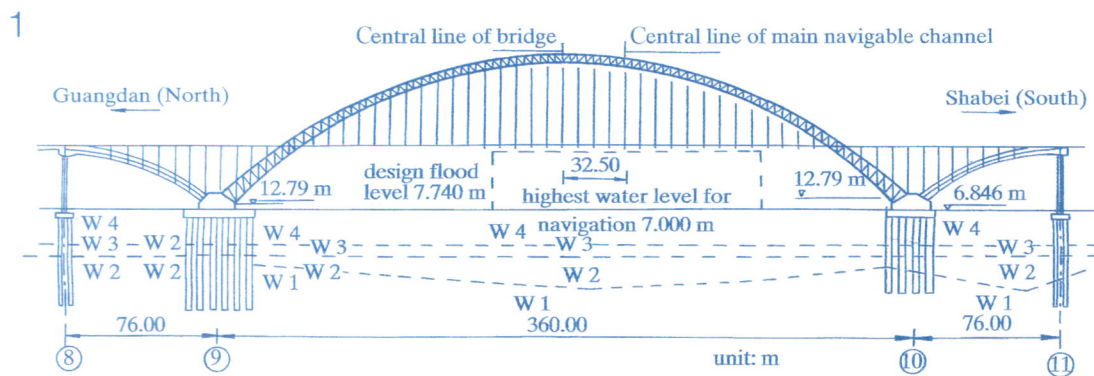

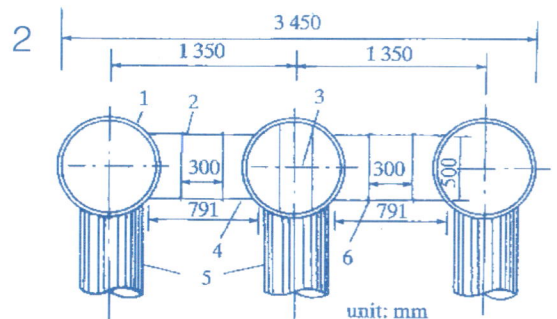

Guangzhou Yajisha Concrete-Filled Steel Tube Arch Bridge

1. BACKGROUND

In the 1960s, concrete-filled steel tube (CFST) has been started to be used in the construction of buildings and Beijing metro station columns and to be studied widely in China. Since 1990–1992, the extensive research has been started, three Chinese Specification CECS28-90, DLGJ99-91 and DLGJ-S11-92 have been successively published to bring about a great advance of CFST in the applications of buildings and some special structures. At the beginning of the 90's of 20th century, CFST has been used in the construction of arch bridges. When the span is not large, such as $L \leq 80m$, single tube can be used, for an example, in the the 80m-span Yiwu Yuanhuang Bridge in Zhejiang Province, single tube of $\phi 800 \times 18mm$ is used. As the span is slightly large, two tubes connected in dumbbell are employed; or three tubes of $3\phi 600 \times 12mm$ are used in 100m-span. Yilan Mudanjiang (jiang means river in Chinese) Bridge with one on top and two in bottom, completed in Heilongjiang Province; and four tubes are used in Huangbai River and Xialao River Bridges, both composed of $2\phi 1\,000 \times 12mm$ with $L=160m$, completed in Hubei Province. Besides, San-an Yongjiang Bridge in Guangxi Province, is a half-through arch with main $L=270m$, open in 1999, a worldwide record of arch bridge in this type at that time.

The Yajisha Bridge at Guangzhou with main $L=360m$, open in June 2000, becomes new worldwide record to replace San-an Yongjiang Bridge, in Yajisha Bridge six tubes are used firstly in China up to completion of Chongqing Wushan Bridge with $L=460m$, in 2005, the details will be given in next section. There is another way to apply CFST in arch bridges, i.e. CFST is used as stiffening skeletons on which the form is hung for pouring concrete box beam such as in Wanzhou Yangtze River Arch Bridge with main $L=420m$, the present worldwide record of decked reinforced concrete arch bridges because in this case, the concrete box beam is still called RC structure and the CFST is considered as the stiff reinforcement in concrete.

The Yajisha Bridge at Guangzhou Bridge in Guangxi Province is constructed as Wanxian Yangtze River Bridge, but is a half-through arch bridge with main $L=312m$ and is a worldwide record of half-through RC arches.

2. YAJISHA ARCH BRIDGE

Yajisha Bridge is an extra-large CFST arch bridge, spanning over Zhujiang on the southwest ring of Express Way at Guangzhou City, the span distribution of main bridge is 76m+360m+76m. Fig.1 shows the elevation of Yajisha Bridge. This Bridge has a half-through mid span and two decked side spans of half arch. The mid-span is an inverted catenary hingeless arch with calculated $L=344m$ and rise $f=76.45m$. In each main rib, six tubes constructed as shown in Fig.2. Two mid tubes in a rib are $\phi 750 \times 20mm$, four side ones are $\phi 750 \times 18mm$

3

图1 丫髻沙桥立视图
Fig.1 Elevation of Yajisha Bridge

图2 弦管和连接板一般构造
1. 弦管；2. 系杆；3. 埋入导管$\phi 220 \times 6$；4. 水平连接板；5. 腹构件；6. 螺栓$\phi 16$
Fig.2 General construction of chord tubes and horizontal connecting plate
1. chord tube; 2. tie; 3. embed conduct $\phi 220 \times 6$; 4. horizontal connecting plate; 5. web member; 6. bolt $\phi 16$

图3 建成的丫髻沙大桥近景（承徐升桥高工惠赠）
Fig.3 Close shot of completed Yajisha Bridge (courtesy of Senior Engr. Xu Shengqiao)

矢高f=76.45m。在每一主肋中，有6只钢管，构造如图2所示。在每一肋内，2中间管为φ750×20mm，4侧管为φ750×18mm，水平连接板厚度为12mm；腹部构件由φ450×12mm竖管、φ350×10mm斜管组成。中拱肋为等宽度3.45m和可变的高度，在拱冠处，上下弦管间中心距为4.00m，而在拱座处则为8.039m。在近拱脚一段的钢管厚度增加至36mm。2肋中心距为39.95m，设置1米字形和1K字形横向支撑。侧边半拱通过可动的橡胶盆式支座支承在边墩上。在两边跨端部，设置通长钢绞线拉杆以平衡由主拱肋传来的水平推力，而组成一3跨连续自锚拱结构，被称为飞燕形，图3、图4分别示建成的丫髻沙大桥近景和远景。

因为全年在珠江需通过万吨大型船只，丫髻沙不能照某些桥，如下牢溪桥在低水位时在河上制造半拱，然后用竖向旋转法提升就位。对丫髻沙桥两个半桥只能分别沿两岸将拱座支承在其桥座制作，桥座则建造于上转盘上（图5），一个拱端两转盘用一钢桁架拉杆连接，拉杆由1m厚混凝土顶板和1m厚底板组成，在顶底板间后浇混凝土；通过竖向旋转24.7014°提升到设计高程，然后通过水平旋转合龙。图5示竖向旋转体系简图和上承盘一般构造。在每一下转盘上设置直径为33m，宽1.1m的环形通道，其上有3mm厚不锈钢镜片，而在每一上转盘下，设置7只由φ800×12mm钢管组成的支承脚以传递由上转盘传至下转盘的重量。图6示北下转盘。在下转盘上，设置2道牵引钢索的反作用支承及2只块体以改换索的方向。水平旋转角分别在北岸为117.1117°，在南岸为92.2333°。下转盘也是桩基的支承平台。

压力灌注钢管混凝土为C60，掺以适量的膨胀剂。为了改善混凝土的和易性，加入些缓凝剂。水灰比为0.35，坍落度为18~20cm。3天抗压强度实际达58.5MPa。压力灌注混凝土的顺序如下：弦杆较早，水平连接板（注入两板的空

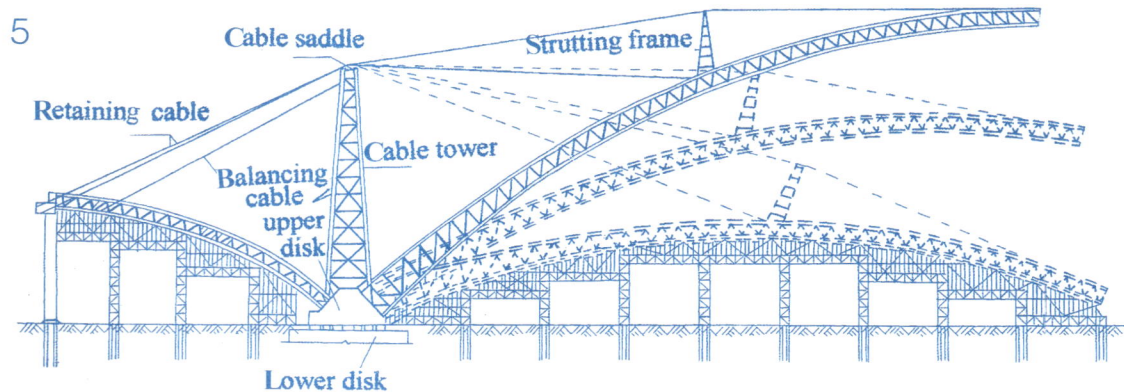

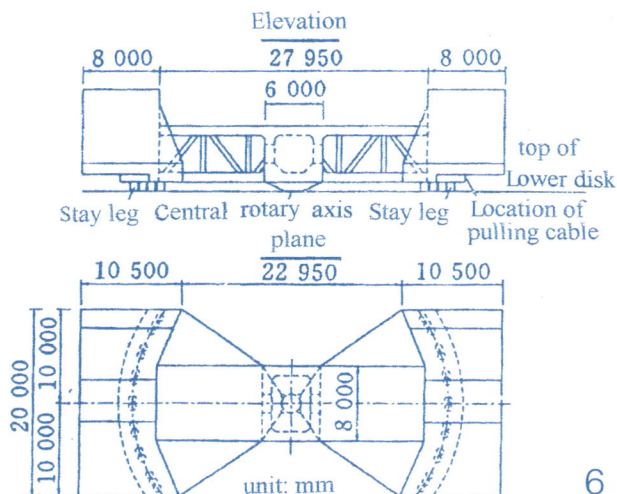

and the thickness of horizontal connecting plate is 12mm; the web members consist of the vertical tubes $\phi450\times12$mm and the inclined tubes of $\phi350\times10$mm. The arch rib has an equal width of 3.45m and a variable depth with a central distance of 4.00m between upper and lower chord tubes at the crown and of 8.039m at the springings. The thickness of tube connecting to abutments is increased to 36mm in a segment from the springing. The central distance of two ribs is 35.95m with 1 米-shaped and 1 K-shaped transverse bracings set between two ribs. The side half arch ribs are supported on side piers through movable rubble pot bearings. Between the ends of two side spans, there are set throughout strand ties to balance the horizontal thrusts from main arch ribs so as to constitute a 3-span continuous self-anchorage arch structure called flying-swallow type. Figs.3, 4 show respectively the close shot and distant shot of the completed Yajisha Bridge.

Because the large ships with capacities of ten-thousand tones must pass through Zhujiang throughout a year, the Yajisha Bridge can not be constructed as some bridges such as Xialao River Bridge with a half arch to be fabricated in river during low water and then to be lifted into position by using vertical swing method. For this Bridge, two halves can only be fabricated respectively on arch frame along two banks with springings to be supported on their abutments which are constructed as upper rotary disks (Fig.5), both of which at one arch end are connected with a steel frame tie constituted of 1m thick top and 1m thick bottom concrete slabs between them concrete will be post-cost; and are lifted to designed elevation through vertical rotation with angle of 24.7014°, then through horizontal rotation to be closed. Fig.6 shows the sketch of vertical rotation system and the general construction of upper disks. On every lower rotary disk, there is set a ring way with diameter of 33m and width of 1.1m, on which there is a 3mm thick stainless mirror steel sheet, and below every upper rotary disk there are set 7 stay leg made of $\phi800\times14$mm tubes to transmit the weight from upper disk to lower one. Fig.6 shows the north lower rotary disk. On the lower rotary disks there are set two reaction supports for pulling cables. The horizontal rotary angles are 117.1117° on the north bank and 92.2333° on the south respectively. The lower disks are also the bearing platforms of pile foundation.

The concrete cast under pressure into tubes is C60 with mixing appropriate expanding agent. For promoting the workability of concrete, some retarding agent is also added. The water cement ratio is 0.35 with slump constant of 18~20cm. The 3-day compressive strength reaches 58.5MPa actually. The sequence of pressure cast concrete are as follows: chord tubes earlier and horizontal connected plates (into cavities of plates) later, lower reaches earlier and upper reaches later, the lower chords earlier and the upper later. Into web tubes and transverse bracings, no concrete will be cast. During pressure cast, it is equivalent to charge the halves of arch rib and to adjust the arch axis. The adjustment is also done by using ropes. After the axis agrees with the design requirement, each of two halves will be closed to use turnbuckles put between chord tubes, then

图5 垂直旋转系统简图
Fig.5 Sketch of vertical rotation system

图6 上转盘一般构造
Fig.6 General construction

腔内）较迟，朝下流的管较早，朝上流的管较迟，下弦较早，上弦较迟。不注入腹管和横撑。在压力灌注中，相当于对半拱肋加载和调整拱轴。调整也可用钢丝绳进行。在拱轴符合设计要求后，每两个半拱用置于两弦管之间的螺丝扣合龙，而后焊接。合龙段长度为1m。图7示两拱肋在两岸作水平旋转。

在所有构造索松开后使内力成为0，主肋变成双铰拱。在所有施工设备移去后，焊接连接桥座的钢管和所有在上下转盘之间连接钢构件，灌注两转盘间混凝土，而拱肋变成无铰拱。

桥面结构包括预制∏-形板和间距为8m的钢横梁以及4根钢纵梁，在板上铺设12cm厚路面，包括4cm改性沥青混凝土和8cm纤维加强混凝土，后者可在计算中考虑。

在下转盘下，设置钻孔桩（图6）桩基础，在北岸承台板下设置36φ3.0m和18φ2.0m，在南岸承台板下设置24φ3.0m和10φ2.0m钻孔桩。南承台板平面尺寸，宽度减小成26.0m，长度增加至54.59m。

welded. The closed segment has a length of 1m. Fig.7 shows the arch ribs on two banks under horizontal rotation.

After all construction cables have been loosed to make the internal forces to be zero, the main ribs become two-hinge arches. After all the construction equipments have been removed and the tubes connecting to abutments and all connecting steel members between upper and lower rotary disks have been welded, and the concrete between two disks has been cast, the ribs become hingeless arches.

The deck structure consists of precast Π-shaped slabs and steel transverse beams with spacing of 8m and four steel longitudinal beams, on slabs there is also a 12cm thick pavement consisting of 4cm modified bituminous concrete and 8cm fiber reinforced concrete, the latter can be considered in calculation.

Under the lower rotary disks, there is set pile foundation with $36\phi 3.0m$ bored piles and $18\phi 2.0m$ under the bearing platforms on north bank (Fig.6) and there are $24\phi 3.0m$ and $10\phi 2.0m$ piles under platforms on south bank. The plane dimensions of south bearing platforms are decreased into 26.0m in width and increased into 54.59m in length.

图7 平转合龙（承徐升桥高工惠赠）
Fig.7 Closure of horizontal rotation
(courtesy of Senior Engr. Xu Shengqiao)

REFERENCES

1.Ding Dajun. New Development of Concrete-Filled Tubular Arch Bridge in China. Travaux n°781. Dec. 2001: 91-94

2.Ding Dajun. Development of Concrete-Filled Tubular Arch Bridges in China. Structural Engineering International, Journal of IABSE, Nov. 2001: 11(4): 265-266

重庆巫山钢管混凝土拱桥

重庆巫山桥（图1）建于重庆市东部，北岸巫山，南岸建始，为一座跨越长江的、中承式钢管混凝土拱桥。主跨460m，从拱座至拱冠高度约为130m（图2）、净矢高对跨度比为1/3.8，其跨度远大于2000年在广州建成的同样形式跨度为360m的丫髻沙拱桥，成为新的世界纪录。在巫山桥中，采用4ϕ1220钢管，上下弦各用2根厚度各为22mm，但下弦2根在靠近拱桥处长度为40.899m一段，厚度加厚至25mm。拱肋宽度为4.14m。弦管通过ϕ711×16mm横管及ϕ610×12mm竖管连接成钢管混凝土桁架，这种桁架一半沿纵向分成11个节段（图3），而沿横向分为2肋，靠近上游和下游，在肋间设置20个横向支撑，故全桥有64节段，最大的吊装节段设计重量为118t，安装节段采用索吊进行而不用支承（图4）。在吊装安装就位后，节段用联结器在吊装状态下进行。在拱腹杆间拱横撑设置在靠近吊杆处以加强拱肋的横向连接。

向每肋上下弦各2根ϕ1 220×22mm主钢管内向、拱肋与桥面连接处的竖腹杆ϕ610×22mm钢管内、向在立柱上横向列宁界管ϕ1 220×22m内、向吊杆处ϕ711×16mm上下横向连接管内注入具有诸多工作特性的、开发的高强混凝土C60，例如高塑性、可收缩补偿、延迟初凝和早期高强，等等。试样28天平均抗压强度达79.3MPa，标准差为3.5MPa，质量完全符合设计规范要求。

注入每一拱肋中主管的混凝土约达600m³，两岸分别从拱座到拱冠分成3个节段，采用连续构筑法进行，压注次序为：①注入靠近下游朝向下江的上弦；②注入靠近上游朝向上江的上弦；③注入靠近下游朝向上江的下弦；④注入靠近上游朝向下江的下弦；⑤注入靠近下游朝向上江的上弦；⑥注入靠近上游朝向下江的上弦；⑦注入靠近下游朝向下江的下弦；⑧注入靠近上游朝向上江的下弦。然后压注混凝土进入竖向腹杆管内和横向连接管。

图1 建成的巫山大桥（承张佐安高工惠赠）
Fig.1 Completed Wushan Bridge (courtesy of Senior Engr. Zhang Zuo'an)

Chongqing Wushan Concrete-Filled Steel Tube Arch Bridge

Chongqing Wushan Bridge (Fig.1) is a concrete filled steel tube (CFST) arch bridge over Yangtze River. The north bank is Wushan and the south is Jianshi. It is a half-through structure with main span of 460m and height from springing to crown of 130m or so (Fig.2), the ratio of clear rise to span is 1/3.8. Wushan Bridge is much larger than the original worldwide record, Guangzhu Yajisha Arch Bridge of the same type, completed in 2000 with main span of 360m and becomes new worldwide record. In Wushan Bridge, $4\phi 1\ 220$ tubes are used, 2 in top row and 2 in bottom, the thickness of 2 tubes in upper and lower chords is 22mm, but the thickness of lower chord tubes in 2 segments near springing with length of 40.899m is increased to 25mm; the width of arch ribs is 4.14m. The chord tubes through transverse tube of $\phi 711 \times 16$mm and vertical tube of $\phi 610 \times 12$mm are connected into CFST truss. A half of this truss along longitudinal was divided into 11 segments (Fig.3) and along transverse into 2 ribs closed to upper and lower reaches, between ribs, there are 20 pieces of transverse bracing, so in whole bridge there are 64 segments, the design weight of the max. hung segment is 118t. The installation of segments was conducted by using cable crane without using supports (Fig.4), after hanging to position, then the segments were spliced in hanging state with coupler. Between web chords, the cross bracings are set near-by hangers to strengthen the transverse connection of arch ribs.

Into 2 upper and lower main tubes in each rib $\phi 1\ 220 \times 22$mm, into the vertical web members at the connection of arch ribs and deck $\phi 610 \times 22$mm tubes, into the transversely connecting tubes $\phi 1\ 220 \times 22$mm above the vertical columns and into the upper and lower transversely connecting tubes of $\phi 711 \times 16$mm at hangers were all injected highstrength concrete C60 developed, possessing many working properties such as extra-plasticity, shrinkage-compensation, delay initial setting and high-early-strength, etc., the 28-day average compressive strength of the specimens was 79.3MPa with standard deviation of 3.5MPa. The quality after practice met the requirements of design code, so it is successful.

The concrete injected into the main tubes of each arch rib amounted approximately to 600m^3, adopted continuously construction method divided in 3 segments along two banks from springing to crown. The sequence of injection was: ① into the upper chord of rib towards lower river near lower reaches; ② into the upper chord towards upper river near upper reaches; ③ into the lower chord towards upper river near lower reaches; ④ into the lower chord towards lower river near upper reaches; ⑤ into the upper chord toward upper river near lower reaches; ⑥ into the upper chord towards lower river near upper reaches; ⑦ into the lower chord towards lower river near lower reaches;

对大桥曾在拱冠、拱座及中间3个截面测了混凝土和钢管在弹性阶段的应变，由此公路设计院牟廷敏高工将之换算成混凝土和钢管所承担的内力，表明两者之比约为80%和20%，即混凝土承担主要内力，按塑性理论计算也基本如此，因此国外有将巫山桥列入钢拱桥是不合适的。

　　对巫山长江大桥钢管，选用电弧热喷铝合金作为长期防腐涂层，其寿命考虑超过30年。涂层设计如下：

（1）底部处理：粗糙度Sa_a，R_2为40~80μm；

（2）喷铝-镁合金厚度160±25μm；

（3）喷环氧密封底部漆，厚30μm；

（4）喷云铁环氧中间漆厚50μm；

（5）喷丙烯聚氨酯面漆，干膜厚80μm；其中40μm是在工厂进行，而其余40μm在桥建成后在现场完成。

上述（1）~（4）也是在工厂完成的。

大桥于2005年元月8日建成通车。

图2　巫山桥总布置图
Fig.2 Sketch of general layout of Wushan Bridge

图3　半拱划分节段
Fig.3 Division of segments in half of arch

图4　用索吊拼接拱（承张佐安高工惠赠）
Fig.4 Arch spliced by cable crane (courtesy of Senior Engr. Zhang Zuo'an)

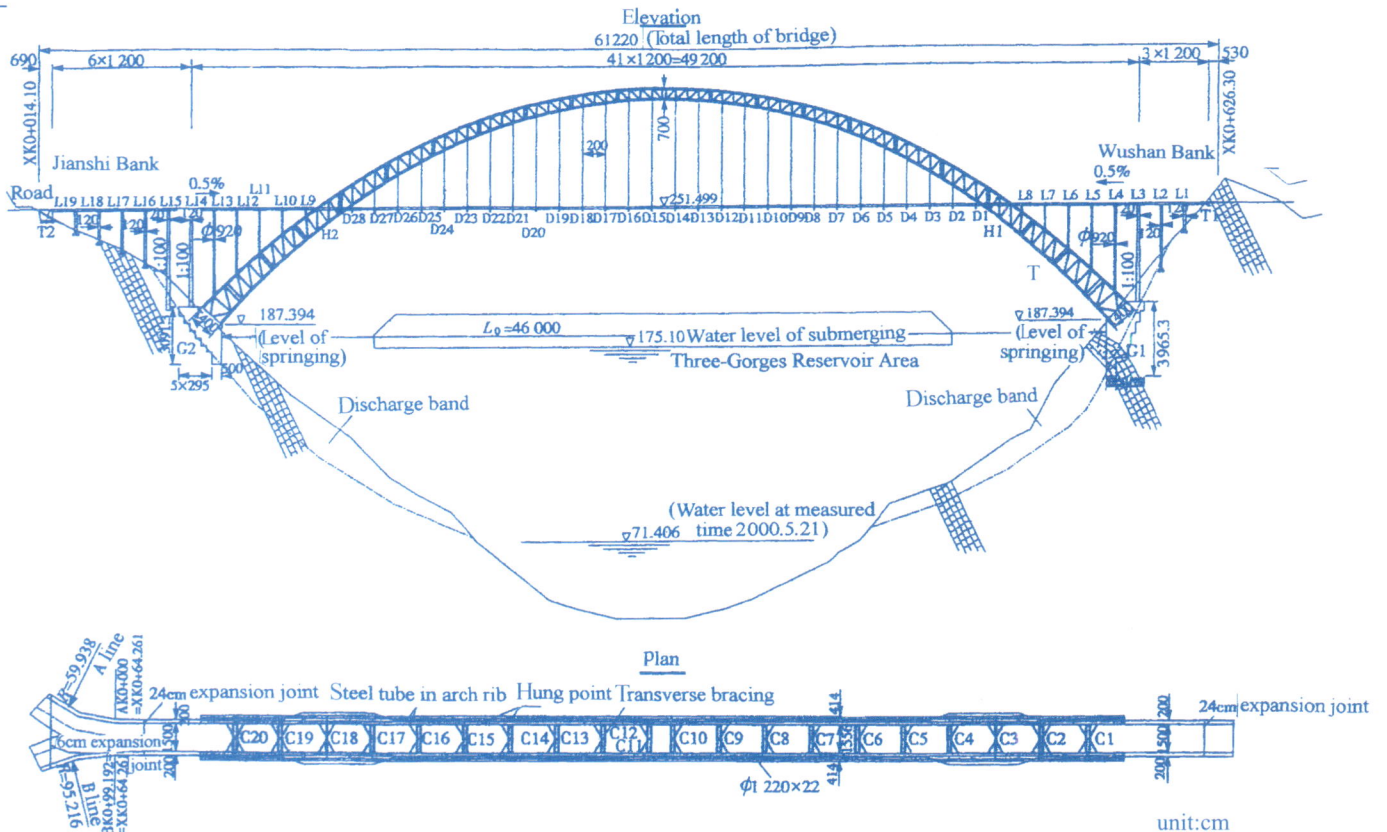

4

⑧ into the lower chord towards upper river near upper reaches. Then inject concrete into the vertical web member tubes and into transverse connecting tubes.

In this bridge, for 3 sections at crown, springing and the median section, the strains in elastic stage were measured, the Senior Engr. Mou Tinmin, Highway Design Institute transformed these into the internal forces in concrete and in steel tube to show these forces being 80% and 20% or so, i.e., concrete undertakes the main internal forces, the calculated results are basically so, hence the concept suggested in foreign country to put the CFST bridges into steel ones is not proper.

For the steel tubes of Wushan Yangtze River, the hot spraying of aluminum alloy with arc was selected as long-acting preservative coating, the life of which is considered for more than 30 years. The design of coating is given as follows:

(1) base treatments: reaching Sa_a roughness R_z40~80μm;

(2) spraying aluminum-magnesium alloy with thickness 160±25μm;

(3) spraying sealing bottom paint of epoxy with thickness of 30μm;

(4) spraying medium paint of micaceous iron oxide epoxy with dry membrane thickness of 50μm;

(5) spraying surface paint of acrylic polyurethane with dry membrane thickness of 80μm, among which the 40μm was conducted in factory and the other 40μm was constructed in site after the completion of bridge.

(1)~(4) in the above design were also finished in factory.

This Bridge was completed and opened on Jan.8, 2005.

3

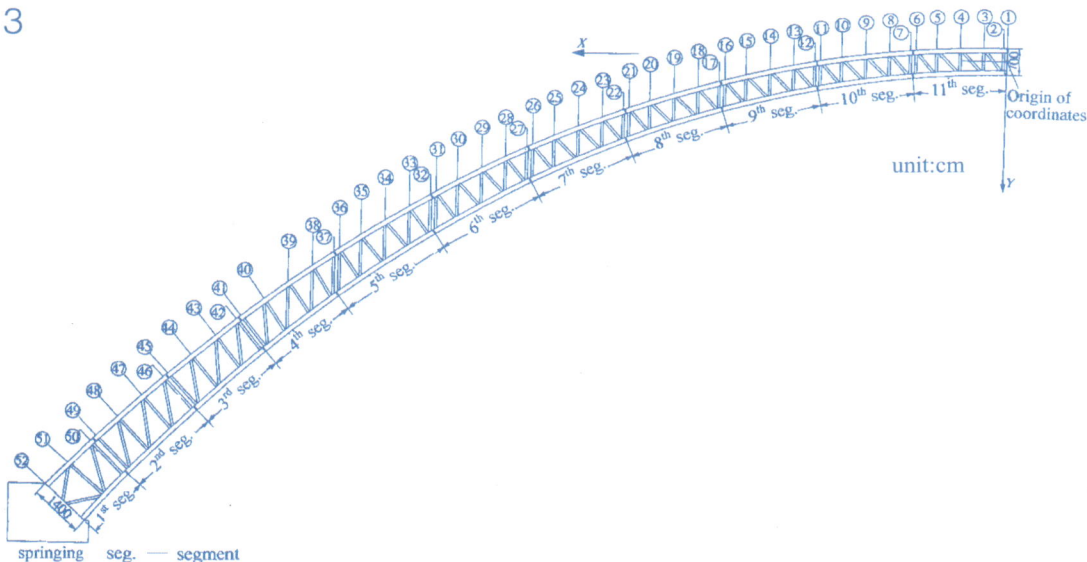

springing   seg. — segment

REFERENCES

1.Zhang Zuo'an, Liu Shilin, Ding Dajun. *Wushan Arch Bridge — The worldwide longest arch constructed of concrete-filled steel tube. Travaux, International. 2006(4): 75-76*

武汉汉江三桥

汉江三桥（图1）是武汉市汉江上建设的又一座大桥，连接着汉口集加咀和汉阳南岸咀，是一座跨径280m的下承式钢管混凝土系杆拱桥。因桥拱红色，亦称"彩虹桥"。1997年12月20日开工，2000年底建成通车。拱肋桁架截面如图2所示。

汉江三桥是为武汉市中心内环线交通枢纽工程，主桥为单孔净跨280m，桥梁全长302.926m，就算跨径 l_c=283.598m，钢管直径为 ϕ1.0m，桥宽20m，矢跨比为1/5，桥的结构示意见图3。共计灌注无收缩混凝土2 306.27m³，其中缀板间填充487.63m³，拱的弦杆钢管内1 818.64m³。

上、中、下三类拱桥是就与道路连接高低而言。下承式拱桥因连接道路低而得名，因通航净空低，大型船只通航困难，又因桥的承载力，拱高不能过低，这对拱的平面稳定性不利，必需加强风撑，使两拱共同工作，故采用少；上承式桥次之，中承拱因连接道路高低适用空间很大，采用极为广泛。

汉江三桥跨越汉江，连接汉阳，故又名晴川桥，因唐诗人崔颢（？— 754年）《黄鹤楼》（在武昌市）七律颈联[①]第一句"晴川[②]历历汉阳树"而得名。

汉江三桥为下承式拱桥的世界纪录。

图1 汉江三桥（承叶见曙教授惠赠）
Fig.1 The 3ʳᵈ Hanjiang Bridge (courtesy of Prof. Ye Jianshu)

图2 拱肋桁架截面
Fig.2 Arch rib truss section

图3 桥的结构示意图
Fig.3 Structural sketch of Bridge

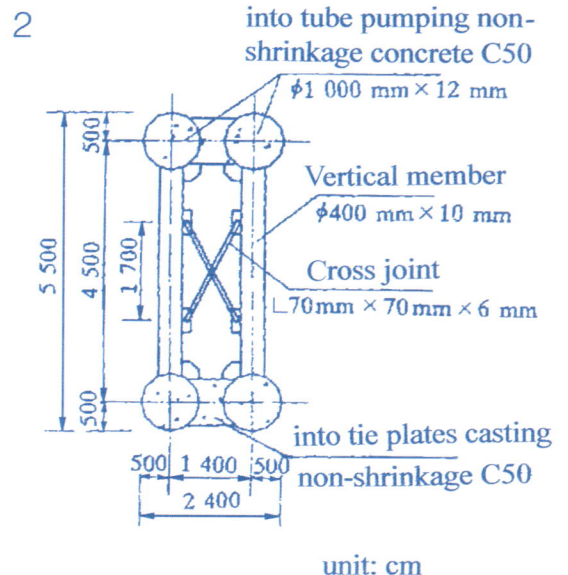

into tube pumping non-shrinkage concrete C50
ϕ1 000 mm × 12 mm

Vertical member
ϕ400 mm × 10 mm

Cross joint
└70 mm × 70 mm × 6 mm

into tie plates casting non-shrinkage C50

unit: cm

The 3rd Wuhan Hanjiang Bridge

The 3rd Hanjiang Bridge (Fig.1) is an another Bridge constructed in Wuhan City over Hanjiang River, it joins Hankou Jijiaju to Hanyang Nan-anju and is a 280m-span low-through concrete-filled steel tube arch bridge with ties. Owing to being red arches, it is also called "Coloured Rainbow Bridge". This bridge started to construct on Dec.20, 1997 and has been completed and opened at the end of 2000. The section of arch ribs is shown in Fig.2.

The 3rd Hanjiang Bridge is the traffic key engineering of the internal ring road in city center, the main bridge has single span with clear span of 280m, its total length is 302.96m, calculated span l_c=283.598m, the diameter of steel tube is ϕ1.0m, the width of bridge is 20m, the ratio of rise to span is 1/5, the structural sketch of bridge is shown in Fig.3. The sum of non-shrinkage concrete cast reached 2 306.27m³, among which 2 tie plates 487.63m³, filling into tube of chord members 1 818.64m³.

The titles of 3-kind arch bridge are different due to being low or high to join road. Low-through arch bridge is called because it joins low road, its navigable clearance is not high, so the large-scale ships are difficult to pass, besides, for increasing bearing capacity of bridge, the arch height can not be two low, it is unfavorable to the stability out of plane of arch, so it is necessary to strengthen the wind bracings to make 2 arches to act as an integral. The deck arch bridges are constructed slightly more, but the half-through arch bridges are adopted extensively, because the space of their adaptability to the height of joined road is large so they are adopted extremely widely.

The 3rd Hanjiang Bridge over Hanjiang River to join Hanyang, so it is also called Qingchuan Bridge, because the poet Cui Hao (?–754) in Tang Dynasty had a poem on "Yellow-Crane-Storied Building (in Wuchang City), this poem is an 8-line poem with 7 characters in a line (sentence), and a strict tonal and rhyme scheme[1], the 1st sentence in neck couplet is "over the sunny[2] river surface, the trees in Hanyang appear extremely clear", so Qingchuan Bridge has also this name.

The 3rd Hanjiang Bridge is a worldwide rocord of low-through arch bridge.

3
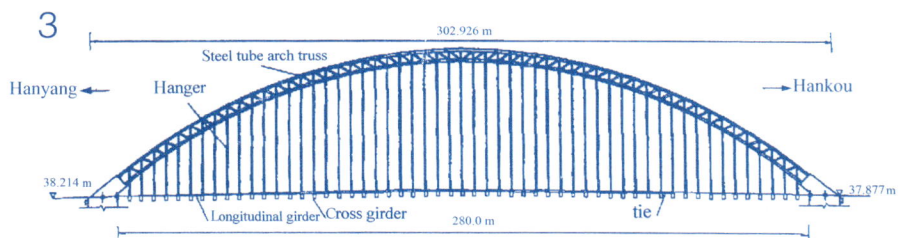

① 律诗8句，第1、2句称首联，3、4句称颔联，5、6句称颈联，7、8句称尾联；颈联第1句即全诗第5句。
② 千家诗（主要为唐宋诗人）中竟将"晴川"误注为"晴川阁"。按"晴川阁"为明朝（1368 — 1643年）人范之箴所建（原本崔诗取名），阁在汉阳东面。

① The 8-line poem includes 4 couplets, the 1, 2 sentences are called head couplet (the 1st couplet), the 3, 4 sentences are called chin couplet, the 5, 6 sentences are called neck couplet and the 7, 8 sentences are called tail couplet (the end couplet), the 1st sentence in neck couplet, i.e., the 5th sentence in the entire poem.
② In the Poem Selection of many poets (mainly from the poets in Tang and Song Dynasties) gives wrong annotation of sunny river as Qingchuan (means sunny river in Chinese) Pavilion. This Pavilion was built by Fan Zhizhen in Ming Dynasty (1386–1643) (the name was from Cui's poem), the Pavilion is located at the east of Hanyang.

参考文献

1.丁庆军，管斌君，胡曙光.武汉市汉江三桥钢管混凝土设计与施工.混凝土，2001（11）：57–59
2.杨齐海，邱国平.武汉市汉江三桥钢管混凝土拱桥施工工艺.桥梁建设，2001（1）：37–40

REFERENCES

1.*Ding Qingjun, Guan Binjun, Hu Shuguang. Design and Construction Technology of New-Style Concrete Filled Steel Tube of the 3rd Jianghan Bridge in Wuhan. Concrete. 2001(11): 57-59*
2.*Yang Qihai, Qiu Guoping. The Construction Technology of CFST Arch of the 3rd Jianghan Bridge in Wuhan. Bridge Construction. 2001(1): 37-40*

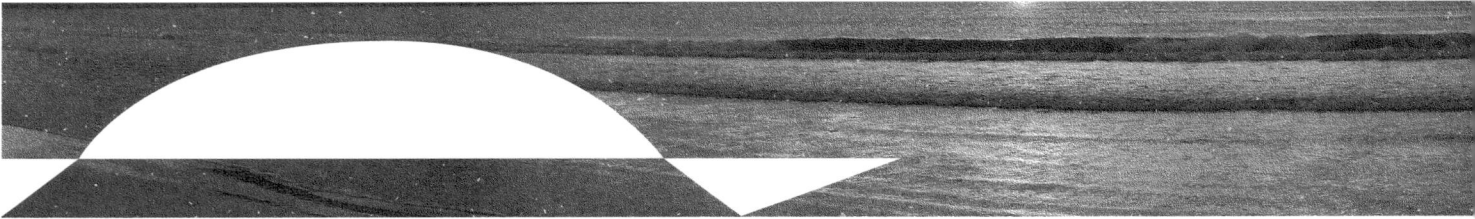

STEEL ARCH BRIDGES

钢拱桥

上海卢浦拱桥

1. 引言

大桥位于上海南部、鲁班路河渡，为城市南北高架桥的关键性连接，也是上海市区第7条河渡设施。这一方案的建设旨在局部获得扩大过河的要求，特别是解除为一繁忙路网环绕的南北高架的负荷。卢浦桥（图1a~e）完成主要架高线和连接上海南北高速路以改善浦东国际机场和市中心的交通状况。

设计主要技术标准如下：

— 路型：城市主要干道；

— 设计速度：60km/h；

— 最大纵坡度：主干线5%，匝道6.4%；

— 桥面宽度：两向6车道，交通车道总宽度24.5m，观光人行道每边2.0m；

— 通航净空：高46m，宽340m；

— 设计荷载：汽20，验算荷载：拖100；规定活荷载，列于中国桥梁规范；

— 行人荷载：4kN/m，在全桥宽度内均匀行人荷载：2.4kN/m²；

— 地震作用：地震烈度7。

2. 设计概念

2.1 建筑和结构特点

最终设计选择箱形拱桥（图2）。从平面图可见两拱内倾，构成"提篮型"拱桥。当时，现有大跨拱桥如美国新河乔治大桥（518m）、澳大利亚悉尼港口大桥（503m）全为桁架拱桥。但从建筑学透视看，箱形拱桥有较少的结构构件，导致视觉上结构较为简洁，这些结构在本质上是较为美学的愉悦。

选择中承式系杆拱桥是因为它适合于上海特别软弱的土壤基础条件。为了平衡主跨巨大水平推力，在双边跨两端间设置强的水平索。加劲梁可直接支承于拱肋上，或从下面由柱支承或由上面吊杆承受。边跨加劲梁与边拱肋和主拱肋固接，同时主跨大梁是由横梁上滑动支座于拱肋和系梁交接处支承的。纵向阻尼装置亦设置在这些横梁上以改善桥的抗震性能。

2.2 桥跨和纵剖面

根据黄浦江的平面，在桥址处的江岸线为480m宽。卢浦大桥将以一跨过江，不允许在江中设墩。卢浦大桥主拱跨为550m，高度为100m（矢跨比：f/l=1/5.5），跨度组合：100m+550m+100m=750m。卢浦大桥桥面垂直曲线半径

1a

1b

Shanghai Lupu Arch Bridge

1. Introduction

The Luban Road river crossing, locating in the south of Shanghai, is the key connection of the city's north-south viaduct, and is also the 7th river crossing facility in the Shanghai urban area. The construction of this project aims at meeting the local expansion requirement of getting traffic across the river, especially in relieving the burden on the North-South viaduct that is surrounded by a busy road network. This bridge (Fig.1a~e) has completed the main north-south elevated line and connects the Shanghai north-south expressway improving the traffic condition between Pudong International Airport and the city center.

The main technical criteria for the design are the following:

— road type: urban main artery;

— design speed: 60km/h;

— maximum longitudinal grade: main route 5%, ramps 6.4%;

— width of deck: 6 lanes in two-directions, total width of traffic lanes 24.5m, width of pedestrian walk for sightseeing 2.0m each side;

— navigation clearance: height 46m, width 340m;

— design load: automobile 20, check load: trailer 100; specified live loads in Chinese bridge code;

— pedestrian load: 4kN/m, uniform pedestrian load on full deck width: 2.4kN/m²;

— seismic effect: earthquake intensity 7.

2. Design Concept

2.1 Architectural and Structural Character

A box-arch bridge is selected for final design (Fig.2). From the plan, it can be seen that 2 arches are inclined inwards to constitute a "carrying-basket-typed" arch bridge. At present, the existing large span arch bridges such as the New River Gorge Bridge in USA (518m) and Sydney Harbor Bridge in Australia (503m) are all truss arch bridges. However, from an architectural perspective, box-arch bridges have fewer structural members resulting in visually simpler structures that are essentially more aesthetically pleasing.

A half-through tied arch bridge is chosen as it suits the particularly soft soil foundation conditions in Shanghai. In order to balance the huge horizontal thrust of the main span, strong horizontal cables are set between the two ends of both side span arches. The stiffening girders may be supported directly on the arch rib or by columns from below or by suspenders from above. The stiffening girders of the side spans are fixed with the ribs of the side arch and main arch, while the girder of the main span is supported with sliding bearings on the crossbeams at the intersections of the arch rib and girder. The damping device in the longitudinal direction is also set on these crossbeams to improve the aseismic behavior of the bridge.

2.2 Span and Profile

According to the plan of the Huangpu River, the shore line at the bridge site is 480m wide. The Lupu Bridge crosses over the river with

1c

1d

图1 建成的卢浦大桥
(a) 正视图（承林元培院士惠赠），
(b) 侧视图（承IABSE2004年上海讨论会惠赠），
(c)拱肋合龙（承Bd&e Iain Masterton博士惠赠），
(d) 桥面合龙（承林元培院士惠赠）

Fig.1 Completed Lupu Bridge
(a) front view (courtesy of Academician Lin Yuanpei),
(b) frank view (courtesy of 2004 IABSE Shanghai Symposium),
(c) closing of arch rib (courtesy of Dr. Iain Masterton, Bd&e),
(d) closing of deck (courtesy of Academician Lin Yuanpei)

图1 建成的卢浦大桥
(e) 大桥夜景（承林元培院士惠赠）
Fig.1 Completed Lupu Bridge
(e) night scene (courtesy of Academician Lin Yuanpei)

为9 000m。桥面纵向最大坡度为2.5%，横向为2%。

3. 结构

3.1 拱肋

拱肋为一扭转刚性形状（图3）。主跨拱肋高度从9.0m变化到6.0m，对边跨从9.0m到7.0m。钢箱上部为矩形截面，5.0m宽，高度从在拱座处的6.0m变化到中跨拱冠处的3.0m，在边跨内从6.0m到4.0m；钢箱下部为梯形截面，3.0m高度，顶宽5.0m，底宽3.0m。

3.2 大梁与横梁

边跨大梁在拱肋之上为一密封箱梁（图4）。箱梁宽41.0m，截面高2.7m，箱梁和拱肋、柱和边跨端横梁固接。

主跨大梁为开口箱梁，由2主箱梁和开口横梁组成（图5）。大梁宽39.5m，截面高度2.7m。主跨大梁由吊杆支承在拱肋上，并由两端支承连接整体拱和边跨大梁段。

3.3 风撑

桥面上有27道风撑，水平距离为13.5m，支撑截面为矩形，上下部钢板分别与拱肋上部和中部钢板平齐。在桥面下2道矩形截面K形支撑设置在边跨和中部每边。

3.4 柱

在每个边跨，总共有4×2根柱。柱截面为矩形：桥座处5m×5m，其余5m×2.5m。

3.5 吊杆和水平索

有27对双吊杆，纵向间距13.5m。吊杆和拱肋在相同平面内（倾斜比为1:5）。

有2组水平索设置在2拱肋端部，每组包含8根索，由预制平行钢丝和锚具组成。索中总力约为20 000t以平衡由中跨自重引起的水平推力。

3.6 基础

ϕ900mm钢管桩用于主跨基础。墩帽由横梁连接。ϕ700mm土壤–水泥搅拌桩用以加固土壤，并相互连接以增强整体性。

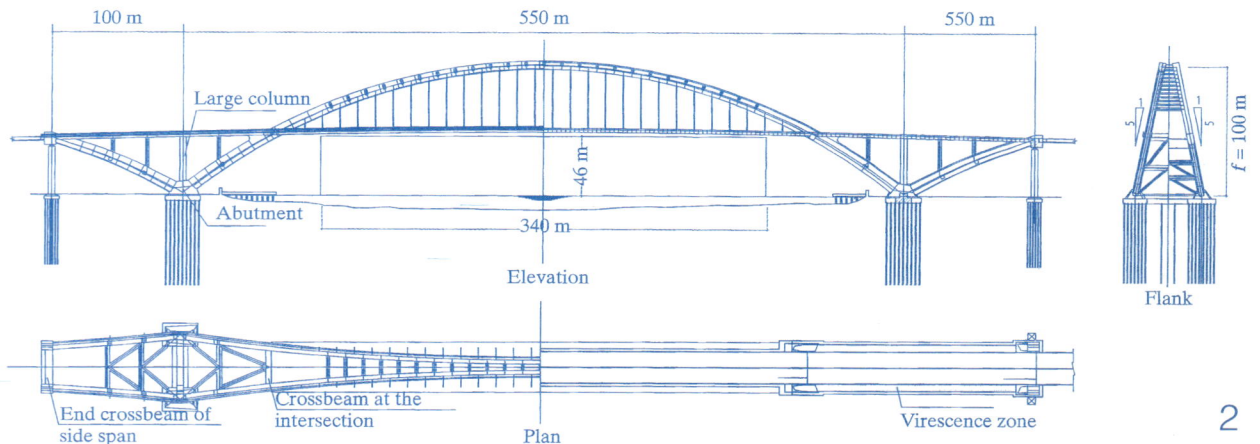

Elevation

Flank

Plan

2

3 000~6 000 mm

6 000~9 000 mm

3000 mm

3 000 mm

3

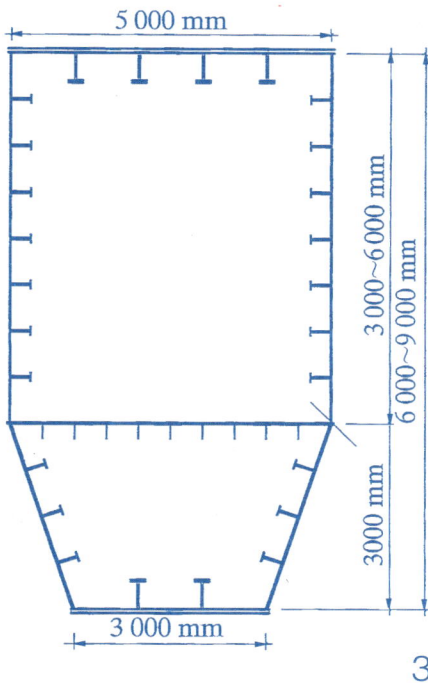

图2 大桥正视及平面图
Fig.2 Bridge elevation and plan

图3 拱肋截面
Fig.3 Section of arch rib

only one span, and no piers are permitted in the river. The main arch span of the Lupu Bridge is 550m, and 100m in height (rise-span ratio: $f/l=1/5.5$), with a span combination of: 100m+550m+100m=750m. The vertical curve radius of the Lupu Bridge deck is 9 000m. The maximum gradient of the bridge deck is 2.5% in the longitudinal direction and 2% in the transverse.

3. Structure

3.1 Arch Rib

The section of the arch rib is a torsionally stiff shape (Fig.3). The arch rib depth of the main span varies from 9.0m to 6.0m, and from 9.0m to 7.0m for the side spans. The upper part of the steel box is a rectangular section with a 5.0m width, and depth varying from 6.0m at the spring to 3.0m at the crown of the mid-span, and 6.0m to 4.0m in the side span; the lower part of the steel box is a trapezoid section with a 3.0m depth and 5.0m width on the top and 3.0m width at the bottom.

3.2 Girder and Crossbeam

The girder in the side span, above the arch rib, is a closed steel box (Fig.4). The box-girder is 41.0m in width and 2.7m in depth. The box girder is fixed with the arch ribs, columns, and end cross beam of the side spans.

The girder of the main span is an open steel box-beam, consisting of 2 main box girders connected by open cross beams (Fig.5). The girder is 39.5m in width and 2.7m in depth. The girder of the main span is supported on the arch rib by suspenders and connected to the integral arch and girder segment of the side span by bearings at the two ends.

3.3 Wind Bracing

There are 27 wind bracings above the deck, with a horizontal distance of 13.5m. The section of the bracing is rectangular, varying in depth, with the upper and bottom plates flush with the upper and middle plates of the arch rib, respectively. Below the bridge deck, 2 K-bracings of rectangular section are set at each side of the side span and the mid-span.

3.4 Columns

There are altogether 4×2 columns on each side span. The column cross section is rectangular; 5m×5m for the column on the abutment, and 5m×2.5m for the others.

3.5 Suspenders and Horizontal Cables

There are 27 pairs of double suspenders spaced at 13.5m longitudinally. The suspenders are in the same plane of the arch rib (slant ratio: 1:5).

There are two groups of horizontal cables set at the end of the two arch ribs, each of which consists of 8 cables made up of prefabricated parallel steel wires and anchorage. The total force in the cables is about 20 000t to balance the horizontal thrust caused by the dead load of the mid-span.

3.6 Foundations

Steel tube piles of ϕ900mm are used in the foundation of the main

3.7 桥座

在桥座处，有主跨肋、边跨肋和桥面柱连接节点。此外它也是钢上部结构和混凝土下部结构连接节点位置。在设计中采用钢和混凝土组合桥座。在中板（箱形拱肋矩形截面）以上边跨和主跨肋部分连接桥座钢的部分。在中板以下肋截面其余部分通过支承端板连接混凝土部分。

4. 施工

4.1 拱肋施工

桥面水平以下拱肋包括边跨和主跨部分，为了安装这部分钢拱肋和加劲大梁，按照它们不同位置，两类施工方法曾予应用。对那些靠在江岸上部分，安装是在脚手架上用350t或300t履带式起重机逐步进行。对那些在江上部分用1 000t船式起重机分阶提升。两座临时钢塔建立在主墩上而临时斜拉索用以建设桥面水平以上桥的主跨拱肋。斜拉索锚固到边跨以提供拱肋的临时支承。通过这种临时斜拉索体系，用一设置在已完成拱肋段端部的起重机可将预制拱肋段提升到它们正确的位置。而后提升的拱肋段被焊接到已建好的拱肋悬臂沙锅内直至两悬臂合拢。

4.2 主跨桥面大梁的施工

两根760m长外部水平索是用于抵抗主拱的巨大推力，索的安装利用悬索桥主索采用的施工方法的施工步道。临时悬挂托架体系用于悬吊超长重水平索。主跨加劲梁段用位于肋上的起重机提升到桥面水平。吊杆安装的锚固于拱肋。在全部桥段到它们正确的位置后，桥段焊接在一起形成全桥。

卢浦大桥于2003年10月28日建成通车。

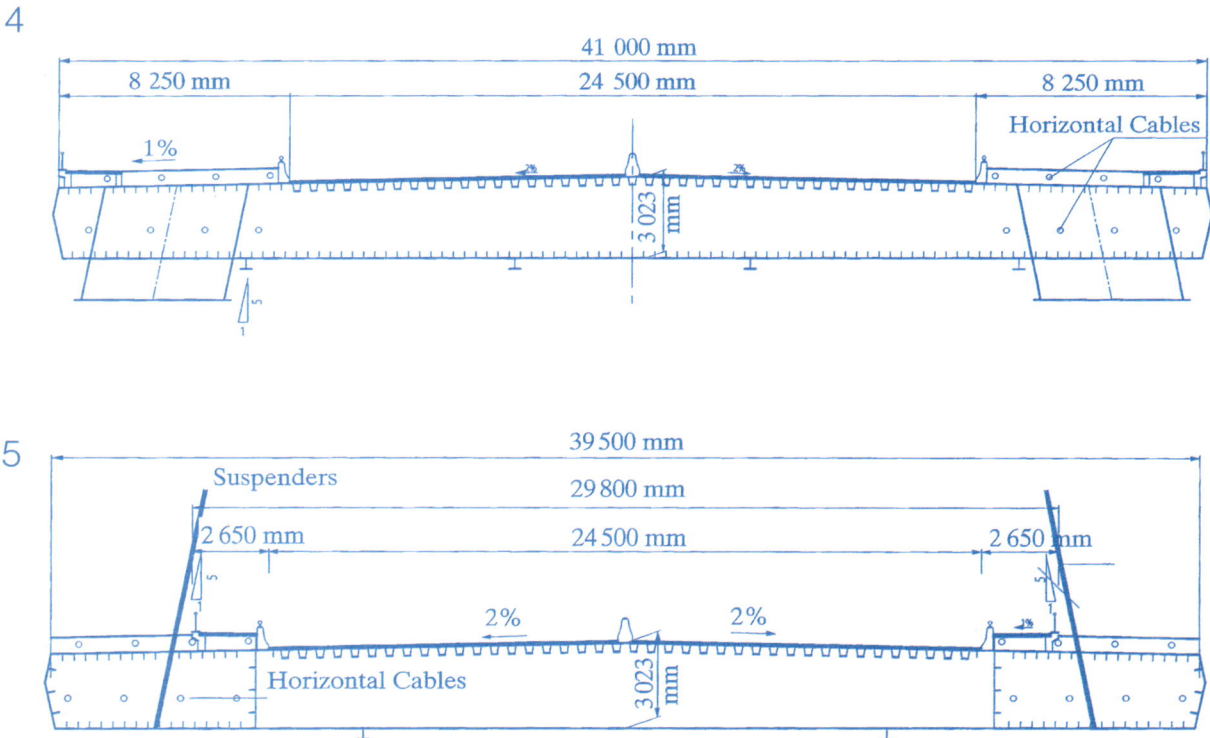

span. The pier caps are connected by cross beams. Soil-cement stirred piles of ϕ700mm are used to strengthen the soil, and are connected to each other to improve the integrity.

3.7 Abutment

At the abutment there is the connecting joint of the main span rib, side span rib and deck column. In addition, it is also the connecting joint location of the steel superstructure and concrete substructure. A steel and concrete composite abutment is used in design. The part of the ribs of the side span and main span above the middle plate (the rectangular section of the box arch rib) is connected to the steel part of the abutment. The other part of the rib section below the middle plate is connected to the concrete part of the abutment through bearing end plates.

4. Construction

4.1 Construction of arch rib

The arch rib below deck level includes the side span and part of the main span. For installing the steel arch rib and the stiffening girders in this part, two kinds of construction methods were used according to their different locations. For those on the riverbank, the installation was performed on falsework with a 350t or 300t crawler crane in stages. For those in the river, staged lifting with a 1 000t barge crane was used. Two temporary steel towers were constructed on the main piers and temporary stays were used for the erection of the arch ribs above deck level in the main span of the bridge. The temporary stays were anchored to the side spans and provided temporary support for the arch ribs. Through this temporary cable-stayed system, the prefabricated arch rib segments could be lifted to their right position with a crane set at the end of the completed arch rib segment. The lifted arch rib segments were then welded to the constructed arch rib cantilever until the closure of the two cantilevers was made.

4.2 Construction of the Main Span Deck-Girder

Two 760m long external horizontal cables are used to resist the huge thrust of the main arch. Installation of the cables employed the catwalk method adopted from the cables employed the catwalk method adopted from the main cable construction method for suspension bridges. A temporary hanging bracket system was used to suspend the super long and heavy horizontal cables. The stiffening girder segments of the main span were lifted to deck level by a crane positioned on the ribs. Hangers were installed and anchored to the arch ribs. After all of the deck segments had been installed to their places, the segments were welded together to form the whole bridge.

Lupu Bridge has been completed and opened on Oct.28, 2003.

图4 边跨大梁截面
Fig.4 Girder section of side span

图5 主跨大梁截面
Fig.5 Girder section of main span

参考文献

2.丁大钧. 中国大陆拱桥和索桥建设新进展. 中国台湾土木水利学会会刊，2004. 31（4）：56-67

REFERENCES

1.Yuanpei Lin, Zenhang Zhang, Biao Ma, Liang Zhou. Lupu Arch Bridge Shanghai. SEI, IABSE Journal, 2004(1): 24-26

2.Ding Dajun. New advance of arch bridges and cable-supported bridges in Mainland China, Taiwan, China, 2004. 31(4): 56-67

重庆朝天门钢桁架拱桥

1.工程概况

重庆朝天门长江大桥（图1a～c）位于重庆朝天门（长江与嘉陵江交汇点，见图2）下游1.2km，是连接长江东西两岸的重要通道，沟通重庆市南岸、江北中央商务区。大桥包括主桥和南北两侧引桥，全长1 741m，其中主桥长932m，采用190m+552m+190m的中承式连续钢桁系杆拱桥。东西引桥分别长495m和314m，均为预应力混凝土连续箱梁桥。大桥采用双层交通布置，上层桥面为双向6车道和两侧人行道，下层桥面中间为双向城市轻轨，两侧为双向2车道。

2.主要技术指标

公路道路等级：城市Ⅰ级主干道，设计行车速度为60 km/h；

桥面车道布置：上层桥面双向6车道，一个车道宽度为3.75 m，两侧人行道，总宽度为2×2.5 m；下层桥面双向2车道，道路净空高度≥5m。

轨道交通标准：双向轨道交通，线间距离4.2m，设计行车速度为80 km/h，允许最大速度100 km/h，轨道交通限界：净宽≥9.2m；轨顶以上净高≥6.5m。

3.设计荷载

3.1 永久荷载

（1）主桁杆件及节点、桥面系、平面联结系、横向联结系及桥门架等均按照构件实际重量计，并按照节点荷载作用于主桁考虑。

（2）上层桥面铺装：22kN/m；下层桥面铺装：12kN/m；上层桥面护栏：1.35kN/m；下层桥面护栏：2.7kN/m；人行道铺装：0.6kN/m；人行道栏杆：1.0kN/m；下层轨道交通明桥面（含检查走道）8.0 kN/m。以上均为每桁荷载，按照节点荷载作用于主桁考虑。

3.2 可变荷载

（1）汽车荷载：计算荷载为城市公路—I级，并按照城—A荷载验算。全桥按照8车道设计，总体加载时根据规范的相关规定进行折减。

Chongqing Chaotianmen Steel Truss Arch Bridge

1. Introduction of Engineering

Chongqing Chaotianmen Yangtze River Bridge (Fig.1a~c) is located at 1.2km of lower reaches from Chaotianmen (the joint of Yangtze River and Jialing River, see Fig.2). It is an important passage connecting west and east banks of Yangtze River and a device facilitating the south bank and the central commercial district in the north of Jialing River in Chongqing City. The total length of the main bridge and both west and east approaches is 1741m, among which the 932m main bridge is a 190m+552m+190m half-through continuous steel truss arch with tie girders, the lengths of west and east approaches are 314m and 495m respectively, both of them are continuous PC box girder bridges (PC = prestressed concrete). Double-level traffic arrangement is adopted with upper deck to be designed in two-way 6 lanes and both side pedestrians, with lower deck in middle two-way municipal light rails and 2 two-way lanes on each side.

2. Main Technical Criteria

Highway grade: 1st-grade municipal main road with design velocity of 60km/h.

Lane arrangement on decks: two-way 3 lanes on upper deck with lane width of 3.75m, and 2 side pedestrians with total widths 2×2.5m; 2 two-way lanes on the lower with the clear road height ≥5m.

Rail traffic standards: two-way light rails with distance between lines of 4.2m, design velocity of 80km/h, allowable max. of 100km/h, boundary of rail traffic with clear width≥9.2m, and clear height over rail top≥6.5m.

1a

图1 建成的朝天门长江大桥(a)，(b)
（承段雪炜高工惠赠）

Fig.1 Completed Chaotianmen Yangtze River Bridge (a), (b)
(courtesy of Senior Engr. Duan Xuewei)

3. Design Loads

3.1 Permanent Load

(1) For members and joints of main truss, bridge deck system, plane joining system, transverse joining system, and portal frames, etc. all their weights are calculated according to the practical ones and considered as joint loads applying to main truss.

(2) Pavement of upper deck: 22kN/m; pavement of lower deck: 12kN/m; guarding railing of upper deck: 1.35kN/m; railing of lower deck: 2.7kN/m; pavement and railing of pedestrian: 0.6KN/m and 1.0kN/m respectively, open bridge of rail communication on lower deck (including inspection footpath): 8.0kN/m, all of the above are the load on a truss, considered following joint loads applying on main truss.

3.2 Variable loads

(1) Traffic load: calculated traffic load according to urban highway grade I and checked following load of urban-A. Total bridge is designed according to 8 lanes, overall loading should be reduced following corresponding stipulations of relevant code.

(2) Rail communication load: executing according to "Agreement Letter of relevant problems about ring line of rail traffic and Chaotianmen Yangtze River Bridge" by the load standard of General

（2）轨道交通荷载：根据重庆市轨道总公司《关于轨道交通环线与朝天门长江大桥相关问题的协商函》的荷载标准执行。轻轨交通车辆采用B型地铁车，5辆车编组，每辆车长19.52m，共4轴，轴间距为2.3m+10.3m+2.3m，车辆最大轴重P_{max} = 140kN。

（3）人群荷载：全桥总体计算时荷载集度采用2.5 kN/m²，人行道局部构件计算时荷载集度采用4.0 kN/m²。

（4）风荷载：设计风速按照平均最大风速为26.7m/s，风荷载对结构的作用按照规范的相关规定计算。

（5）温度作用：设计温度为最高+45℃，最低−5℃，体系温度按20℃计，温差按照±25℃考虑。

（6）活载组合：公路车道荷载与轻轨荷载组合作用时，不考虑组合折减系数，按照最不利加载进行组合。

3.3 偶然荷载

地震荷载：地震基本烈度为Ⅵ度，大桥按Ⅶ度设防。

4.材料及基本容许应力

4.1 主要材料

主桁构件钢材采用Q420qD、Q370qD和Q345qD等三种；桥面系构件主要采用Q345qD，部分采用Q370qD；联结系构件主要采用Q345qD。材料技术条件应符合国家标准《桥梁用结构钢》（GB 714-2000）的要求。连接型钢的材质均采用Q345qD，材质和外形尺寸等技术条件应符合国家现行相关标准的要求。

高强螺栓：10.9S级，M30高强度螺栓材质采用35VB；M24和M22高强螺栓材质采用20MnTiB；螺母、垫圈采用45号优质碳素钢。高强螺栓、螺母、垫圈等应符合国家标准《钢结构用高强度大六角头螺栓、大六角螺母、垫圈与技术条件》（GB/T 1228—1231）的要求。

4.2 材料容许应力

钢材的屈服强度σ_s按照国家标准《桥梁用结构钢》（GB/T 714−2000）采用。设计安全系数K = 1.7，容许应力按照不同板厚取$[\sigma] = \sigma_s / K$。

5.结构设计概况

5.1 总体布置及主要结构特点

本桥正桥钢梁采用190m+552m+190m三跨连续钢桁系杆拱桥，钢梁全长934.1m（包括端横梁），主桥全宽

1c

Railway Company in Chongqing City adopting B-typed metro trains as those of light rail traffic with 5 trains in a team with every train length of 19.52m, having 4 axes, axis distances 2.3m+10.3m+2.3m and max axle load P_{max}=140kN.

(3) Crowd load: adopting calculated density of 2.5kN/m$_2$ on whole bridge in general calculation, adopting the density of 4.0kN/m$_2$ on pedestrian in calculation of local members.

4) wind load: design wind velocity according to average max. wind velocity of 26.7m/s, calculating the action of wind load to structure according to relevant stipulations in code.

5) thermal action: highest design temperature +45℃, lowest -5℃, system temperature following 20℃, considering temperature difference following ±25℃.

6) combination of live loads: without considering the reduction coefficient as combining the action of highway lane load and light rail load in most unfavorable combination.

3.3 Ancient action

Seismic action: fundamental intensity of degree VI, defence of this bridge according to degree VII.

4. Materials and Fundamental Allowable Stresses

4.1 Main materials

For the main truss, the kinds of steel Q420qD, Q370qD and Q345qD are adopted; for deck system, Q345qD is mainly adopted and Q370qD is partially; for the members in joining system, Q345qD is mainly used. The technical conditions of material should meet the requirements stipulated in National Standard "Structural Steel for Using in Bridges" (GB 714-2000). For the connecting section steel, Q345qD is all utilized, the technical conditions of quality and external shapes should meet the stipulations in current relevant national standard.

High-strength bolts: 35VB is used for the quality of high-strength bolts of grade 10.9S, M30; 20MnTiB is used for the quality of high-strength bolts of M24, M22; 45# high-quality carbon steel is used for nuts, washers, high-strength bolts, nuts and washers, etc should all meet the requirements in National Standard "Technical Conditions of High-Strength Large Hexagonal Head Bolts, Large Hexagonal Nuts, Washers Used for Steel Structures" (GB/T1228-1231).

4.2 Allowable stresses of materials

The yield strength σ_s of steel is adopted according to National Standard "Structural Steel for Use in Bridges" (GB/T 714-2000)". The design safety coefficient K=1.7 and the allowable stresses $[\sigma]=\sigma_s/K$ according to different thickness.

5. General Situation of Structural Design

5.1 General layout and main structural characteristics

3-span 190m+552m+190m continuous steel truss arch bridge with tie girders has whole length of 934.1m (including end cross beams). The full width of main bridge is 36.5m and that of truss 29m, with truss of variable depth in end span, the middle span is steel truss arch with

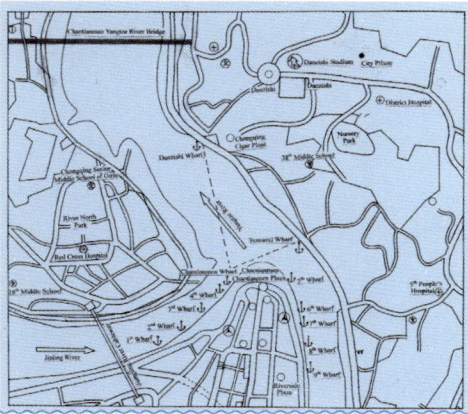

图1 建成的朝天门长江大桥
（承段雪炜高工惠赠）(c)
Fig.1 Completed Chaotianmen Yangtze River Bridge (courtesy of Senior Engr. Duan Xuewei)(c)

图2 重庆跨长江大桥位置图
（承段雪炜高工惠赠）
Fig.2 Location of the bridge in Chongqing, across Yangtze River (courtesy of Senior Engr. Duan Xuewei)

2

36.5m，桁宽29m，两侧边跨为变高度桁梁，中跨为钢桁系杆拱。拱顶至中间支点高度为142m，拱肋下弦线形采用二次抛物线，其矢高为128m，矢跨比1/4.31；拱肋上弦部分线形也采用二次抛物线，并与边跨上弦之间采用$R = 700$m的圆曲线进行过渡。主桁采用变高度的N形桁架，拱肋桁架跨中桁高为14m，中间支点处桁高73.13m（其中拱肋加劲弦高40.45m），边支点处桁高为11.83m。全桥采用变节间布置，共有12m、14m、16m等三种节间长度，边跨节间布置为$8 \times 12m + 14m + 5 \times 16m$，中跨节间布置为$5 \times 16m + 2 \times 14m + 28 \times 12m + 2 \times 14m + 5 \times 16m$。中跨布置有上下两层系杆，其中心间距为11.83m，下系杆与加劲腿处中弦及边跨下弦贯通。上层系杆采用H形截面，下层系杆采用"王"形截面面＋辅助系索，钢结构系杆端部与拱肋下弦节点相连接，下层辅助系索锚固于节点端部。

主桥支承体系布置：纵向支承体系布置为西中支点（P7墩）设置不动铰支座，其余各墩均设置活动铰支座。横向支承体系布置为另一中支点（P8墩）设置固定支座，边支点设置横向活动支座，边支点下横梁中心设置两个横向限制位移支座，以避免轨道变形。

主桥伸缩缝布置：西边支点与引桥交界处采用伸缩量为640mm的模数式伸缩缝，东边支点与引桥交界处采用伸缩量为960mm的模数式伸缩缝（伸缩缝在选择按照温度和活荷载下支座位移幅度确定，不仅考虑温度效应）。

图3、图4分别示桥的纵剖面和平面图以及桥面横截面。

5.2 主桁杆件截面

主桁弦杆为焊接箱形截面，采用弦杆中内力最大变化，截面宽度有1 200mm和1 600mm两种，截面高度在1 240~1 840mm范围内变化，板厚24～50mm。杆件按照沿四边拼接设计，拼接处杆件高度、宽度均相同，不同宽度和高度杆件之间采用变宽（高）度设计，对于同一杆件，宽度和高度不在相同截面变化。

腹杆采用箱形、H形及"王"形截面，箱形截面高1 240~1 440mm，板厚24～50mm；H形截面高700~1100mm，板厚16~50mm，杆件端部按照两边拼接设计。

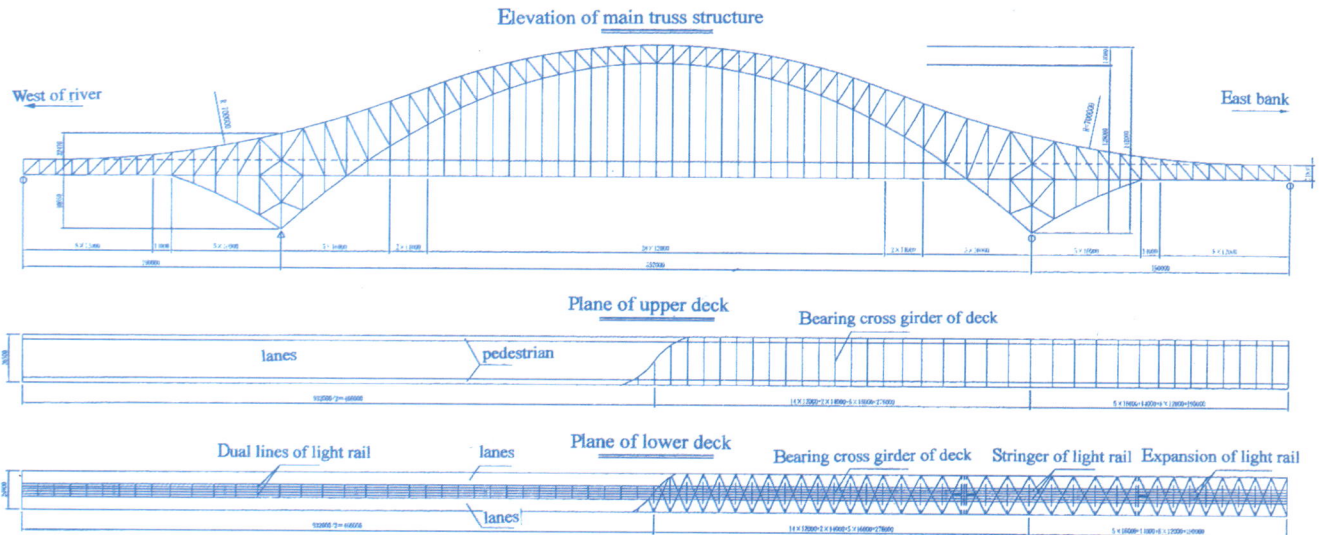

Notes: 1. unit: mm; 2. upper & lower chords in parabola; 3. △—unmovable support, ○—movable support

3

tie girders. The height from arch top to middle supports is 142m, the lower chord is in quadratic parabola with rise of 128m and ratio of rise to span is 1/4.31; the major part of upper chord is also in quadratic parabola and to adopt circular curve with $R=700m$ for transition between the upper chords of middle and end span. The N-type truss is adopted for the main one with central depth of 14m, the depths at middle support and at end support are 73.13m (including the depth of stiffening chord being 40.45m) and 11.83m respectively. 3 various panel lengths of 12m, 14m, 16m are adopted for entire bridge, for end span arrangement: $8\times12m+14m+5\times16m$, for middle span: $5\times16m+2\times14m+28\times12m+2\times14m+5\times16m$. For the tie girder in middle span, the upper and lower decks with central distance of 11.83m are arranged, the lower tie of middle span is through the middle chord of stiffening leg and the lower chord of end span. For upper tie, section "H" is adopted and for lower one, section "王" + auxiliary cables are adopted, the end of steel tie is connected with the joint of the lower chord in arch rib, the lower auxiliary tie cables are anchored at the end of joint.

The layout of support system in main bridge: layout of longitudinal support system is designed to set immovable hinged support at west middle support (pier No.P.7), on the other piers there are all set moved hinged supports. The transverse support system is arranged to set fixed supports on the other middle pier (No. P.8) and to set transversely movable supports on end supports, under which at the centers of transverse girder, 2 devices for limiting transversely displacement due to thermal action in main truss to both side so as to avoid the rail deformation.

The layout of expansion joints in main bridge: on the west side, at end support connecting to the approach there is set an expansion joint with width in modulus 640mm, on the east bank, at the connection set an expansion joint with width in modulus of 940mm (the selection of expansion joint is determined following the range of support displacement under temperature and live load, not only considered following temperature effect).

Fig.3, 4 shows respectively the longitudinal profile and plane of the bridge, and cross-section of the deck.

5.2 Member section of main truss

The chords of main truss have welded box section. To adapt the large variety of internal forces in chords, the width and depth are varied corresponding; there are 2 widths of 1 200mm, 1 600mm, and the depths are varied in the field of 1 240~1 840mm, the plate thicknesses of 24~50mm. Member is designed according to welding together edgewise (along 4 edges), at spliced place the depth and width of member are the same, between the members with various width and various depth, it is designed according to various width (depth), for a same member, the width and depth are not varied at same section.

For web members, box, H and 王-shape sections are adopted with box section depths of 1240~1440m and plate thicknesses t of 24~50mm, with H-shape section depth of 700~1100mm and

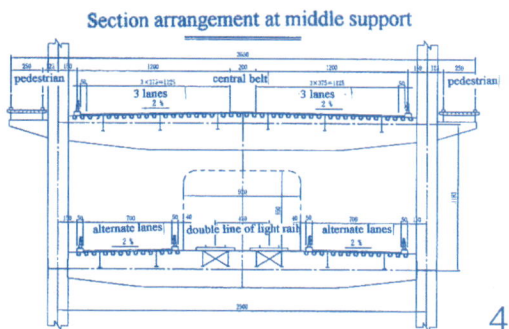

Section arrangement at middle support

Notes: 1. unit: mm; 2. 8-cm thick modified bituminous mastic pavement of steel deck; 3. steel railing on lane sides, stainless rail for pedestrian; 4. light rail deck: wood shapers of stringers, upon which 60kg/m rail to be set.

图3 纵剖面和平面图
（承段雪炜高工惠赠）
Fig.3 Longitudinal profile and plane of the bridge
(courtesy of Senior Engr. Duan Xuewei)

图4 桥面横截面图
（承段雪炜高工惠赠）
Fig.4 Cross-section of the deck
(courtesy of Senior Engr. Duan Xuewei)

上层系杆采用焊接H形截面，截面高1 500mm，宽1 200mm，板厚50mm。下层系杆采用焊接H形截面，截面高1 700mm，宽1 600mm，板厚50mm。

主桁杆件所采用的最大板件厚度50mm，最大长度44m，最大安装吊重80t。

图5、6和7分别示上下层桥面工程图和桥面系工程图。

5.3 主桁节点

主桁节点除中间支承节点（E15）采用整体节点外，其余均采用拼装式节点。节点板最大厚度80mm（E15节点），最大规格为5570mm×7620mm（E18节点）。

5.4 起顶点布置

对每一桁架，在端支点和中间支点处均设置4个起顶点，起顶点设在支座两侧的节点板下方。其中中支点最大起顶反力为130 000kN。

5.5 桥面系

上层桥面采用正交异性钢桥面板，板厚16mm，采用U形闭口肋，沿桥纵向设置横隔板，其间距不大于3m，沿桥横向布置6道纵梁，在主桁节点处设置一道横梁。下层桥面两侧车道采用正交异性钢桥面板，桥面板板厚16mm，采用U形闭口肋，纵桥向设置横隔板，其间距不大于3m，横桥向每侧布置2道纵梁，在主桁节点处设置一道横梁；下层桥面在边车道，设厚16mm的正交异性板，采用U形闭口肋；沿桥纵向，设置横隔板，在下层主桁每一节点间距大于3m，在横向，在每边设两纵梁；对轻轨部分，在中间采用纵横小梁体系，其中横小梁与两边钢桥面板横梁共为一体，共设置两组轻轨，其中心间距为4.2m，每组轻轨（小）纵梁由两片纵梁组成，两片纵梁通过平联和横联连为一体，纵梁端部通过鱼形板和连接角钢与横梁连接。轻轨纵梁上设置木质枕轨和60kg/m钢轨，作为城市轻轨交通行驶轨道。

对上层桥面，在主桁节点外侧设置人行道托架，在这些托架之上设置∏形各向异性板作为人行道桥面。

5.6 平纵联

下层桥面平纵联为交叉型设置，杆件采用焊接工形构件，横梁作为下平联撑杆。拱肋上、下弦平纵联采用钻石形桁式，加劲弦平纵联采用K形桁架。由于相邻节间存在一定的夹角，平联节点板应采用弯折方式进行过渡。上弦A9—A11平联作为施工期间的临时平联，在主桁合拢后予以拆除。

5

6

t=16~50mm, member end is designed according to splice along two edges.

For the upper tie, it is adopted welded H-shape section with depth of 1 500mm, width of 1 200mm and t=50mm. For the lower tie, it is adopted welded 王-shape section with depth of 1 700mm, width of 1 600mm and t=50mm.

For the adopted plate member in main truss, the max. thickness t is 50mm, the max. length is 44m and the max. hoisted weight for installation is 80t.

Figs.5, 6 and 7 show the Engineering pictures of upper and lower decks and deck system.

5.3 Joints of main truss

Except that middle support joint (E15) is to construct into integral joint, the other joints arc to construct into spliced ones. The max. thickness of gusset is 80mm (joint E15), the max. dimensions are 5570mm×7620mm (joint E18).

5.4 Arrangement of lift points

For each truss, there are all set 4 lift points at end and middle supports, these points are set under gusset on both sides of support. The max. lift reaction of middle support is 130 000kN.

5.5 Deck system

For upper deck system, it is adopted the orthotropic steel plate of 16mm thick with closed U-type ribs. Along the longitudinal direction of bridge, there are set diaphragms with spacing not larger than 3m on upper deck, in the transverse, there are arranged 6 longitudinal beams and at the joint of main truss there is set a transverse girder. On both side lanes in lower deck, there is set the orthotropic steel plate of 16mm thick with closed "U" ribs adopted, along the longitudinal of bridge, there are set diaphragms with spacing not larger than 3m on lower deck and at every joint point of main truss, in the transverse, there are set 2 longitudinal beams on each side, for the part of light rails in the middle, there is adopted the system of stringers and cross beams among which the cross beams are the same bodies of the transverse girders in steel deck on both sides, on this system, 2 light rails with central spacing of 4.2m are set, each group of stringers is constituted of 2 which are jointed together into a body through horizontal and transverse connections, the ends of longitudinal girder are connected with cross ones through fish pieces and connecting angles. On the top of light rails there are set wood sleepers and steel rails with 60kg/m to be used for driving as urban light communication rail roads.

For upper deck, there are set the brackets for pedestrian beside the external sides of main truss joints, on these brackets, Π-shaped orthotropic plates are set as pedestrian deck

5.6 Horizontal longitudinal joining

The horizontal longitudinal joining of lower deck is set crosswise with welded I-shape members adopted, and also the transverse girder as the bracings of lower horizontal joining. For the horizontal longitudinal joining, in the upper and lower chords, diamond-type trusses are adopted, for this joining in the stiffening chords, K-type

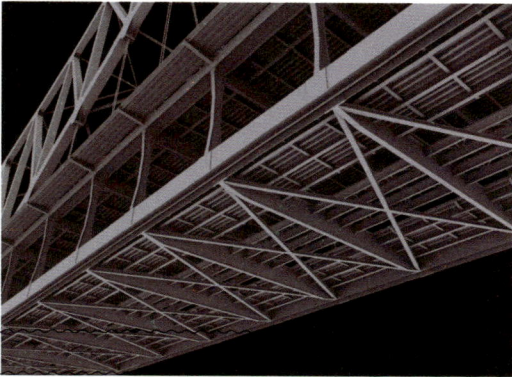

图5 上层桥面工程图（承段雪炜高工惠赠）
Fig.5 Engineering picture of upper deck (courtesy of Senior Engr. Duan Xuewei)

图6 下层桥面工程图（承段雪炜高工惠赠）
Fig.6 Engineering picture of lower deck (courtesy of Senior Engr. Duan Xuewei)

图7 桥面系工程图（承段雪炜高工惠赠）
Fig.7 Picture of deck system engineering (courtesy of Senior Engr. Duan Xuewei)

5.7 横联与桥门架

主桁拱肋每两个节间设置一副桁架式横联，位于拱肋上下平纵联"米"字形形心处；加劲腿区段每个节间均设置一桁架式横联。中间支点处设桁架式桥门架，边支点A1-E1和E18-E19等处均设板式桥门架，E19-E20处设置桁架式桥门架。

5.8 结构预拱度的设置

主桁预拱度按照恒载+1/2静活载挠度曲线值反向设置，并适当修正。根据计算成果，边跨不需要设置预拱度，中跨预拱度的设置采用如下方法：M16-M19（E19）各节点采取将上、下层横梁顶面加高的方法；M20-M36、C20-C36各节点采用调整细杆件中心线、横梁顶面加高和缩短吊杆的方法。

5.9 高强螺栓连接

主桁架采用M30高强螺栓，ϕ33栓孔，设计有效预应力为360kN；桥面系、联结系采用M24、M22高强螺栓，分别为ϕ26、ϕ24栓孔，设计有效预应力240kN、200kN。摩擦面摩擦系数按照f＝0.45计。高强螺栓连接部分的摩擦面，要求出厂时的抗滑移系数不小于0.55，构件安装前抗摩擦系数不小于0.45。

5.10 钢梁防腐

钢结构构件防腐涂装参照采用中国技术标准《铁路钢桥保护涂装》（TB／T 1527－2004）中的涂装体系的油漆种类、涂装数和干膜厚度进行适当调整。为了节约篇幅，本文略。

6.钢桁安装

边跨采用部分鹰架结合临时墩的伸臂法架设。首先钢桁两节间E1-E3设置鹰架，利用墩旁塔吊架设，钢梁及平衡梁共长48m；在钢桁上弦拼装架梁吊机，分别在E6和E10节点设置临时墩，利用架梁吊机分别伸臂36m、50m、80m，利用悬臂法架设钢梁至中间墩，伸臂架设时应在锚跨适当压重，保证抗倾覆安全系数大于1.3。江东侧边跨不具备通航

8a

trusses are set. Because there are included angles between adjacent panels, the gussets of horizontal joining must adopt to transit with bending. For upper chords A9-A11, horizontal joining is taken as temporary one during construction and will be removed after the main truss is closed.

5.7 Transverse joining and portal frames

For the arch ribs of main truss, in every 2 panels a trussed transverse joining is set, located at the centroid of "米"-typed upper and lower horizontal longitudinal joining in arch rib; for every panel in the segments of stiffening leg, there is set a truss-type transverse joining. At middle support, there is set truss-type portal frame, at end supportA1-E1 and at E18-E19, panel-type portal frames are set, at E19-E20 truss-type portal frame is set.

5.8 Setting pre-camber of structure

The pre-camber of main truss is set in reverse according to the deflection due to dead load +1/2 (statical life load) and appropriately revised. Following calculated results, the pre-camber in end span is unnecessary to set, in middle span, the pre-camber is set according to the following method: for the joints M16-M19 (E19) to rise the tops of transverse girders in upper and lower decks; for joints M20-M36, C20-C36 to adjust the centerlines of steel member, to rise the tops of transverse girders and shorten the hangers.

5.9 Connections with highstrength bolts

For main truss, highstrength bolts M30 are adopted, the effective design prestressing force of bolt hole $\phi 33$ is 360kN; for deck system, joining system, highstrength bolts M24, M22, the effective prestressing forces of bolt holes $\phi 26$, $\phi 24$ are 240kN, 200kN respectively. The friction coefficient of friction surface is adopted following $f=0.45$. For the friction surface of connection of highstrength bolts, it is required that f is not less than 0.55 as ex-factory and not less than 0.45 before installation of members.

5.10 Anti-corrosion of steel girders

The antirust coating of steel structure is referred to adopting the kinds of paint, layers of painting and thickness of dry film in Chinese Technical Standard "Protection Coating for Steel Railway Bridges" (TB/T 1527-2004) and adjusted appropriately. For saving space, the details are neglected in this article.

6. Installation of Steel Truss

The end span should be installed by cantilever method, on trestles and temporary piers. First, two panels E1-E3 of steel truss are installed on the trestles by means of tower crane beside end pier, the total length of steel girder of 2 panel and equalizing girder was 48m; next, the erecting gantry was assembled on the upper chord of steel truss; at joints E6 and E10, set temporary piers respectively; then using this gantry with cantilevers of 36m, 50m, 80m to install the steel girders from end pier to middle one, by cantilever method. While installing steel truss, some balanced weight should be used on the end span to make sure that the stability coefficient is larger than 1.3. The end span in the east does not possess the navigable conditions,

图8 建成后的灯光夜景图
（承段雪炜高工惠赠）(a)
Fig.8 The light night scenec of completed bridge (courtesy of Senior Engr. Duan Xuewei)(a)

条件，西岸侧边跨位于岸上，因此边跨安装时考虑采用施工栈桥供料。

中跨采用两侧对称的全伸臂辅以吊索塔架的施工方法，在跨中合拢，安装时考虑从江面供料。中跨安装时钢梁先整体安装至108m（7个节间），随后逐步架设拱肋桁架及吊杆直至跨中合拢。吊索塔架高按照100m（指外拉索塔上锚固点至A15节点中心距离）考虑，共设两层拉索，前索锚固点分别位于A25、A31节点（距中间墩分别为144m和216m），后索锚固点分别位于A2、A3节点（分别为166m和178m），塔架顶部锚固点间距2m。中跨钢梁架设时首先对称伸臂架设至168m，同时可以进行吊索塔架的安装，然后挂设内索并进行初张拉，继续架设钢梁，随后挂外索、初张拉、架设钢梁，最后进行跨中合拢。中跨伸臂架设过程中还应对边跨端部48m范围内进行逐步压重，最大压重量为1 150 kN/m，全桥压重量总计为110 000kN。拱肋桁架合拢时先合拢下弦再合拢上弦。待拱肋跨中合拢后，安装临时系杆并张拉，完成结构的体系转换，然后逆序逐根撤除拉索及吊索塔架，架梁吊机同时后撤。再利用桥面吊机在上层桥面走行，逐节间安装其余上、下层系杆和上层桥面横梁直至跨中合拢，系杆中跨合拢时先合拢上系杆再合拢下系杆，系杆合拢完成后拆除临时系杆。然后桥面吊机由跨中后撤并逐节间吊装下层桥面横梁、平联、轻轨纵梁和上、下层钢桥面板。为部分消除钢桥面板与主桁的共同作用影响，此前所安装的钢桥面板与横梁之间均采用临时连接，全部主构件安装完成后再进行钢桥面板与横梁之间的正式连接。

主结构安装完成后安装并张拉辅助系索。全桥附属结构、桥面铺装等全部完成后，辅助系索和吊杆进行全面调索并达到设计要求。

图8(a)、(b)示建成后灯光夜景图。

7.静力、动力分析

7.1 结构平面受力分析

按照平面杆系仅对主桁结构进行建模，同时考虑杆件的刚度。主要计算成果详见表1。

8b

and that in the west is one bank, hence it was considered to provide materials by adopting construction trestler during the installation of end spans.

The steel truss of middle span would be installed by full cantilever method symmetrically with the assistance of sling pylon, and was closed at the middle, it was considered to provide materials from during the installation of middle span, the steel girders were firstly installed integrally to 108m (7 panels), then the arch rib truss and hangers would be installed step by step until the middle of span is closed. The sling pylon is 100m high (the central distance of anchoraged point on external sling pylon to joint A15) and had two levels of cable; the anchoraged points of the former cable are at A25 and A31 (144m and 216m from the middle pier), the back cable was anchored at A2 and A3 (166m and 178m respectively), the spacing between anchor points on the pylon was 2m. While installing the steel girders in middle span, they were firstly installed symmetrically to 168m by cantilevers, the sting pylons could be installed at the same time, then the internal cables were set and tensioned initially, the steel girders were installed continuously, then the external cables were set, tensioned initially and the steel girders were installed, finally the middle span was closed. During the process of installation of middle span by cantilevers, it was necessary to press weight gradually in the field of 48m at the end edge span, the max. weight to be pressed was 1150kN/m of bridge, total weight over the entire bright was 110 000kN. During the closed the arch rib was closed, the temporary ties were installed and tensioned, the transformation of structural system was finished, then the tensioned cables and sling pylons removed back at the same time. Then utilizing the deck cranes to go on upper deck, the ties of upper and lower decks and the transverse beams on upper deck were installed panel by panel until they were closed in span center, during the closure of this in middle span, the upper ties were done firstly, then the lower ties, after the ties were closed, the temporary this were removed. Then deck cranes were removed back, the transverse beams, horizontal joining, the stringers of light rails and the steel deck plates were installed panel by panel. For eliminating partially the influence of the integral action of steel deck plate and main truss, between the steel deck plates and cross beams installed previously, the temporary connections were adopted, the permanent connection should not be done until all members are installed completely.

After the installation of main structure was finished, auxiliary facilities and pavement were all completed, the forces in assistant cables and hangers would be adjusted to meet design requirements.

Fig.8(a), (b) shows the light night scene of completed bridge.

图8 建成后的灯光夜景图
（承段雪炜高工惠赠）(b)
Fig.8 The light night scenec of completed bridge (courtesy of Senior Engr. Duan Xuewei)(b)

7. Static and Dynamic Analyses

7.1 Structural plane analysis

The calculation model is only made for main truss according to plane bar-system and taking account of the stiffnesses of members.

表1 结构平面静力计算成果

杆件最大内力		系杆内力			支座反力（一桁）		静活载作用下的最大竖向挠度			
拉力	压力	上层系杆	下层系杆	辅助系杆	边支点	中间支点	边跨挠度△（绝对值）		中跨挠度△（绝对值）	
kN	kN	kN	kN	kN	kN	kN	cm	$\triangle/L_p$	cm	$\triangle/L_p$
57 138	88 398	28 209	56 991	20 000	9 739	145 000	16.6	1/1 145	31.9	1/1 730

由上表的分析成果可以看出：①对于本桥所设置的双层系杆来说，起主要作用的仍然是下层系杆，而上层系杆拉力尚不到系杆总拉力的30％；②结构中跨静活载作用下的挠跨比（1/1 730）远小于规范的规定值（1/800）。因此可以认为，钢桁拱桥一般具有较大的结构竖向刚度，结构竖向刚度不是其控制结构设计的主要因素。

7.2 结构静力稳定性分析

本桥的结构稳定性计算采用空间有限元法进行，有限单元法采用通用的空间分析程序ANSYS进行计算。计算模型按照结构构件的空间布置进行模拟，所有构件均采用空间梁单元，对于上下层桥面板，将其刚度与质量等效分配到纵横梁上，模型边界条件按照成桥支承体系设置。结构静力稳定性分析结果表明成桥状态的稳定安全系数为6.8，满足规范中的有关规定。

7.3 结构动力特性分析

结构动力特性分析采用与静力稳定性分析相同的模型。主要分析成果详见表2。

图9示朝天门桥合龙。

图9 朝天门桥合龙（承段雪炜高工惠赠）
Fig.9 Closure of Chaotianmen Bridge (courtesy of Senior Engr. Duan Xuewei)

The main calculation results are given in details in Tab.1.

Tab.1 Plane static calculation results of structure

one max. internal force in members		internal force in tie		
tension	com-pression	in upper tie	in lower tie	in auxi-liary tie
kN	kN	kN	kN	kN
57 138	88 398	28 209	56 991	20 000
support reaction (in one truss)		max vertical deflection under static and life loads		
at end support	at middle support	$\triangle$ in end span (absolute value)		$\triangle$ in middle span (absolute value)
kN	kN	cm	$\triangle/L_p$	cm	$\triangle/L_p$
9 739	145 000	16.6	1/1 145	31.9	1/1 730

From the calculation results, it can be seen that: ① in the double-level ties, the force in lower one plays dominating role, the force in upper tie is only 1/3 of the total; ② the ratio 1/1 730 of structure deflection to its span under static and life loads is far less than the stipulated value 1/800 in the Code. Therefore it can be concluded that the steel truss arch bridge generally has larger vertical structural stiffness, which is not major factor to control the design of structure.

7.2 Static stability analysis of structure

The stability calculation of this bridge structure is conducted by space FEM adopting current space analysis program ANSYS. The calculation model is simulated according to the space arrangement of structural members, all of which are adopted in space beam elements, the stiffnesses and masses of the upper and slower decks are equivalently distributed to longitudinal and cross girders, the boundary conditions are set according to the support system after bridge completion, the calculation model structural space shows in Fig.9. The result of structural static stability analysis indicates that the safe coefficient of static stability in the phase of bridge completion is 6.8 and meets the requirements of related stipulation in Code, the state of instability in bridge completion phase is shown in Fig.10.

7.3 Analysis of structural dynamic characteristics

For the analysis of structural dynamic characteristics, the same model used in static stability analysis is adopted. The main analysis results are given in Tab.2.

Fig.9 shows the closure of Chaotianmen Bridge.

表2 主桥成桥状态动力特性

NO.	振型向	自振频率(Hz)	自振圆频率f_v(rad/s)	自振周期(s)
1	梁、拱横弯曲	0.1 978	1.2 428	5.0 556
2	全桥纵向振动+梁拱竖弯曲	0.2 756	1.7 316	3.6 284
3	梁拱横向弯曲	0.3 678	2.3 110	2.7 189
4	梁拱横向弯曲	0.3 776	2.3 725	2.6 483
5	梁拱竖向弯曲	0.3 952	2.4 831	2.5 304
6	梁拱横向弯曲	0.4 075	2.5 604	2.4 540
7	梁拱横弯	0.4 731	2.9 726	2.1 137
扭弯频率比 $\varepsilon = f_{11}/f_2 = 2.42$				

8.结束语

朝天门长江大桥主体结构的设计和下部结构的施工已完成。2006年6月开始钢梁的架设。全桥在2008年10月建成通车。现在该桥成为世界上跨度最大的钢拱桥，充分说明了我国拱桥建设水平已暂居世界前列。目前钢桁拱桥在中国已得到越来越多的应用。

图10示已建成的朝天门大桥。

10a

Tab.2 Results of dynamic characteristics in completion state of main bridge

No.	vibration mode	self-vibration frequency (HZ)	self-vibration circular f_v (rad/s)	self-vibration period (s)
1	transverse bending of truss, arch	0.1 978	1.2 428	5.0 556
2	longitudinal vibration + arch vertical bending	0.2 756	1.7 316	3.6 284
3	transverse bending of truss, arch	0.3 678	2.3 110	2.7 189
4	transverse bending of truss, arch	0.3 776	2.3 725	2.6 483
5	vertical bending of truss arch	0.3 952	2.4 831	2.5 304
6	transverse bending of truss, arch	0.4 075	2.5 604	2.4 540
7	vertical bending of truss arch	0.4 731	2.9 726	2.1 137

contortion frequency ratio $\varepsilon = f_{11}/f_2 = 2.42$

图10 建成的朝天门大桥（承段雪炜高工惠赠）(a)

Fig.10 Completed Chaotianmen Bridge (courtesy of Senior Engr. Duan Xuewei)(a)

Conclusion

The structural design of Chaotianmen Yangtze River Bridge and substructure engineering have been finished. The manufacture of steel girders was conducted in factory in June 2006. This bridge has been completed and opened in Oct. 2008. Now, this Bridge becomes the longest arch bridge in the world, it shows fully that the level of arch bridge construction in China occupies temporarily the worldwide leading position. The steel truss arch bridges have been adopted in this country more and more.

Fig.10 shows the completed Chaotianmen Bridge.

REFERENCES

1.Duan Xuanwei, Juhani Virola, Ding Dajun. The Chaotianmen Bridge — world's longest-span steel arch. RIA. 2007(1): 60-67

2.Duan Xuanwei, Juhani Virola, Ding Dajun. Chaotianmen Bridge — maaibman pitkajanteisin teraskaarisilta rakenteilla kunaassa, 2007(1): 46-49

图10 建成的朝天门大桥（承段雪炜高工惠赠）(b)
Fig.10 Completed Chaotianmen Bridge
(courtesy of Senior Engr. Duan Xuewei)(b)

重庆菜园坝双层公轨两用拱桥

重庆菜园坝大桥（图1）是在嘉陵江与长江汇合前跨越长江的一座南北向大型拱桥。该桥上游离鹅公岩长江大桥（悬索桥，跨度211m+600m+211m）4km，下游距石板坡长江大桥1.2km。根据桥位通航净空论证，大桥主跨不宜小于400m，取420m。

在大桥工程可行性研究和初步设计阶段，曾进行过多方案比较，最后与国内普遍应用的经济、成熟的两种桥型进行了经济比较：

① 100m+420m+100m跨度中承式钢管混凝土系杆拱桥；

② 220m+420m+120m跨度高低双塔斜拉桥；

③ 88m+102m+420m+102m+88m跨度中承式刚构、钢箱系杆拱组合结构。

比较结果表明方案③主桥长度达800m为最长，造价却最低。作为重庆菜园坝长江大桥付诸实施方案，既经济，又创新。

大桥主桥设计为88m+102m+420m+102m+88m，主桥总长800m。图2示大桥主桥的总体布置。从平面图看，拱向内倾，即构成所谓"提篮式"。

为了提高结构的整体性，大桥设计在三个层面上使用了"组合"技术：①在材料上将混凝土与钢组合（图3），提高材料使用效率；②在直接承受活载梁体设计中采用将正交异性桥面板与桁架钢梁组合（图4），提高梁体承载效率；③在主体承载结构设计中将预应力混凝土Y形刚构与提篮钢箱系杆拱组合（图5），提高主体结构跨越能力。

组合式正交异性桥面钢桁架梁采用"组合"概念设计，令正交异性桥面板与钢桁架梁联合作用，使公轨荷载与梁共同承担，进而使公轨双用钢梁重降至最轻；由于在主体承载结构设计中将预应力混凝土Y形刚构与钢箱系杆拱进行组合，从而使系杆中拱的有效跨度从420m减小到320m，极大地降低了大桥的水平推力，提高结构总体效率；在主体结构的下部结构采用预应力混凝土Y形刚构也带来其他优点：充足的强度与刚度、优良的防（船舶）撞能力与耐久性、良好的建筑可塑性及经济指标。此外，对大桥提篮拱肋仅设6道横撑，在保证主体结构有足够的稳定性的前提下，对主拱自重有所降低。

正是由于这些关键材料，结构"组合"技术使大桥主桥具有很高的材料与结构效率，与功能类似规模相当的大桥相比，大大节约钢材，估计可达约1 300t。

图6示建成大桥夜景。

1

图1 建成的菜园坝大桥（承鲁渝京高工、张佐安高工惠赠）
Fig.1 Completed Caiyuanba Bridge (courtesy of Senior Engr. Lu Yujing and Senior Engr. Zhang Zuo'an)

Chongqing Caiyuanba Double-Deck Arch Bridge with Dual Purpose for Highway & Light Rail

Chongqing Caiyuanba Bridge (Fig.1) is located on Yangtze River in front of that it joins with Jialing River, and is a large scale arch bridge. This Bridge has a distance of 4km from Egongyan Yangtze River (suspension bridge with spans: 211m+600m+211m) on upper reaches and 1.2km to Shibanpo Yangtze Bridge on lower reaches. Following the demonstration of navigable clearance at bridge cite, the main span of bridge is not proper to be smaller than 400m, adopts 420m.

During the feasibility research of arch preliminary design, many projects were conducted for comparing, finally an economic comparison was carried with 2 economic and ripe bridge types of adopting commonly in China:

① concrete-filled steel tube half-through tied arch bridge with spans of 100m+420m+100m;

② unequally high bi-pylon cable-stayed bridge with spans of 220m+420m+120m;

③ composite structure of half-through rigid frame & steel box tied arch with spans of 88m+102m+420m+102m+88m.

The compared results show in the project ③ that the length of main bridge reaches 800m being the max, and the construction cost is least. The practice project of Chongqing Caiyuanba Yangtze River is economic and also creative.

The bridge is designed with spans: 88m+102m+420m+102m+88m, its total length is 800m. Fig.2 show the general layout of Caiyuanba Yangtze River Bridge. From the plane sketch, the arch is inclined inwards, thus it constitute into a type, called "carrying basket".

In order to strengthen the integrity of structure, in 3 fields, the composition technique is used: ① on materials, concrete and steel are composite (Fig.3) to raise the application efficiency of material; ② in the design of girder to directly carrying live load, the orthotropic deck plate and steel truss girder are composite (Fig.4) to raise the bearing efficiency of girder; ③ in the structural design of main body, PC Y-shape rigid frame and carrying-basket tied steel box arch are composite (Fig.5) to raise the spanning capacity of main structure.

Composite orthotropic bridge deck and steel truss girder are designed by using "composition" conception to make the orthotropic deck to simultaneously work with steel truss girder, i.e., to make the loads of highway and light-rail to be carried with girder, hence to decrease the weight of bi-purpose steel girder for highway and light rail to the minimum, because PC Y-shape rigid frame is designed to be composite with steel box tied arch in the main bearing structure, so it reduces the effective span from 420m to 320m, thus the horizontal thrust is decreased greatly, then the total efficiency of structure is raised; in the substructure of main structure PC Y-shape rigid frame is adopted, it brings the other advantages: sufficient strength and stiffness, higher capacity and durability for preventing impact, good architectural plasticity and economic index. Besides, for the arch ribs

参考文献

1.孙峻岭，邓文中，刘孝标. 重庆菜园坝长江大桥主桥设计概念与实践. 全国桥梁学术会议论文集（上册），重庆，2006：91-102

2.刘孝标. 重庆菜园坝长江大桥刚构、钢桁架、系杆拱组合结构设计. 全国桥梁学术会议论文集. 昆明，2004：240-245

REFERENCES

1.Sun Junling, Deng Wenzhong, Liu Xiaobiao. Conception and Practice of design for main bridge of Chongqing Caiyuanba. Proceedings of National Symposium for Bridges (the 1st of 2 vols). Chongqing, 2006: 91-102

2.Liu Xiaobiao. Design of composite structure of rigid frame, steel truss and tied arch. Proceedings of National Symposium for Bridge. Kunming, 2004: 240-245

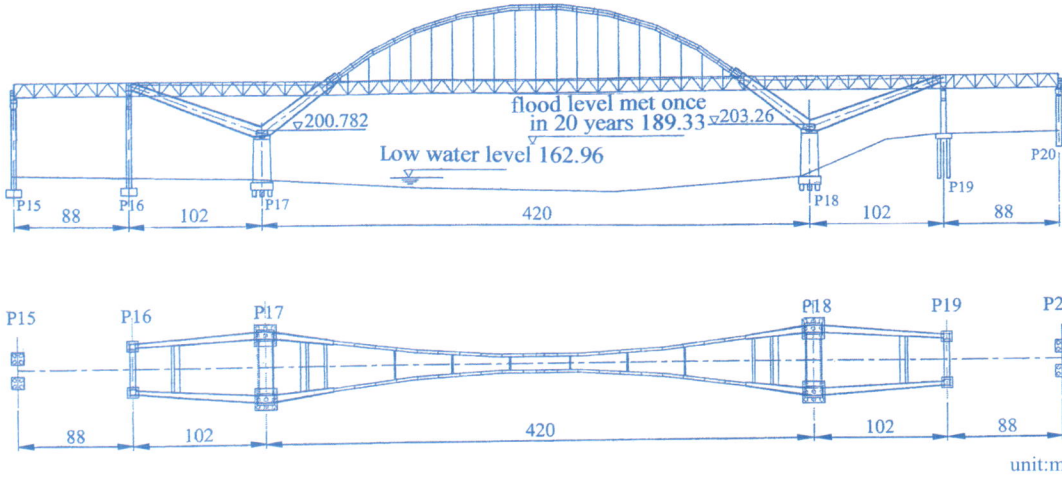

North ←   → South   2

▽200.782
flood level met once
in 20 years 189.33 ▽203.26
Low water level 162.96
▽

P15   88   P16   102   P17   420   P18   102   P19   88   P20

P15   P16   P17   P18   P19   P20

88   102   420   102   88

unit:m

3

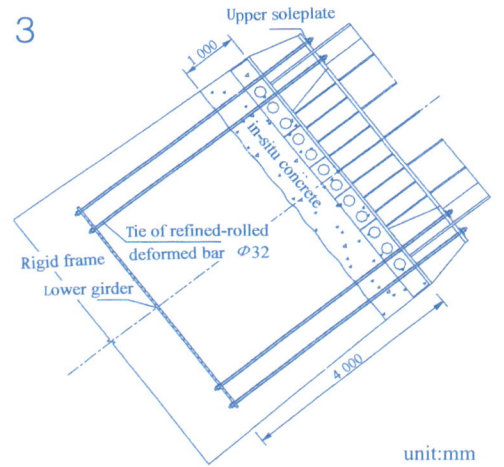

Upper soleplate
1 000
in-situ concrete
Tie of refined-rolled
deformed bar Φ32
Rigid frame
Lower girder
4 000

unit:mm

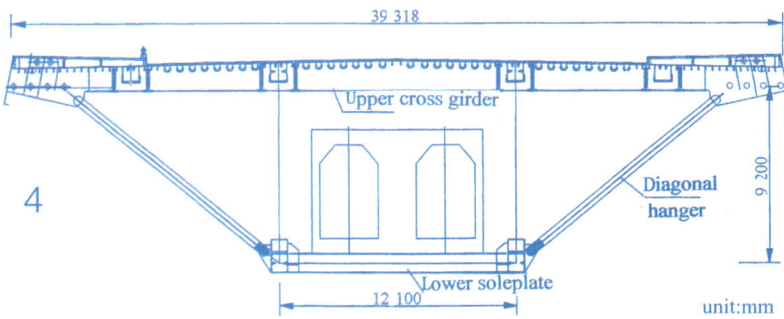

39 318

Upper cross girder

9 200

4

Diagonal
hanger

Lower soleplate

12 100

unit:mm

of carrying basket bridge, there are only set 6 transverse bracings, the dead weight is reduced somewhat.

Owing to these key "composition" technique of this bridge has very high efficiency of materials and structures, as compared to a bridge with function and similar corresponding scale, estimating to reach 1 300t or so.

Fig.6 shows the night scene of completed Bridge.

6

5

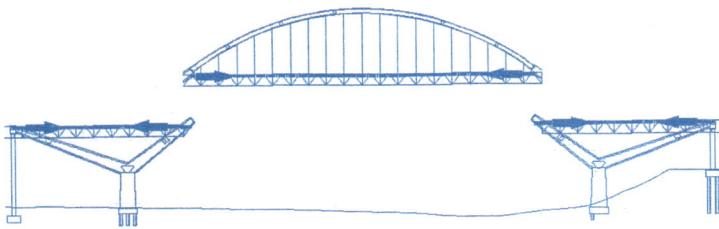

图2 菜园坝长江大桥总体布置
Fig.2 General layout of Caiyuanba Yangtze River Bridge

图3 钢与混凝土接头
Fig.3 Joint of steel and concrete

图4 正交异性桥面钢桁架梁
Fig.4 Steel truss girder with orthotrapic deck

图5 一对对称的预应力混凝土连续刚构—系杆中拱
Fig.5 A pair of symmetrical PC continuous rigid frame-tied central arch

图6 建成的大桥夜景（承张佐安高工惠赠）
Fig.6 Night scene (courtesy of Senior Engr. Zhang Zuo'an)

南京大胜关长江铁路钢桁架拱桥

京沪高速铁路大胜关长江大桥（图1）已于2006年9月14日开始兴建，预计将于2009年11月30日建成，2010年通车。该桥不仅是我国第一座高速铁路过江桥，主桥跨度也是世界同类桥梁中最大的，桥面共设6条轨道，可同时行驶三种速度的列车，设计荷载超过20座南京长江三桥。

南京大胜关长江大桥位于南京长江三桥1.55km处，南京长江大桥约20km处，全长14.789km，主桥长1 615m。该桥为双孔通航的6跨连续钢桁架拱桥，跨度分布为：109m+192m+2×336m+192m+109m，矢高84m，矢跨比1/4，拱肋跨中处高12m，支座处高53m，连续钢桁连续梁桁高16m，节间长均为12m。所用混凝土总量为南京长江一、二、三桥总和。

大胜关大桥上铁轨按6线布置，分别为京沪高速铁路双线，设计速度为300km/h，沪汉蓉铁路双线，客车设计速度为200km/h和南京地铁双线，行车速度为80km/h。根据规划，地铁8号线从沧波门地区向东接原宁芜铁路，利用原宁芜铁路改造为城市轻轨。

大桥钢轨枕木下是格子梁，乘客探头窗外，可看到桥下的奔腾江水，至为壮观。

大胜关大桥拥有四个"世界第一"，即列车时速最快、桥面载重最大、江中跨度最大、施工水域最深。

图2(a)，(b) 示桁拱施工，图3示临下水前的沉箱，其平面尺寸为80m×38m，高26.5m，图4示钢筋混凝土桩的沉放，桩的直径为2.8m，长112m，支承在泥岩上。

1b

2a

2b

Nanjing Dashengguan Yangtze River Railway Steel Truss Arch Bridge

The Beijing-Shanghai High Speed Railway Dashengguan Bridge over Yangtze River (Fig.1) has been constructed at Nanjing has been started to be constructed on 14th Sept. 2006 and scheduled to be completed on 30th Nov. 2009 and opened in 2010. This bridge is not only the 1st one of high speed railway over river, but the main span is also the largest of same-typed bridges in the world on deck, there are set 6 rails on which 3 trains with different speeds can run at same time, the design loads exceed those of 20 times of 3rd Nanjing Bridge.

The bridge site is located at the upper reaches with a distance of 1.55km to the 3rd Nanjing bridge 'and at the upper reaches with distance of 20km or so to the 1st Nanjing bridge. The total length is 14.789km and the length of main bridge is 1 615m. The main bridge is a continuous steel 6-span truss arch structure with dual navigable passes. The spans distribute as: 109m+192m+2×336m+192m+109m, the rise is 84m, the ratio of rise-span is 1/4, the depth of arch rib at span center is 12m, that at support is 53m, in side spans, the depth of steel-truss continuous girder is 16m with all panels of 12m. The consumption of concrete was the sum total of the 1st, the 2nd and the 3rd Nanjing Yangtze River.

The rails on Dashengguan Bridge are arranged following 6 lines, they are respectively dual lines of Beijing high-speed railway with design speed of 300km/h, dual lines of Shanghai-Hankou-Chengdu with design speed of 200km/h and that of Nanjing metro with design speed of 80km/h. Following the programme, the line No.8 of metro towards the east from Cangbomen Area to connect the original Nanjing-Wuhu railway, the original Nanjing-Wuhu railway will be refounded into city light rail.

Under sleepers of rails in this bridge, there are cellular beams, when the passengers stick their heads out of the window, they can see the galloping river water under bridge, this scene is very magnificent.

The Dashengguan Bridge has 4 "Worldwide First", i.e., the velocity of train is most fast, the load of bridge is most large, the span in river is most long and the water area of constructing is most deep.

Fig.2(a), (b) show the construction of trussed arch, Fig.3 shows the caisson before sinking, its plane dimension are 80m×38m with height of 26.5m, Fig.4 shows the sinking of reinforced concrete piles, the diameter of which is 2.8m and the length is 112m, supported on mudstone.

图1 南京大胜关钢架铁路大桥
(b)近视（承秦顺全教授级高工惠赠）
Fig.1 Nanjing Dashengguan Yangtze River Railway Bridge (b) close view (courtesy of Senior Engr. Prof. Qin Shunquan)

图2 桁架施工（承秦顺全教授级高工惠赠）(a), (b)
Fig.2 Construction of trussed arch (courtesy of Senior Engr. Prof. Qin Shunquan) (a), (b)

图3 沉箱在下水前（承秦顺全教授级高工惠赠）
Fig.3 Caisson before sinking (courtesy of Senior Engr. Prof. Qin Shunquan)

图4 沉桩（承秦顺全教授级高工惠赠）
Fig.4 Sinking piles (courtesy of Senior Engr. Prof. Qin Shunquan)

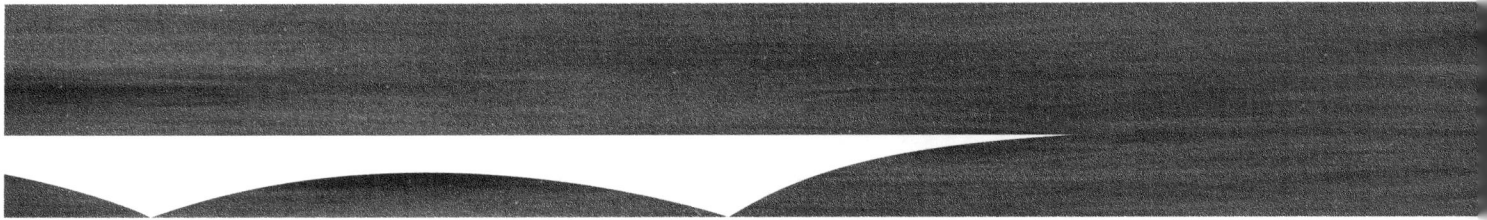

RIGID FRAME BRIDGES
刚构桥

广东虎门大桥中辅航道桥

广东虎门大桥全桥由东引桥、880m悬索主桥、中引桥、辅航道桥和西引桥组成。辅航道桥（图1）跨度为150m+270m+150m（图2），上部结构由两座单桥组成，每座均为单室单箱梁预应力混凝土连续刚构桥，桥面总宽度为31m，其中行车道为2×14.25m，桥墩为箱形截面双柱式空心薄壁结构，下部为群桩基础。该桥采用三向预应力体系，纵向预应力采用张拉吨位为4297kN的VSLEC6-22和EC612型钢丝束；竖向预应力采用ϕ32精轧螺纹粗钢筋；横向预应力为6-3型扁钢管预应力，并采用一端张拉一端轧花固定锚工艺。

辅航道桥采用对称悬臂施工法，最大悬臂长度达128m，施工过程中的抗风稳定性和抗风问题十分突出，设计上将上、下游两座单桥在0号梁处用体外横隔板联成整体，使两座单桥的主墩和下部桩基可共用抗御风载。该桥于1997年7月建成通车。

在1998年10月挪威的298m的Raftsundet桥（位于Lofoten岛）或301m的Stolmsundet桥（位于Auotevoll岛）建成前，我国辅航道桥跨长超过当时跨度同为260m的澳大利亚门道桥和挪威Kistiunsand桥（260m的门道桥为双墩支承中心线间距离）而跃居连续刚构桥的世界第一位。

1

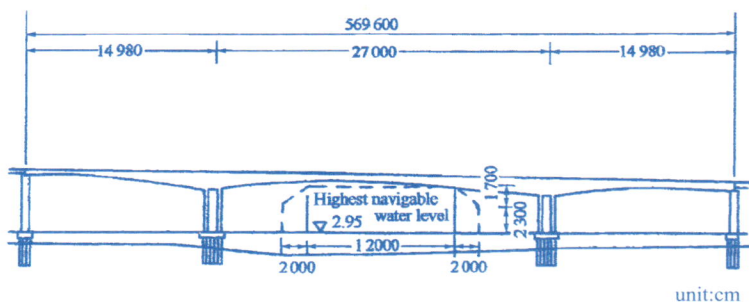

2

unit:cm

Auxiliary Navigable Pass Bridge in Guangdong Humen Bridge

The whole bridge of Guangdong Humen Bridge is constituted of east approach, 880m suspension bridge, middle approach, auxiliary navigable pass bridge and west approach. The spans of Auxiliary Navigable Pass Bridge (Fig.1) are 150m+270m+150m (Fig.2), the superstructure consists of 2 single bridges, each of which is a PC continuous rigid frame bridge with single cell and single box, the width of entire deck is 31m, among which the running lanes are 2×14.25m, the bright piers are hollow double-column-typed thin wall structures, the substructures are pile group foundations. For this bridge, the 3 dimensional prestressing system is adopted, the longitudinal prestressing adopts VSLEC 6-22 with a tonnage of 4 297kN and EC612-type wire bundle; the vertical prestressing adopts threaded thick bars ϕ32 with finish rolling; the transverse prestressing adopts 6-3 typed noncircular tube, and tensioning at one end and fixing anchorage technique through rolling thread at the other end are used.

For the Auxiliary Navigable Pass Bridge, the symmetrical cantilever construction method was adopted, the max. cantilever length reached 128m, during construction, the stability and problems of wind resistance were outstanding, on the design the two single bridges on upper and lower reaches were connected into an integral by using external diaphragm at No.0 girders, so that the mainpiers of 2 single bridges and their pile foundation in the lower can resist wind together. This bridge was completed and opened in July 1997.

Before Norwegian Raftsundet Bridge (located on Lofoten Island) with span of 298m and Stolmsundet Bridge (located on Auotevoll Island) with span of 301m were completed in Oct. 1998, the span of Chinese Auxiliary Navigable Pass Bridge was over Australian Gateway Bridge and Norwegian Kistiunsund Bridge, both with spans of 260m (for Gateway Bridge, 260m is the distance between the support center line of double piers and leaps to the 1st place in the world.

图1 辅航道桥（承石国彬教授级高工惠赠）
Fig.1 Auxiliary Navigable Pass Bridge (courtesy of Senior Engr. Prof. Shi Guobin)

图2 辅航道桥纵剖面图
Fig.2 Profile of Auxiliary Navigable Pass Bridge

参考文献

1.丁大钧. 现代混凝土结构学. 北京：中国建筑工业出版社，2000：826-864

REFERENCES

1.Ding Dajun. A Science on Modern Concrete Structures. Beijing: China Building & Architecture Press, 2000: 826-864

2.Ding Dajun, Liu Weiqing. New Entwicklungen bei Hochbausern und grossen Brücken aus Beton in China. Beton und Stahlbetonbau. 1999. 94(4): 178-185

黄石长江连续刚构桥

黄石桥（图1）位于湖北黄石市，主桥为5跨预应力混凝土连续刚构，其跨度分布为162.5m+3×245m+162.5m，为单室箱形截面，在支座处截面高度为13.0m，跨中4.1m，按二次抛物线变化。桥面宽度20m，其中机动车道15.0m，非机动车道两边各2.5m（图2）。黄石岸引桥长840.7m，由连续箱梁桥和桥面连续简支T形梁桥组成，浠水岸引桥长679.21m，由桥面连续简支T形梁桥组成。主桥墩采用直径28m双壁钢围堰加16根φ3.0m（及3.3m?）钻孔灌注桩基础，具有较高的防船舶撞击能力，通航净空为20m×24m，可容5 000t单体轮船或32 000t大型船队上下通航。

大桥采用高强混凝土C55建造，于1991年10月开始施工，1995年建成。在重庆石板坡连续刚构桥建成前，它可能是预应力混凝土连续刚构桥的世界纪录。

图1 黄石5跨连续刚构桥
（承老友史尔毅教授级高工惠赠）
Fig.1 Huangshi 5-span Continuous Rigid Frame Bridge
(courtesy of old friend Senior Engr. Prof. Shi Eryi)

图2 黄石桥截面图
Fig.2 Box section of Huangshi Bridge

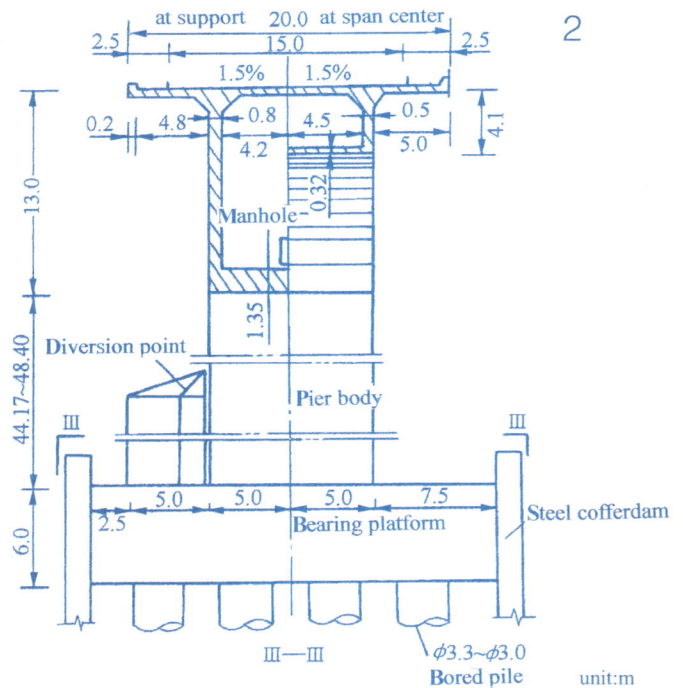

Huangshi Continuous Rigid Frame Bridge over Yangtze River

Huangshi Bridge (Fig.1) is located in Huangshi City, Hubei Province, the main bridge is a 5-span continuous PC rigid frame, of which the spans are distributed as follows: 162.5m+3×245m+162.5m with single-cell box section, the section depth is 13.0m at supports, that is 4.1m at span center, varied following a quadratic parabola. The deck width is 20m, among which the lane for motor vehicles is 15.0m and that for non-motorized vehicles is 2.5m on each side (Fig.2). The approaches on Huangshi bank having a length of 840.7m consist of continuous box girder bridge and simply supported T-typed girder bridges with continuous deck; the approaches on Xishui bank having a length of 679.21m consist of simply supported T-typed girder bridges with continuous deck. For the pier of the main foundation of steel cofferdam with $16\phi3.0m$ (and 3.3m?) bored filling piles is adopted, this construction possesses higher capacity of preventing the impact from ships, the clear navigable clearance is 20m×24m, it can allow the navigation of 5 000t single steamships or large-scale 32 000t ship groups to run upwards and downwards.

This bridge was constructed by using high-strength concrete C55, it started to construct in Oct. 1991 and completed in 1995. Before Chongqing Shibanpo continuous rigid frame bridge has been completed, this bridge might be the worldwide record of PC continuous rigid frame bridges.

参考文献

1.李国豪主任编委，项海帆主编. 中国桥梁. 上海：同济大学出版社；香港：建筑与城市出版有限公司，1993：270

2.丁大钧. 高性能混凝土及其在工程中的应用. 北京：机械工业出版社，2007：274

REFERENCES

1.Chairman Li Guohao, Editor-in-Chief Xiang Haifan. Bridges in China. Shanghai: Tongji University Press; HK: A & U Publication Ltd., 1993: 270

2.Ding Dajun. High Performance Concrete and its Applications in Engineering . Beijing: China Machine Press, 2007: 274

重庆石板坡连续刚构大桥

原重庆长江大桥（图1）位于重庆市，1980年7月1日建成通车，正桥全长1 120m，跨度分布：86.5m＋4×138m＋156m＋174m＋104.5m，最大跨度174m，悬臂端梁高3.2m，支座处梁高11.0m，该桥用跨度为35m吊梁连接，桥宽21.00m，上部桥面结构由两个分开的单室箱梁组成，肋厚46~32cm（在中部），箱间净距离为484cm，在距支座6.65m范围内用底板连接，采用三向预应力。桥墩采用等截面空心钢筋混凝土结构，墩中竖隔与箱梁肋对应设置，自基础边至桥面高60~70m，采用滑模施工。

原桥宽21m、4车道，交通十分繁重，因此必须拓宽，而水道交通，航道要求净空292m。在大桥拓宽工程建成前，原桥仍需使用，因此不得不在原桥上游净5m处建新桥，这样便于建造新基础，而将原⑥号墩（图2）省去以符合航道净空要求，新桥跨度为：86.5m＋4×138m＋330m（主跨）＋104.5m，即成主跨为330m连续刚构桥，它超过挪威301m跨的Stolmasundet桥（在挪威文中sundet意为海峡）而成为新的世界纪录。在新桥建成复线工程后，原桥也将改造，统称石板坡长江大桥。新桥其余墩与原桥双双对应，在建筑上也是美观的。

330m大跨度在跨中采用长103m、重约1400t的钢箱，在武汉制造，逆流水运至重庆，于2006年5月2日吊装，于两端桥墩伸出各长220m的悬臂，通过80多个对接板，用1 288个螺栓连接。钢箱准确就位在2006年6月7日才完成，误差不超过1mm。焊接后大跨成为连续刚构。

图3、图4分别示新桥施工时330m跨在远处和330m跨局部，图中示出这时新桥墩已建成，而330m大跨梁待建，对面原⑥号墩仍清晰可见。

新桥各部分的混凝土强度分别为（林文修教授提供赐告，在此谨志谢忱）：

正桥预应力混凝土刚构4号、5号、7号梁及南岸现浇梁采用C60，北岸1号、2号、3号梁采用C50，墩身采用C40。承台及桩采用C30，合拢段采用C60，加入了GNA和杜拉纤维[①]。

在新桥于2006年8月通车后，即改造原桥，将原桥⑥号墩拆除，而后照新桥将该桥建成330m的连续刚构，于2007年6月通车。

图5示拓宽新桥已建成，其中330m跨赫然在目；因桥尚未建成，原⑥号墩依稀可见。

5

4

2

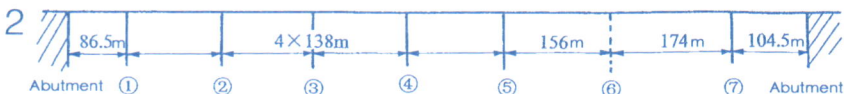

① GNA为高效抗裂膨胀剂，系中国建筑材料科学院经多年研究、改进开发的科研成果，获国家发明专利（专利号：cn 01118138.9号），GNA具有低掺量、低碱含量、分散性能好等优点。可取消外防水、取消后浇带、连续无缝施工、缩短工期、节约资金、提高建筑物的整体防水性和耐久性。

　　杜拉纤维为聚丙烯纤维，在钢筋混凝土中适量掺入杜拉纤维可有效地抑制钢筋腐蚀。

① GNA is a highly effective new expansion agent against cracking, it is an achivement from scientific research, studied, improved and developed by China Academy of Construction Meterical Sciences and gains state invention patent (the patent No: cn 01118138.9). GNA possesse some advantages low amount of addition, low amount of alkali and good dispersion, etc. Thus, the external waterproofing can be omitted, post–cast belt can be also, and continuous constrction can be done without joint, the construction period can be shortened, the fund can be saved, the integral waterproofing and durability can be elevated.

　　Dura fiber is poly propylene fiber. When proper Dura fiber is mixed into reinforced concrete, it can restrain the corrosion of bars.

图1 原重庆长江大桥（承项海帆、范立础院士惠赠）
Fig.1 Original Chongqing Yangtze River (courtesy of Academician Xiang Haifan, Fan Lichu)

图2 新桥跨度分布
Fig.2 Span distribution of new bridge

图4 330m跨局部视图（承林文修教授惠赠）
Fig.4 Local view of 330m span (courtesy of Prof. Lin Wenxiu)

图5 建成的拓宽工程（承张佐安高工惠赠）
Fig.5 Completed widening Engineering (courtesy of Senior Engr. Zhang Zuo'an)

参考文献

2.丁大钧. 高性能混凝土及其在工程中的应用. 北京：机械工业出版社，2007：274

REFERENCES

1.Ding Dajun, Juhani Virola. The Shibanpo Bridge — Longest-span concrete rigid frame bridge. RIA (Construction Engineer and Architect). 2006(2): 64-65

2.Ding Dajun. High Performance Concrete and Its Applications in Engineering. Beijing: China Machine Press, 2007: 274

Chongqing Shibanpo Continuous Rigid Frame Bridge

　　The original Chongqing Bridge over Yangtze River (Fig.1) is located at Chongqing City, completed and opened on July 1st 1980, the total length is 1 120m, with span distribution: 86.5m+4×138m+156m+174m+104.5m, the max. span is 174m, the girder depth at cantilever end is 3.2m, that at girder end 11.0m, this Bridge is connected by using hanging beams with span of 35m, the bridge width is 21.00m, the top deck structure is constituted of 2 separate single-cell box girders with rib thicknesses of 46~32cm (in center), clear distance between boxes is 484cm, connected with bottom slab in the field of 6.65m at support, prestressed in 3 ways. The hollow reinforced concrete piers of constant section are adopted, the vertical diaphragms in pier are correspondingly set with girder ribs. The heights of pier from foundation edges to deck are 60~70m, built up by slip-form method.

　　The original bridge width is 21m with 4 lanes, the traffic is too heavy, so a widening engineering should be made, however, for the communication over water channel, a clear space for navigable pass is required to be 292m. Before the widening engineering of bridge has been completed, the original bridge should be kept in service, so the new bridge has to be constructed at a place with clearance of 5m on the upper reaches, thus it is easy to construct the new foundation and the pier No.6 is omitted, so as to meet the requirement of the clearance for navigable pass, the spans of new bridge are 86.5+4×138+330 (main span) +104.5m and constructed into continuous rigid frame bridge. On the original bridge during construction rigid-frame bridge with main span of 330m, which is over the Norwegian Stolmasundet Bridge with span of 301m and becomes the new worldwide record. After the new bridge has been completed into a multiple line engineering, the original one will be reformed, both are celled by a joint as Shibanpo Yangtze River Bridge. The other piers in new bridge are corresponding with the original every other, it is also beautiful in architecture.

　　The structural type of rigid frame of this 330m span is adopted with a 103m steel box weighing 1 400t being used, which was manufactured in Wuhan, then transported to Chongqing in Yangtze River against current. On May 2, 2006, The box was hoisted and connected to the cantilevers stretching 220m from pier columns through more than 80 joint plates and 1 288 bolts, the steel box was taken precisely to its place on June 7, 2006 with error not more than 1mm. After being welded, the largest span changes into continuous rigid frame.

　　Fig.3, 4 show the 330m-span at a distant and its local view, from this figure, it can be seen that the new piers have been completed and the 330m-girder is waiting for constructing, the original pier No.6 on the opposite side can be seen clearly.

　　The concrete strengths in different parts of new bridge are given as follows (courtesy of Prof. Lin Wenxiu to tell the Editor, he appreciates his kindness herewith):

　　For the No.4, No.5 and No.7 girders in PC rigid frame of main bridge and the cast – in – cite girder on south bank, C60 was used, for the No.1, No.2 and No.3 girders on north bank, C50 was adopted, for the bodies of pier, C40 was done, for the bearing platforms and piles C30 was used, and for the closed segment C60 was utilized with adding GNA and fiber①.

　　After the new bridge was opened in Aug. 2006, the No.6 pier in original bridge was removed, the largest span of 330m would be constructed following the new one into continuous rigid frame and opened in June 2007.

　　Fig.5 shows the 330m – span has been completed, but the original pier No.6 without being reformed can be seen vaguely.

图3 重庆石板坡大桥330m跨在远处（承林文修教授惠赠）
Fig.3 The 330m span of Chongqing Shibanpo Bridge at far distance (courtesy of Prof. Lin Wenxiu)

丰城赣江Y形墩连续刚构桥

　　V形墩桥是20世纪60年代中最先由T. Y. Lin International在设计美国加利福尼亚州Hegenberger桥时采用的；T. Y. Lin International设计、于1981年建成的我国台湾台北市忠孝桥为一座多孔Y形墩桥，桥长1 145m，间距80m，宽31.5m，梁高2.6m。我国广西雄山桥，跨度为67.5m+95.0m+67.5m，中间距两边悬臂长27.5m，悬臂间设置40m挂梁均为箱形截面，墩顶梁高3.0m向两侧对称伸长16m，按直线变化成2.0m，V形墩上口宽20m，节约是明显的。

　　丰城赣江桥（图1）位于江西省丰城市，总长1 207m，分跨为12×40m+55m+4×70m+55m+8×40m，桥宽2×1.0m+11m。正桥为Y形墩6孔预应力混凝土连续刚构桥；引桥采用桥面连续的跨度40m的预应力混凝土简支梁桥。正桥和引桥均采用相同的4箱单室等高度箱梁，梁高1.9m。V型托架及其上30m主梁采用斜撑式贝雷支架就地浇筑；托架之间的40m主梁与简支梁均采用相同的工艺预制，相同的双导梁架设；主桥墩采用浮运承台外壳（外壳平面尺寸与承台相同，但高度大于承台厚度）施工；施工速度很快，工期仅18个月，于1992年11月竣工。

　　图2示丰城赣江桥在施工中。

1

2

Fengcheng Ganjiang Continuous Rigid Frame Bridge with Y-Shape Piers

Bridge with V-shaped piers was firstly adopted by T. Y. Lin International in designing American Hegenberger Bridge in California USA in 1960's; the Zhongxiao Bridge in TaiPei City, Taiwan, China was also designed by T. Y. Lin International and completed in 1981 is a multi-span one with Y-shaped piers, the length of main span is 1 145m, the spacing 80m the width 31.5m and the depth of girder 2.6m. The spans of Zhishan Bridge in Guangxi Province: 67.5m+95.0m+67.5m, the cantilever length from both sides of middle span is 27.5m, between cantilevers there is set a 40m hanging girder, all of them are box sections, the girder on pier top has depth of 3.0m and extends symmetrically 16m in two ways and the depth is decrease to 2.0m linearly. The top width of V-shaped pier is 20m, save effect is obvious.

Fengcheng Ganjiang Bridge (Fig.1) is located at Fengcheng City, Jiangxi Province, has a total length of 1 207m with spans: 12×40m+55m+4×70m+55m+8×40m, bridge width: 2×1.0m+11m, the main one is a 6-span PC continuous rigid frame bridge with Y-shaped piers; the approaches adopt 40m PC simply supported girder bridges with continuous deck. Both the main bridge and approaches adopt the same single-cell 4-box girder with equal depth of 1.9m. V-shaped brackets and the 30m main girders on them were cast-in-situ by using diagonal-struted Bailey trusses; both of the 40m main girders between bracket and simply supported girder were prefabricated by using the same technology and erected by using double guide girder; the main bridge piers were constructed by floating the external sleeves of bearing platform (the plane dimensions of sleeves were the same as bearing platform, but the height was larger than the thickness of platform); the construction progress was very quick and period was only 18 months and completed in Nov.1992.

Fig.2 shows the Fengcheng Ganjiang Bridge under construction.

图1 建成的丰城赣江桥（承项海帆院士惠赠）
Fig.1 Fengcheng Ganjiang Bridge (courtesy of Academician Xiang Haifan)

图2 在施工中的丰城赣江桥（承范立础院士惠赠）
Fig.2 Fengcheng Ganjiang Bridge under Construction (courtesy of Academician Fan Lichu)

参考文献

2.李国豪主任编委，项海帆主编. 中国桥梁. 上海：同济大学出版社；香港：香港建筑与城市出版社有限公司，1993：269

REFERENCES

1.T. Y. Lin International. Engineering Bulletin. 1983-2, 12. p.1

2.Chairman Li Guohao, Editor-in-Chief Xiang Haifan. Bridges in China. Shanghai: Tongji University Press; HK: A&U Publication Ltd., 1993: 269

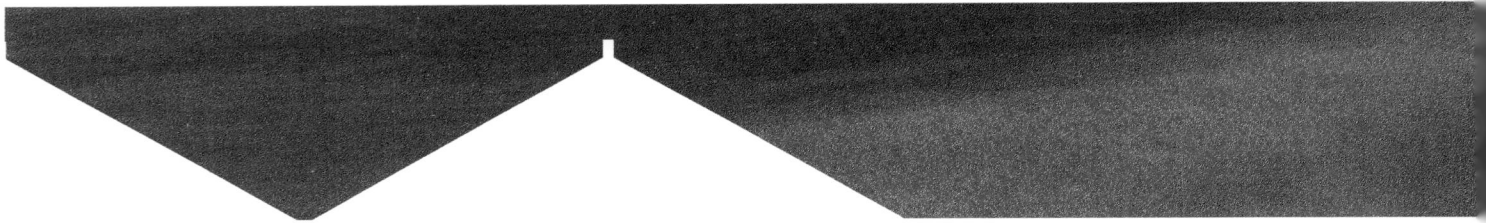

CABLE-STAYED BRIDGES

斜拉桥

三县洲独塔斜拉桥

　　福建福州三县洲是闽江中一小岛，其下游约1km为跨越闽江的解放大桥。用三县洲岛作为踏板，于其上建设桥塔，建造跨越闽江的独塔斜拉桥，即三县洲桥（图1）。主桥立面布置如图2所示，预应力混凝土箱梁截面见图3。大桥北起工业路，沿白马河向南，经大庙路，过江后接上山路，至六一路三叉街，全长4 913m，其中引道长3 487m，宽43m，桥梁全长1 376m，其中引桥长799m，主桥长577m，宽28m，全线按城市一级主干道设计。大桥施工时间为自1998年5月至1999年2月，全桥于1999年5月正式通车。

　　三县洲大桥主桥设计成独塔单索面斜拉桥，倒Y形塔高117.5m，采用在两个内斜塔柱间设置A形支座辅助施工。索成扇形布置；北汊一跨过江，跨径238m；南汊利用地形，结合实际，多跨布置，斜拉桥部分长160m。大桥设计与周围环境协调，巍巍桥塔耸立洲上，与两岸建筑斗艳，与南岸风光争辉。

　　三县洲大桥建成后，与六一路、湖东路、白马路等连接成内环。同时与二环路一、二期工程连接形成准二环。从而大大发挥了市区路网功能，有效地缓解了市区交通拥挤，解决市区西部南北过江难问题，并且带动市区西部开发，极大地推动城市建设和经济发展。

图2　全桥立面图
Fig.2 Elevation of main bridge

图3　主桥箱梁截面
Fig.3 Box girder section of main bridge

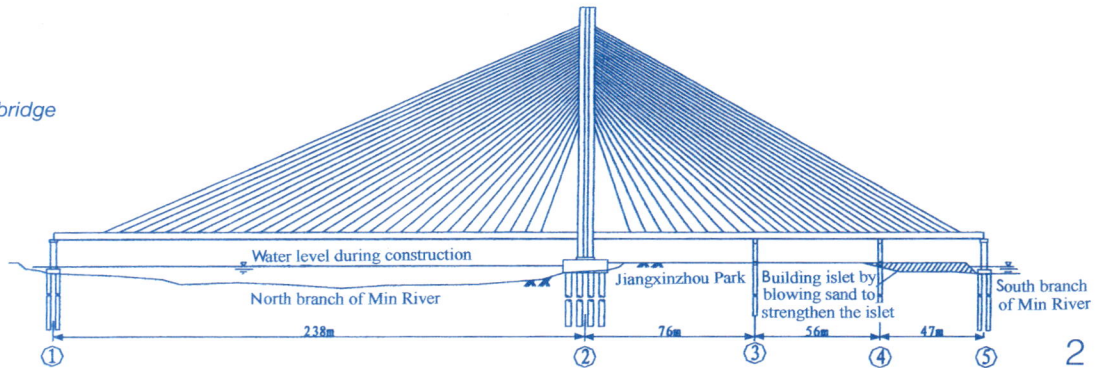

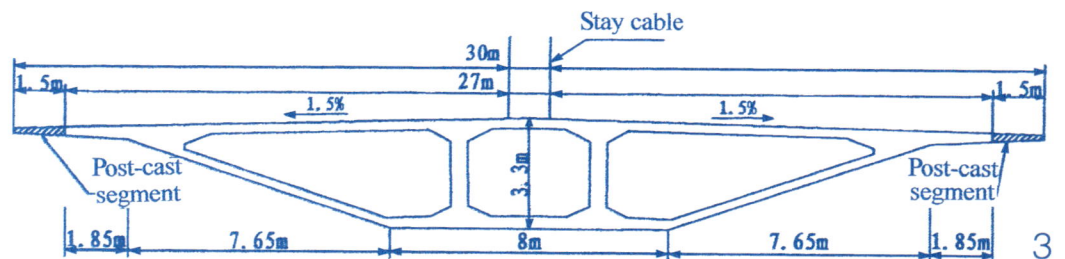

Sanxianzhou Single-Pylon Cable-Stayed Bridge

Sanxianzhou is an island in Minjiang near Fuzhou, Fujian Province, at a distance of 1km in the lower reaches, there is the Jiefang Bridge. Utilizing the Island Sanxianzhou as a bridge site on which the pylon is constructed, then a single-pylon cable-stayed bridge to span Minjiang is completed, i.e., Sanxianzhou Bridge (Fig.1). The elevation of the main bridge is shown in Fig.2 and the PC box girder section in Fig.3. This bridge starts from Gongyelu (lu means road in Chinese) in the north and along Baimahe (he means also river in Chinese) towards the south, and through Damiaolu, then over Minjiang to connect Shangshanlu, and reaches Liuyilu, Sanchajie (jie means street in Chinese), the total length is 4 913m, among which there is the approach length of 3 487m with width of 43m, the total length of bridge is 1 376m with approaching bridge length of 799m and main bridge length of 577m, the width of 28m. The entire line is designed following urban main line of 1st grade. The construction time was from May 1998 to Feb. 1999, and the entire bridge was opened formally in May 1999.

The main bridge of Sanxianzhou Bridge is designed as a single-pylon and single-plane cable-stayed one with inverted Y-typed pylon of which the height is 117.5m, by using A-shaped support set between 2 inclined pylon columns to conduct auxiliary construction. The cables are arranged in fan shape; a span over the north branch of Minjiang, the span is 238m over the south branch, utilizing the topography and combining the practice, a multiple-span arrangement is adopted, the partial length of cable-stayed bridge is 160m. The design of bridge is harmonized with the environment, the towering bridge pylon stands on the island to win over being novel as the buildings on two banks and to win over being beautiful with the scenery of banks.

After the completion of Sanxianzhou Bridge, it has connected with Liuyilu, Hudonglu, Baimalu etc, to form an internal ring, at the same time, it connects with the 1st and 2nd-period engineering of the 2nd ring road to constitute the quasi 2nd ring. Hence the effect of the road net in urban area is greatly developed and the traffic congestion is effectively eased, the difficulty of passing over the river from the west part of urban area in northsouth way is solved, the final effect brings on the west part to develop and greatly advances the city construction and economical development.

参考文献

1.李茂清，戴忠诚，薛峰. 福州市三县洲斜拉桥边跨施工. 铁道建筑，2003（12）：3-6

REFERENCES

1.Li Maoqing, Dai Zhongcheng, Xuefeng. Construction of the side span of Sanxianzhou cable-stayed bridge, completed in Fuzhou City, Railway Building. 2003(12): 3-6

图1 三县洲桥（侧视图）（承丁汉山教授、宁平华高工惠赠）
Fig.1 Sanxianzhou Bridge (lateral view) (courtesy of Prof. Ding Hanshan and Senior Engr. Ning Pinghua)

台湾高屏独塔斜拉桥

高屏桥（图1a~c）为台湾南部第2公路一部分，跨越高雄县和屏东县之间的高屏河。该桥梁体系由36座常用的连续桥和1座斜拉桥组成。常用桥短跨跨长为36.2~45.3m，用先进的支撑法建造，而这些桥在60~120m的长跨则用悬臂梁法施工，斜拉桥也许是该体系中最重要和最困难的部分，因此被设计成屏东县的一项标志。

设计于1995年的斜拉桥于2000年建成，为一座不对称的2跨斜拉桥结构（图2），短跨桥面长180m，长跨330m，使该桥成为世界第4长的独塔斜拉桥，第1、2、3长的桥顺次为俄罗斯的鄂毕河桥、伏尔加河（中游）桥、德国莱茵河桥，它们跨长分别为2×408m、2×407m和368m（长跨）（参看本书绪论表4-8）。

混凝土桥塔，高183.5m。桥面由两种型式加劲梁构成，短跨为现场浇筑的混凝土箱梁，而长跨则为预制的就地焊接钢箱梁。两种型式箱梁剖面和尺寸相同，并施加纵横向预应力。箱梁宽为34.5m，截面高度3.2m。作用在短跨混凝土梁横向中的预应力束如图3所示.

桥塔（图4）为一带有横撑的混凝土塔，高度相当于短跨。桩支承塔的底部，中间桩支承连接梁，梁水平地连接两塔脚。4根斜拉索距塔顶12.75m处与塔相连，其余的则从第一连接处每隔3.85m相连。

斜拉索为两种型式，二者都包含7股钢丝束。A型索达91根束，而B型则不多于61束。所有索施加预应力以减小索的垂度和保持桥面初始和希望的外形。

高屏县为台风地震区。因此斜拉桥设计成足够强以抵抗这些自然力。因为主跨长度为330m，风的作用为桥的设计重要因素之一，必须进行风洞试验。风洞试验曾按3种模型进行：截面型、全模型、施工期间全模型。这些试验考虑使用条件、稳定极限、颤振反应、涡流发散反应、平均静荷载及空气动力导数。风洞尺寸为15m×13.6m×1.7m，阻尼

1b

1a

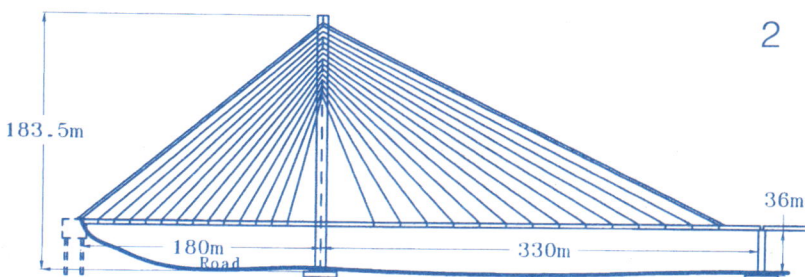

2

183.5m

36m

180m
Road

330m

1c

Taiwan Kao-Pin Single-Pylon Cable-Stayed Bridge

The Kao-Pin Bridge (Fig.1a~c) is a part of the 2nd Highway in the southern Taiwan and crosses the Kao-Pin River between Kao-Hsing County and Pin-Tung County. This bridge system consists of 36 conventional continuous bridge and a cable-stayed bridge. The short spans of the conventional bridges, ranging in lengths from 36.2m to 45.3m were constructed by the advanced shoring method, while the long spans of these bridges, ranging from 60m to 120m were done by cantilever method. The cable-stayed, perhaps, the most important and most difficult part of the bridge system, was designed to be a landmark for Pin-Tung County.

The cable-stayed bridge, designed in 1995 and completed in 2000, is an unsymmetrical two-span cable-stayed structure (Fig.2), the bridge deck of the short span is 180m and that of the long span 330m, making this bridge to be the 4th longest one-pylon cable-stayed bridge in the world, because the 1st, 2nd and 3rd longest bridges are respectively the Russian OB River Bridge, the Volga River (middle reaches) Bridge and Rhine River Bridge, their spans are 2×408m, 2×407m and 368m (long span) (see Tab.4-8 in the Introduction of this book).

The pylon is an A-type concrete tower with height of 183.5m. The decks consist of stiffening girder with 2 types: the shorter span is a site-cast concrete box girder and the longer one is a steel box girder prefabricated and welded in place. The 2-type box girders have the same section and dimensions, and prestressed in the longitudinal and transverse directions. The width of the box girders is 34.5m and their depth 3.2m. The prestressing tendons acting on the concrete box girder in the transverse direction are shown in Fig.3.

The bridge pylon (Fig.4) is a tower with a strut supporting the highway , its height being equivalent to the length of the shorter span. Piles support the bottom of pylon and the middle piles support the connecting beam which horizontally connects the 2 legs of the pylon. 4 stay cables are attached to the pylon at 12.75m from its top and the remaining cables are attached at 3.85m intervals from the 1st attachment.

The stay cables are of two types, A and B, both consist of 7-strand wire tendons. Type-A cables consist of up to 91 tendons, while type-B cables consist of no more than 61 tendons. All the cables are prestressed in order to reduce the cable sag and to keep the bridge deck in the initial and desired shape.

Pin-Tung County is a typhoon and earthquake area. Therefore, the cable-stayed bridge is designed to be strong enough to withstand such natural forces. Because the main span length is 330m, the wind effect is one of the most important factors for the bridge design, and it was necessary to carry out wind tunnel tests. The wind tunnel tests were carried out on three models: a section model; a full model; and a full model during construction. These tests took into account, in-service conditions, stability limit, buffeting response, vortex-shedding response, mean static loads, and aerodynamic derivatives. The

比为2%~3%之间。

对截面模型，采用1：80比例模型和在试验期间考虑几种荷载条件。对全模型和施工期间的全模型，模型比例1：150。对全模型的风洞试验结果如表1所示。

因为用悬臂法施工和主跨长为330m，桥在施工期间的空气动力性能对空气动力稳定是重要的。对全模型，承受附加活荷载，由于施工适当的设备和附加活荷载进行风洞试验。对施工期间全模型试验结果如表2所示。对全模型和施工期间全模型的误差在理论和决定数值之间是可以接受的。

表1 全模型风洞试验结果

模型数	模型形状	频率（Hz） 理论结果	频率（Hz） 试验结果	误差（%）
1	弯曲	2.866	2.825	1.4
2	弯曲	5.609	5.525	1.5
3	倒向	7.238	6.900	4.7
4	弯曲	7.398	7.000	5.4
5	扭转	8.353	8.550	2.3

表2 施工期间全模型风洞试验结果

模型数	模型形状	频率（Hz） 理论结果	频率（Hz） 试验结果	误差（%）
1	倒向	1.905	1.875	1.6
2	弯曲	2.431	2.325	4.3
3	扭转	5.548	5.875	5.9

Long-span deck

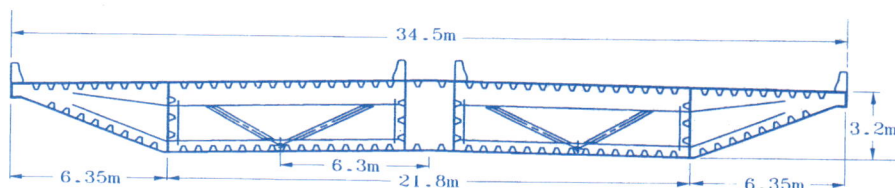

Short-span deck

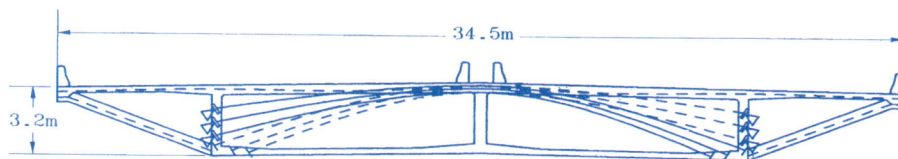

dimensions of the wind tunnel were 15m×13.6m×1.7m, and damping ratios were considered between 2% and 3%.

For the sectional model, a 1:80 scale model was used, and several load conditions were considered during the tests. For the full model and the full model during construction, the scale of the models was 1:150. The results of the wind tunnel tests on the full model are given in Table 1.

Because the cantilever method is used during construction, and because the main span length is 330m, the aerodynamic behaviour of the bridge during construction is important for the aerodynamic stability. Wind tunnel tests were performed on the full models subjected to additional dead loads, due the equipment and additional live loads due to construction. The results of the wind tunnel test on the full model during construction are listed in Table 2. For the full model and the full model during construction, the errors between the theoretical and the determined values were acceptable.

4

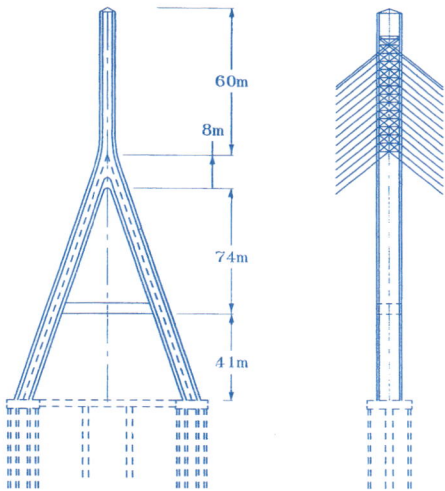

图3 长短跨箱梁截面
Fig.3 Cross section of box girders in long and short spans

图4 桥塔正视和侧视图
Fig.4 Front and side views of the pylon

Fig.1 Wind tunnel test results of the full model

Model number	Model shapes	Frequency(Hz) Theoretical result	Frequency(Hz) Test result	Error(%)
1	flexural	2.866	2.825	1.4
2	flexural	5.609	5.525	1.5
3	lateral	7.238	6.900	4.7
4	flexural	7.398	7.000	5.4
5	torsional	8.353	8.550	2.3

Fig.2 Wind tunnel test results of the full model during construction

Model number	Model shapes	Frequency(Hz) Theoretical result	Frequency(Hz) Test result	Error(%)
1	lateral	1.905	1.875	1.6
2	flexural	2.431	2.325	4.3
3	torsional	5.548	5.875	5.9

REFERENCES

1.Yang-Cheng Wang. Kao-Pin His Cable-Stayed Bridge, Taiwan, China. Structural Engineering International, IABSE Journal. 1999(2): 94-95

南京长江三桥

南京长江三桥（图1）位于长江江苏境南京区段，在已建成的南京长江大桥上游约19km处，距长江入海口约350km。

南京长江三桥为钢塔钢箱梁双索面五跨连续斜拉桥，跨度布置为63m+257m+648m+257m+63m，主桥全长1 288m，采用半漂浮结构体系，总体布置如图2所示。

索塔为"人"字形，高215m，塔柱外侧圆曲线部分半径720m，设4道横梁，其中下塔柱及下横梁为钢筋混凝土结构，其余部分为钢结构，下塔柱36.318m，塔柱高178.682m，横桥向截面宽度6.2~8.4m，顺桥向宽度为8.0~12.0m，截面尺寸上下相等，横桥向宽5.0m，顺桥向宽6.8m。

除钢混合段外，一个钢塔柱共分为21个节段，节段长7.7~11.42m，一个节段的最大吊重不超过160t，钢塔总重约12 000t。钢塔柱构造及节段划分见图3。

钢塔柱主体结构采用Q370qD，壁板厚30~48mm，腹板厚32mm，壁板加劲肋厚22~24mm，腹板加劲肋厚24mm，横隔板加劲肋厚10mm，见图4。

图5示桥塔在施工中。

图6示南京长江三桥采用的钢箱梁。

南京长江三桥北桥塔承台呈哑铃形，包括钢套箱外墙，平面尺寸为84.00mm（横桥向）×29.00m（顺桥向），承台高度为7.0m，封底混凝土厚3.80m，采取无底双壁钢套箱为挡水结构进行承台干施工，哑铃两端下各设24根钢管桩，另壁下各4根。哑铃中部下6根。

图7示哑铃承台在施工中。

南京长江三桥获古斯塔夫斯—林德恩斯国际奖。

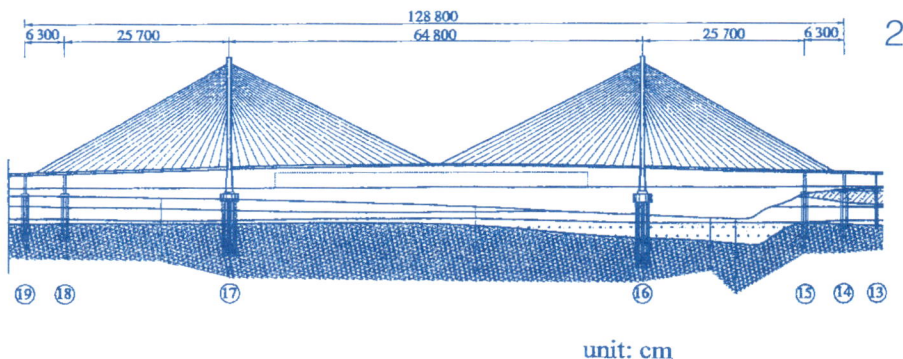

1a

2

unit: cm

The 3rd Nanjing Yangtze River Bridge

The 3rd Nanjing Yangtze River Bridge (3NYRB) (Fig.1) is located at the Nanjing segment within Yangtze River Jiangsu Province boundary and has a distance of 19km or so in the upper reaches from the completed Nanjing Bridge and a distance of 350km or so to the mouth of Yangtze River entering the sea.

The 3NYRB is a 5-span continuous cable-stayed bridge with steel pylons, steel box girder and double cable planes, the arrangement of its spans: 63m+257m+648m+257m+63m, the total length of main bridge is 1 288m and a semi-floating system is adopted, the general layout is shown in Fig.2.

The cable pylon appears to be a herringbone with height of 215m, the radius of external circular curve of pylon columns is 720m, when there are set 4 transverse beams, the lower pylon columns and the lower transverse beam are reinforced concrete structures, the other parts are steel structures, the 36.318m lower pylon columns have section with width of 6.2~8.4m cross bridge direction and with width of 8.0~12.0m along bridge direction. The column height of steel pylons is 178.682m, the section dimensions are equal in upper and lower parts, the width is 5.0m cross bridge direction and 6.8m along bridge direction.

Except of steel composite segments, each steel pylon column is divided into 21 segments, the segment lengths are 7.7~11.42m, the max. hoisted weight is not over 160t, the total weight of steel pylons is 12 000t or so. The construction of steel pylon column and the division of segments are shown in Fig.3.

The main structure of steel pylon columns adopts Q370qD, the wall thickness are 30~48mm, the web thickness is 32mm, the thickness of stiffening rib of wall are 22~24mm, the thickness of stiffening rib of web is 24mm, the thickness of stiffening rib of diaphragms is 10mm, see Fig.4.

Fig.5 shows the bridge pylon column under construction.

Fig.6 shows the steel box girder adopted in the 3NYRB.

The bearing plate using in the north pylon of the 3NYRB appears to be dumbbell, the plane dimension including the external wall of steel sleeve box of which are 84.00m (cross bridge direction) ×29.00m (along bridge direction), the thickness of bearing plateform is 7.0m and that of concrete for sealing bottom is 3.80m, a double-wall steel sleeve box without bottom as water-retailing structure was adopted to conduct the construction of bearing platform body. Under 2 ends of dumbbell, there are set respectively 24 steel pipe piles, additionally, under walls, 4 steel pipe piles. Under the middle part, there are 6 steel pipe piles.

Fig.7 shows the dumbbell bearing platform under construction.

3NYRB gained the International Prize of Gustafus-Lindens (transliterated from Chinese).

1b

图1 南京长江三桥（承娄学全教授级高工惠赠）
(a) 正视图；(b) 侧视图
Fig.1 The 3rd Nanjing Yangtze River (courtesy of Senior Engr. Prof. Lou Xuequan)
(a) front view, (b) side view

图2 桥型总体布置（尺寸单位：cm）
Fig.2 General layout of bridge type (dimension unit: cm)

3

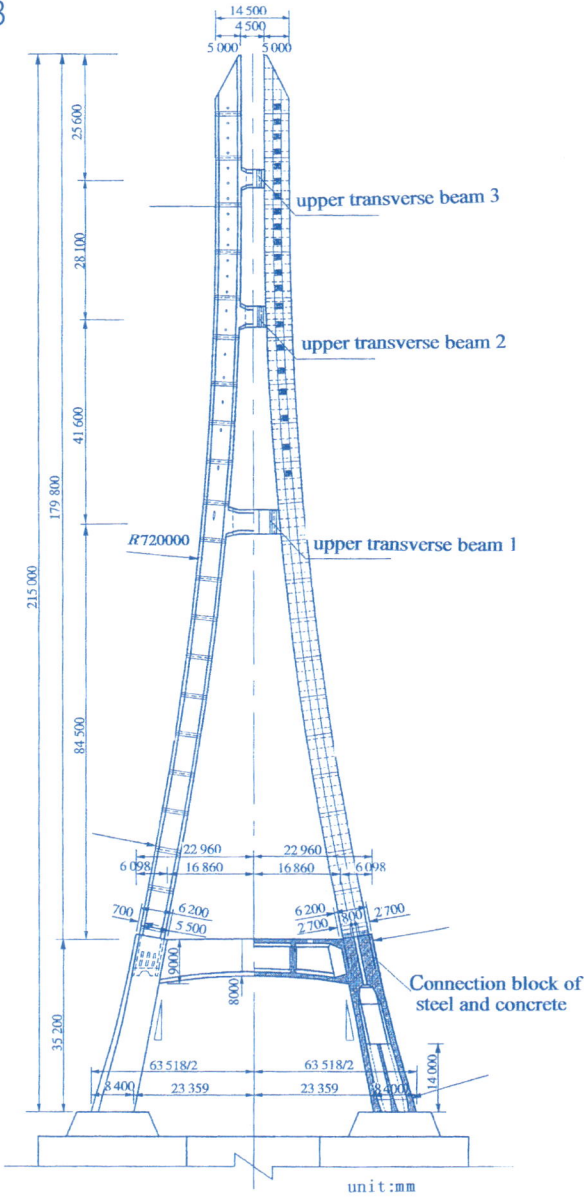

14 500
4 500
5 000　5 000

25 600

upper transverse beam 3

28 100

upper transverse beam 2

41 600

179 800

215 000

R720000　upper transverse beam 1

84 500

22 960　22 960
6 098　16 860　16 860　6 098

700　6 200　6 200　800　2 700
5 500　2 700

9000
8000

Connection block of
steel and concrete

35 200

63 518/2　63 518/2
8 400　23 359　23 359　8 400

14 000

unit:mm

图3　钢塔柱构造及节段划分
Fig.3 Construction and segment division of steel pylon column

图4　钢塔柱截面
Fig.4 Section of steel pylon column

图5　桥塔在施工中（承娄学全教授级高工惠赠）
Fig.5 Pylon under construction (courtesy of Senior Engr. Prof. Lou Xuequan)

图6　钢箱梁
Fig.6 Steel box girder

图7　哑铃承台在施工中（承娄学全教授级高工惠赠）
Fig.7 Dumbbell bearing platform under construction (courtesy of Senior Engr. Prof. Lou Xuequan)

4

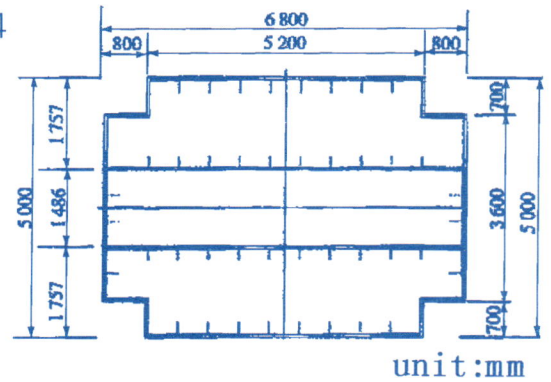

6 800
800　5 200　800

1757
5 000　1 486　3 600　5 000
1757

700
700

unit:mm

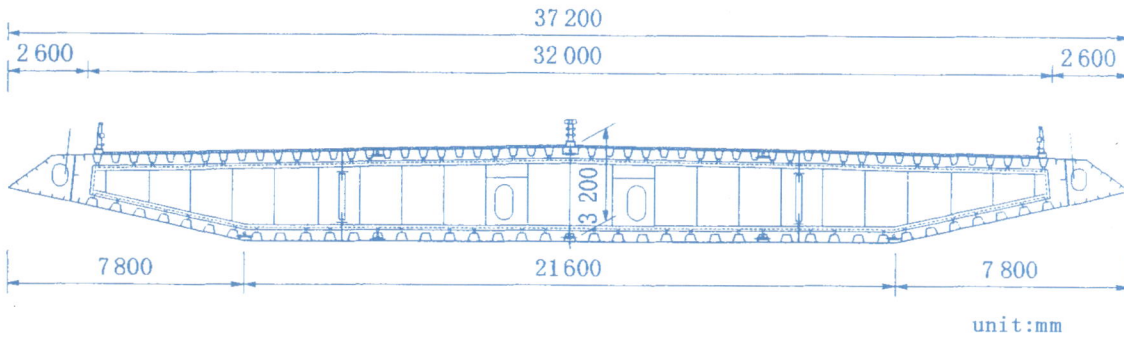

37 200
2 600　　32 000　　2 600

3 200

7 800　　21 600　　7 800

unit:mm

6

5

7

参考文献

1.南京长江三桥建设指挥部. 南京长江三桥（彩
色画册），2004：9

2.崔冰，等4人. 南京长江第三大桥钢塔柱设计与
施工. 2004年全国桥梁学术会议论文集. 北京：人
民交通出版社，2004：92-101

REFERENCES

*2.Cui Bing, et al 4 persons. Design and
construction of steel pylon column in the 3NYRB.
The Proceedings of National Symposium on
Bridges. Beijing: The People's Communication
Press, 2004: 92-101*

*3. Lou Xuequan, Ding Dajun. Ivan Balaz. 3rd
Bridge in Nanjing (in Czech), EUE Stav. 2006(3):
48-51*

安庆长江斜拉桥

安庆长江公路大桥（图1a~c）位于长江安庆河段，是继安徽省铜陵和芜湖长江大桥后第三条过江通道，大桥东距铜陵大桥约100km，西距九江长江大桥约164km，北起京福、沪蓉国道主干线在安徽境内共用线合安高速公路，南接沿江高速公路。大桥由北岸高架桥、圣埠匝道桥、分离式立交、北岸跨堤引桥、**主桥**、南漫堤引桥、南引桥及引道组成。全长5 985.66m，其中引桥为20m、25m、40m和51m跨的双幅等高单箱预应力混凝土连续箱梁，跨堤、跨新河为主跨60m、70m变截面预应力混凝土连续梁，钻孔桩基础。

大桥主桥为50m+215m+510m+215m+50m5跨连续双塔双索面全焊扁平流线形钢箱梁斜拉桥（图2），全长1 040m。主桥加劲梁截面高度3m，梁宽30m（含风嘴）（图3）。

索塔为钢筋混凝土分离式倒Y形结构，高184.781m；索塔基础为直径32m，高51m或59m双壁钢围堰，内设直径3.0m钻孔桩复合基础。为克服营运荷载下过渡墩与辅助墩内产生负反力，在辅助墩跨钢箱梁内压重960t。

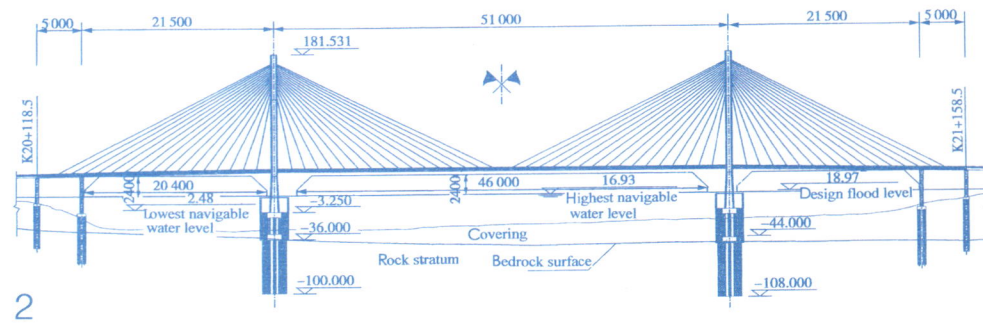

2

1a

1b

1c

Anqing Yangtze River Cable-Stayed Bridge

Anqing Yangtze River Highway Bridge (Fig.1a~c) is located on the Anqing segment of Yangtze River, it is the 3rd passage over the river after Tongling and Wuhu Yangtze River Bridges completed in Anhui Province, and has a distance to Tongling Bridge of 100km or so in the east, and that to Jiujiang Bridge of 164km or so in the west. This Bridge starts in the north from the common line Hefei-Anqing express highway on the main highway lines of Beijing-Fujian and Shanghai-Chengdu national roads, and connects the express highway along river in the south. Anqing Bridge is constituted from north bank of viaduct, Shenghua ramp bridge, separate overcrossing, north approach over bank, **main bridge**, south approach overflow, south approach and approach road. The entire length 5 985.66m, among which, the approaches are dual constant depth and single-box PC continuous girders with spans of 20m, 25m, 40m and 51m, the bridges over bank and over new river are variable depth PC continuous girders with spans of 60m, 70m and bored pile foundation.

The main bridge is a 50m+215m+510m+215m+50m 5-span continuous cable-stayed one with double pylon and double cable planes and all welded shallow streamlined steel box girder (Fig.2), its entire length is 1 040m. The depth of stiffening girder in main bridge is 3m, and the width is 30m (including wind fairing) (Fig.3).

The cable pylon is a separate inverted Y-shaped RC structure with height of 184.781m, and the pylon foundation is a double-walled steel cofferdam with diameter of 32m, heights of 51m or and 59m, in the cofferdam there is set a complex foundation constituted of 18 bored piles with diameter of 3.0m. In order to overcome the negative reactions produced in transitional and auxiliary piers under operating loading it should set pressure weight of 960t in the steel box girder of auxiliary span.

图1 建成的安庆长江大桥（承教授级高工陈其祖惠赠）
(a) 全景；(b) 侧视；(c) 夜景
Fig.1 Constructed Anqing Yangtze River Bridge (courtesy of Senior Engr. Prof. Chen Qizu) (a) full view, (b) side view, (c) night scene

图2 安庆长江大桥主桥跨度布置图（尺寸单位：cm）
Fig.2 Span arrangement of the main bridge in Anqing Yangtze River Bridge (dimension unit: cm)

图3 主桥钢箱梁构造图
Fig.3 Construction of steel box girder of main bridge

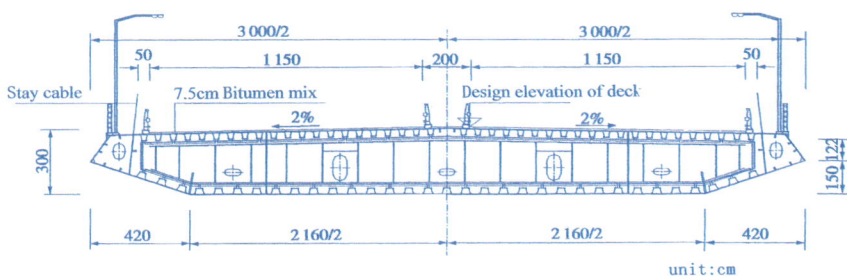

参考文献

1.胡明义. 安庆长江公路大桥设计与施工. 全国桥梁学术会议论文集. 昆明，2004：173-181

REFERENCES

1.Hu Mingyi. Design and construction of Anqing Yangtze River Highway Bridge. Proceedings of National Symposium on Bridges. Kunming, 2004: 173-181

香港昂船洲斜拉桥

香港昂船洲大桥（图1）是全长为13.5km的9号干线青衣至长沙湾段的重要组成部分，横跨蓝巴勒海峡，连接昂船洲岛（在新界之南、与九龙靠近）和8号货柜码头，这有助于分散3号干线的交通流量。

国际大桥设计竞赛于1999年11月22日开始，通过几轮评选，最后由英国的Flint & Neill Partnership公司、中国的上海市政工程设计院、丹麦的Architect Dissingt Weithing Arkitektfirma公司组成、由英国Halcrow集团领导的小组获胜。最后主跨确定为1 018m，它仅次于苏通大桥，为国际第二的斜拉桥。为通航净空要求，至少需要73.5m，因此采用高架引桥。

昂船洲大桥全长1 596m，每边4个边跨部分，分别长79.75m、70m、70m和69.25m（图2）。圆形独柱式桥塔由地面至175m为混凝土结构，混凝土最外一层的垂直钢筋和箍筋采用不锈钢钢筋，而175~298m部分则为钢与混凝土组合结构，钢外壳用不锈钢制造（图3），这在世界上为首次。根据理论模拟方法预测，可提供超过120年的使用寿命。

采用不锈钢使桥塔造价预算增加15%，在此尚未考虑因毋须使用极高耐久性的混凝土而节省的费用。有关增加费用会因节省日后的维修费用而将以抵消。

桥面主跨度两端延伸至边跨49.75m长的部分为钢箱梁结构，两个钢箱由横梁连在一起，在主跨部分，间距为18m，而在边跨则为15m。桥面箱内部的空气湿度会受到控制，以便提供低于相对湿度60%的环境。桥面外层涂漆系统保护。底层：锌环氧树脂40μm；第一层防护漆：环氧云母氧化铁150μm；第二层同第一层；饰面聚氨酯50μm。所有涂料均须在预制现场处理。

昂船洲大桥原计划于2008年8月建成。由于气候恶劣，大桥推迟而可望于2009年建成。

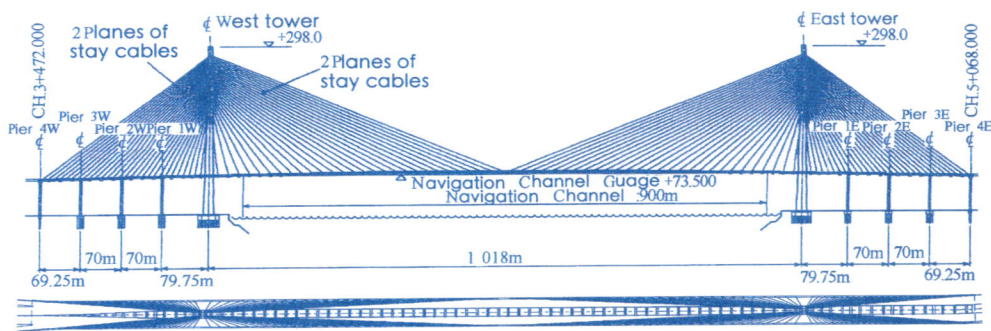

2

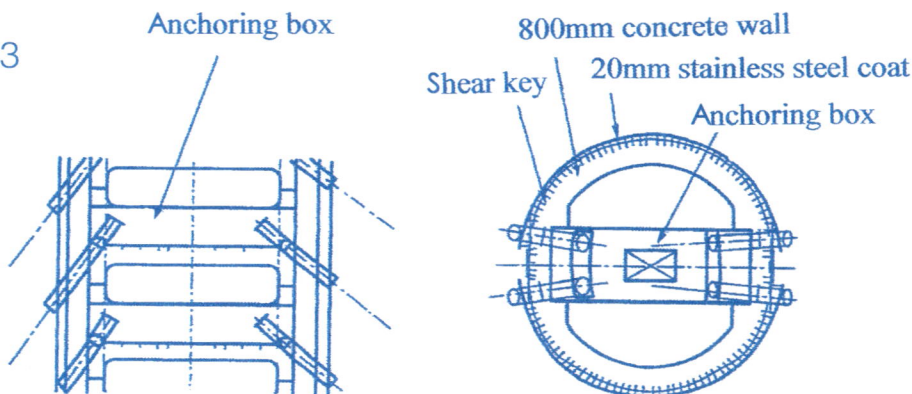

3

Hongkong Stonecutters Cable-Stayed Bridge

1

Hong Kong Stonecutters Bridge (Fig.1) is an important component of Tsingyi to Changshawan segment in the artery No.9 with total length of 13.5km, it spans Ramble Channel and connects Stonecutters Island (in the south of New Area, near Jiulong) and the wharf No.8 of packing boxes and contributes to disperse the communication flows on artery No.3.

The international competition of bridge design started on Dec.12, 1999, through some Choices, finally the group constituted of English Flint & Neill Partnership Co., Chinese Shanghai Design Institute for Municipal Works, Danish Architect Dessingt Weithing Arkitektfirma A/S, led by English Halcrow Group won. The main span was determined finally to be 1 018m, which is only smaller than Sutong Bridge and becomes worldwide cable-stayed bridge in the 2nd place. Because of the requirement of navigation clearance, it needs 73.5m at least, so high-level approaches are constructed.

The total length of Stonecutters Bridge is 1 596m, the lengths of 4 side spans on each end are 79.75m, 70m, 70m and 69.25m respectively (Fig.2). Circular single-column pylon from ground to 175m high is reinforced concrete structure, of which the rebars and stirrups in external layer adopt stainless steel, the segment from 175m to 298m is composite structure of steel and concrete, its external shell is manufactured with stainless steel (Fig.3), this is the first construction in the world. Following theoretical simulation, it can predict that this method will provide service life more than 120 years.

Adopting stainless steel increases the cost budget of pylons by 15%, there is not to consider the cost saving due to not using high-durability concrete. The relative increase of cost may be offset due to saving cost of maintenance in the future.

The deck of main span and edge spans of 49.75m extending from 2 ends is a steel box structure, constituted of 2 boxes connected with transverse beams, the spacing of which in the part of main span is 18m, and that in the part of side span is 15m. The humidity in box interior should be controlled so as to provide some circumstances with the relative humidity lower than 60%. The external surface is protected will painting system bottom layer: zinc epoxy resin 40μm; the 1st layer protective painting: epoxy micaceous oxide iron 150μm; the 2nd layer is the same as the 1st layer; the decorative surface polyurethane 50μm. All the paintings should be handled in prefabricated site.

Stonecutters Bridge was originally scheduled to be completed in Aug. 2008, but because the weather is adverse, it is postponed and may be expected to be completed in 2009.

参考文献

1.许志豪，黄剑波.昂船洲大桥耐久性、维修和安全考虑.全国桥梁学术会议论文集（上册）.重庆，2006：46-53

2.丁大钧.中国大陆拱桥和索桥建设新进展.中国台湾土木水利学会会刊，2004.31（1）：265-267

REFERENCES

1.Xu Zhihao, Huang Jianbo. Considerations on durability, maintenance and safety of stonecutters bridge, Proceedings of the National Symposium on Bridge (the 1ˢᵗ of 2 vols). Chongqing, 2006: 46-53

2.Ding Dajun. New advances of the construction of arch bridges and cable supported bridges in Mainland China. Proceedings of Civil and hydraulic engineering society, Taiwan, China. 2004. 31(4): 265-267

香港汀九桥

香港汀九桥为三塔斜拉桥（图1），图2、图3分示该桥塔施工已到顶和桥在施工中。汀九桥及高架引道为大榄隧道及3号干线青衣段之间提供重要连接通道，以桥梁跨过汀九及青衣西北面的900m宽蓝巴勒海峡，将新界的西面及西北面与九龙及港岛的市区连接，并经青屿干线连接位于赤蜡角的香港国际机场。

汀九桥全长为1 177m，桥塔为单柱式，从桥塔的顶部起四面斜拉索以扇形向下伸展至距离13.5m处锚固，斜拉索支承两块相连接的面板，每块面板各容纳兼有坚固（钢制）硬路肩的三线混凝土行道。

桥的汀九塔和青衣塔分别高168m和162m，建于基岩上的筏形基础，而中塔高195m，则设置在钻孔桩上并建于特别设计以免船只撞击的人工岛上，所有塔柱用滑模建造。

桥面以174件合成桥面节段组成，每件典型节段长度为13.5m。钢梁在工场制造，船运往工地，并直接起吊到桥面，然后栓接到已架设的节段上，在钢梁上安放预制混凝土板，而后将板间空缝浇灌混凝土造成以钢和混凝土合成的桥面。

汀九桥独一无二的特点是单支柱桥塔通过斜拉索横向地稳固下来，这些斜拉索由桥塔顶经过桥面下钢横梁再向下延至桥塔在42m高（以主水平基准计起）的部分。中央塔通过将桥塔顶部分连接汀九及青衣塔旁的桥面的纵向斜拉索作进一步稳固。这一安排使桥塔有足够的稳定性以抵抗极端台风荷载。这些斜拉索配备震动气流阻尼器，限制在恶劣天气下的位移。所有斜拉索均由一股15mm直径高强钢绞线组成。每一条钢绞线由7根镀锌钢丝做成，用高密度聚乙烯塑料保护，这些套内空隙则注满石油蜡质料，每根斜拉索再以聚乙烯塑料套管保护，这些套管外有旋转纹，以减低风及雨带的震动。

汀九桥连接一条双程三线分离高架引道以及两条双线匝道，总长3.5km，一半建在地面，另一半是高达62m的桥，桥跨的长度达115m。

汀九桥及高架桥于1998年5月通车。

3a 3b

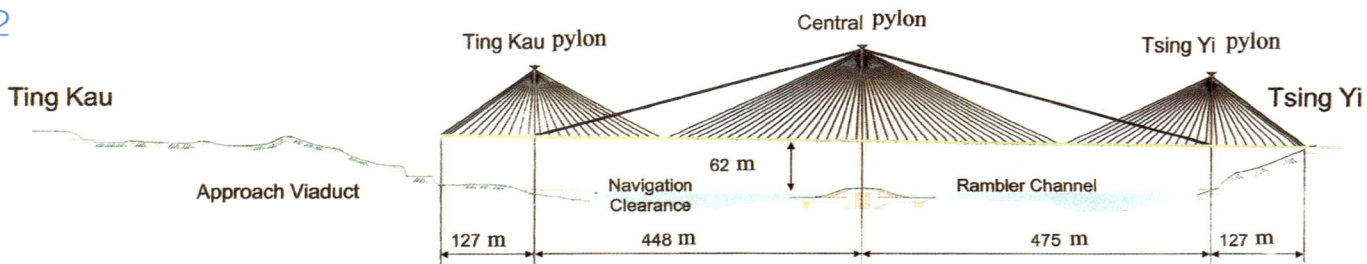

2

Hongkong Ting Kau Bridge

Ting Kau Bridge is a cable-stayed one with 3 towers (pylons) (Fig.1) which were constructed to tops and the bridge was started to construct, both are shown in Figs.2, 3. Ting Kau Bridge and Approach Viaduct provide the crucial link between the Tai Lam Tunnel and Tsing Yi secting of Route 3 by bridging the 900m wide Rambler Channel between Ting Kau and northwest Tsing Yi Island. It connects the west and northwest New Territories to the urban areas of Kowloon and HK Island and also the HK Iternational Airport at Chek Lap Kok via Lantau Link.

The whole length of Ting Kau Bridge is 1 177m, the tower is single-column type, from tops of 3 towers, four planes of stay cables in fan configurations radiate downwards to anchorages at 13.5m centers. The stay cables support 2 interconnected decks each of which accommodates a 3-lane carriageway with a hard steel shoulder.

The heights of towers at Ting Kau and Tsing Yi are 168m and 162m respectively and founded on spread footings to bedrock, the center tower is 195m high and founded on bored piles within a purposed designed ship impact protection island. All towers were constructed by slipforming.

The deck was formed by 174 numbers of composite deck panels. Each typical panel was 13.5m long. The steel girders were fabricated in a yard, transported by barge to site and lifted directly to the deck level where they were bolted to the previous panel. Precast concrete slabs were added with insitu concrete joints to form a steel/concrete composite deck.

A unique feature of the Ting Kau Bridge is the arrangement for the single-column towers which are stabilized transversely by stay cables passing from the tower top to cross struts below the deck and downwards to the tower at a level +42m PD. The center tower is further stabilized with longitudinal stay cables connecting the tower top to the deck close to Tsing Yi and Ting Kau towers. These arrangements are necessary to provide the towers with sufficient stability to withstand the extreme typhoon wind loads. These stay cables are provided with vibration dampers to limit the range of movement in adverse conditions. All stay cables consists of a bundle of 15mm diameter high tensile strands. Each strands is made up of 7 galvanized steel wires protected by a high density polyethylene (HDPE) sheath with petroleum max infill. The whole cable is further protected within a HDPE duct with helical lines to minimize the effects of wind/rain induced vibration.

Tsing Kau Bridge connects a dual 3-lane approach viaduct and two 2-lane ramps totaling 3.5km of roads half constructed and grade and half elevated up to 62m above ground with spans up to 115m in length.

Tsing Kau Bridge and viaduct was opened to traffic in May 1998.

1

图1 汀九桥（承冯铭硕教授惠赠）
Fig.1 Ting Kau Bridge (courtesy of Prof. Feng Mingshuo)

图2 汀九桥桥塔施工已结顶（编者自拍摄）
Fig.2 Pylon of Ting Kau Bridge constructed up to top (taken by the Editor)

图3 汀九桥在施工中（编者自拍摄）(a), (b)
Fig.3 Ting Kau Bridge under construction (taken by the Editor) (a), (b)

参考文献

1.香港民政事务总署. 汀九桥及高架引桥，中英双解，6页（承冯铭硕教授惠赠）

REFERENCES

1.HK Home Affairs Department. Tsing Kau Bridge and Approach Viaduct, in Chinese-English, 6pp (courtesy of Prof. Feng Mingshuo)

香港汲水门桥

汲水门大桥（图1，图2）连同马湾高架道路是直接通往位于赤蜡角的香港国际机场之青屿干线中两座重要桥梁。

汲水门大桥主跨430m，为公铁两用斜拉桥，在世界这类桥中占第三位，因为丹麦欧儿海峡桥主跨为490m，而我国武汉天兴洲桥主跨则为504m。

汲水门大桥全长820m（图3），它上层承载双向3车道，下层则承载2条铁路路轨及2条单线有盖的行车道（图4）。

与青马大桥一样，汲水门大桥在一般情况下，上层开放通车，下层用作维修通道，或在强风或发生紧急事故时，作交通改道之用。高7.89m的桥身外形与上下层中心特设的通气隙，经过风洞测试，验证确保桥梁气体动力稳定性。

混凝土桥塔高150m，塔脚用跳模建造，两塔柱用预应力横梁连接，桥塔顶部亦加上预应力以抵抗斜拉索锚碇所产生的爆破力。

主跨桥身构件长8.7m，用钢腹板与混凝土桥面板、底板构成。整座桥以176根斜拉索支承，每根拉索由51～102根直径15.7mm高强钢绞线，每股钢绞线由7根镀锌钢丝组成，外层包胶并注入软脂保护。斜拉索再用重型胶层外套保护。

在下层承托路轨的铁路道盘，承载时速达135km的火车，是一种特别设计的隔声及弹性系统，该系统以预应力混凝土板组成，承托于弹性支座上。

长503m的马湾高架道路基本上是一座大型桥梁，包括6个横跨马湾的桥跨，与长70m的大屿山引跨及汲水门桥边跨相似，它以预应力钢筋混凝土箱梁建成；其桥墩采用手挖沉箱为基础，深至基岩上。

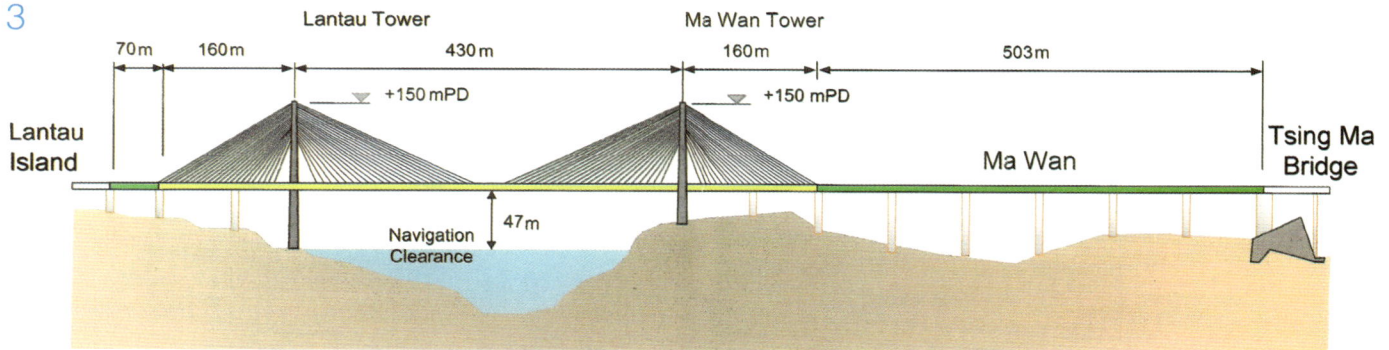

3

1

2

Hongkong Kap Shui Mun Bridge

Kap Shui Mun Bridge (Fig.1 and Fig.2) and Mawan Viaduct are 2 important structures in the Lantau Link which provides a direct access to the HK International Airport at Chek Lap Kok.

Kap Shui Mun Bridge is a cable-stayed one with main span length of 430m carrying both road and rail traffic. In the worldwide bridges with this type, it occupies the 3rd place, because the main span of Danish Oresund (sund means strait in Danish) Bridge is 490m, and that of Tianxingzhou Bridge is 504m.

The Kap Shui Mun Bridge is 820m long (Fig.3), its upper deck carries a dual 3-lane expressway, lower one 2 railway tracks and 2 single-lane sheltered carriageways (Fig.4).

Similar to Tsing Ma Bridge, in general case, the upper deck of Kap Shui Mun Bridge is open to traffic; the lower deck caters for maintenance access or traffic diversion during high winds or in emergencies. The shape of the 7.89m deep bridge deck, including the deliberate provision of an air gap at the center in both the upper and lower decks, has been verified by wind tunnel testing for aerodynamic stability.

The concrete tower is 150m high, the legs of tower were constructed by a jump-form process and joined together by post-tensioned struts. The tops of towers were also post-tensioned to resist the bursting forces caused by the stay cable anchorages.

8.7m long main span units with steel webs and concrete top and bottom slabs are built. The whole bridge is supported by 176 stay cables, each made up of 51 to 102 high-strength strands of 15.7mm diameter. Each strand is made up of 7 galvanized wires greased and protected by plastic sheathing. The stay cable is further protected by a heave duty plastic sheathing.

Truckform for the railway, which carries train running at speeds up to 135km/h on the lower deck, is a special sound-deadening and resilient system of post-tension concrete slabs, supported on elastomeric bearings.

The 503m long Mawan Viaduct consists of 6 spans over Mawan. Similar to the 70m Lantau approach span and Kap Shui Mun Bridge side spans it is constructed of post-tensioned reinforced concrete boxes with columns founded on hand dug caissons resting on bedrock.

图1 汲水门大桥（承冯铭硕教授惠赠）
Fig.1 Kap Shui Mun Bridge (courtesy of Prof. Feng Mingshuo)

图2 汲水门大桥（编者于1997年10月自拍摄）
Fig.2 Kap Shui Mun Bridge (taken by the Editor in Oct. 1997)

图3 汲水门大桥及马湾高架道路总布置图（承冯铭硕教授惠赠）
Fig.3 General layout of Kap Shui Mun Bridge and Ma Wan Viaduct (courtesy of Prof. Feng Mingshuo)

图4 汲水门大桥主梁透视图（承冯铭硕教授惠赠）
Fig.4 Perspective drawing of Kap Shui Mun Bridge (courtesy of Prof. Feng Mingshuo)

参考文献

1.香港民政事务总署. 汲水门桥及马湾高架道路，6页（承冯铭硕教授惠赠）

REFERENCES

1.HK Home Affairs Department . Kap Shui Mun Bridge and Mawan Viaduct, 6pp (courtesy of Prof. Feng Mingshuo)

苏通长江大桥

1. 引言

苏通大桥（图1）位于长江南岸苏州地区常熟的牛金镇和长江北岸的南通市，故简称苏通大桥。在西边，距离主跨为1 385m江阴悬索桥82km，在东边距离长江入海口108km，主桥主跨1 088m，为世界最长的斜拉桥。全长总布置（自北到南）：[（12×30m）+3×（11×50m）+（50m+ 9×75m）+（10×75m）]预应力混凝土连续梁桥+（2×100m+300m+1 088m+300m+2×100m）全钢箱梁斜拉桥+（5×75m）预应力混凝土连续梁桥+（140m+268m+140m）预应力混凝土连续刚构桥+3×（11×50m）预应力混凝土连续梁桥，除桥座全桥长8 146m（图2）。

2. 主桥

2.1 总体布置

主桥为双塔双索面斜拉结构，边跨具有3座桥墩。主要技术标准：①6−车道全封闭高速公路；②设计速度为100km/h；③桥结构标准设计周期，对主桥为100年，而对次主桥和引桥为60年；④汽车荷载为超20级，120级拖车；⑤桥标准宽度为34m；⑥纵向坡度≤3%，横向为2%；⑦通航净空：对主通航跨（有双通道的单孔），宽×高=891m×62m；对次通航跨（单通道单孔），220m×24m；对特殊通航跨（双通道单孔），220m×39m。至于抗震设防、风的设计标准、设计洪峰频率、设计水位和船舶撞击等在此不予详述。

2.2 结构体系

在桥塔拉和加劲大梁间，仅设置横向抗风支座及纵向具有限位功能的黏滞阻尼器，不设置垂直支承，阻尼器为消耗由风的脉冲、汽车制动和地震引起的动力效应，但不约束由温度和车辆引起的缓慢位移；当由静风、温度和车辆引起的相对纵向位移在阻尼器设计行程之内时，阻尼器将不约束主梁的运动，当超过时则将对主梁起约束作用。在塔柱和主梁间设置的阻尼器对每塔4只，全部8只。在主梁和过度墩和辅助墩间，设置纵向滑动支座并约束横向相对位移。

2

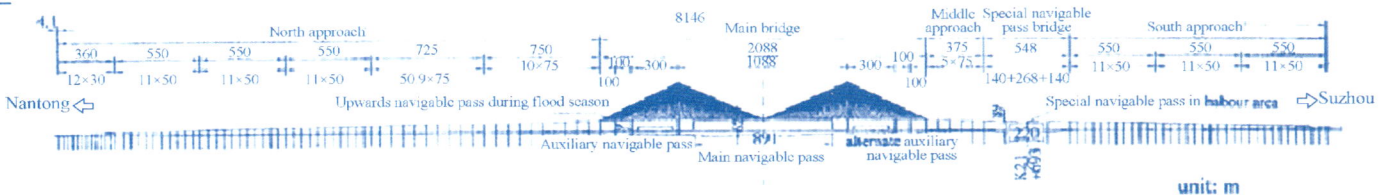

3

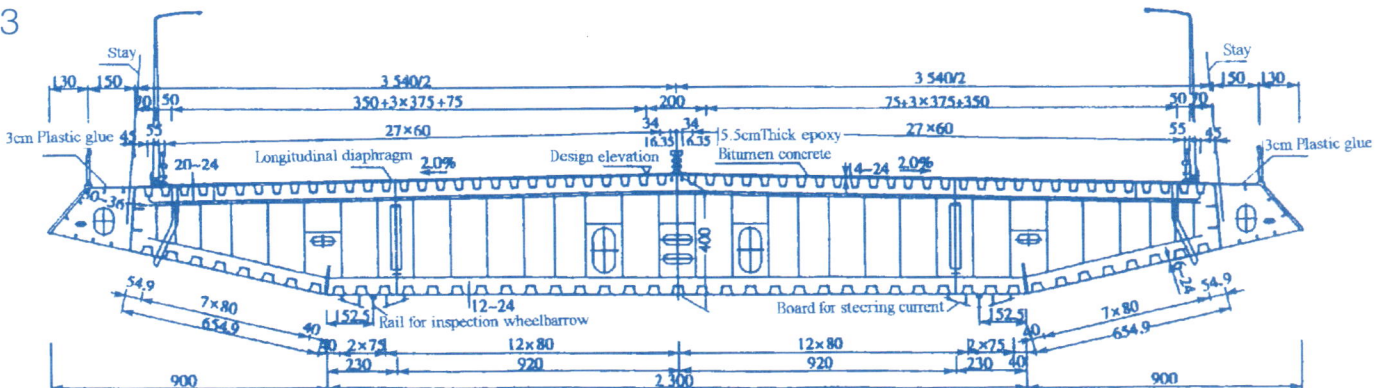

Sutong Yangtze River Bridge

1. Introduction

A large bridge (Fig.1) across the Yangtze River, in China, between Niujin Town of Changshu which belongs to Suzhou Region on the south bank and Nantong City on the north bank of the river; hence comes the abbreviation Sutong. Its distance is 82 km to the Jiangyin suspension bridge (main span 1 385m) in the west, and 108km to the mouth of entering sea of Yangtze River in the east. The main bridge is the world's longest cable-stayed bridge with a main span of 1 088m. The general layout combination of the whole bridge is (from north to south): [(12×30)+3×(11×50)+(50+9×75)+(10×75)]m PC (Prestressed concrete) continuous girder bridge + (2×100 +300 +1 088+300+2×100) m steel-box girder cable-stayed bridge +(5×75) m PC continuous girder bridge + (140+268 +140) m PC continuous rigid frame bridge +3×(11×50) m PC continuous girder bridge. The bridge has a total length of 8 146m excluding abutments (Fig.2)

2. Main Bridge

2.1 General layout

The main bridge is a cable – stayed structure with bi-pylon double cable plane and 3 piers in side spans. Main technical standards: ① fully closed 6-lane express highway; ② design speed 100km/h; ③ standard design period of bridge structure 100 years for main bridge and 60 years for secondary main bridge and approaching bridges; ④vehicle load: grade super 20, grade 120 trailer; ⑤standard width of bridge 34m; ⑥ longitudinal slope≤3%, transverse slope 2%; ⑦ navigable clearances: for main navigable span (single opening with double passages), width×height =891m×62m; for sub-navigable span (single opening with single passage), 220m×24m; for special navigable span (single opening with double passages), 220m×39m. Seismic fortification design standard, design standard for wind, design frequency of flood, design water level and ship impact load, etc., are not described here.

2.2 Structural system

Between pylon and stiffening girder, there are only set transverse bracings against wind and longitudinal viscous dampers with function to limit place and without setting vertical support. The damper has damping energy dissipation for the dynamic effects due to pulse wind, braking and earthquake, but does not restrain the slow displacements due to temperature and cars. When relative longitudinal displacements due to static wind, temperature and cars. When relative longitudinal displacements due to static wind, temperature and cars are in the design travel of damper, then dampers do not restrain the movement of main girder, when over, they will play the limitation role to main girder. The dampers are set between pylon and girder, and to each pylon 4 dampers are set, 8 in whole. Between main girder and transition and auxiliary piers, there are set longitudinal slide supports and restrain transverse relative displacements.

2.3 加劲大梁

采用封闭式流线形空心钢箱梁，并在每边设置风嘴。对大梁的外腹板，在塔区段，顶、底板和锚箱构件，采用较厚Q370q钢板。对其他构件可采用Q345q钢板。带风嘴的钢箱全宽41.0m，不包括风嘴顶板全宽35.4m，底板宽度为9.0m+23.0m+9.0m。在中心线处箱高4.0m，标准节段长度为16.0m，在边索区段，标准节段长度为12.0m，主梁构造如图3所示。

按照应力要求，对顶板，沿纵向在不同区段采用四种不同厚度14~24mm厚钢板，索塔附近厚度最大。沿横向，在靠近外腹板范围，采用两种厚20mm、24mm钢板，在顶板上，设置8~10mm厚U形加劲肋；对底板在不同区段沿纵向采用12~24mm厚度钢板，在底板上，设置6~8mmU形加劲肋。在钢箱内，设置横隔板，标准间距4.0m；一般其厚度为10mm，在索的吊点处，采用不同厚度横隔板，即靠近外腹板采用16mm厚钢板，在中心部12mm厚。在钢箱梁中，设置2纵向隔板，除在垂直支承处，压力大的区域和靠近塔座处，采用实腹横隔，其余处采用桁式的。

为了锚固斜拉索于主梁上，采用锚箱，它整体焊于腹板外侧，为保证索内内力合理地分布于主梁，主梁腹板内边和支承板在设计中予以加强。

图4示建成的主桥。图5示大桥通车。图6示大桥夜景。

2.4 斜拉索

采用强度为1 770MPa的平行钢丝索，最大规格为PEST-313，单索最大重量为59t。索在钢箱上的锚点标准间距为16.0m，在边跨边索区段为12.0m，在塔上锚点的间距为2.3~2.7m。索的设计寿命为50年，其更换能力曾予考虑。斜拉索的消能目的是控制最大侧向振幅不大于其长度的1/1 700。根据有关研究，在这座大桥中采用阻尼器和气动措施的组合，它们也是预设的，然后按实际情况考虑是否对辅助索应安装辅助索用构件。

5a

5b

2.3 Stiffening girder

A closed and streamlined shallow steel box girder with fairing (wind mouth) set on each side is adopted. For the external web of girder, the top and bottom plates in the segments of pylon area and for the anchorage box, thicker plate is required to use steel Q370q. For the other members, it is to adopt steel Q345q. The whole width of steel box with fairings is 41.0m, the width of top deck excluding fairings is 35.4m, the width of bottom plate is (9.0+23.0+9.0)m. The depth of box at central line is 4.0 m, the standard length of segment is 16.0m, that is 12.0m in end cable area. The construction of main girder is shown in Fig.3.

According to the requirements of stress, for the top plate 4 different thicknesses of 14~24mm are adopted in various segments along longitudinal direction, those near eable pylons are the max. Transversely in the field near external web 2 thicknesses 20mm and 24mm are used, and on top plate 8~10mm thick U-shaped stiffening ribs are set. For bottom plate different thicknesses of 12~24mm in various segments along longitudinal direction are used. On bottom plate 6~8mm thick U-shaped stiffening ribs are set. In steel box, there are set transverse diaphragms with standard spacing of 4.0m. Generally its thickness is 10mm, at hung point of cable the diaphragms with variable thicknesses are adopted, i.e., near external web it is 16mm thick and in center 12mm thick. In steel box girder, 2 longitudinal diaphragms are set, except that at vertical supports, the areas with heavy compression and near pylon, solid-web diaphragms are used; at the other place, they will be trussed.

For the anchorage of cable stays on main girder, anchorage boxes are used, welded integrally on external side of web plate. To guarantee the reasonable distribution of the force in cable stays to main girder, the internal side of web plate of girder and bearing plate has been strengthened in design.

Fig.4 shows the completed main bridge, Fig.5 shows the opening to traffic. Fig.6 shows the night scene of bridge.

2.4 Cable stays

Parallel wire cable stays with strength of 1 770MPa are used, the max. standard is PEST-313, and the max. weight of a single cable is 59t. The standard spacing of anchorage points of stays on steel box is 16.0m, and it is 12.0m in end cable area of side spans. The spacings of anchorage point on pylon are 2.3~2.7m. The design life of stays is 50 years and their replace ability has been considered. The damping aim of cable stays is to control the max. Lateral amplitude not larger than 1/1 700 of their length. Following related study, in this bridge the combination of dampers and pneumatic measures is adopted; also in stays and main girder, they are preset. Then it can be considered whether the auxiliary cable members should be installed according to practical cases.

2.5 Cable pylon

Two inverted Y-shape pylons are adopted and a lower transverse beam is set under main girder. Pylon height is 300.40m and that over deck is 230.41m. Hollow box section is adopted for the pylon:

图5 大桥通车（承游庆仲教授级高工惠赠）
Fig.5 Bridge open to traffic (courtesy of Senior Engr. Prof. You Qingzhong) (a), (b)

图6 苏通大桥夜景（承游庆仲教授级高工惠赠）(a)
Fig.6 Night scene of Sutong Bridge (courtesy of Senior Engr. Prof. You Qingzhong) (a)

2.5 索塔

采用Y形混凝土塔和在主梁下设置横梁，塔高300.40m，在桥面上高230.41m。对塔采用空箱截面；上部塔柱为对称单室单箱，外部尺寸由9.0m×8.0m变化到10.0m×17.4m，在斜拉索锚固平面壁厚为120cm，而在非锚固平面为100cm。塔柱中部和下部为非对称的单室单箱，外部尺寸由10.8m×6.5m变化到15.0m×8.0m，壁厚为120cm和150cm。图7示索塔构造，图8示主桥塔和索。

对斜拉索在塔上的锚固，1~3号桥墩，直接锚固于塔的混凝土体上，其余则锚固于埋入上塔柱混凝土内的钢锚箱上。钢锚箱成段制造，长7.12~8.52m，宽度2.40m，高度2.30~3.55m，节段采用高强螺栓连接；钢锚箱和塔的侧向接触面用剪力钉连接，而最下端则直接支承于混凝土底座上。

2.6 桥墩

对辅助墩和过渡墩，采用普通钢筋混凝土分离式薄壁墩，高约60m；单幅平面尺寸为850cm×500cm，标准壁厚为50cm；因支座布置等构造需要，距墩顶450cm范围内向主桥和引桥侧各加宽150cm，墩顶平面尺寸为850cm×800cm。

2.7 基础

对桥塔基础，设置131根、直径d=2.8m/2.5m钻孔灌注桩（附加4个保留桩位）。主墩No.4（主桥下8个桥墩自北向南编号为Nos.1-8）下桩长117m，而主墩No.5下桩长114m。桩的承台为哑铃形，在每一塔柱下，承台平台尺寸为51.3m×48.1m，基础厚度：在边缘为5.0m变化至最后处的13.3m。承台顶面垂直于下塔柱中心线。两承台用一平面尺寸为11.0m×28.1m、厚6.0m的系梁连接。

对近塔辅助墩塔基础采用36根、d=2.8m/2.5m钻孔灌注桩（钢护筒内径280cm），对主墩No.3，桩长98m，而对主墩No.6，桩长101m。承台平面尺寸为52.0m×32.5m，厚度从边缘的4.0m变化到最厚处的10.3m。

对远塔辅助墩和基础，均采用19根、d=2.8m/2.5m钻孔灌注桩，对主墩No.1、No2和No.8桩长为108m，而对No.7，则长110m。全部承台平面尺寸均为43.2m×19.3m，厚度从边缘的4.0m变化到最厚处的8.3m。

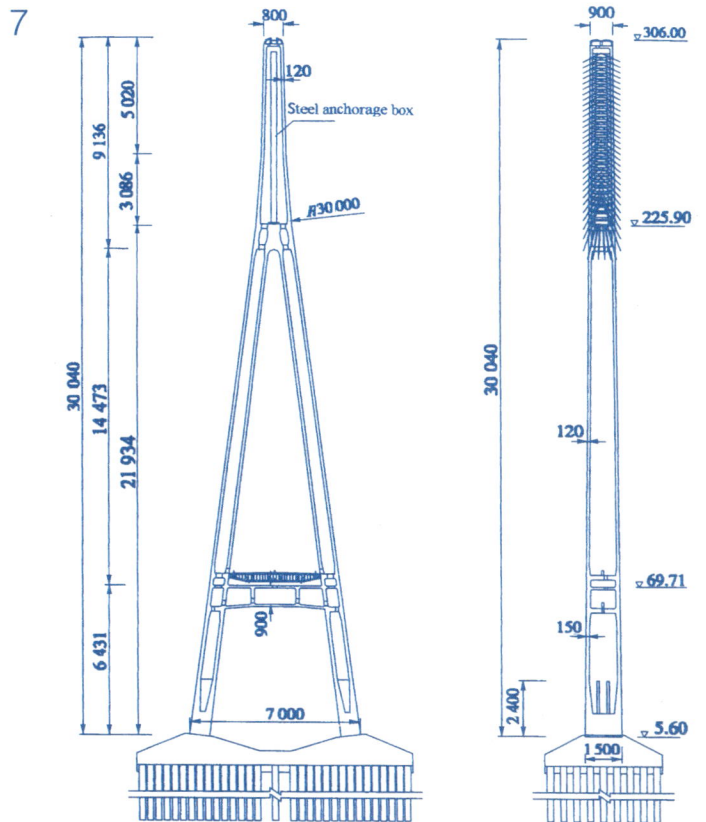

the upper pylon column is asymmetrical single-cell single box with external dimensions varying from 9.0m×8.0m to 10.0m×17.4m with wall thickness of 120cm at anchorage plane and 100cm at non-anchorage plane. The shape of mid and lower pylon columns is unsymmetrical single-cell single box with external dimensions varying from 10.8m×6.5m to 15.0×8.0m with wall thickness of 120cm and 150cm. Fig.7 shows the construction of cable pylon, Fig.8 shows the pylon and cables of main bridge.

For the anchorage of stays on pylon, the 1st~3rd piers are anchored directly on concrete body of pylon, and the others are on steel anchorage boxes which are embedded in concrete of upper pylon column. Steel anchorage box is manufactured in segment with length of 7.12~8.52m, width of 2.40 m and height of 2.30~3.55m, and segments are connected with high-strength bolts. The lateral contact face of steel anchorage box and pylon is connected with shear nails and the lowest end is supported directly on concrete plinths.

2.6 Pier

For auxiliary and transition piers, common reinforced concrete separate thin-wall structures are used with height of about 60m. The plane dimensions of single width pier are 850cm×500cm, standard wall thickness is 50cm. Because of the construction requirements of arranging support etc. in the field of 450cm over pier top, each of 150cm is increased towards the main and approaching bridge to transition pier top, with plane dimensions of 850cm×800cm.

2.7 Foundation

For pylon foundation, 131 bored and filling piles (additionally, 4 reserve pile sites) are set with d=2.8m/2.5m. Under main pier No.4 (numbering 8 pier under main bridge into Nos.1-8 from north to south) the pile length is 117m and 114m under main pier No.5. The bearing platform of pile is dumbbell-shaped. Under every pylon column, its plane dimension are 51.3m×48.1m with foundation thicknesses of 5.0m at edge varying to the thickest of 13.3m. The top of bearing platform is perpendicular to the central line of lower pylon column. 2 platforms are connected by a tie beam of 11.0m×28.1m with thickness of 6.0m.

For the foundation of auxiliary pier near pylon, 36 bored and filling pile with d=2.8m/2.5m (the internal diameter of steel protecting sleeve is 280cm) are used. The pile length of main pier No.3 is 98m and that of No.6 is 101m. The plane dimensions of bearing platform are 52.0m×32.5m with thickness of 4.0m at edge varying to the thickest of 10.3m.

For the foundation of auxiliary and transition piers far from pylon, both of 19 bored filling piles with d=2.8m/2.5m are used. The pile length of main piers No.1, 2 &8 is 108m and that of No.7 is 110m. All the plane dimensions of platforms are 43.2m×19.3m with the thickness of 4.0m at edge varying to the thickest of 8.3m.

Considering the importance of Sutong Bridge and the non-uniformity of stress distribution of group piles, to guarantee the safety of foundation structure, all the pile foundations under main bridge are required to jet mortar to the bottom of pile to increase the bearing capacities of single

图7 索塔构造（尺寸单位：cm）
Fig.7 Construction of cable pylon (dimension unit: cm)

图8 主桥塔和索（承游庆仲教授级高工惠赠）
Fig.8 Pylon and cables of main bridge (courtesy of Senior Engr. Prof. You Qingzhong)

图9 主桥减振阻尼器（承游庆仲教授级高工惠赠）
Fig.9 Damper on main bridge for absorbing vibration (courtesy of Senior Engr. Prof. You Qingzhong)

考虑苏通大桥的重要性和群桩应力分布的不均匀性，为保证基础结构的安全可靠，主桥下所有桩基础要求桩底注浆以增强单桩承载力40%以上。

对苏通大桥，设置了减振阻尼器（图9）以防地震时发生破坏。

图10（a~d）示大桥在施工中。图11示4号墩基础构造。

3. 副桥及引桥

3.1 副桥

副桥为一座连续刚构结构，主跨268m，位于主航通道南侧河谷内，供进出常熟港船只使用。在两通航通道中心距离约为1.7km。为了减小对主桥景观的影响，在跨步设计曾对梁桥进行分析和研究：钢连续梁桥和连续刚构桥。考虑我国缺乏建造钢连续梁桥的经验，最后预应力混凝土连续刚构桥方案被采用。上部结构设计为分开的双桥，在主墩顶部，两箱梁用横隔梁连接，两主墩整体固结于主梁。在两过渡顶部，设纵向滑动支承，在横向靠近中心分隔带，支座为固定的，而在另侧，可横向移动。对主梁，采用单室单箱截面，顶宽16.4m，底宽7.5m，在支座处梁高15.0m，在跨中为4.5m，按1.6次抛物线变化。最小顶板厚度为32cm，腹板厚度按70-60-50-45cm等级逐渐变化，底板则按17~32cm变化。

对主墩，采用双薄壁空心截面，墩柱平面尺寸为2.5m×7.5m，长侧壁厚60cm，短侧80cm，沿墩底在200cm范围内为实心，对过渡墩，也采用混凝土空心截面，平面尺寸为4.0m×7.5m，长边壁厚70cm，短边100cm，顶底在一定范围内为实心。

对主墩，采用42根、d=280cm/250cm钻孔灌注桩整体基础。北墩下桩长102m，南墩113m，承台平面尺寸为49.6m×33.2m，厚7.0m。对过渡墩采用分离式基础，9根钻孔灌注桩，d=180cm，桩长110m，承台平面尺寸为14.0m×14.0m，厚4.0m。

3.2 引桥

引桥也建成分离式双桥，每桥为单箱截面，从北岸，第一单元为12×30m跨预应力混凝土连续梁，引桥截面高度1.8m。第2、第3和第4单元为11×50m预应力混凝土连续梁，等截面高度为2.8m，而后两单元9×75m和10×75m预应力混凝土连续梁，等截面高度4.0m。通过主桥，有一个单元5×75m预应力混凝土连续梁等截面高度。然后通过副桥

10b

pile by more 40%.

On Sutong Bridge, there are set dampers (Fig.9) for absorbing vibration to avoid the failure in earthquake.

Fig.10(a~d) shows the bridge under construction. Fig.11 shows the construction of No.4 pier.

3. Secondary bridge and approaching bridges

3.1 Secondary bridge

The secondary bridge is a continuous rigid frame structure with main span of 268m. It is located over river valley on south side of main navigable passage and it is used for the ships to pass in and out Changshu Harbour. The central distance between these 2 navigable passages is about 1.7km. For decreasing the influence to landscape of main bridge, in preliminary design the analysis and study of girder bridge were conducted: steel continuous girder bridge were continuous rigid frame bridge. Considering that there is lack of experience in China in constructing steel continuous girder bridge, finally the project of PC continuous rigid frame bridge is adopted. The super structure is designed to be separate into dual bridges. On the top of main pier 2 box girders are connected with diaphragm beam, and 2 main piers are integrally fixed with the main girders. On the top of 2 transition piers, longitudinal slide supports are set. In transverse direction, near central separate strip the supports are fixed, and on the other side they can move transversely. For main girder, the section of single-cell single box is adopted with top width of 16.4m, and bottom width of 7.5m. The girder depth is 15.0m at support and 4.5m at span center varying following parabola with power of 1.6. The min. top slab thickness of box is 32cm, web thicknesses vary following 70-60-50-45cm, the thicknesses of slab bottom vary following 170~32cm.

For the main pier, double thin-wall hollow section is adopt. The plane dimensions of pier column are 2.5m×7.5m with wall thicknesses of 60cm in long side and 80cm is short side, and being solid in 200cm field along pier top and bottom. For transition pier, a concrete hollow section is also adopted; the plane dimensions are 4.0m×7.5m. The wall thickness of long side is 70cm and that of short size is 100cm; the top and bottom are solid in definite fields.

For the main pier, the integral foundation is used with 42 bored filling piles of d=2.8m/2.5m. The length of piles under north pier is 102m and that under south pier is 113m. The plane dimensions of bearing platform ate 49.6m×33.2m with thickness of 7.0m. For the transition pier, the separate foundation is used with 9 bored and filling piled of d=180cm and pile length of 110m. The plane dimensions of bearing platform are 14.0m×14.0m with thickness of 4.0m.

3.2 Approach spans

The approaching bridges are also constructed to be separate into dual bridge each with single box section.

From north bank, the 1st unit with (12×30)m-spans PC continuous girder of north approaching has depth of 1.8m. The 2nd, 3rd and 4th units are (11×50)m of PC continuous girder with equal depth of 2.8m, then there are adopted 2 units of (9×75)m and (10×75)m PC

10a

图10　大桥在施工中（承游庆仲教授级高工惠赠）
(a) 北引桥；(b) 5号墩（靠苏州侧）
Fig.10 Bridge under construction (courtesy of Senior Engr. Prof. You Qingzhong)
(a) north approaching bridge, (b) pylon on No.5 pier
(near the side of Suzhou)

有3单元11×50m以连接南岸。图10示75m跨箱梁。其他构造细部、预应力钢筋的安排和下部结构等在此不予赘述。但应说明上部结构为分段预制的采用用架桥机悬拼工法进行施工。节段连接采用密型齿剪刀键，环氧树脂接缝，采用横梁转向块。在箱梁纵向，在预应力混凝土箱内采用体外预应力束。体外束体系包括可更换锚固部分、转向设施以及可拆卸的体外束限位装置。

4. 四项世界纪录

（1）主跨为1 088m的斜拉桥，超过原世界纪录、主跨为890m的日本多多拉斜拉桥198m；

（2）300.4m高的主塔，从塔顶到塔底垂直误差控制不超过10cm；

（3）262根钻孔灌注桩（每墩131根），国际标准2%缺陷，苏通大桥是0。262根桩支承主桥承台、索塔，上部结构共约50万t重量；

（4）苏通大桥共有272根斜拉索，每根均由313根ϕ7钢丝组成，钢丝强度为1 770MPa，全由上海宝钢生产，使用寿命由30年延长至50年。272根斜拉索中有56根长度打破世界纪录，其中最长的8根长度为577m。

5. 国际荣誉

苏通大桥获得乔治·理查德森奖，是迄今为止我国获得的桥梁工程的最高奖。

11

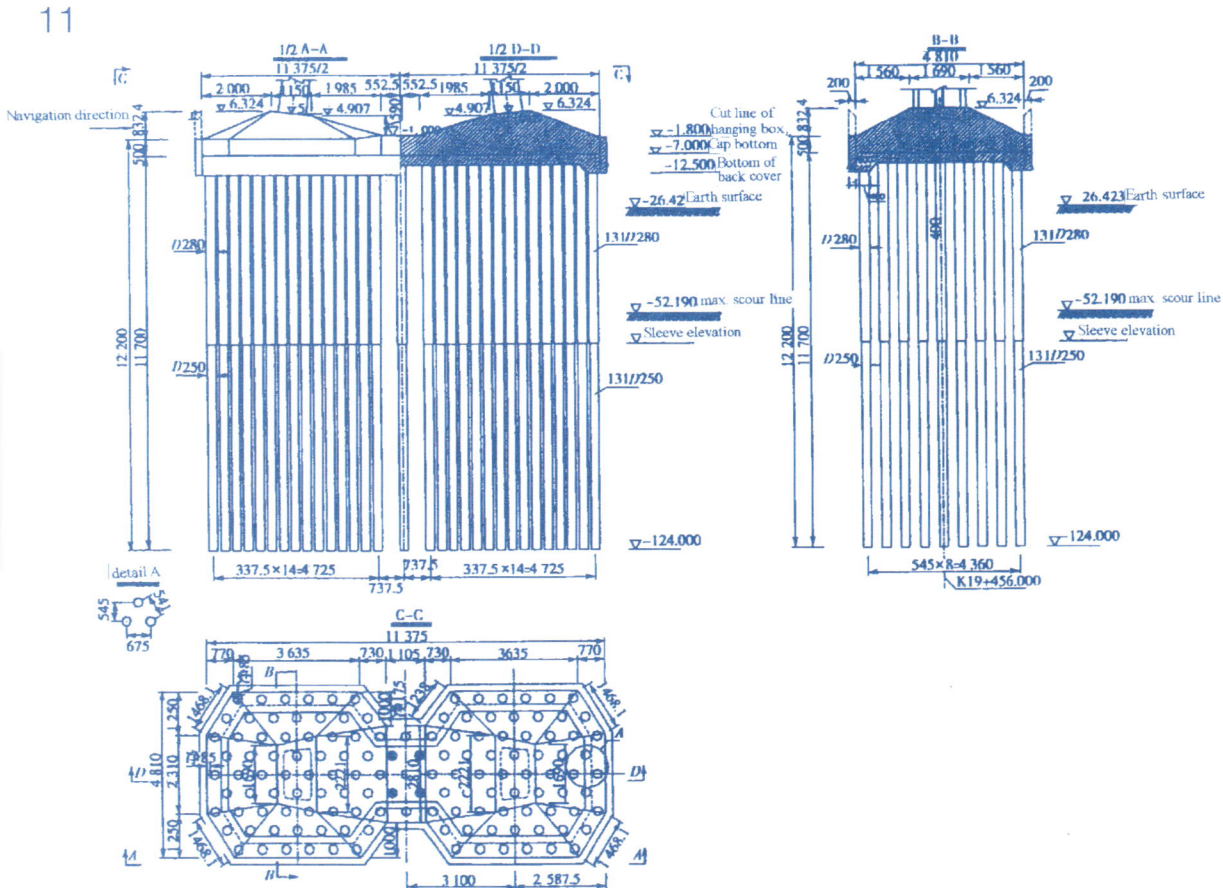

图10 大桥在施工中（承游庆仲教授级高工惠赠）
(c) 远视；(d) 4号墩（靠南通侧）
Fig.10 Bridge under construction (courtesy of Senior Engr. Prof. You Qingzhong)
(c) distant view, (d) No.4 pier (near the side of Natong)

图11 4号墩基础构造
Fig.11 Foundation construction of No.4 pier

10c

10d

continuous girders with equal depth of 4.0m. Through main bridge, there is a unit of (5×75)m PC continuous girder with equal depth. Then through secondary main bridge, there are 3 units of (11×50)m equal depth PC continuous girder to connect south bank. Fig.10 shows the section of 75m-span box girder. The other construction details and the arrangement of prestressed steels and substructure, etc. are not described here. But it should be mentioned that the superstructures are prefabricated in segments and constructed by splicing in hanging state with erecting bridge machine. The connection of segments if conducted by adopting close tooth shear keys and filling the joints with epoxy resin, and the type of transverse beam is adopted as the device for changing direction. In the longitudinal direction of box girder, there are adopted the external prestressed tendons in PC box. The external prestressed tendons system consists of: changeable anchorages, devices for changing direction, tendons and dismountable limit devices of external tendon.

4. 4 Worldwide Records

(1) Cable stayed bridge with main span of 1 088m, exceeds Japanese Tatara Cable Stayed Bridge with main span of 890m by 198m.

(2) For main pylons with height of 300.4m, the construction error of perpendicularity from bottom up to top is controlled not exceeding 10cm.

(3) The defect of 262 bored filling piles (131 piles under each pier) is zero, the International Standard allows 2%. The 262 piles support 5×10^5t weight or so from the bearing platforms of main bridge, cable pylons and superstructures.

(4) In Sutong Bridge, there are 272 stayed cables in total, every cable is constituted of $313\phi 7$ wires with strength of 1 770MPa, all of wires were produced by Shanghai Baogang Company, the service life of wires is extended from 30 years to 50 years. Among the 272 stayed cables, there are 56 cables with length more than that of the original worldwide record, the length of the longest 8 cables reaches 577m.

5. International Honour

Sutong Bridge gain George Richardson Prize, up to now, it is the highest bridge prize gained by Chinese bridge.

REFERENCES

1.Ding Hanshan, Ding Dajun. The Suzhou-Nantong Bridge — worldwide longest-span cable stayed bridge. RIA. 2006(3): 49-54

武汉天兴洲公铁两用斜拉桥

　　武汉天兴洲公铁两用长江大桥（图1a~d）位于武汉二桥（斜拉桥，*l*=400m，1995年建成通车）下游9.5km处，跨越长江中小洲——天兴洲，建成后是世界最长的公铁两用桥。主桥为双塔3索面斜拉桥，跨越南支流，跨度分布为95m+196m+504m+196m+95m，其南引桥为15×40.7m箱梁桥，上层为公路6车道，下层为4线（8轨），其中2线按1级铁路干线设计，另2线为客运，3根加肋梁为新型板桥结构，由宽度为2×15m的N形钢桁架组成，桁高为15.2m，节间长度为14m（图2）。对公路桥，采用正交异性板或混凝土桥面和钢桁架组合体系；对铁路桥，采用混凝土桥面和钢桁架组合体系，跨越长江北支流：62×40.7m箱梁+（54.2m+2×80m+54.2m）混凝土连续梁+4×40.7m箱梁。公路和铁路建造在一起的长度为2 842m，而后分开成公路和铁路平行，公路位于上游，铁路则在下游。6车道公路引桥全长为8 043m。公路按运营速度80km/h设计，客运铁路设计速度为200km/h，其模拟动力设计速度为250km/h。该大桥于2004年9月28日开始兴建，计划于2008年8月31日建成，但因故推迟于2009年建成。桥塔为混凝土结构，倒Y形，在桩帽上的高度为188.5m，在塔的两边，有用镀锌平行钢丝组成的3×16ϕ 7拉索。直径3.4m钻孔桩用作塔的基础，2号墩有32根桩，3号墩则有40根，采用在由软硬物体组成的非匀质砾岩中用新技术打桩，首次在国内采用由承建单位开发的抗扭能力为30t·m的动力钻头。在塔上设置大吨位的液压阻尼器。采用双壁钢围堰作为桩帽。在2号桩墩双壁钢围堰浮运就位后，采用从锚固墩预应力准确定位技术施工。3号墩钢围堰尺寸为70m（长）×44m（宽）×15.5m（高），是亚洲最大的，整体成功浮运就位。图3示3号塔墩，用以浇筑混凝土直径3.6m的保护套，图4示桩的钢筋框笼。

1

1a

Wuhan Tianxingzhou Highway-Railway Bi-Purposed Cable-Stayed Bridge

1b

The Wuhan Tianxingzhou highway-railway bi-purposed Bridge over Yangtze River (Fig.1a~d) in located on the lower reaches 9.5km to the 2nd Wuhan Bridge (cable-stayed bridge with main l=400m, completed and opened in 1995). This bridge is constructed to span the Tianxingzhou which is an islet standing in Yangtze River, and will be the largest one in the world after completion. The major bridge spanning over south river branch is a cable-stayed one with 2 pylons and 3 cable planes, the spans of which distribute as follows: 95m+196m+504m+196m+95m, with south approaching 15×40.7m box girders, its super deck is designed for 6-lane highway, and the lower for 4-line (8 tracks), among which 2 are designed following 1st grade truck line and the other 2 following the special use passenger transport, 3 stiffening girders are new-type plate-truss composite structures of N-shape trusses with the width=2×15m, the height of

图1 天兴洲大桥（承段雪炜高工惠赠）
(a) 建成全景；(b) 建成前一刻
Fig.1 Tianxingzhou Bridge (courtesy of Senior Engr. Duan Xuewei)
(a) full view completed, (b) a moment before completion

图1 天兴洲大桥（承段雪炜高工惠赠）
(c) 建成的主跨；(d) 在朝晖中
Fig.1 Tianxingzhou Bridge (courtesy of Senior Engr. Duan Xuewei)
(c) completed main span, (d) in morning sunshine

图2 建成的钢加劲桁架（承段雪炜高工惠赠）
Fig.2 Completed steel stiffening truss (courtesy of Senior Engr. Duan Xuewei)

图3 No.3塔墩用以浇注混凝土直径3.6m的保护套
Fig.3 Pylon pier for pouring concrete of protecting sleeve with diameter of 3.6m

图4 桩的钢筋框笼
Fig.4 Reinforcement frame of pile

truss=15.2m and panel length=14m(Fig.2). For highway bridge, the composite system of orthotropic plate or concrete deck and steel truss is adopted; for railway bridge the composite system of concrete deck and steel truss is used. The major bridge spanning north river branch: 62×40.7m box girders+ (54.2m+2×80m+54.2m) continuous concrete girders+4×40.7m box girders. The length with highway and railway constructed together is 2 842m, then is separated into highway and railway running parallel with highway being located on upper reaches and the railway on lower. The whole length of 6-lane highway approaching is 8 043m. The highway is designed following operating velocity 80km/h, and the design velocity of railway for passenger transport is 200km/h, with a simulating dynamical design of velocity of 250km/h. This Bridge had been constructed on 28th Sept. 2004 and the constructed completion will be scheduled on 31st Aug. 2008, but has been postponed to be completed in 2009 for some reason. The main pylons are concrete structures with inverted Y-shape, its height on pile cap is 188.5 m, on both sides of pylon there are 3×16ϕ7 stays constituted of galvanizing parallel wires. The bored piles with diameter of 3.4m are used as the foundations of pylon, there are 32 piles under No.2 pier and 40 under No.3, these piles were driven by using the new technique in non-uniform conglomerate composed of soft and hard matter, the dynamical bit developed by constructer with torsional capacity of 30t · m was adopted firstly in China. On the pylon, there are set hydraulic dampers with large tonnage. A double-walled steel cofferdam is adopted as the cap of piles. After the double-walled steel coffer dam of No.2 pile pier was moved floating into place by transport, it was constructed by precise prestressing locating technique from anchored pier. The dimensions of steel cofferdam No.3 pier are 70m (length) × 44m (width) × 15.5m (height) is the largest one in Asia which was integrally transported by floating method and located successfully. Fig.3 shows the driving of the steel protecting sleeve with diameter of 3.6m for casting concrete piles. Fig.4 shows the reinforcement frame of pile.

参考文献

1.武汉天兴州道桥投资有限公司. 武汉天兴州公铁两用长江大桥简介, 4页

REFERENCES

1.Wuhan Tianxingzhou Road-Bridge Investment-Development Co. Ltd. Simple Introduction of Wuhan Tianxingzhou Highway-Railway Bi-purpose Yangtze River Bridge, 4pp

2. Ding Dajun, Ivan Balaz. Tianxingzhou bridge with span of 504m — the world's record in the category of dual-purpose cable-stayed bridge (in Czech). Konstrukce. 2006(1):60-62

澳门双层斜拉桥

澳门双层斜拉桥（图1，图2，图2中塔为高348m的澳门塔）是从澳门半岛通向凼仔岛（澳门大学在此岛上）的第3座桥，因为1974年和1994年建造的前两座大桥，在交通高峰时通常拥挤，不得不建新桥。新桥位于珠江三角洲，因此在近50年内有概率超过10%发生动力峰值为0.1g的地震。

场地土壤状况分为3层，每层的厚度、密实情况和塑性特性不同。顶层厚8~10m，由淤泥、流动塑性黏土、散砂组成；中间层厚6m，为软塑黏土或低密度砂；底层厚10~40m，为中等密实和密实的砂以及硬塑或硬黏土；下卧层为花岗岩床，在深22~61m处从北向南倾斜。

在高潮位时，竖向通航净空28m，航道至少净宽150m。桥按通过4 000DWT、速度为8m/s的船只设计。在航道两边作了防护桥墩对特殊碰撞的防护。

主桥设计为预应力混凝土等截面单箱梁，主跨跨度为180m，两侧跨跨度各为110m。新桥分别在上层每向设有3车道，下层每向有2车道，在后些时候可能改成双轨轻型铁道。包括在下层上还有2根直径为800mm的给水管线和600mm宽7层缆索管道。引桥每跨60m，为预应力混凝土等截面箱梁，共22跨。

为了简化施工和对截面提供合理的横向力，桥设计成单室双箱梁，上层桥面宽13m，承担3个3.5m宽车道和1m宽人行道，底层宽8m，设计极限承担单车道和一4m宽轻钢铁轨。在两箱梁间有3.1m宽空间，用以安置中间桥塔。但是为了提供足够的位置锚固斜拉索，锚固区被扩大，在这些点桥几乎有16m宽。

主桥为混凝土斜拉桥，斜拉索设置在平行的平面内，为竖琴式安排。每一侧跨具有5%纵坡，用半径为3 500m的曲线与中跨连接。混凝土主梁截面高度为6.13m，由锚固为10m间距的斜拉索悬支。侧跨支承在竖向可移动的支承上，在主梁和塔之间设置有侧向支承。斜拉桥的纵向移动由一纵向"浮动"体系所约束。由于跨长，在一预期的地震时产生的最大跨

1

Macau Double-Deck Prestressed Concrete Cable-Stayed Bridge

Macau double-decked cable-stayed bridge (Figs.1, 2, the tower in Fig.2 is the Macau tower with height of 348m) is the 3rd bridge from Macau Peninsula to Dangzai Island (Macau University is located on this Island). Because 2 former bridges constructed in 1974 and 1994 were generally crowded during traffic peaks, so it is necessary to construct a new bridge. The new bridge is located on Zhujiang Delta, hence in recent 50 years, there an earthquake will occur with dynamic peak of 0.1g, the probability exceeds 10%.

The state of site soil is divided into 3 layers, the thickness, density and plastic property of every layer are different. The top layer is 8~10m thick and mud flowing plastic clay and loose sand; the middle layer is 6m thick and consists of soft plastic clay or low-density sand; the bottom is 10~40m thick and there are sand with mid-dense to dense sand and hard plastic clay or hard clay, the underlying granite bedrock with embedded depth of 22~61m, dipping from north to south.

When the tide water level is high, the vertical navigable clearance is necessary to be 28m, the vertical navigable clearance is necessary to be 28m, the least navigable clear width 150m. This bridge is designed to accommodate vessels of 40 00DWT and ship velocity of 8m/s. Both sides of navigation channel, the piers are protected for special impact.

The main bridge is designed as single PC box girder with equal section; the main span is 180m and 2 side spans are 110m. On the upper deck of new bridge, there are set 3 lanes in each way, on the lower, 2 lanes in each way, after sometime, they are possible to be reformed into double-track light railway. There are also 2 supply lines with diameter of 800mm and 7-layer cable ducts with width of 600mm included on the lower deck. Every span of approaches is 60m PC box girder, totaling 22 spans.

For simplifying construction and providing reasonable transverse forces, the bridge is designed into single-cabled box girder for the section, the width of upper deck is 13m on which there are 3 3.5m wide lanes and a 1m-wide side walk, the width of lower deck is 8m with ultimate capacity to carry out a single lane and a 4m-wide light railway. Between 2 box girders, there is 3.1m-wide space to set the middle pylon of main span. For providing sufficient place to anchor the stayed cables, the anchored area is enlarged, where the width of bridge is almost 16m.

The main bridge is concrete cable-stayed one with the stayed cables in parallel plane, i.e., in harp arrangement, each side span has a 5% longitudinal gradient to connect the middle span by using a curve with radius of 3 500m. The section depth of concrete girder is 6.13m, suspended with stayed cables anchored in spacing of 10m, the side span is carried on movable bearing in vertical. Between girders and pylons, there is set lateral bearings. The longitudinal displacement of cable-stayed bridge is restrained with a floating longitudinal system. Owing to the max. span displacement of 150mm

图1 澳门双层斜拉桥（承谢蔚鸿高工惠赠）
Fig.1 Macau Double-Stayed Cable Bridge
(courtesy of Senior Engr. Xie Weihong)

度位移为150mm，这可很容易为跨端伸缩缝所吸收。因此浮式体系使二塔在其间可吸收水平地震力，而不至使桥墩承受超额的地震力。该体系也可降低由温度波动引起的热应力。

在此设有如通常斜拉桥中所采用的弹性约束，因为箱梁中没有横隔。

主桥箱梁设计为薄壁截面高度为6.13m的箱形截面，而桥面具有1%的横向坡度。为了改进箱梁的强度，支座处底板厚度为1.4m，相应地在两腹板间设置垂直横隔。在顶板底部，设置横撑以防止在箱梁内产生屈曲和扭曲应力。在塔墩支承点处2m厚的横隔，在端支承处和索锚处减小为1.2m。

为了抵抗由在上、下桥面上的交通荷载所引起的拉应力，箱梁的顶底板配置了侧向预应力钢绞线。为了减小箱梁的主拉应力，沿桥腹板用垂直预应力筋和束加强，侧向预应力位置在腹板和底板连接处箱梁节点。有一种风险，即预应力管道可能削弱箱形截面，为了预防这点，在箱梁底板和腹板外面有一道U形"边箍"，在此预应力钢铰线可安排过底板，斜拉索则锚固于主梁腹板下面的块体内。在钢预应力索和腹板的外部，设置U形"护梁"。由于在箱梁内部通行车辆，通风、防火和消防设施必需在箱内设置。垂直净空应限制，因此必须充分利用侧向空间。底板宽度对箱梁内力是敏感的，因此不得不尽可能减小以提供足够的净空。因此在箱梁中采用倾斜的腹板，这样可简化索力传递并有较好的分布。

桥的高跨比为1/29.4，表明结构的厚重。箱梁外面的"边板"是为改善层次而设计的，而在腹板中心，接近中性轴处，沿梁每隔5m设置0.8m直径孔洞以流通空气和从隧道来的烟气。主梁足够刚劲，但比较主塔略柔。从结构受力观

occurring in a predicted earthquake, it is easy to be absorbed by the expansion joint at span end. Therefore the floating system can make the space between 2 pylons to absorb horizontal seismic action, and does not make the piers to bear the over loaded seismic action, this system can decrease also the thermal stress due to temperature.

There is set elastic restraint as adopted generally in cable-stayed bridges, because in box girder there is no diaphragm.

Main box girder is designed as a thin-walled box section with depth of 6.13m, the deck has 1% transverse slope. For promoting the strength of box girder, the thickness of bottom slab at bearing is 1.4m and vertical diaphragms is correspondingly set within the web. On the bottom of top deck, there will be a cross-strut to prevent warp and distortion stress produced in box girder. At the bearing point of pylon pier, there is set 2m thick diaphragm, at the end support and cable anchorage position, the thickness of diaphragm is decreased to 1.2m.

For resisting the tension stress produced due to traffic loads, on the upper and lower decks, in top and bottom slabs, there are set lateral prestressed strands. For minimising the principal tensile stress on the box girder, the web slabs are strengthed by using vertical prestressed bars and tendons along the bridge. The anchorages of lateral prestressed steel strands, vertical bars and longitudinal tendons, are located at the connection of web and bottom slabs of the box girder joint. There is a risk that the prestressing ducts might weaken the box section; for preventing this, outside the bottom and web slabs of the box girder, there is a U-shaped "brim" where ducts can be arranged for prestressing lateral steel strands across the bottom slabs. The stay cable in anchored in the block beneath the web slabs of the main girder. Because traffic is also carried within the box girder, ventilation, fire protection and fire-fighting facilities must be set inside the box. Vertical headroom is restricted, hence full use must be made of the lateral space. The width of bottom slab is so sensitive to the forces on the box girder that it had to be minimized as far as possible to provide sufficient headroom. Therefore the box girder is adopted in a titled web slab which will simplify the transmission of cable forces to allow for better distribution . On the externals of steel prestressed cables and webs, there are set U-shaped "protecting beams". Because the cars pass through the inside of box girder, it is necessary to set the ventilation and fire protection devices in box. The vertical clearance should be limited, hence it needs to utilize fully the lateral space. The width of bottom slab is sensitive to the internal forces of box girder, this width should be decreased to provide sufficient clearance. Hence, in box girder, the sloped webs are adopted so as to make the cable forces to transmit easily and to distribute better.

The rise-span ratio of bridge is 1/29.4, it shows the structure to be thick and heavy. Outside the box girder, "brim plate" is designed for promoting stratification, along the girder and web center near the neutral axis, there is set openings ϕ0.8m every 5m for ventilating the air and the smoke from tunnel. The main girder is stiff sufficiently compared, the main pylon has less flexibility. From the view of being stressed in structure, this bridge can be defined as "partial cable-stayed bridge",

点，桥可定义为"部分斜拉桥"，桥上索力仅用于改善主梁的应力状态。对这一特殊桥，索的间距范围为6m、7m、8m、10m和12m，曾予计算，所有都能满足要求。采用索距10m是根据一系列理由。首先，较宽的间距减少分段数，结果在较短的施工期间以较快的进度完成。较宽间距也为驾乘人员提供了明朗的和改善的视觉效果，对抗风也有利，使索尽全能工作而使结构更有效。用更大的间距将要求大节段施工，造成施工较为困难和费用较大。在此共有96根索。混凝土索塔从桩帽起高85m，从桥面计则高48m，成3柱形，构成字母M，2柱在主梁外，中间柱则在两箱梁中间，M为澳门Macau第一字母。4个横梁完成塔结构 —— 2个上横梁和2个下横梁。

新桥于2002年10月开始兴建，2005年建成。

桥的主梁和桥塔均用普通混凝土非高性能混凝土B50（澳门标准），基本相当C50混凝土建造，其耐久性采取增加保护层厚度、混凝土表面涂装措施解决（主梁和塔混凝土表面均涂装）——武汉中铁大桥局设计院谢尉鸿工程师为了解赐告，特附此致谢。

2

the cable forces is used only to promote the stress state in bridge. For this special bridge, the ranges of cable spacing are 6m, 7m, 8m, 10m and 12m, as being calculated, all these spacing can meet this requirements. To adopt 10m cable spacing is decided following a series of reasons. Firstly, wider spacing can decrease the number of segments, in result this engineering can be completed in a more short construction period and faster progress. Wider spacing can also provide also the effects of bright, clear and promote sight view for the motorists, and is also favorable to resist wind, so as for developing the full capacities of cables to make the structure more efficient. To use too large spacing will require to construct large segments as to make the construction more difficult and the cost larger. There are 96 cables. The height of concrete pylon is 85m from pile cap and that is 48m from bridge deck, the pylons form 3-column shape to constitute a letter M; 2 columns stand beside main girder and the middle between 2 box girders, M is the 1st letter of Macau, and 4 transverse beams — 2 upper and 2 lower — constitute the structure of pylons.

New bridge was started to be constructed in Oct. 2002 and completed in 2005.

The main girder and pylon are constructed by using common high-strength concrete B50 (Macau Standard), not high performance concrete, which corresponds basically to C50 in Code (50010-2000). The durability is solved to increase the cover thickness and coating measure (all the concrete surface of main girders and pylons are all coated). These states were told kindly by Engineer Xie Weihong of the Design Institute, China Zhongtie Major Bridge Bureau, the author express his thanks here.

图2 澳门大桥（承叶雄高工惠赠）
Fig.2 Macau Bridge (courtesy of Senior Engr. Ye Xiong)

参考文献

2.丁大钧. 高性能混凝土及其在工程中的应用. 北京：机械工业出版社，2007：274

REFERENCES

1.Zheng Qiang, Wei Jun, Wen Wusong. Macau in the Making. Bd&e. 2005(1): 24-25

2.Ding Dajun. High Performance Concrete and its Applications in Engineering. Beijing: China Machine Press, 2007: 274

上海南浦斜拉桥

在重庆石门独塔斜拉桥（跨度为230m+220m）建设时，北京交通设计研究院老友即曾告知，我国已在酝酿建设大跨度双塔斜拉桥，认为0.8~0.9（230×2）=368~413m，即可越过建设300m斜拉桥而一跃建设400m双塔斜拉桥。后经专家反复论证，乃决定在上海黄浦江上建设主跨为423m的南浦大桥（图1）。

1988年12月15日，在浦东原上海港务局混凝土厂址上，打下第一根钢管桩，1981年6月20日，当时我国最大的斜拉桥铺上最后一块桥面板，主跨423m的大桥全线贯通。

南浦大桥全长8 346m，分主桥、主引桥、分引桥三部分，主桥长846m，以一跨423m过江。主桥桥面用钢材与混凝土两种建筑材料叠合而成。桥面下一层用大型I字钢制成框架，上一层是用钢筋混凝土桥面板，钢框架与桥面板用电焊焊接，结合处再浇上混凝土，使二者联成一体，这在我国是首次采用。

主桥桥面的钢框架共有438根钢梁，其中有一根重86t；制作钢梁用的钢板最厚达80mm，拼装钢框架用的10多万套高强螺栓直径达30mm。

大桥主桥面用180根钢索吊在桥塔上，其中最粗的一根是用265根直径7mm高强钢丝绞合而成，直径146mm，重21t。钢索长达223m，180根钢索都是用千斤顶拉后固定在桥塔上的。

南浦大桥的通航净空为46m。

浦东引桥长3 746m；浦西引桥长3 754m，后者由于受地区空间的限制，设计成复曲线螺旋形，其造型独特。游客乘车盘旋而上，如同进入了盘山公路。

主桥桥面宽30.35m（图2），其中6车道车行道宽23.45m，设计荷载汽超20级，全重3 000kN平板车验算。主桥两侧各设2m宽人行道，车行道与斜拉桥之间以及人行道间设防护栏杆。

桥塔高150m，采用折线H形钢筋混凝土门架，双索面成扇形布置。塔柱每侧索面各22对斜拉索，在塔柱中央设置一对垂直索以代替梁下竖向支承，使主梁在纵向成为漂浮体系。主梁采用钢-混凝土组合梁构造，主桥两端及边墩处设置640mm组合式大位移伸缩缝。

据所知，大桥针对加拿大465m跨的安娜雪丝桥混凝土桥面因两边斜拉索的空开段由于索力而被拉裂的缺陷，而在中间100m对混凝土桥面施加了预应力，解决了这一问题。

2

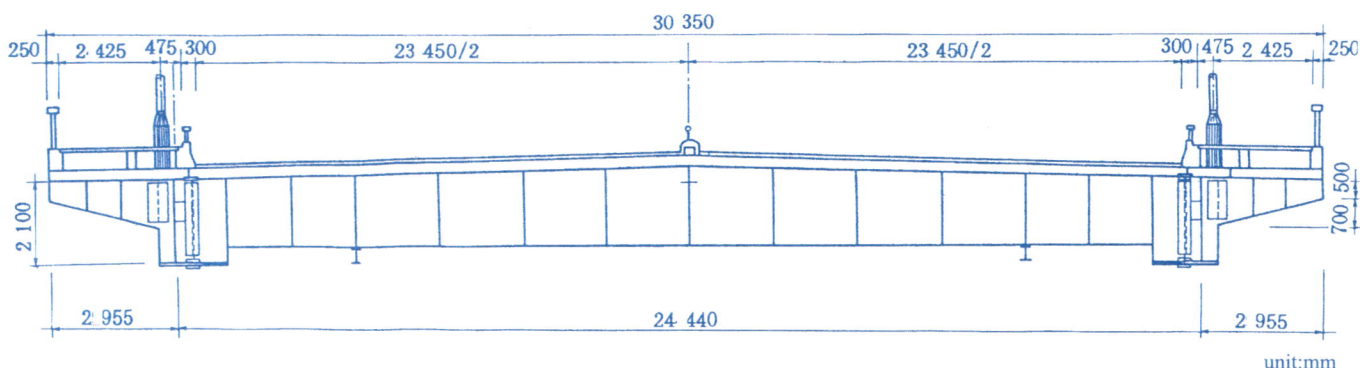

unit:mm

Shanghai Nanpu Cable-Stayed Bridge

During the construction of Chongqing Shimen single pylon cable-stayed bridge (spans: 230m+220m), an old friend working in Communication Design Research Institute in Beijing told the author that it was brewing to construct a cable-stayed bridge in China with span of 400m, because it deemed that 0.8~0.9 (230×2)=368~413m, namely it was possible to jump up over 300m to construct a bi-pyloned cable-stayed bridge with main span of 400m. Through careful and repeated demonstration by experts, hence it was decided to construct Nanpu Bridge (Fig.1) over Huangpujiang (jiang means river in Chinese) with a main span of 423m.

On Dec.15,1988, on the concrete site of factory of original Shanghai Port Office, the 1st steel tube pile was driven, on June 20, 1991, the last deck slab of the largest cable-stayed bridge in China at that time was paved, then, the full bridge with main span of 423m has been joined up all along the line.

The total length of Nanpu Bridge is 8 346m, divided into 3 parts: main bridge, main approaches and branches of approach, the length of main bridge is 846m, a span of 423m passes over the river. The deck of main bridge is laminated with 2 construction materials of steel and concrete. The lower layer of deck is frame built with large I steel, the upper layer is constituted by using reinforced concrete slabs, steel frame is welded with deck slab, at the connection concrete was poured to make them monolithic, the method was used firstly in China.

In the steel frame of main bridge deck, there are 438 steel beams, among which a beam has weight of 86t; the thickness of steel plate for manufacturing beam reaches to 80mm, the diameter of more 10×10^4 sets of high-strength bolts used reaches 30mm.

The main bridge of this engineering is suspended on pylons with 180 steel cables, among which a thickest one is twisted together by using 265 high-strength wires of ϕ7mm, the diameter of this cable is 146mm, weighted is 21t. The length of cable reaches to 223m, 180 cables were fixed on the pylons after being tensioned by using jack.

The clearance for navigation of this bridge is 46m.

The length of Pudong (dong means east in Chinese) approach is 3 746m, that of Puxi (xi means west in Chinese) is 3 754m, the latter is limited due to area space and designed into a compound curve—spiral curve, its modeling is special. The visitors take car upwards helically, it seems to enter into a highway spiraling up to mountain.

The deck width of main bridge is 30.35m (Fig.2), in which, the traffic way of 6 lanes is 23.45m, the design load follows extra-motor grade 20 and checked following total weight of 3 000KN of flatbeds. Beside 2 sides of main bridge, on each of both, there is set a pedestrian walk with width of 2m, between traffic way and stayed cables, and at the external side, there are set protective railings.

The height of pylons is 150m, the broken-line H-shape reinforced concrete portal frame is adopted, double cable plane is arranged in fan shape, on each side of pylon columns, there are 22 pairs of cables, in the center of column, there is set a pair of vertical cables to replace the vertical supported below girder to make the main girder into a floating system in longitudinal. The main girder adopts the composite construction of steel-concrete. At 2 ends of main bridge and side piers there are set expansion joints of 640mm large displacements.

As known, for preventing cracking of concrete deck in the segment between the tensioned cables as occurred in Canadian Annacis Bridge with span of 465m, in this bridge, in the 100m central segment, there is set prestressing to deck for solving this problem.

图2 大桥一般段横截面
Fig.2 Cross section of bridge in general segment

参考文献

1.李国豪主任编委，项海帆主编. 中国桥梁. 上海：同济大学出版社；香港：建筑与城市出版社有限公司，1993：269

REFERENCES

1.Chairman Li Guohao. Edior-in-Chief XiangHanfan. Bridges in China. Shanghai: Tongji University Press; HK: A&U Publication Ltd., 1993: 269

图1 南浦大桥（承项海帆、范立础院士惠赠）
Fig.1 Nanpu Bridge (courtesy of Academician Prof. Xiang Haifan, Fan Lichu)

上海杨浦斜拉桥

上海在建成主跨为423m的南浦桥后，乃能越过500m而建成主跨为602m的、双塔双索面杨浦斜拉大桥（图1a~d），将我国斜拉桥的设计和建桥技术推上一个新的水平。

杨浦大桥位于上海杨浦区宁国路地区，桥址离苏州河5.3km，离吴淞口20.5km，与南浦大桥相距11km，该桥是市区内跨越黄浦江、连接浦西老区与浦东开发区的重要通道，是上海市区内环线的重要组成部分。

大桥全长8 354m（包括主桥、引桥、匝道、引道），主桥全长1 178m，跨度分布为：过渡孔45m+边孔（99m+144m）+主孔602m+边孔（144m+99m）+过渡孔45m。主孔采用一跨过江方案，跨度602m，两侧边孔243m，中间各设辅助墩（图2），主桥桥面总宽度30.35m（图3）。图4示建成的杨浦大桥跨度结构，图5示支座视图。

主桥为双塔空间双索面钢—混凝土组合梁斜拉桥结构。桥墩固结，上部结构为纵向悬浮体系，横向设置限位和抗震设施。

钢筋混凝土柱塔高为200m，塔形呈钻石状。主塔基础采用钢管桩。辅助墩、锚墩、边墩均为柱式墩，钢筋混凝土预制桩基础。钢主梁采用箱形断面，主梁中距25m，钢横梁间距4.5m，工字形断面，车道板采用预制钢筋混凝土板。过渡孔为简支预应力混凝土T梁。

每座索塔两侧各有32对拉索，全桥长256根。最大索长330m，拉索最大断面由313根直径ϕ7高强钢丝组成。浦东引桥长3 764m，浦西引桥长3 430m，引桥全长7 176m(?)。上部结构为简支桥面连续体系，下部结构为柱式墩，钢筋混凝土预制桩基础。

大桥于1991年4月29日动工，于1993年10月1日通车。全桥斜拉索总长度超过2万m，总重约2 900t。桥的建筑精度和质量均属第一流，主桥钢结构由高强螺栓连接，无一误差。大桥主塔设计要求垂直精度为1/2 000，而实际达到1/15 000。

1993年9-10月编者应邀访问日本，10月1日晨9时，在宾馆打开电视机，恰逢杨浦大桥在桥头举行通车仪式，印象深刻。

1d

1a

1b

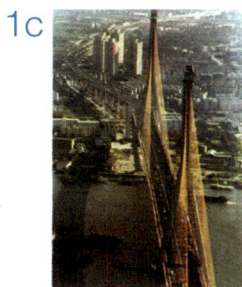

1c

Shanghai Yangpu Cable-Stayed Bridge

After Nanpu Bridge with main span of 423m has been completed in Shanghai, overstepping the span of 500m to complete bi-pylon and double cable plane Yangpu Bridge (Fig.1a~d) with main span of 602m, it push up the design and the technique of constructing bridges to a new level.

Yangpu Bridge is located in Ningguolu (lu means road in Chinese) Area, Yangpu District, Shanghai City, the distance to Suzhouhe (he means river in Chinese) is 5.3km, to Wusongkou (kou means the mouth of a river) 20.5km, to Nanpu Bridge 11km. This Bridge is an important passage of civic area over Huangpujiang to connect old area of Puxi (xi means west in Chinese) and developed area of Pudong (dong means east in Chinese), an important component part of internal ring line of Shanghai City.

The total length of Yangpu Bridge is 8 354m (including main bridge, approaches, circuit road and approach roads) and that of main bridge is 1 178m, the distribution of spans: transition span 45m + side span (99m+144m) + main span 602m + side span (144m+99m) + transition span 45m. The main span adopts the project to pass over river with one span of 602m and each side span of 243m, where is set an auxiliary pier (Fig.2). The deck of main bridge is 30.35m wide (Fig.3). Fig.4 shows the completed span structure of Yangpu Bridge, Fig.5 shows the view of support.

The main bridge is a cable-stayed bridge structure with bi-pylon spatial cable plane and steel-concrete composite girder. The piers are fixed, the superstructure is a longitudinal floating system and in the transverse, there are set the devices of limiting position and resisting earthquake.

The height of pylon with reinforced concrete columns is 200m with diamond shape. The foundation of main pylon adopts steel tube piles. The auxiliary piers, anchorage piers and side pier adopt column ones and reinforced concrete precast pile foundation. The steel main girder adopts box section with central distance of 25m and the spacing of steel cross beams is 4.5m with I-section, the precast reinforced concrete slabs are used as traffic lane. The transition span are simply supported PC T-girder.

Beside each pylon, there are 32 pairs of cables, totaling 256 cables in whole bridge. The max cable length is 330m, the max section is constituted from 313 high-strength wire with diameter of 7mm. The approach length of Pudong is 3 764m, and that of Puxi 3 430m, the total length is 7 176m(?). The superstructure is simply supported continuous deck system, and the substructure column piers and precast reinforce concrete pile foundtion.

Yangpu Bridge started to construct on April 29, 1991 and opened on Oct.1, 1993. The total length of stayed cables in whole bridge is more than twenty-thousand m and total weight is 2 900t or so. Both construction precision and quality occupy the 1st position, the steel structure was connected with high-strength bolts and there was not an error. The design vertical precision of the pylon requires 1/2 000, and the practical one reaches 1/15 000.

During Sept.-Oct. 1993, the author was invited to visit Japan, at 9 o'clock in the morning of Oct.1, 1993, as he opened TV, the opening ceremony was held in the front of Yangpu Bridge, so the impression is deep.

图1 杨浦大桥（承田炜博士惠赠）
(a)~(d)
Fig.1 Yangpu Bridge (courtesy of Dr. Tian Wei) (a)~(d)

参考文献

1.李国豪主任编委，项海帆主编. 中国桥梁. 上海：同济大学出版社；香港：建筑与城市出版社有限公司，1993：269

REFERENCES

1.Chairman Li Guohao, Edior-in-Chief Xiang Haifan. Bridges in China. Shanghai: Tongji University Press; HK: A&U Publication Ltd., 1993: 269

2

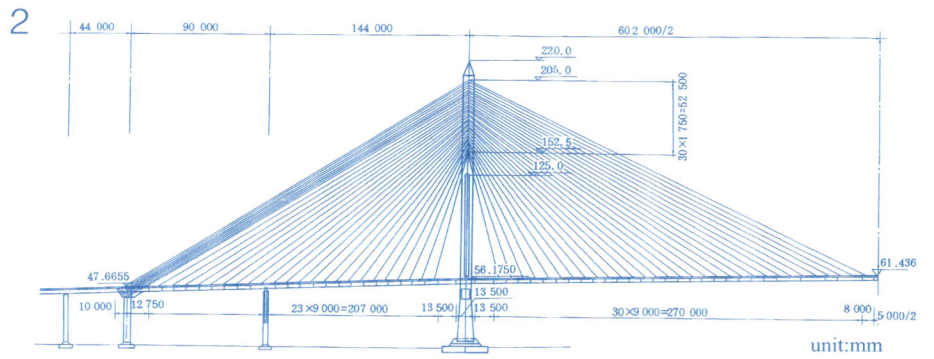

44 000 | 90 000 | 144 000 | 60 2 000/2

220.0
205.0
152.5
125.0
30×1 750=52 500

47.6655 | 56.1750 | 61.436

10 000 | 12 750 | 23×9 000=207 000 | 13 500 | 13 500 | 30×9 000=270 000 | 8 000 | 5 000/2
13 500

unit:mm

3

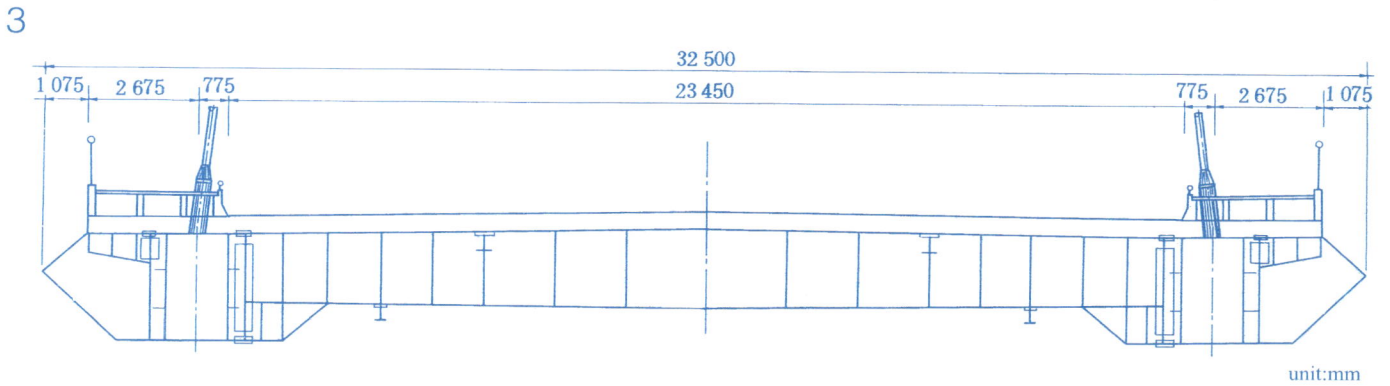

32 500

1 075 | 2 675 | 775 | 23 450 | 775 | 2 675 | 1 075

unit:mm

图2 纵剖面图
Fig.2 Longitudinal profile

图3 横截面图
Fig.3 Cross section

图4 建成的杨浦大桥跨度结构（承蒋森荣教授惠赠）
Fig.4 Completed span structure of Yangpu Bridge
(courtesy of Prof. Jiang Senrong)

图5 支座视图（承蒋森荣教授惠赠）
Fig.5 View of support (courtesy of Prof.
Jiang Senrong)

4

上海徐浦斜拉桥

1. 概况

徐浦大桥（图1a~e）是继南浦大桥、杨浦大桥之后，上海市区第3座跨越黄浦江的特大型桥梁。它位于徐汇区龙华乡和浦东新区三林镇附近的江面上，下游距南浦大桥10.2km。大桥全长6 017m，主桥长1 074m，主跨590m，总宽35.95m，主塔高217m；设双向8车道，设计时速80km；最大荷载为汽一超20级。

徐浦大桥西接朱梅路，东连新辟的杨高南路，纵贯东西，形成一条长余10km的通街大道，为外环线西南段划上了第一条线。它和建成后的外环线一期工程连成一体，成为沪宁和沪杭高速公路进入上海的交通枢纽，也是今后虹桥机场和浦东国际机场之间最便捷的主要通道。

徐浦大桥首次全面采用国产STE355钢板代替进口桥梁钢板加工制作构件，推动了我国特种钢材冶炼和轧制水平的提高。

大桥于1994年4月正式开工，1997年6月24日建成通车。

2. 选择结构形式

在桥址处黄浦江宽约520m，水深在8~13m之间变化，通航净空要求46m。桥址处土壤为典型的长江三角洲冲击层。

主跨为590m。当决定为单跨时，只有两种桥型可供考虑，即悬索桥和斜拉桥。在已知桥址软弱土的条件下，悬索桥方案被认为是过于昂贵的，特别是其锚固 —— 在施工期间也太干扰行船。

主桥塔为A形，升高至217m（图2）。桥面宽36m，8车道，每边有一宽0.75m维修车道（图3）。

对设计跨度近600m的双塔斜拉桥，有4种型式大梁可以考虑：钢一混凝土组合梁、预制混凝土梁、预制和钢混合梁和全钢梁。钢一混凝土组合梁有很多优点，例如较低自重、较高制造精度（工厂条件）、施工简单、快速及较低费用。

上海地区前2座斜拉桥，南浦桥和杨浦桥都是钢一混凝土组合设计。在已知这种型式结构中积累了可观经验，因此决

1a

1b

Shanghai Xupu Cable-Stayed Bridge

1. Introduction

Xupu Bridge (Fig.1a~e) is the 3rd extra-large bridge after Nanpu and Yangpu Bridges to pass over Huangpujiang. It is located on the river near Longhuaxiang of Xuhui District and Sanlin Town of Pudong New District, the distance of 10.2km from Nanpu Bridge on the lower reaches. The total length of bridge is 6 017m, main bridge is 1 074m long, the main span 590m with total width of 35.95m, the main pylon 217m high; there are set 2-way 8 lanes with design velocity of 80km/h; the max. load is the grade of extra-car 20.

Xupu Bridge joins Zhumei Road in the west, and connects Yanggao South Road newly constructed in the east, and extends from west to east to form a thoroughfare with more than 10km long, and constitute the 1st line for the south-west segment of external ring road. This bridge joins with the engineering in the 1st period of external ring roads into an integral traffic net, forms a communication centre enter Shanghai from Shanghai-Nanjing and Shanghai-Hangzhou Express Highways and will become a most convenient main passage between Hongqiao airfield and Pudong international airport.

The steel plates STE355 made in this country are fully used in the 1st time for Xupu Bridge to replace the imported plates for bridge to manufacture members, it pushes ahead with the level of smelting and rolling special steel to be raised in China.

Xupu Bridge started to construct formally in April 1994 and has been completed and opened on June 24, 1997.

图1 建成的徐浦大桥（承林培元院士惠赠）(a)~(d)
Fig.1 Completed Xupu Bridge (courtesy of Academician Prof. Lin Yuanpei) (a)~(d)

1c

1d

2. Selecting the Structural Form

The river at the bridge site is about 520m wide. Water depth is various from about 8m to 13m. Clearance for navigation needs 46m. The soil at the site is the typical soft alluvium of the Changjiang Delta.

The main span is 590m long. As a single-span crossing was decided, only two types of bridges of suspension bridge and cable-stayed bridge could be considered. Under the given site's soft soil conditions, the suspension bridge alternative was deemed to be too expensive — especially its anchorages — and too interfering with shipping during construction.

The main pylons are A-shaped, rising to a height of 217m (Fig.2). The deck is 36m wide for 8 lanes of traffic, with a 0.75m maintenance lane on each side (Fig.3).

For a two-pylon cable-stayed bridge with design span nearly 600m, four types of girders can be considered: steel-concrete composite, precast concrete, mixed precast and steel and all steel. A steel-concrete composite girder has many advantages, such as lower self-weight, higher manufacturing accuracy (factory conditions), simpler, faster construction and lower cost.

The two previous cable-stayed crossings in the Shanghai region, the Nanpu and Yangpu bridges, were steel-concrete composite designs. Given the considerable experience accumulated in this type of structures, hence it was decided to use the same method for the

图1 建成的徐浦大桥（承林培元院士惠赠）(e)
Fig.1 completed Xupu Bridge (courtesy of
Academician Prof. Lin Yuanpei)(e)

定对徐浦桥采用相同方法。这也使能在手边的早先方案很多工具和设备可重复利用。

3. 施工考虑

采用组合斜拉桥，建造边跨将较主跨大大简单。如果设置多个辅助墩，架设边跨和架设引桥上部结构以相似方式完成。因为采用相同的施工方法，为架设大梁的工具和设备可以重复使用。因此，架设边跨大梁像建设引桥一样继续进行。

如果边跨和主塔同时完成，在主跨和边跨索上的工作可同时进行。比较斜拉桥对称的构造，这种方法可减少桥面吊车数一半，因此大大地加速施工。这是中跨大梁、混凝土梁和边跨用预制斜拉桥体系的一项明显优点。

4. 设计特征

如前所述，相同的预制I字梁方法用于边跨桥面梁和引桥桥面梁。在用吊车就位后，I字梁横向浇筑形成混凝土多室箱梁。用这种方式，不需有临时桥面支承。

在边跨多个辅助墩大大增强了桥的刚性。这种安排使可能设计风速超过90m/s。在闭合前的建设期间，甚至在台风季节，在这样的强风中结构是安全可靠的。

5. 连接

在主跨钢—混凝土组合大梁与侧跨预制箱梁之间的连接是极其重要的。当边跨截面与主跨形状不同时，在中跨主梁中强的轴力、弯矩和剪力将由连接结构均匀传递至边跨截面。

连接为一长7.5m的梁，其中纵横向预应力钢绞线和边跨及主跨纵向钢绞线连接。在钢主梁中靠近连接段有许多加劲肋。钢箱用高等级混凝土填充。厚的钢板安装在端面，而内力由销杆和角钢传递。此外，在连接处有4个刚性滑动球铰支承以改进支承力状态并有助于桥塔和大梁之间的临时的强化。

6. 基础

对590m主跨，两座主塔不均匀沉降影响曾予细致考虑。直径900mm的钢管桩用作基桩。承力层在大约-56~-79m之间。两塔基础沉降在100mm以内。

在辅助墩之间某些沉降不可避免，而主塔和第一辅助墩之间将引起边跨梁内很大内力。采用800mm直径的钻孔桩，每个墩的桩尖设置在相同土层同一高程上以便控制沉降。此外，高度可调节的支承安装在每个辅助墩上。一旦沉降量测超过设计容许值时，支承高程和内力将人工调节以防止混凝土梁开裂。

7. 架设

在桥面架设时，如果吊车在主跨上架设桥面板和在裸露的钢横梁上架设钢主梁，钢横梁尚未形成组合梁，桥面刚性严重地受损而弯曲变形很大。如果容许发生，这将导致钢梁过大的扭转变形，造成安装主梁的困难。因此，为了保持刚性，曾采取下列措施：

—— 在组合梁形成横梁后，利用桥面吊车架设以增加刚性。

—— 在形成组合梁之前和之后，对钢横梁"反向顶进"以调节内力和变形。

—— 当钢主梁连接到工厂预装配的钢横梁时，横梁支承条件尽可能地接近实际架设情况。

Xupu Bridge. This also enable a great deal of tools and equipment of hand from these earlier projects to be re-used.

3. Construction Considerations

With composite cable-stayed bridges, the side spans are much simpler to construct than the main span. If multiple auxiliary piers are set, erecting the side spans is a accomplished in a manner similar to that used in erecting the superstructure of the approach spans. Since the same construction method is used, the tools and equipment for erecting the girders can be used repeatedly. Thus, erection of the girders on the side spans proceeds continuously, like the construction of the approaches.

If the side spans and the main pylons are completed at the same time, the work on the cables for the main span and side spans can proceed simultaneously. Compared with the symmetrical construction of cable-stayed bridges, this method can reduce the number of bridge deck cranes by half, thus greatly speeding construction. This is a distinct advantage for the cable-stayed bridge system using a steel-concrete composite girder for the central span and precast concrete beams for the side spans.

4. Design Characteristics

As noted, the same construction method is used as for the deck beams of precast I-beams on the side spans as on the approaches. After positioning by crane, the I-beam is transversely cast to form the concrete box beams with multiple cells. In this way, it is not necessary to have temporary deck supports.

The multiple auxiliary piers on the side spans greatly increase the rigidity of the bridge. This arrangement has allowed for a design wind velocity of more than 90m/s. During any construction stage before the closure, even in typhoon season, the structure is safe and reliable in such strong wind.

5. Connection

The connection between the steel-concrete composite girder on the main span and precast box beams on side spans is of critical importance. As the sections of the side spans and the main span differ in shape, the strong axial, moment and shear forces in the main girder of the central span will be uniformly transferred to the section of the side span from the connection structure.

The connection is a precast beam with 7.5m long, in which longitudinal and transverse prestressed strands are connected with the longitudinal strands of the side spans and the main span. There are many rib stiffeners in the steel main girder near the connection segment. The steel box is filled with high grade concrete. Thick steel plates are installed on the terminal face and the internal force is transferred with welded dowels and angle-irons. Moreover, there are four rigid sliding ball hinge bearings at the connection to improve the bearing force state and favor the temporary consolidation of the structure between the pylons and girders.

2

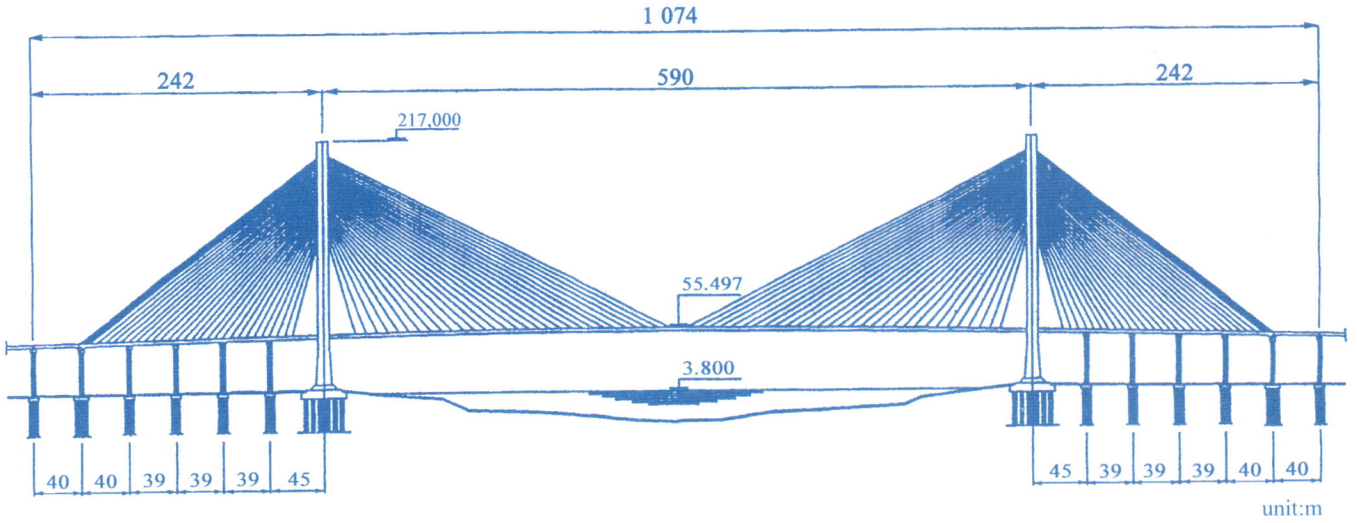

1 074

242   590   242

217,000

55.497

3.800

40 40 39 39 39 45   45 39 39 39 40 40

unit:m

3

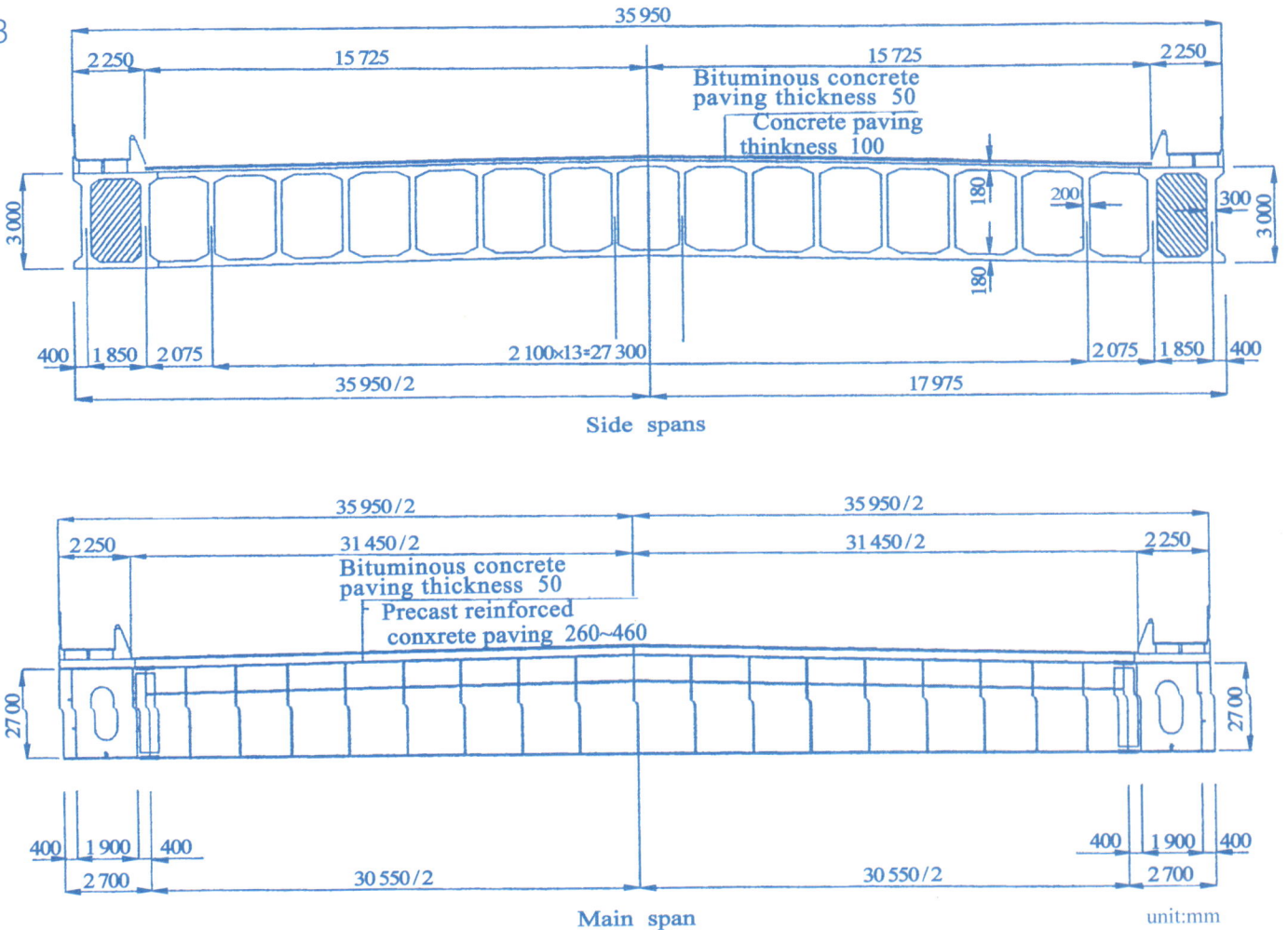

35 950

2 250   15 725   15 725   2 250

Bituminous concrete
paving thickness 50
Concrete paving
thinkness 100

180

200

180

3 000   3 000

300

400 1 850 2 075   2 100×13≡27 300   2 075 1 850 400

35 950/2   17 975

Side spans

35 950/2   35 950/2

2 250   31 450/2   31 450/2   2 250

Bituminous concrete
paving thickness 50
Precast reinforced
conxrete paving 260~460

2 700   2 700

400 1 900 400   400 1 900 400

2 700   2 700

30 550/2   30 550/2

Main span   unit:mm

6. Foundation

For the 590m main span, the influence of uneven settlement of the two main pylons has been carefully considered. Steel pipe piles 900mm in diameter are used as foundation piles. The bearing stratum ranges from about -56m to -79m. The settlement of the foundations of two pylons is within 100mm.

Some settlement between auxiliary piers is unavoidable, and the uneven settlement between the main pylon and the auxiliary piers on the first span will result in great internal force in the beams of side spans. Bored piles 800mm in diameter were used and the pile tip of every pier was set at the same elevation on the same soil stratum in order to control settlement. In addition, height-adjustable bearings have been installed on every auxiliary pier. Once the settlement has been measured to exceed the value allowed design, the bearing elevation and internal force will be manually adjusted so as to prevent the concrete beams from cracking.

7. Erection

During deck erection, if the crane on the main span erects the deck slabs and the steel main girder on the bare steel cross beams, and the steel cross beams has not yet formed the composite girder, the rigidity of the deck is severely compromised and flexural deformation is great. If allowed to occur, this would lead to excessive torsional deformation of the steel girder, making it difficult to assemble the main steel girder. Therefore, in order to maintain rigidity, the following measures have been adopted:

—After the composite girder forms the cross beams, the erection is made by using the deck crane so as to increase rigidity.

—Before and after forming the composite girder, "reverse jacking" for the steel cross beams adjusts the internal forces and deformations.

—When the steel main girder is joined to the steel cross beams preassembled in the factory, the support conditions of the cross beams are as close as possible to that of the actual erection.

图2 立视图
Fig.2 Elevation

图3 桥面横截面
Fig.3 Deck cross section

REFERENCES

1.Yuan Pei Lin, Zeng Huan Zhang, Bian Ma. Xupu Cable-Stayed Bridge, Shanghai, China. Structural Engineering International, IABSE, 1996(3): 166-168

湖北鄂黄长江斜拉桥

　　湖北鄂黄长江大桥（图1）是北京至广州106国道跨越长江，连接鄂城、黄冈两座中等城市的特大桥梁，是湖北省交通重点工程项目，建设鄂黄长江大桥对完善国家路网布局、提高106国道的通行能力，提升城市功能，促进湖北省特别是鄂东经济发展意义重大。

　　鄂黄大桥全长2 690m，主桥为5跨连续双塔双索面预应力混凝土斜拉桥，跨度分布为55m+200m+480m+200m+55m，主塔高172.3m。桥面宽24.5 m（不含布索区宽度），设计为双向4车道。荷载标准：汽车-超20级，挂车-120。鄂州岸桥为4×50m+26×30m，黄州岸引桥为20×30m+2×50m大桥索塔基础采用直径ϕ3.0m大桩，钢围堰。

　　2002年8月中旬，大桥顺利通过静载、动载试验。

　　鄂黄大桥于1999年10月15日正式动工建设，至2003年4月建成通车。

1

图1 鄂黄大桥
Fig.1 E-Huang Bridge

Hubei E-Huang Cable-Stayed Bridge over Yangtze River

Hubei E-Huang Yangtze River Bridge (Fig.1), a special great bridge is located on the National Highway No.106 from Beijing to Guangzhou to span Yangtze River, to link 2 middle cities of E-City and Huanggang, and is a major communication project of Hubei Province, the significance of constructing E-Huang Yangtze River Bridge is great for perfecting the layout of national nets, improving the passable capacity of 106 National Highway, promoting city function, advancing economic development of Hubei Province, especially E-East Area.

The total length of E-Huang Bridge is 2 690m, the main bridge is a 5-span continuous PC cable-stayed structure with double pylons and double cable planes, the spans are distributed of follows: 55m+200m+480m+200m+55m, the main pylons are 172.3m high. The width of deck is 24.5m (without including the area for distributing cables), there are 4 lanes in 2 ways. Load specification: motor-super 20, trailer-120. The approaches on Ezhou Bank are 4×50m+26×30m, those on Huangzhou Bank are 20×30m+2×50m. The foundation of bridge pylon adopts large piles with diameter of ϕ3.0m, steel cofferdam.

In the middle ten days of Aug. 2002, this Bridge was smoothly passed the tests of statical and dynamical loads.

E-Huang Bridge started formally to be constructed on Oct.15, 1999 and has been completed and opened to traffic on April, 2003.

参考文献

1.丁大钧. 中国大陆拱桥和索桥建设新进展. 中国台湾土木水利学会会刊，2004. 31（4）：56-67

2.鄂黄大桥.
http://baike.baidu.com/view/374823.htm

REFERENCES

1.Ding Dajun. New Advances of Construction of Arch Bridges and Cable Supported Bridges in Mainland China. Proceedings of Civil and Hydraulic Engineering Society, Taiwan, China, 2004. 31(4): 56-67

2.E-Huang Bridge, http://baike.baidu.com/view/374823.htm

荆州长江大桥

荆州长江公路大桥(图1)[1]建在长江中游的荆江河段，与318国道、宜黄高速公路、襄荆高速公路、荆常高速公路相连，是207国道跨越长河的咽喉工程。大桥由北岸引桥、荆州大堤桥、北岸滩桥、北汊通航孔桥、三八洲桥、南汊通航孔桥、南岸滩桥、荆南干堤桥和南岸引桥等9个部分组成，全长4 397.6m，桥面宽24.5m，双向4车道，日通车能力可达2万辆以上。大桥构成复杂，技术含量高，桥梁结构包揽国际国内大跨度桥梁多种形式。北汊通航孔桥为主跨500m预应力混凝土斜拉桥。三八洲连续梁桥，主跨150m，连续长度1 100m。

荆州长江大桥的建成通车，宣告207国道全线贯通，沟通了湘鄂两省，使中原地区形成一条南北公路交通大动脉，对促进两湖平原的经济发展，推动荆州市城市建设以及长江防汛抗洪等都将发挥重要作用。

荆州长江公路大桥位于湖北省荆州市，是207 国道跨长江的一座特大型桥。桥梁全长为4 177. 60 m。设计行车速度：100 km/h。设计荷载：汽2超20，挂2120。桥面宽度：行车道净宽21.5m，桥面总宽为24.5m (斜拉桥段27.0m)，不设非机动车道和人行道。大桥共由9个桥段组成，自北向南依次为：

(1) 北岸引桥　22×20 m 预应力混凝土简支空心板；

(2) 跨荆江大堤桥　93m+150m+93m预应力混凝土连续梁；

(3) 北岸滩桥　5×30m 预应力混凝土简支T梁。主桥：长为2 557m；

(4) 北汉通航孔桥　200m+ 500m+200m 预应力混凝土斜拉桥；

(5) 三八洲桥　100m+6×150m+100m预应力混凝土连续梁；

(6) 南汉通航孔桥　160m+ 300m+ 97m 预应力混凝土斜拉桥。南岸桥：长270m；

(7) 南岸滩桥　8×30m预应力混凝土简支T梁；

(8) 跨荆南干堤桥　50m+80m+50m预应力混凝土连续梁；

(9) 南岸引桥　9×30m预应力混凝土简支T梁。

图2示荆州大桥主桥示意图。

从上可见整个荆州大桥规模是很大的。

Jingzhou Yangtze River Bridge

The Jingzhou Yangtze River Highway Bridge(Fig.1)[1] is constructed at the Jingzhou River segment of Yangtze River middle reaches and connected with the 318 National Road, Yihuang Express Highway, Xiangjing Express Highway, Jingchang Express Highway, and is the key engineering of the 207 National Road to span Changsha. This Bridge consists of 9 parts: north approach, bridge over Jiangzhou Bank, bridge over north beach, navigable span of north branch, bridge over Sanba Islet, navigable span of south branch, bridge over south beach, bridge over Jing south main bank and south approach et ect., the entire length is 4 397.6m, the bridge width is 24.5m with 4 lanes in 2 ways, the traffic potential in every day was over 2×10^4 cars. This Bridge is constituted complicatedly, the technicality is high and the bridge structures consist of multi-type bridges adopted in aboard and at home. The bridge over north branch is a cable-stayed bridge with the main span of 500m and a Sanba Islet Bridge is a continuous girder bridge with the main span of 150m and total length of 1 100m.

The completion and open of Jingzhou Yangtze River Bridge showed the total line of 207 National Road to be through, it links Hunan and Hubei Provinces and makes the middle area of China to become the main artery of the northsouth highway communication, to improve the economic developments of Hunan-Hubei flatlands, to promote the urban construction of Jingzhou and to prevent flood and highwater in Yangtze River will develop an important affect.

The Jingzhou Yangtze River Highway Bridge located at Jingzhou City, Hubei Province is an extra-bridge on 207 National Road over Yangtze River, the full length of bridge is 4 177.60m. The design traffic speed: 100km/h, the design loads: Motor 2 extra 20 and trailer 2 120. The deck width: the clear lane width for driving vehicles is 21.5m, the total width of deck 24.5m (the width of cable-stayed bridge segment 27.0m), there are not set the lane for not motor driven vehicles and walk. This bridge consists of 9 bridge segments, from the north to the south are respectively:

(1) north approach, 22×20m PC simply supported hollow slabs;

(2) bridge over Jingzhou bank 93m+150m+93m PC continuous girders;

(3) bridge over north beach 5×30m PC simply supported T girders, the main bridge is 2 557m long

(4) navigable span of north branch 200m+500m+200m PC cable-stayed bridge;

(5) bridge over Sanba Islet 100m+6×150m+100m;

(6) navigable span over south branch 160m+300m+97m PC cable-stayed bridge, south bank bridge is 270m long;

(7) bridge over south beach 8×30m PC simply supported T-girder;

(8) bridge over Jing south main bank 50m+80m+50m PC continuous girders;

(9) south approach 9×30m PC simply supported T-girders.

Fig.2 shows the sketch of the main bridge of Jingzhou Bridge.

From the above, it can be seen that the scale of Jingzhou Bridge

图1 荆州长江大桥
Fig.1 Jingzhou Yangtze River Bridge

北汉通航孔桥主梁采用预应力混凝土肋板式结构。双主肋高2.4m，标准梁段肋宽1.7m，梁顶宽26.5m（底面宽27.0m），桥面板厚32cm。为消除边墩支座负反力，两梁端各70m范围内采用加大主肋宽度的方法，增加自重。

北汉通航孔桥采用H形索塔。北塔高为139.15 m，南塔高为150.25 m。两塔每根塔柱下边均设有5m高的塔座。桥塔上横梁截面高度为4m，下横梁截面高度为6m，均设置了预应力筋。

北汉斜拉索采用PES7 热挤聚乙烯拉索，PESM7冷铸镦头锚固体系。拉索最小间距为4m，标准间距为8m，塔下第一对斜索与直索间距为11.5m，拉索最小倾角为23.554°。全桥采用PES72139~PES72283 等8 种规格的斜拉索。

主梁设计成飘浮体系，仅在两端交界墩上设4个拉压球型支座，支座设计竖向压力为5 000kN，竖向拉力为2 500kN，位移量为±400 mm，转角1°。

南汉通航孔桥主梁采用预应力混凝土肋板式结构，双主肋高2.2 m。根据受力和静力平衡的需要，桥面板厚度分别采用32 cm、76 cm、108 cm、132 cm 及实体梁5 种不同的截面型式。

南汉斜拉桥两塔为高度不等的H形塔。高塔高度为124.8 m，低塔高度为89.4 m。

南汉斜拉桥斜拉索采用与北汉斜拉桥相同的材料，在拉索的布置上南汉斜拉桥塔下不设直索，塔下无索区长20.0m，拉索标准间距为8.0m，最小间距为4.0m。拉索最小倾角为25.75°。

南汉斜拉桥亦为飘浮体系，仅在两端交界墩上设4个拉压球型支座，由于结构的不对称性，小边跨梁端的拉压支座需要承受较大的竖向拉力。

两座斜拉桥主塔均采用大块整体钢模（10m高）爬模施工技术，保证了混凝土质量和外观。

三八洲预应力混凝土箱形连续梁桥，分两幅布置，主梁设计成两个分离的箱梁。箱梁墩顶梁高为8.0m，跨中及梁端

is very great.

The navigable span of north branch adopts PC rib-slab structure. The depth of double main ribs is 2.4m, the rib width of standard segments is 1.7m, width of girder top 26.5m (the width of bottom 27.0m), the thickness of deck slab 32cm. For the sake of eliminating the negative reaction in the edge support, in the 70m field of both ends of the girder, a method to widen the width of the main ribs to increase the dead weight is adopted.

For the north navigable span, the H-typed pylons are adopted. The height of the north pylon is 139.15m, that of south pylon is 150.25m. Under each pylon column, there is a 5m high pylon seat. The section depth of the upper transverse beam is 4m and that of the lower one is 6m, in both of them, there are set prestressed reinforcements.

For the north branch stayed cables, the hot-working polyethylene PES7 and the anchorage system with chill casting heads PESM7 are adopted. The minimal spacing of stayed cables is 4m, standard one is 8m, the spacing of the straight cable under pylon between the 1st pair of inclined cables is 11.5m, the minimal slope angle is 23.554o. For the entire bridge, 8 specifications of stayed cables PES72139 to PES72283 etc. are used.

The main girder is designed to be a floating system, only on the boundary piers at 2 ends, the tension-compression spherical bearings are set, the vertical compression is 5 000kN and the vertical tension is 2 500kN in the bearing design, the displacements: ±400mm, rotation angle 1°.

For the south navigable span, the main girder adopts PC rib-slab structure, the depth of double main ribs is 2.2m. Following the requirements of stressing and the statical equilibrium, the deck slabs adopt respectively 5-typed different sections with the thicknesses of 32cm, 76cm, 108cm, 132m and solid girder body.

Two H-typed pylons of the cable-stayed bridge over the south branch have different heights. The height of the higher pylon is 124.8m, that of the lower one is 89.4m.

The same materials are adopted as those used in the cable-stayed bridge over north branch, on the arrangements of stayed cables, under the pylon of south branch bridge, there is not set the straight cables, the length of cableless area is 20.0m, the standard spacing of stayed cables is 8m, the minimal spacing is 4.0m, the minimal slope angle is 25.75°.

For the cable-stayed bridge over the south branch, the floating system is also adopted, only on the boundary piers at 2 ends, 4 tension-compression spherical bearings are set, but owing to the unsymmetry of structure, the tension-compression bearings at the girder ends of smaller side span will bear larger vertical tension.

For the main pylons of 2 cable-stayed bridges, the construction technique of climb formwork of large integral steel form (height of 10m) was used, it guaranteed the quality and appearance of concrete.

The PC continuous girder bridge over Sanba Islet is arranged in dual lanes, the main girders are designed with box section into 2

高为3.3 m。单幅箱梁顶宽为12.5m，底宽为7.0m。

　　主桥基础全部设计为钻孔灌注桩基础。北汉通航孔桥两塔下均为22根直径2.5m桩基，承台直径33.0m，承台厚6.0m；三八洲桥中墩每幅采用5根直径2.0m桩基，承台厚度为5.0m；南汉斜拉桥高塔下采用22根直径2.0m桩基，承台直径为27.2m，承台厚度为6.0m，低塔下采用15根直径2.0m桩基，矩形承台厚度为6.0m。

　　对荆州大桥，曾进行过静力模型试验检验设计计算的正确性，保证斜拉桥的整体强度和稳定，对北汉主跨500m预应力混凝土斜拉桥进行了1：30的铝合金模型静力稳定性试验，以全面掌握结构在自重、汽车荷载以及不平衡施工荷载作用下，索力和主梁内力的分布变化情况，确定结构在最大悬臂状态和成桥状态下失稳时的荷载条件，同时进行结构非线性对结构静力稳定性的影响分析。对主跨300m、500m斜拉桥进行了节段模型风洞试验、抖振响应分析、裸塔气动弹性模型试验，对主跨500m预应力混凝土斜拉桥做了全桥模型风洞试验。通过设置合理的临时墩解决了最大双悬臂长度达248.6m的风稳定性问题。

　　此外还进行了仿真分析和地震反应分析以及施工监控。

2

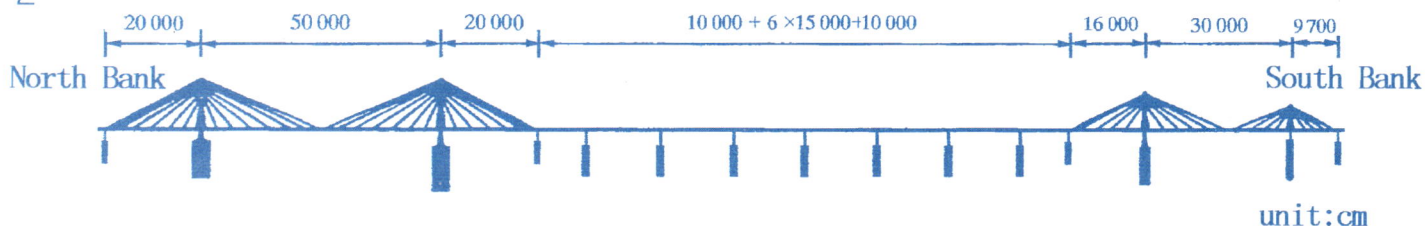

North Bank　　　20 000　　　50 000　　　20 000　　　10 000 + 6 ×15 000+10 000　　　16 000　　　30 000　　　9 700　　　South Bank

unit:cm

separate box girders. The depth of box girder is 8.0m on pier top, that in the middle of span and at the girder ends is 3.3m. The top width of box girder in single lane is 12.5m, the bottom width is 7.0m.

All foundations used in the main bridge are designed into bored filling piles. Under both of the two pylons of the navigable span over north branch, there are set $22\phi2.5m$ pile foundation, the bearing plateform diameter is 33.0m and its thickness is 6.0m; in each lane of Sanba Islet, there set $5\phi2.0m$ pile foundation with the thickness of 5.0m; under the high-pylon of the cable-stayed bridge over south branch, there is set a foundation with $22\phi2.0m$ piles, the bearing platform diameter is 27.2m and its thickness is 6.0m, under the lower pylon there is $15\phi2.0m$ set a pile foundation with rectangular bearing platform and the thickness of which is 6.0m.

For the Jingzhou Bridge, the test of statical model was conducted to check the correctness of the design and calculation so as to guarantee the integral strength and the stability of the cable-stayed bridge, for the PC cable-stayed bridge over the north branch with the main span of 500m, an aluminium alloy model on statical stability with 1:30 scale was carried out so as to overall master the variety of the internal forces in the cables and in the main girder when the structure was under the dead weight, the vehicle load and the unbalanced loads during construction in order to determine the condition of loads during unstability as the structure was under the states of the max cantilever and completion, at the same time, the influence analysis the nonlinearity of structure on the statical stability. For the cable-stayed bridges with the main spans of 300m and 500m, the wind tunnel tests on the segmental models, the analysis on the response of shake and the pneumatio elastic model on exposed pylon were conducted, for the PC cable-stayed bridge with the main span of 500m, the wind tunnel test on whole bridge (model) was also done. Through reasonably setting temporary piers, it solved the problem on wind stability of the double cantilever with the length of 248.6m.

Additionally, the analyses of imitating true and earthquake response, as well as the construction monitoring were conducted

参考文献

1.丁大钧. 中国大陆拱桥和索桥建设的新进展. 中国台湾土木水利学会会刊，2004. 31（4）：56-67

REFERENCES

1.Ding Dajun. New advances of the construction of arch bridges and cable supported bridges in Mainland China. Proceedings of Civil and Hydraulic Engineering Society. Taiwan, China, 2004. 31(4): 56-67

芜湖双层斜拉桥

1. 引言

芜湖长江大桥（图1）为一座铁道与公路合并的双层承担双轨铁道和4车道交通的大桥。铁道桥总长10 511m，而公路桥长5 681m。跨越长江桥长2 184m，包括钢桁架斜拉主桥。跨度排列：120m+2×144m+ 2×(3×144m)+（180m+312m+180m)+2×120m=2 184m。

2. 结构外形

主桥为一座双层斜拉桥，主跨312m、边跨180m跨越主通航道。桥的立面和主梁截面如图2、图3所示。在公路桥面之上塔高33.27m形成低塔斜拉桥，亦即拱背斜拉桥。8对平行钢丝斜拉索安装在每座塔上，而水平纵索则安排在钢主梁和两塔之间横梁墩顶之上。钢桁架截面高度和宽度分别为13.5m和12.5m。悬臂托架延伸到钢桁架之外以作斜拉索锚碇，在两索平面中心线之间的距离为23.4m。包括人行道在内的公路桥面宽为21.94m。

桥址紧靠一机场和一座现有的铁道编组场。因此桥的尺寸严格受航空要求和空间要求控制，限制高度使飞机有安全空间和连接线高程，限制坡度以使火车得以从桥上到编组场。桥址条件，例如水文、地质等也影响桥的设计。最后桥塔高度（33m）对跨长（312m）之比仅为0.109。因为通航净空要求，不能加设辅助墩以改进大梁刚度，所以边跨长度为180m，边跨长度与中跨长之比为0.577。因为引桥通航净空和坡度限制（引）桥的结构高度不大于3m，选择加劲桁架而铁道和公路布置在两个不同水平，桁架对增进桥的垂直刚度有利，但对侧向刚度不利。如对该大桥，跨度是长的，而主要结构参数偏离通用值很多，对铁道桥活载重大，而火车动力作用是大的，因此桥的刚度（特别是侧向刚度）问题是严重的。采用增进刚度的主要措施是结合道路桥面板和钢桁架组合使其共同工作。这一措施在增进大梁的垂直刚度，特别是侧向刚度是有效的。

1

Wuhu Double-Deck Cable-Stayed Bridge

1. Introduction

Wuhu Yangtze River Bridge (Fig.1) is a combined rail and highway bridge with a double-deck carrying two railway tracks and 4 lanes of traffic. The total length of the railway bridge is 10 511m, and the length of the highway bridge is 5 681m. The length of the bridge across the Yangtze River is 2 184m, comprised of steel trusses with a main cable-stayed bridge. The span configuration over the river is: 120m+2×144m+ 2×(3×144m)+(180m+312m+180m)+2×120m= 2 184m.

2. Structural Configuration

The main bridge, a double-deck cable-stayed bridge has a main span of 312m across the main navigation channel with side spans of 180m. The bridge elevation and girder cross section are shown respectively in Figs.2 and 3. The height of the pylon above the roadway deck is 33.27m to form a cable-stayed bridge with low pylon, i.e. and extradosed cable-stayed bridge. Eight pairs of parallel-wire stay cables are mounted on each pylon, and horizontal longitudinal cables are arranged between the steel girder and the cross beams between the two pylon legs on top of the piers. The depth and width of the steel truss is 13.5m and 12.5m, respectively. Cantilevered brackets extend outside the steel trusses for the stay cable anchorages with a distance of 23.4m between the two cable plane centerlines. The total width of the highway deck, including sidewalks, is 21.94m.

The bridge site abuts an airport and an existing railway marshalling yard. Thus, the bridge dimension are strictly governed by the required navigation clearance, a limited height to allow for safe aircraft clearance and the connecting line's elevation and limited grade to get trains from the bridge to the marshalling yard. Site conditions, such as hydrology, geology, etc. also influence the bridge design. Consequently, the ratio of pylon height (33m) to span length (312m) is only 0.109. Because of the navigation clearance requirements, auxiliary piers can not be added to improve the stiffness of the girder, so the length of the side span is 180m with a length ratio of side span to mid span of 0.577. Because the navigational clearance and longitudinal grade of the approach spans restrict the structural depth of the bridge not to more than 3m, a stiffening truss is selected and the railway and highway are laid out on two different levels. The truss is favorable for improving vertical stiffness of the bridge, but unfavorable to lateral stiffness. As for this bridge, the span is long, and the main structural parameters deviate much from conventional values; live load for railway is heavy, and the dynamic action of the train is large, so the stiffness issue of the bridge (especially lateral stiffness) is severe. The main measure taken to improve stiffness is to combine the roadway deck slab compositely with the steel truss to make them work together. This measure is efficient in improving vertical stiffness, and especially lateral stiffness of the girder.

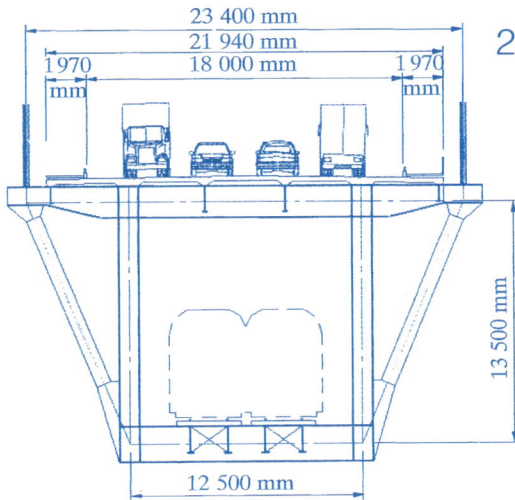

图1 芜湖长江大桥全视图（承方秦汉院士惠赠）
Fig.1 General view of Wuhu Yangtze River Bridge (courtesy of Academian Fang Qinhan)

图2 侧视图
Fig.2 Elevation view

所有桁架构件焊成箱形。隔板节点为刚性节点，而全部辅助构件，例如侧向支撑隔板、节点板以及端部横向构件焊到格板节点。对大梁，采用具有极限强度为500MPa和屈服强度为350MPa的结构钢；最大钢板厚度为50mm。

3. 桁架架设

钢桁架架设是用平衡悬臂法从两桥塔进行，而大桥在中跨合龙。公路斜拉桥大梁是柔性的，故加劲大梁对系统挠度不是如此重要，起拱可用于控制挠度。当对铁道斜拉桥，主桁架很刚性，不可能用起拱控制挠度，因为和斜拉索具有很小倾斜角，梁的挠度不确定性，故系统的调节必须是在桁架合拢时间内。合拢段和螺栓孔是按施工图在工厂制造的。当架设不容许加大螺栓孔而禁止制作新孔，故开发双铰合拢法。直径32.85mm柱螺栓打入ϕ33mm螺孔内，而达成准确合拢，大桥纵剖面变成平滑。

4. 基础

对主跨，采用在不同水平（图2）、直径3m具有高桩帽的钻孔桩基础，双壁钢围堰直径为30.6m。

5. 结束语

由铁道荷载引起的动力作用是很大的。大桥竖向和横向刚度应符合铁道运行安全要求，但很难确定大桥横向刚度。最方便增进横向刚度的方法是加宽桁架。对一座在相同平面内担负铁道和公路的大桥和宽桁架是不经济的。优化解决是合并道路混凝土板与钢桁架的组合作用，同时增进横向和竖向刚度并保持相对小的桁架宽度和截面高度。

大桥于1997年3月正式动工建造，而在2000年9月30日通车。

3

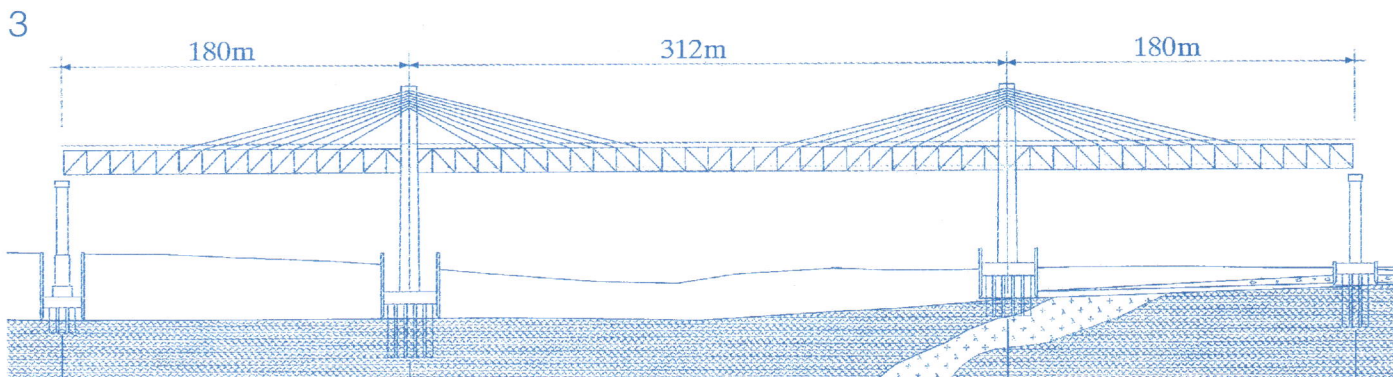

180m   312m   180m

All truss members are welded into a box shape. The panel points are rigid joints, and all the subsidiary members, such as diagrams, gusset plates of the lateral bracing, and end transversal members are welded to the panel points. Structural steel with a 500MPa ultimate strength and 350MPa yield strength is employed for the bridge; maximum steel plate thickness is 50mm.

3. Truss Erection

The erection of the steel truss was proceeded by balanced cantilever method from the two pylons, and the bridge was closed at mid-span. The girder of the highway cable-stayed bridge is flexible, so the stiffening girder is not so important to the system deflection, and camber could be used to control deflections. As for the railway cable stayed bridge, the main truss is much stiffer, and controlling deflections with camber is not possible because of the uncertainty of the beam deflection with the small inclination angle of the stay cables, so system adjustments were necessary during closure of the truss. The closure segments and the bolt-holes were fabricated in a factory according to working drawings. During erection it was not allowed to enlarge the bolt-holes, and it was forbidden to make new holes, so a double-hinge closure method was developed. Studs with a diameter of 32.85mm were driven into ϕ33mm bolt-holes and precise closure was achieved, the bridge profile turns out to be smooth.

4. Foundation

For the main span, it is adopted ϕ3m bored pile foundation with high pile cap on 2 different levers, the diameter of (Fig.2) double-walled steel cofferdam is 30.6m.

5. Conclusion

The dynamic action induced by the railway load is very large. The vertical and transversal stiffness of the bridge should meet the safety requirements of the railway operation, but it is very difficult to determine the transversal stiffness of the bridge. The most convenient way to improve the transversal stiffness is to widen the truss. For a bridge carrying a railway and highway in the same plane it is not economical to widen the truss. The optimal solution is to combine the roadway concrete slab with the steel truss for composite action, improving both the transverse and vertical stiffness and maintaining a relatively small truss width and depth.

The bridge started formally to construct in March 1997 and opened on Sept.30, 2000.

图3 主梁截面
Fig.3 Cross section of main girder

参考文献

2.丁大钧. 中国大陆拱桥和索桥建设的新进展. 中国台湾土木水利学会会刊，2004. 31（4）: 56−67

REFERENCES

1.Qin-han Fang. Wuhu Double-Deck Cable-Stayed Bridge. SEI, Journal of IABSE. 2004. 14(1): 32-33
2.Ding Dajun. New Advances of Arch Bridges and Cable-Supported Bridges in China Mainland. Proceedings of Civil and Hydraulic Engineering Society, Taiwan, China, 2004. 31(4): 56-67

夷陵多跨长江斜拉桥

1. 引言

夷陵大桥（图1）位于湖北省宜昌市，跨越长江，此处是著名的三峡水利枢纽所在地。于此平均江宽730m，在不同季节，水深在15m和35m之间变化。

桥面承担4车道和2条各宽2m的人行道。主桥面宽23m，包括防护索锚的中间分隔带。用于设计的活载为中国标准卡车道荷载（20t标准卡车间距15m及一超20卡车、轴荷载30t），速度60km/h。最大的单车荷载（轴压120t）曾用于试验和核算。人行道活载3.5kN/m²。河床为沙/砾石覆盖，其深度从北岸20m降至南部河中心线的4m。南岸为大厚度的裸露岸石。

三塔预应力混凝土箱梁单索面斜拉桥及2主跨348m方案的选择是基于建议的比较和充分考虑通航要求、费用和周围的和谐。该大桥在那些跨江结构中是独特的。

2. 桥的布置和特点

夷陵长江大桥为一座有348m主跨及120m边跨支承在40m间隔的墩上的连续斜拉桥，总长936m（图2）。3座混凝土塔在桥面上呈倒Y形，有着和周围和谐的几乎相同的形状。两边塔同高，较中间塔略矮。主箱梁截面高度为3m，在两边悬挑翼缘各3.5m。两座中间墩将每个锚碇边跨分成3个小跨，每个40m长。大桥具有单索面，多根索安排成扇形，沿大梁间距为8m，在锚碇边跨某些部分，索距为5.5m。平衡重沿锚碇边跨100m分布，作为在自重下结构平衡和抵抗在营运中端墩的上举力。主梁固定在中塔处，而在边塔纵向是自由的。

主跨长由航行要求和费用考虑两者确定。348m主跨两边塔位于这一区域，此处在枯水季河床是暴露的。作为结果，建设费用可予减少。边跨长度由桥址限制确定，故增加梁长将是不经济的。这样由于较短的支承跨，造成边塔低于中心塔。

在两岸4只中间墩有效地工作以增进体系的刚性和降低作用到大梁和塔上的力。中间墩保持由活载引起的边跨位移于很低的水平。这样，锚碇在大梁的索可以有效地限制塔顶的位移，而作用到边塔以及中间塔的力被减小。也是采用混凝土大梁和中间墩，体系获得足够的刚度，结果在施工中传到塔和大梁上合理的力的条件以使不须引入稳定索。在中间

Yiling Multi-Span Cable-Stayed Bridge over Yangtze River

1. Introduction

The Yiling Bridge (Fig.1) crosses the Yangtze River in Yichang City, where the famous Three Gorges Hydropower Station Project is located. Here, the average river width is 730m, and water depth is variable between 15m and 35m at the river center in different seasons.

The deck carries 4 lanes and 2 pedestrian walkways, each 2m wide. The main bridge deck is 23m wide including a 3m wide median strip that protects the cable anchorage. The live load used in design is for a Chinese standard truck lane load (20t standard trucks at 15m intervals and one super 20 truck with a 30t axle load) at a velocity of 60km/h. A large single truck load (120t axle load) was used for testing and checking calculations. The pedestrian live load used in design is $3.5kN/m^2$. The riverbed is covered with sand/gravel with the depth decreasing from 20m at the north bank to 4m at the river centerline in the south. The south bank is exposed rock of great thickness.

The 3-pylon PC box girder, cable-stayed bridge project with a single cable plane and two 348m main spans is selected on the basis of proposal comparisons, and full consideration of navigation requirements, costs, and harmony with the surroundings. This bridge is unique among those crossing the Yangtze River.

2. Bridge Layout and Characteristics

Yiling Yangtze River Bridge is a continuous cable-stayed structure with 2 main spans of 348m and side spans of 120m supported by piers at 40m intervals with a total length of 936m (Fig.2). The three concrete pylons have an inverted "Y" shape above the deck, and are almost of the same shape harmonizing with the surroundings. The two side pylons are of the same height, slightly shorter than the central one. The main box girder is 3m in depth with flange cantilevers of 3.5m on both sides. Two intermediate piers divide each anchor side span into three smaller spans, each 40m in length. The bridge has a single cable plane with multiple cables arranged in a fan shape at a spacing of 8m along the girder, 5.5m in some parts of the anchor side span. Counterweights are distributed along 100m of the side anchor spans for structural balance under dead load and to resist uplift forces to the end piers during operation. The main girder is fixed at the central pylon and free longitudinally at the side pylons.

The main span length is determined by both navigation requirements and cost considerations. The two side pylons of the 348m main spans are located in an area where the riverbed is exposed in dry season. As a result, the construction cost can be reduced. The side span lengths are determined by site restraints and so that an increase in girder length will not be economical. This results in the side pylons being shorter than the central pylon due to the shorter supporting span.

The four intermediate piers on both banks work efficiently in improving system rigidity and reducing forces applied to the girder

图1 夷陵长江大桥总视图（承邵长宇教授惠赠）
Fig.1 General view of Yiling Yangtze River Bridge (courtesy of Prof. Shao Changyu)

塔上控制力为在施工中不平衡荷载状态引起。降低营运力不能进一步减小柱的尺寸。

3. 上部结构

　　主钢筋混凝土桥塔在桥面以上为单室箱形截面，对中柱和边柱纵向宽度分别为7.0m和5.5m。上部塔包括索的锚碇区，在壁中分布有预应力钢筋。在桥面以上主塔为双室箱形截面，其横向宽度从桥面到基础逐步减小，并在顶部施加预应力，中塔和边塔分别示于图3及图4。

　　主混凝土大梁为3室箱形截面。主、边跨典型截面示于图5。横隔壁在主塔及墩处加强大梁。在箱梁内附加横隔壁在主跨内分布在4m间距，在边跨内则分布在5.5m间距。预应力钢绞线则分布在箱梁顶部相应横隔处；有6个单元4ϕ15.2mm钢绞线相应于主跨横隔，有10个单元4ϕ15.2mm钢绞线在边跨是由于横隔较大的间距和平衡重。在索锚区竖向腹板和横隔用10单元ϕ32mm竖向预应力筋施加预应力。用于主梁的纵向预应力可分为3组：在施工中40根ϕ32mm预应力钢绞线用于主跨，20根用于边跨；7根ϕ15.2mm、12根ϕ15.2mm、19根ϕ15.2mm内部钢绞线分布在主边跨，按变化的量考虑力的条件；19根ϕ15.2mm外部钢绞线分布在主梁底部翼缘上，这是约1/4总的预应力钢筋。

　　斜拉索按照尺寸可分成6组，最小的索包括27-ϕ15.2mm的钢绞线，最大的包括47根钢绞线。镀锌钢绞线标准强度为1 770MPa，在营运中容许应力为0.45标准强度，钢绞线体系应用于结构中。

4. 施工

　　因为两边跨靠近两江岸，而江床在枯水季是裸露的，钻孔桩和桩帽的施工可无需借助大型设备来完成。在建造边塔

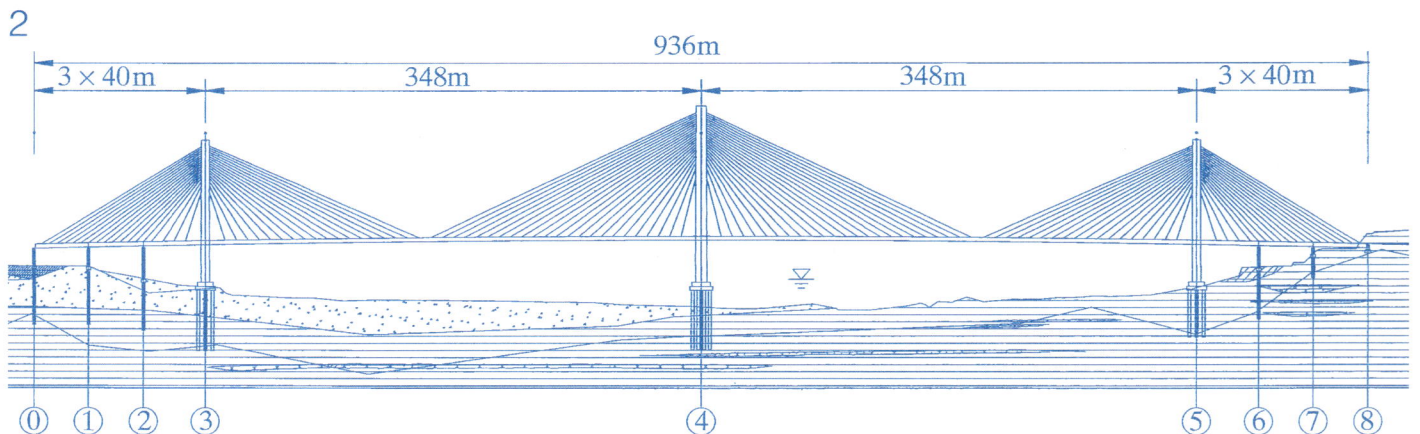

2

936m

3×40m　　348m　　348m　　3×40m

⓪ ① ② ③ ④ ⑤ ⑥ ⑦ ⑧

3

4 m

45 m

126 m

55 m

7 m

26 m

13.8 m

7 m

7 m

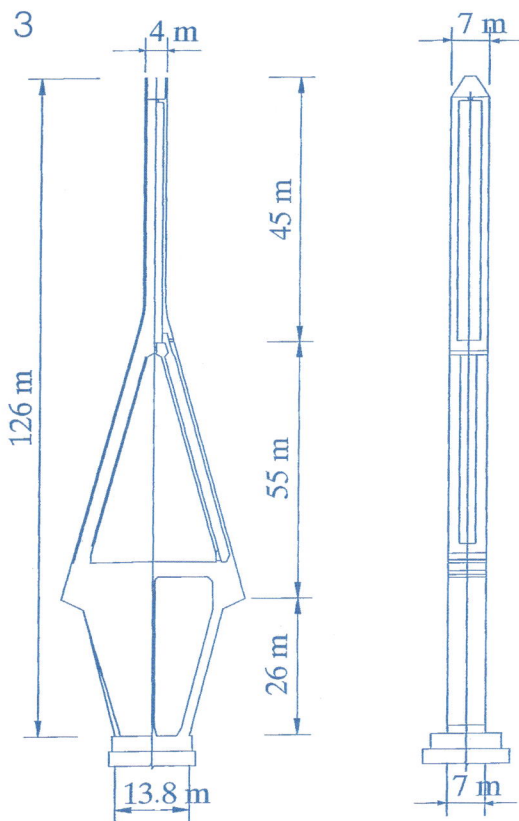

and pylons. The intermediate piers keep the displacements in the side spans due to live load at very low levels. Thus, the cables anchored in the girder can limit the displacement of the pylon top efficiently, and the forces applied to the side pylons as well as to the central pylon are reduced. Also, with the adoption of the concrete girder and intermediate piers, the system gains sufficient stiffness resulting in rational force conditions to the pylon and girder during construction so that it is unnecessary to introduce stabilization cables. The controlling force on the central pylon is in the unbalanced load state during construction. Reduction of the operation forces can not reduce the pylon size further.

3. Superstructure

The reinforced concrete pylons are a single cell box section, above the deck, with a longitudinal width of 7.0m and 5.5m for the central and side pylons, respectively. The upper pylons consists of cable anchorage zones with prestressed bars distributed in the walls. The main pylon below the deck are double-celled box-section whose transverse widths decrease gradually from the deck to the foundation, and are prestressed in the top. The structures on the central and side pylons are shown respectively in Figs.3 and 4.

The main concrete girder is a box-section with three cells. Typical sections of the main and side spans are shown in Fig.5. Diaphragm walls strengthen sections of the girder at the main pylons and piers. In the box girder additional diaphragms are distributed at 4m intervals in the main span and 5.5m in side spans. Prestressing strands are distributed in the top of the box corresponding to the diaphragm walls; there are six units of $4\text{-}\phi15.2$mm strands corresponding to diaphragm walls in the main span and ten units of $4\text{-}\phi15.2$mm strands in the side span due to larger distances between diaphragms and counterweights. The vertical webs and diaphragm walls within cable anchorage areas are prestressed by ten units of $\phi32$mm vertical prestressing bars. The longitudinal prestressing used in the main girder can be classified into three groups: forty $\phi32$mm prestressing strands are used in the main spans and twenty in the side spans during construction; seven $\phi15.2$mm, twelve $\phi15.2$mm, and nineteen $\phi15.2$mm internal strands are distributed in the main and side spans in varying amounts with respect to force conditions; nineteen $\phi15.2$mm external strands are distributed on the bottom flange of the main girder, which are about 1/4 of the total prestressing steel.

The stay cables can be classified into six groups according to size, the smallest cable consists of $27\text{-}\phi15.2$mm strands and the largest consists of 47 strands. Standard strength of the galvanized strands is 1 770MPa with an allowable stress in operation of 0.45 times the standard strength. The strand system is applied in the structure.

4. Construction

Because the two side pylons are near the riverbanks, and the

中，简单的栈桥可用于运输。为此费用显著降低。桥塔用升降模板现浇，泵送混凝土到塔上。

中塔位于江的中心，支承塔的钻孔桩借助平台来完成，而桩帽在枯水季节当水位差在围堰中和之外很小，用悬吊箱形围堰施工。为了降低费用，驳船设备用于建造中塔。中塔用一升降机现浇，混凝土则由流动的混凝土工厂泵送。

现浇混凝土主梁的长度在两边跨为131m，环绕中塔22m；两段324m主跨为预制，而用平衡悬臂法架设。主梁预制段在桥下运输，而用特殊起重机提升。混凝土箱梁典型段为4m，而特殊段为3.5m长(50mm接缝)，合拢段3m。在悬臂施工时，每40m安排500mm现浇接缝以加速施工和减小在剖面中的积累误差。两主跨同时合龙，在预制段提升后和混凝土浇筑后锁定临时连接钢结构。

5. 结束语

对夷陵长江大桥选择3塔斜拉方案，以符合通航及桥址要求。中塔和基础位于深水中和两边塔靠近江岸的事实也是经济合理的。总的说来，3跨或多跨斜拉方案也表明其竞争力。随着超越时代的发展，更多的挑战以符合调和文化和自然环境增长要求，以及各种可能出现的科技问题。设计者应借引入国内、国际可应用的建设经验试着提高技术进步。具有348m跨的3塔斜拉桥对桥址和环境应具适应性，从2001年12月28日已成功地服务于宜昌区域。

5

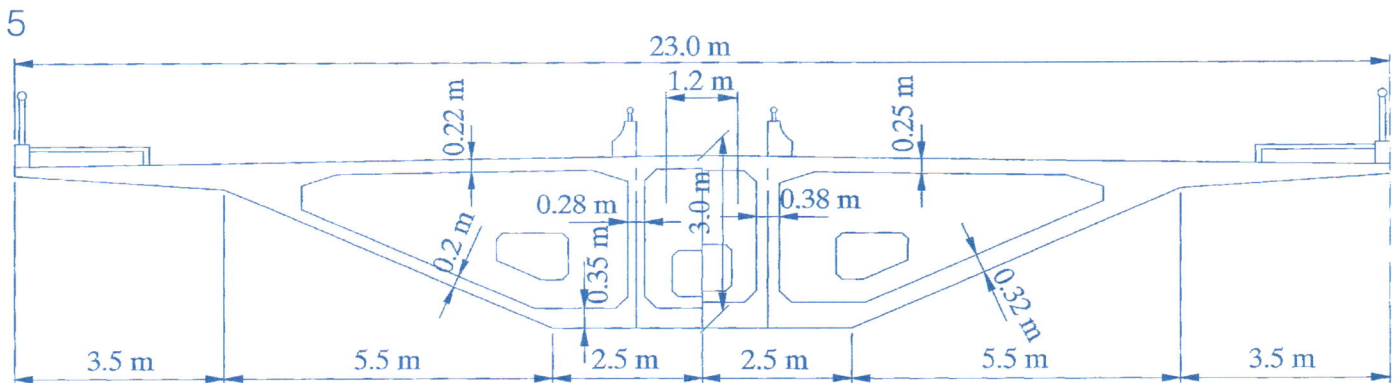

4

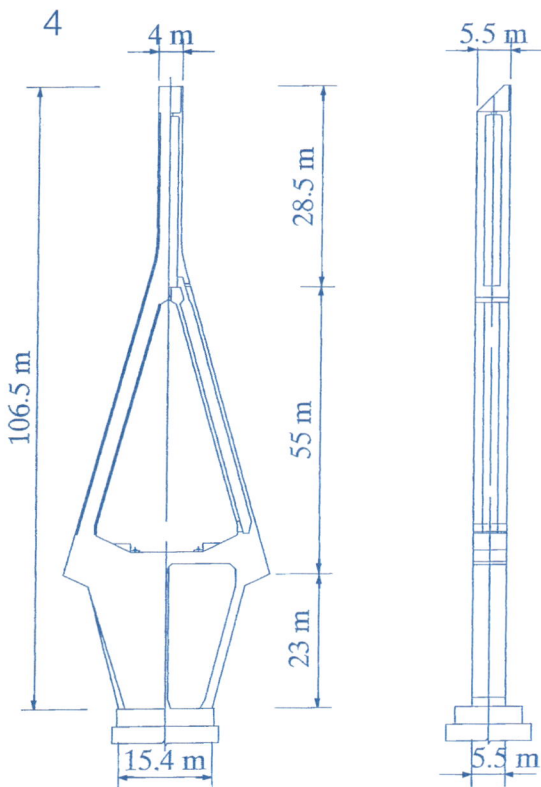

図4 边塔结构
Fig.4 Structure of side pylon

図5 大桥大梁典型截面
Fig.5 Typical girder section of bridge

参考文献

2.丁大钧. 中国大陆拱桥和索桥建设新进展. 中国
台湾土木水利学会会刊，2004. 31（4）：56—67

REFERENCES

*1.Changyu Shao. Yiling Multispan Cable-Stayed
Bridge over the Yangtze River. SEI, IABSE Journal,
2004. 14(1): 27-28*

*2.Ding Dajun. New Advances of Arch Bridges
and Cable-Supported Bridges in China Mainland.
Proceedings of Civil and Hydraulic Engineering
Society. Taiwan, China, 2004. 31(4): 56-67*

riverbed is exposed in the dry season, the construction of bored piles and pile caps could be completed without the assistance of barge equipment. Simple trestles were employed for transportation during construction of the side pylons. The cost was reduced remarkably because of this. The pylons were cast-in-situ using lift formwork and pumping concrete to the pylons.

The central pylon is located at the center of the river, the bored piles supporting the pylon were completed with the assistance of platforms, and the pile caps were constructed using suspended box cofferdams in the dry season when the water level difference in and out of the cofferdam was small. To reduce costs, barge equipment was used during construction of the central pylon. The central pylon was cast on site using a lift and concrete was pumped from the floating concrete plant.

The cast-in-situ length of the main girder was 131m on both side spans and 22m around the central pylons; two 324m main spans were prefabricated and erected using the balanced cantilever method. The prefabricated segments of the main girder were transported under the bridge and lifted using special cranes. A typical segment of the concrete box is 4m and some special ones are 3.5m long (with 50mm joints). The closure segment is 3m. During cantilever construction, the 500mm cast-in-situ joints were arranged every 40m to speed up construction and decrease accumulating error in the profile. The two main spans were closed at the same time, and temporary connecting steel structures were locked after the prefabricated segments were lifted and the concrete was cast.

5. Conclusion

The 3-pylon cable-stayed project is selected for the Yiling Yangtze River Bridge to meet the navigation and site requirements. The fact that the central pylon and the foundation are located in deep water and that the two side pylons are located near the banks is also economically rational. All in all, the cable-stayed solution with three or multiple pylons has shown their competitiveness. With developments over time, more challenges will be encountered in bridge design to meet the increasing requirements of harmonizing the cultural and natural environments, and the various technical problems that may appear. The designer should try to promote technical progress by introducing applicable domestic and international construction experience. The 3-pylon cable-stayed bridge with 348m spans is selected because of its appropriate suitability to the side environment and has been successfully serving the region of Yichang since its completion on Dec.28, 2001.

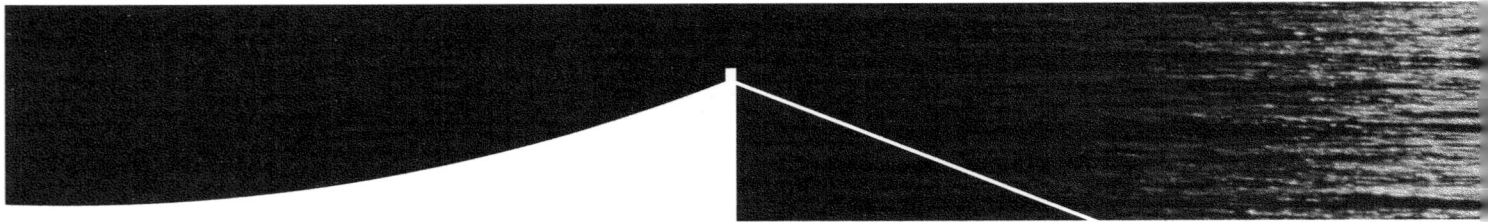

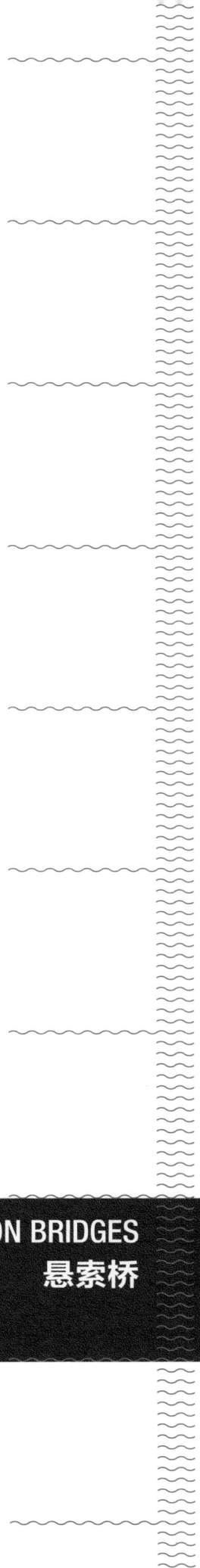
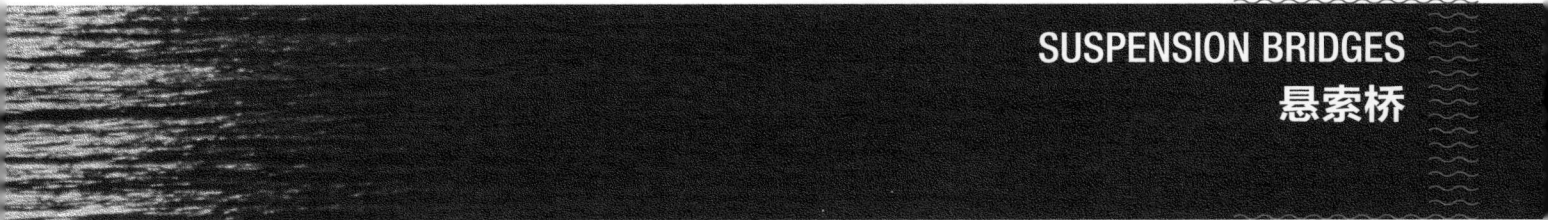

SUSPENSION BRIDGES
悬索桥

武汉阳逻悬索桥

武汉阳逻长江悬索大桥(图1)[1]建于武汉，位置在市的东北郊，距离武汉二桥（预应力混凝土斜拉桥主跨400m，1995年建成）下游27km。阳逻桥主跨1 280m，恰好与美国1937年建成的旧金山的金门大桥跨度相同。桥北岸为新洲区阳逻镇，其南岸则属洪山区。工程总长度共10km，桥梁长度2 725m，其中主悬索桥的跨度为250m+1 280m+440m(图2)[1]。引桥总长度1 445m，包括70m和55m长连续梁，其余长度为连接线7 275m。

南北桥塔为钢筋混凝土箱形截面门式框架结构(图3)，上、下横梁用预应力混凝土建造。两桥塔高度分别为169.8m和163.3m，X形支撑为钢结构。两主索中心间距为35m，每索包括很多钢绞线，每一钢绞线由127ϕ5.35mm平行钢丝组成，标准强度为1 670MPa。中跨矢跨比为1：10.5。在南边跨（440m）和中跨（1 280m），每一主索（ϕ83cm）由154股钢绞线组成，每索总共19 558ϕ5.35mm钢丝。在北边跨（250m）中，由于边中跨比较小，主索由162股钢绞线组成，其中额外8股锚固于北塔塔顶的索鞍上。吊索采用ϕ5.1mm、强度为1 670MPa平行钢丝，采用标准间距16m。

在悬索桥桥面中，采用全焊流线形截面扁平钢箱加劲梁，用Q345-D合金钢制造，标准梁段长度为16m。根据风洞试验及截面总体计算结果，钢箱梁高度取3.0m，桥面宽度为38.5m（包括两侧风嘴50cm宽的导流板），高宽比为1：12.8。桥面板为正交异性板：顶板厚14mm，底板厚10mm，U形加劲肋厚6mm，间距为300mm。在钢箱梁中，每隔3.2m设一道横隔板，在吊点处厚10mm，非吊点处厚8mm。在梁端部区域，由于有竖向支座、横向限位支座和伸缩缝装置，横隔板应予适当加厚。钢箱梁外部防腐蚀采用电弧喷铝方法；对内部防腐蚀采用抽湿系统。在钢桥面上铺设6cm厚环氧沥青。在桥塔下横梁处，设4个竖向支座，4个抗风支座和4个纵向阻尼缓冲支座。图4示主桥型布置。

在塔柱下设置分离式桩帽。在每一北塔柱基础，设置14根ϕ2.8m钻孔桩，横向排列为3，4，4，3，成梅花形。在每一南塔柱下，设置5×5ϕ2.0m钻孔桩。柱帽高度为6m。

1

3

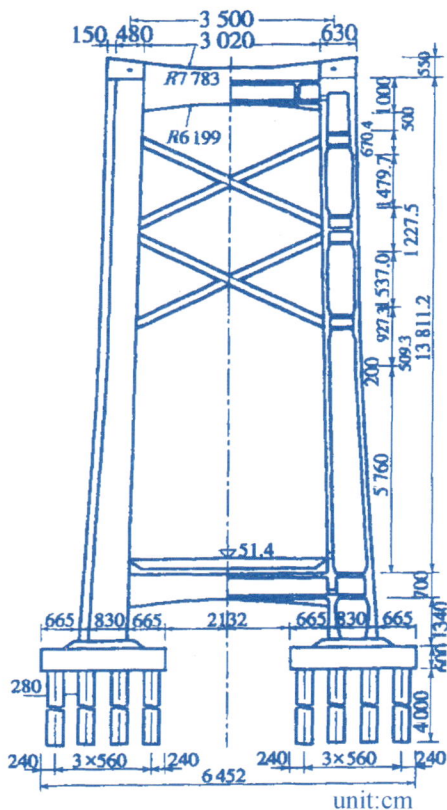

Fig.1 图中标注 (unit:cm)

图1 武汉阳逻桥效果图（承徐国平教授级高工惠赠）
Fig.1 Effect picture of Wuhan Yangluo Bridge (courtesy of Senior Engr. Prof. Xu Guoping)

图2 阳逻桥塔一般构造
Fig.2 General construction of pylon

图3 桥塔在施工（承徐国平教授级高工惠赠）
Fig.3 Pylon under construction (courtesy of Senior Engr. Prof. Xu Guoping)

Wuhan Yangluo Suspension Bridge

Yangluo Yangtze River Bridge (YYRB) (Fig.1)[1] constructed in Wuhan, is located at a place in city northeast suburbs with a distance of 27km in the lower reaches from the 2nd Wuhan Bridge (PC cable-stayed bridge with main span of 400m, completed in 1995). Its main span of 1 280m is exactly the same as that of the famous Golden Gate Bridge, dated 1937, situated in San Francisco, USA. In the north bridge bank there is Yangluo Town of Xinzhou District, and the south bank belongs to Hongshan District. The total length of engineering amounts to 10km, with bridge length 2 725m, among which the spans of main suspension bridge: 250+1 280+440m (Fig.2)[1]. The total length of approaching is 1 445m constituted of 70m and 55m long continuous girders, and the remaining length is the connecting line of 7 275m.

The south and north pylons are RC (reinforced concrete) portal frame structures of box section(Fig.3), with upper and lower transverse beams constructed of PC (prestressed concrete). The pylon heights are 169.8m and 163.3m respectively, and the X-bracings are steel structures. There are 2 main cables with central spacing of 35m, each constituting of a number of steel wire strands, each strand is made of 127ϕ5.35mm parallel steel wires with standard strength of 1 670MPa. Its ratio of rise to middle span is 1:10.5. In south side span (440m) and middle span (1 280m), each main cable (ϕ83cm) constitutes of 154 strands, totaling 19558ϕ5.35mm wires per cable. In north side span (250m), owing to being smaller ratio to main span, the main cable consists of 162 strands, of which the 8 extra strands are anchored in socket of cable saddle. For hangers, parallel steel wires ϕ5.1mm with strength of 1 670MPa are used at normal spacing of 16m.

In the suspension bridge deck, a shallow steel box stiffening girder with an all-welded streamline section is used, made of alloy steel Q345-D; and the length of normal girder segment is 16m. According to the wind tunnel test and general calculation result of the section, the steel box girder depth of 3.0m is adopted, the width of the deck is 38.5m (including 50cm wide baffle set on the sides of wind mouths), the ratio of depth of width being 1:12.8. The bridge deck is an orthotropic structure: 14mm thick top plate, 10mm thick lower plate, and 6mm thick U-shaped stiffening ribs with the spacing of 300mm. In steel box girder, there is a diaphragm plate spacing every 3.2m, with thickness of 10mm at hung point and 8mm at the other places. In the area of girder ends, there are vertical supports, transverse limited supports and expansion joint devices, and the transverse diaphragm plates should be thickened appropriately. For the external corrosion resistance of steel box girder, the arc aluminium blasting method is used; for resisting internal corrosion, the moisture-extracting system is adopted. Onto the steel deck, 6cm thick epoxy asphalt is paved. Under each lower transverse beam of pylon, there are set 4 vertical supports and 4 longitudinal damping buffer supports. Fig.4 shows Layout of main bridge type.

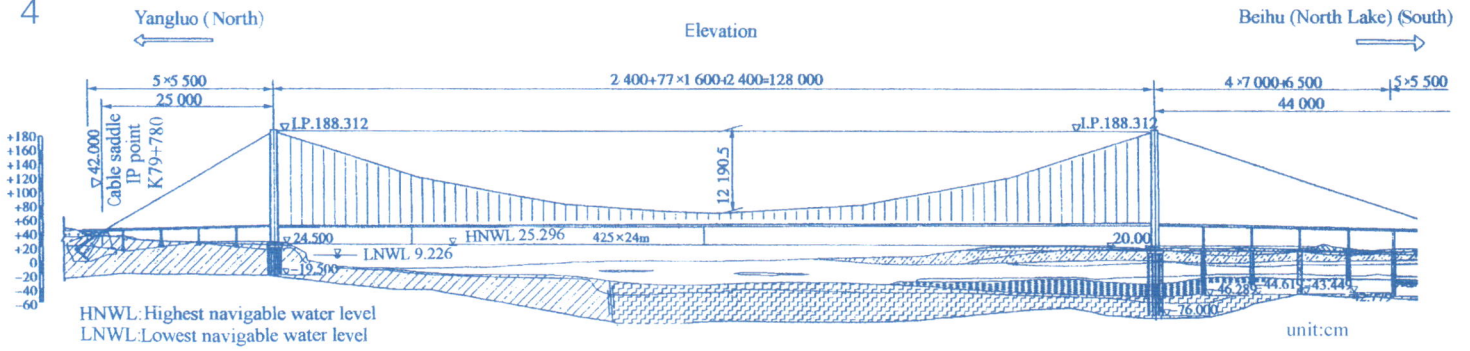

4

Elevation

Yangluo (North)

Beihu (North Lake) (South)

5×5 500   25 000

2 400+77×1 600+2 400=128 000

4 ×7 000+6 500   5×5 500

44 000

I.P.188.312   I.P.188.312

12 190.5

+180 +160 +140 +120 +100 +80 +60 +40 +20 0 -20 -40 -60

▽42.000 Cable saddle IP point K79+780

▽24.500

LNWL 9.226

HNWL 25.296   425×24m

20.00

▽-19.500

16.000

-46.28 -44.61 -43.44

HNWL:Highest navigable water level
LNWL:Lowest navigable water level

unit:cm

7a

4 主桥型布置
Fig.4 Layout of main bridge type

图5 南锚碇
Fig.5 South anchorage pier

图6 北锚碇
Fig.6 North anchorage pier

图7 建成的武汉阳逻桥（承郭宏磊教授惠赠）
(a), (b)
*Fig.7 Completed Wuhan Yangluo Bridge
(courtesy of Senior Engr. Prof. Guo Honglei)*
(a), (b)

254/255 中国桥梁建设新进展(1991–) / **悬索桥** NEW ADVANCES OF BRIDGE CONSTRUCTION IN CHINA (1991–) / SUSPENSION BRIDGES

4

6

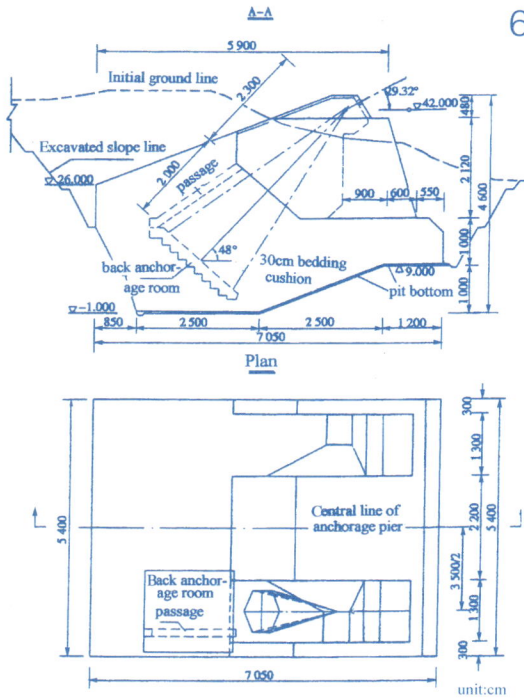

A-A

5 900

Initial ground line

2 300

19.32° ▽42.000

480

2 120

4 600

Excavated slope line

▽26.000

2 000

passage

900 600 550

1 000

48°

30cm bedding cushion

△9.000

pit bottom

1 000

back anchorage room

▽-1.000

850 | 2 500 | 2 500 | 1 200

7 050

Plan

300

1 300

2 200

5 400

Central line of anchorage pier

3 500×2

1 300

5 400

Back anchorage room passage

300

7 050

unit:cm

Separate pile caps are set under cable pylon columns. Under each north pylon column foundation, 14 bored piles ϕ 2.8m are set to be arranged transversely into 3, 4, 4, 3 in quincuncial shape. Under each south pylon column, 5×5 bored piles ϕ 2.0m are placed. The depth of caps is 6m.

Owing to thick cover and large scale of south anchorage pier (Fig.5) and close distance (only 150m) to Yangtze River embankment, the flood control requirement of which is high, the design and construction of deep foundation pit is difficult. Finally it was decided to adopt circular slurry wall (Fig.5), with external diameter of foundation to be ϕ 7.3m, wall thickness 1.5m and total depths 54.5~61.5m. This slurry wall is constructed with grade C35 underwater concrete. The internal lining thicknesses are variable: in 6m depth it is 1.5m, in 6~21m 2.0m, in 21~41m 2.5m, and the lining is constructed of C30 concrete. The gravel level surfaces are excavated to -20.32~ -24.0m, a 0.3~0.4m thick concrete bedding is cast and then a 6m thick RC bottom slab is constructed. After finishing the C15 filled concrete, a 8~10m thick RC top slab is poured. For improving the uniformity

5

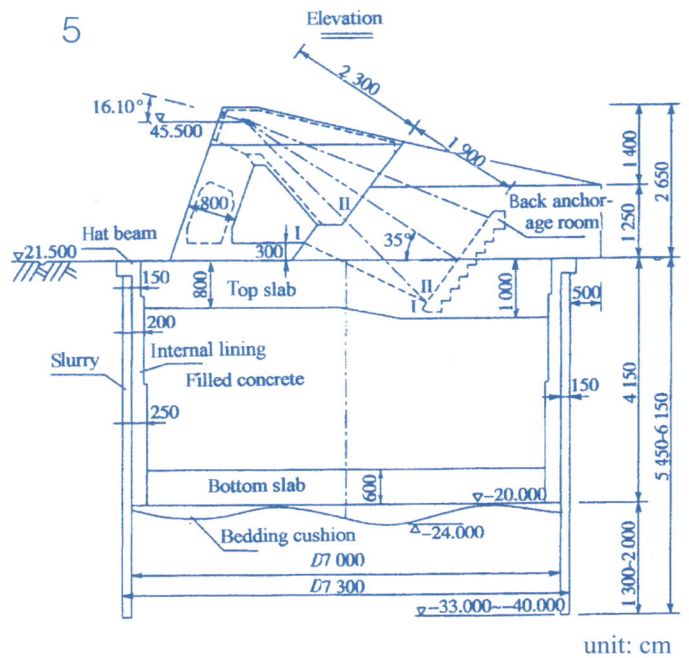

Elevation

2 300

16.10° 45.500

1 900

1 400

2 650

800

II

Back anchorage room

1 250

Hat beam

35°

300

I

▽21.500

150

800

Top slab

II

1 000

500

200

Slurry

Internal lining

4 150

150

5 450-6 150

Filled concrete

250

Bottom slab

600

▽-20.000

Bedding cushion

△-24.000

Ø7 000

Ø7 300

1 300-2 000

▽-33.000~-40.000

unit: cm

7b

由于南锚碇（图5）厚的覆盖和大的尺度和靠近（仅150m）长江堤岸，其洪控要求是高的，深基坑的设计和构造是困难的。最后决定采用圆形地下连续墙（图6），基础外径为ϕ73m，壁厚1.5m，总深度为54.5~61.5m。地下墙用水下混凝土C35建造。内衬厚度是变化的：在6m深度内厚度为1.5m，在6~21m，厚2.0m，在21~41m，厚2.5m，衬砌采用混凝土C30建造。开挖至卵石层表面标高−20.3~24.0m，浇筑0.3~0.4m厚的垫层混凝土，然后浇筑6m厚的钢筋混凝土底板。填芯混凝土C15施工完成后，浇筑8~10m厚的钢筋混凝土顶板。为了提高基底应力分布的均匀性，在基锚碇前半部设置26个空隔仓，并对前趾区卵石层进行压浆加固处理。在锚体尾部设置16根直径ϕ1.2m钻孔灌注桩和1.5m厚承台以支承锚块尾部混凝土自重。

　　在北锚碇（图6）中，采用自然开挖的重力锚体。总深度46.0m，基础长度70.5m，宽度54.0m。基础底部分成两个台阶：第一台阶底面标高为−1.0m，第二台阶底面标高为+9.0m，中间水平距离25.0m范围设计成斜坡，对锚体，除索鞍支承顶部用混凝土C40建造外，对其余部分采用混凝土C30。在锚系中ϕ15.24mm预应力钢绞线标准强度为1 860MPa.

　　北锚碇混凝土用量为87 440m³，钢筋1 750t，预应力钢绞线126t，钢材531t（不计定位架）。南锚碇基础混凝土用量为172 524m³，钢筋6 648t，钢材79t。锚体混凝土用量为40 259m³，钢筋1 144t，预应力钢绞线114t，钢材（不计定位架）382t。施工于2003年10月开始，于2007年建成。图7示建成的武汉阳逻桥。

世界最长的10座悬索桥

编号	桥名	跨度（m）	位置	建成年份
1	明石海峡桥	1 991	日本神户—Kobe	1998
2	西堠门大桥	1 650	中国舟山岛	2008
3	大海带桥	1 624	丹麦科瑟（Korsor）	1998
4	润扬大桥	1 490	中国镇江	2005
5	亨伯尔大桥	1 410	英国赫尔（Hull）	1981
6	江阴大桥	1 385	中国江苏	1999
7	青马大桥	1 377	中国香港	1997
8	维拉扎诺海峡桥	1 298	美国纽约	1964
9	金门大桥	1 280	美国旧金山	1997
10	阳逻大桥	1 280	中国武汉	2007

　　从上可见从1997—2008年的短短11年中我国在世界10座悬索大桥中不仅建成5座，而且最长桥跃居第二位，建设速度之快和规模之大，确是惊人的。当然我们还应不断前进。

of the stress distribution under foundation, in the front part of the anchorage pier 26 empty cells are set, and around the toe of the pier a gravel layer a strengthening of pressure gravity is conducted. Under the tail part of pier, 16 bored and filling piles ϕ 1.2m and a 1.5m thick cap are set to support the dead load of concrete from pier tail.

In the north anchorage (Fig.6), a gravity anchorage body with natural excavation is adopted. Its total depth is 46.0m with foundation length of 70.5m and width 54.0m. The foundation base is divided into 2 steps: the base level of the 1st one is −1.0m, that of the 2nd is +9.0m, and the mid horizontal distance 25.0m is designed into a slope. For the anchorage body, except that the support top of cable saddle is constructed of C40 concrete, for the other part C30 concrete is used. The ϕ 15.24mm PC strand with standard strength of 1 860MPa is used in anchorage system.

The amount of concrete in north anchorage pier is 87 440m^3, steel bars 1 750t, PC strands 126t and steel (uncounted of positioning frame) 531t. In south anchorage pier foundation: amount of concrete is 172 524m^3, steel bars 6 648t, steel 79t. In anchorage body: amount of concrete is 40 259m^3, steel bars 1 144t, PC strands 114t and steel 382t (uncounted of positioning frame). This construction was commenced in Oct. 2003, and has been completed in 2007. Fig.7 shows the completed Wuhan Yangluo Bridge.·

The leading 10 long-span suspension bridges worldwide

No.	Bridge	Span(m)	Location	Year
1	Akashi-Kaikyo	1 991	Kobe, Japan	1998
2	Xihoumen	1 650	Zhoushan Island, China	2008
3	Great Belt East	1 624	Korsor, Denmark	1998
4	Runyang South	1 490	Zhenjiang, China	2005
5	Humber	1 410	Kingston-upon-Hull, UK	1981
6	Jiangyin	1 385	Jiangsu, China	1999
7	Tsing Ma	1 377	Hong Kong, China	1997
8	Verrazano-Narrows	1 298	New York, NY, USA	1964
9	Golden Gate	1 280	San Francisco, CA, USA	1997
10	Yangluo	1 280	Wuhan, China	2007

It can be seen that in a short time of 11 years since 1997 to 2008, China has completed 5 longest suspension bridges among the 10 longest worldwide and the longest occupies the 2nd position. The construction speed is faster and the scale is large, certainly both are worthy to be admired. Of course China should go forward continuously.

参考文献

1.徐国平，邓海. 武汉阳逻长江大桥总体设计. 中国公路学会桥梁和结构分会. 2004年全国桥梁学术会议论文集. 北京：人民交通出版社，2004：116-123

2.徐国平，刘明虎，刘化国. 武汉阳逻长江大桥锚碇设计. 中国公路学会桥梁和结构分会. 2004年全国桥梁学术会议论文集. 北京：人民交通出版社，2004：129-138

REFERENCES

1.Xu Guoping, Deng Hai. *Overall design of Wuhan Yangluo Yangtze River Bridge. The Proceedings of the National Symposium on Bridge. Branch Society for Bridges and Structures, China Highway Society. Beijing: Press of People's Communication. 2004: 116-123*

2.Xu Guoping, Liu Minghu, Liu Huaguo. *Anchorage Design of Wuhan Yangluo Yangtze River Bridge. Ibid, The Proceedings of the National Symposium on Bridge. Branch Society for Bridges and Structures, China Highway Society. Beijing: The People's Communication Press. 2004: 129-138*

3.Xu Guoping, et al 5 person. *The Yangluo Bridge—a large suspension bridge under construction in Wuhan, China. RIA. 2005(5)*

齐勒哈仁钢丝网水泥悬索桥

在我国，钢丝网水泥在桥梁工程中的应用开始于1973年。1974年在山西省太谷县一试验性13m净跨混凝土敞肩拱，用钢丝网水泥扁壳板填充成功地建成跨越香玉河。1975年，一座单跨20m净跨、用钢丝网水泥扁壳板建造的混凝土敞肩式拱桥跨越山西东山河。重庆市开县70m跨临江桥于1976年建成，它是一座双曲单拱桥，由5个预制30mm厚钢丝网水泥节段在纵向组成，而在横向是整体节段。在预制钢丝网水泥节段吊起闭合成拱后，砌石以组成组合拱。该桥看起来优美轻巧。

在四川省南充市跨越嘉陵江的6跨拱桥，每跨跨长为70m，于1975年建成，桥的总长为775.51m。拱圈侧壁是用30mm厚的钢丝网水泥建造，而组成钢筋混凝土箱形截面。

在重庆市云阳县跨越潭溪的195.66m桥是我国第一座钢丝网水泥斜拉桥。桥面用钢丝网水泥建造，加劲梁为钢筋混凝土单箱截面，宽度1.9m。桥的跨长为34.91m、78.84m和89.91m。桥面系统用正交、厚度t=35mm钢丝网水泥带肋板，用3层网2层钢筋、肋高215mm（扣除 t），宽35mm，桥面很轻，迄今（至1993年编者撰写参考资料2时，今不详）仍基本保持良好的使用条件。

齐勒哈仁桥跨越新疆自治区额尔齐斯河（在新疆之北），于1992年7月建成，为一座3跨悬索公路牧道两用桥（图1），跨长为36m、108m和36m。该桥净宽度为4.5m+2×0.25m（安全带）。加劲梁为一高1.41m的钢丝网水泥梯形箱梁，带纵横向肋，而用钢筋混凝土边梁在两侧边加强（图2）。箱梁底和侧板用5层网和3层钢筋（习称5网3筋）预制成8m节段，同时厚度为40mm。横肋用4层网和3层钢筋（习称4网3筋），厚40mm，高度200mm。纵横肋间距分别为500mm和800mm。桥面系构成正交各向异性钢丝网水泥板，4只小的不相连接的梯形箱梁，其中距为1.0m，厚

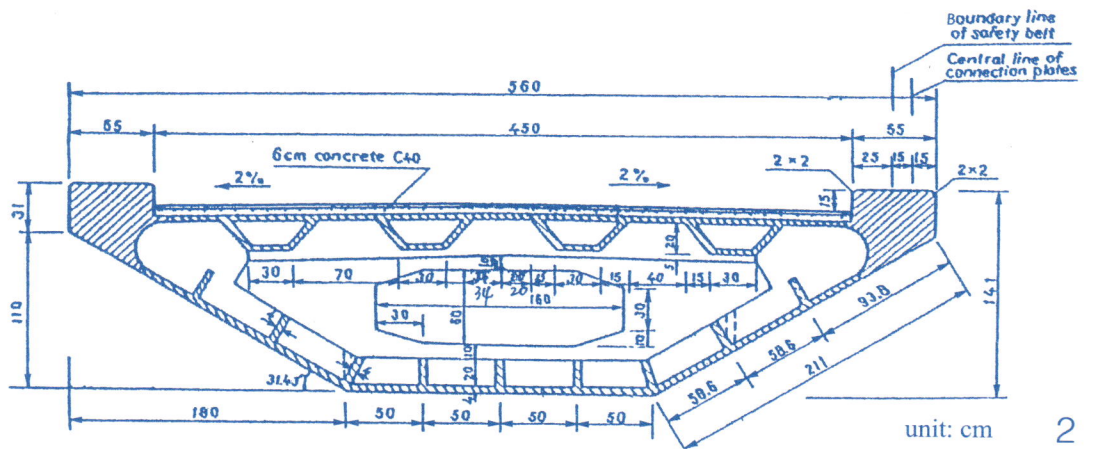

unit: cm

2

258/259 中国桥梁建设新进展（1991-）/ **悬索桥** NEW ADVANCES OF BRIDGE CONSTRUCTION IN CHINA (1991-) / SUSPENSION BRIDGES

Qileharen Ferrocement Suspension Bridge

In China, the use of ferrocement in bridge engineering started in 1973. In 1974 in Taigu County of Shanxi Province, an experimental 13m clear span spandrel concrete arch bridge filled with ferrocement shallow shell slabs was successfully completed over Xiangyu River. In 1975, a single-span open spandrel concrete arch bridge of 20m clear span with ferrocement shallow shell slabs was constructed over Dongshan River in Shanxi Province. The 70m span Linjiang Bridge in Kai County of Sichuan Province, completed in 1976 is a single arch double curvature bridge assembled from 5 precast 30mm thick ferrocement segments in longitudinal direction and monolithic segment in the transverse direction. After the precast ferrocement segments were hoisted to be closed into arch, stones were built so as to constitute a composite arch bridge. This bridge appears very exquisite and very light.

The 6-span arch bridge over Jialing River in Nanchong City of Sichuan Province with span length of 70m for each span was completed in 1975. the total length of the bridge is equal to 775.71m. the lateral walls of the arch ring were made of 30mm thick ferrocement and constituted of reinforced concrete section.

The 195.66m bridge cover Tanxi River in Yunyang of Chongqing City is the first ferrocement cable-stayed bridge in China. The deck is made of ferrocement and the stiffening girder is made of single reinforced concrete box section with 1.9m width. The span lengths of this bridge are 34.91m, 75.84m and 84.91m. the deck system was formed by using of orthogonal ferrocement ribbed slab with thickness t equal to 35mm, 3 layers of mesh and 2 layers of bar with rib depth (deducing t) of 215mm and width of 35mm, the deck of the bridge is very light and up to now (up to 1993 as the Editor wrote Ref.2, now the situation is not understood), it is kept basically in good service conditions.

The Qileharen Bridge over Erqisi River in Xinjiang Autonomous Region (in the north of XAR), completed in July 1992, is a bi-purposed suspension for highway and herd with three spans (Fig.1) with length of 36m, 108m and 36m. This bridge has a clear width of 4.5m+2×0.25m (safety belts). The stiffening girder is 1.41m high ferrocement trapeze box beam with longitudinal and transverse rib, and stiffened with reinforced concrete edge beams on both lateral sides (Fig.2). The bottom and lateral plates of the box beam were made of 5 layers of mesh and 3 layers of bars (be used to call 5 meshes-3 bars) precast in 8m segment simultaneously with thickness of 40mm. The transverse ribs was made of 4 layers of mesh and 3 layers of bars (be used to call 4 meshes-3 bars) with thickness of 40mm and depth of 200mm. The spacings of longitudinal ribs and transverse ribs are equal to 500mm and 800mm respectively. The deck system is made of orthogonally anisotropic ferrocement plates with longitudinal ribs of 4 small disconnected trapeze boxes, of which the central spacing is 1.0m and the thickness is 40mm. It is made of 4 layers of mesh and 2 layers of bars. The width of box bottom is equal to 300mm. The 40mm thick transverse rib is made of 4 layers of

图1 齐勒哈仁桥（承牛铁汉教授级高工惠赠）
Fig.1 Qileharen Bridge (courtesy of the Senior Engr. Prof. Niu Tiehan)

图2 齐勒哈仁桥截面
Fig.2 Section of Qileharen Bridge

1

40mm。小箱用4层网和2层钢筋构成。箱底宽为300mm。40mm厚横肋由4层网和3层钢筋构成，高度250mm，间距800mm。在纵向，建造120mm厚横向钢筋混凝土（C40）横隔，间距4.0m，用以加强小箱梁抗扭刚度。C40混凝土于钢丝网水泥桥面上铺成厚度60mm。钢丝网（5mm直径）100mm×75mm设置在混凝土加预应力以防止开裂。在悬索内涂层和隔离层的外表面10~12mm，保护层用3层钢丝网并敷设M5水泥浆构成。

图3示钢丝网水泥箱梁下半部的制造。

齐勒哈仁桥桥塔采用钢筋混凝土门式结构，塔柱为1.2m×1.8m的削角多边形。每个塔柱基础为4根直径1.2m的钻孔灌注桩。锚碇为重力式箱形结构。每根索缆由7束61钢丝共427ϕ5的平行钢丝束组成。

大桥为公路、牧道两用桥，于1992年7月竣工。

齐勒哈仁桥的薄壁钢丝网水泥箱梁、正交异性桥面系和用于悬索的防护方法曾获得国家专利。

钢丝网水泥也用于修理桥面，广东省洛溪大桥主跨180m，曾是我国当时最长的刚架桥。在通车一年后，约400m² 桥面铺砌显示出剥落迹象。用细粒石混凝土配以钢纤维（用熔抽法生产）和15mm×15mm网格的11mm直径钢丝制成的一种组合材料修理桥面。这种组合材料的强度、延性、韧性和耐磨性是非常好的。

在20世纪70年代中，用钢丝网水泥制造的浮式沉井开始获得承认。在四川宜宾建造的100m钢筋混凝土拱桥主墩用外直径12m、高度6~9m的沉井构成，双井壁之间距离为1.3m，内外壁厚度为30mm。它们是用4层网和2层钢筋构成，内壁下3m长采用6层网和2层钢筋。

除沉井外，钢丝网水泥套管也用以建设桥墩下的桩基础。

mesh and 3 layers of bars with 250mm depth and 800mm spacing. In longitudinal direction, a 120mm thick transverse reinforced concrete (C40) diaphragm with 4.0m spacing is constructed for strengthening the stiffness of the small box beams against torsion. C40 concrete was paved to a thickness of 60mm on the top of the ferrocement deck. Wire mesh (5mm diameter) 100mm×75mm placed in concrete is prestressed to prevent cracking. On the external surface of the internal coating and insulating layers of the suspending cables, ferrocement cover 10~12mm thick is made using a 3 layer wire-mesh plastered with M5 cement mortar.

Fig.3 shows the fabrication of the half part below of the ferrocement box girder.

The pylon of Qileharen Bridge adopts reinforced concrete portal frame structure, pylon columns are 2 polygons of 1.2m×1.8m with cut edges. The bored-filling piles with diameter of 1.2m are used as the foundation of each pylon column. The anchorage piers are gravity-type box structures. Each main cable consists of 7 tendons of 61 wires, totalling 427ϕ5 parallel wires.

This bridge has highway herdway bi-purpose and was completed in July 1992.

Ferrocement is also used to repair the deck of bridge. Luoxi Bridge in Guangdong Province with a main span of 180m was the longest rigid frame bridge at that time in China. After one year behind its opening, about 400m^2 of deck pavement showed the signs of spalling. A composite material, made of fine-grained stone concrete reinforced with steel fiber (produced by melt and drawn method) and 15mm×15mm mesh of 11mm diameter wires was used to repair this deck. The strength, ductility, toughness and wearability of this composite material are considerably good.

In the 1970s, floating caissons made of ferrocement started to gain acceptance. The main piers of the 100m reinforced concrete arch in Yibin of Sichuan Province are made of caissons with external diameter equal to 12m and heights ranging from 6m to 9m, the distance between two walls is 1.3m and the thickness of both the internal and external walls is equal to 30mm. They are made of 4 layers of mesh and 2 layers of bars, for the internal wall, 6 layers of mesh and 2 layers of bars are used for the height of 3m below.

Except caissons, ferrocement casing pipes are also used in the construction of pile foundation under bridge piers.

图2 齐勒哈仁桥截面
Fig.2 Section of Qileharen Bridge

图3 钢丝网水泥箱梁（下半部）的制造
（承牛铁汉教授级高工惠赠）
Fig.3 Fabrication of ferrocement box girder (half part below) (courtesy of the Senior Engr. Prof. Niu Tiehan)

参考文献

1.牛铁汉，唐德熊. 采用钢丝网水泥薄壁箱梁加劲的悬索桥 —— 跨越额尔齐斯齐勒哈仁桥设计简介. 新疆公路运输四川科学技术，1992（4）：2-9

REFERENCES

1.Niu Tiehan, Tang Dexiong. The suspension bridge stiffened with ferrocement thin-wall box girder — A brief introduction of design to Qileharen Bridge spanning Erqisihe. Xinjiang Highway Transport Sichuan Scientific Technique. 1992(4): 2-9

2.Ding Dajun. Ferrocement Structures in China. Journal of Ferrocement. 1993. 23(3): 213-222

香港青马大桥

在香港主要居住区和大屿山岛上的新机场之间的必经之路上有3个结构：马湾高架桥、汲水门斜拉桥、青马悬索桥和隧道。青马大桥的上层布置2个3车道的公路，下层是双轨铁路线和2个单车道的封闭公路。

青马大桥（图1，图2）主跨1 377m（图3），全长2 160m。香港的气候条件，尤其是台风的发生和腐蚀性大气，以及铁路通往机场的要求是设计的主要影响因素。其他的重要因素有海上和空中的通航净空，对轮船可能撞击的保护措施，以及进行深水施工的各种困难。

青马大桥从靠大陆一侧的青衣跨越马湾岛，除了马湾塔的基础以外，其他的基础都是支承在坚实基岩上的扩大基础，马湾塔建造在离岸350m左右的一个海底大陆架附近，大约12m深的沉箱上，塔四周还建造了一个防船撞击的保护岛（图4）。这个方案决定了1 377m的中跨和355.5m的马湾一侧悬索边跨。

在青衣一侧，地形陡峭，严重限制了新建3号高速公路线的立体交叉。由于靠岸的水很深，公路线型方案要求引道从桥塔处的主线开始分道。

青衣岸边的水深，要求桥塔建在接近水滨的岸上。公路立交定线妨碍了选跨方案的采用。在青衣一侧，在锚碇桥座结构和主塔之间，有3个桥墩；在马湾一侧，则有2个墩身用爬模法建造基础。钢筋加环氧涂层，给以海蚀环境中的额外保护。最终完成的悬索桥不仅是世界上净跨最长的公路铁路两用桥[①]，而且也将是世界上最不对称的悬索之一。

206m高的钢筋混凝土桥塔采用滑模施工，每个塔柱宽6m（沿横桥向），并沿纵向从18m收分到9m。塔柱在竖向倾斜的坡度为1/100，并用预应力混凝土门式深梁连接，以抵抗侧向力。为了保证塔柱在施工中可能出现大风时的稳定，在滑模施工过程中，钢桁架被设置在门梁处。这些钢桁架最终浇注在永久性的混凝土梁中。桥塔基础的控制设计标

3

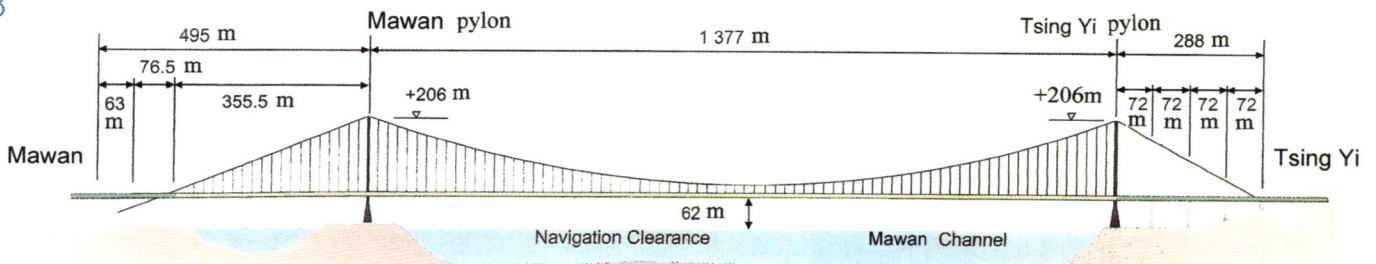

① 日本明石海峡桥（Akashi-Kaikyo Bridge）最先方案是设在本州—四国连线中线上公铁两用悬索桥，跨度分布为890m+1 780m+890m，1986年施工时已改至东线上，为主跨1 990m的公路悬索桥。

① The first project of Japanese Akaski-Kaihyo Bridge was located on the middle line of Honshu-Shikokiu highway and railway bi-purpose connection with spans: 890m+1 780m+890m, before construction in 1986, it was shifted to east line and changed into a suspension bridge for highway with main span of 1 990m.

图1 香港青马悬索桥（承冯铭硕教授惠赠）
Fig.1 Hong Kong Tsing Ma Suspension Bridge (courtesy of Prof. Feng Mingshuo)

图2 青马大桥（1997年编者自拍）(a)
Fig.2 Tsing Ma Bridge (taken by the Editor in 1997)(a)

图3 青马大桥总体布置（承冯铭硕教授惠赠）
Fig.3 General layout of Tsing Ma Bridge (courtesy of Prof. Feng Mingshuo)

2a

Hongkong Tsing Ma Bridge

Along the road necessary to pass from the main housing territories of Hong Kong to the airport on the Lantau Island, there are 3 important structures: Mawan Viaduct, Kap Shui Mun Cable-Stayed Bridge, Tsing Ma Suspension Bridge and tunnel. On the upper deck, there are arranged two 3-lane highways, on the lower, there is a close line consisting of a double truck railway and two single-lane highways.

The main span of Tsing Ma Bridge (Fig.1, 2) is 1 377m with entire length of 2 160m (Fig.3). The climate conditions in HK, especially the occurrence of typhoon and corrosive atmosphere as well as the requirements of railway passing to airport are the main influence factors in design. The other important factors are navigation clearances on sea and in sky, protective measures against the possible collision of ships and various difficulties during construction in deep water.

Tsing Ma Bridge spans Mawan Island from Tsing Yi River near the mainland, excepting the foundation of Mawan Pylon, the other ones are extended foundations supported on solid rock, the Mawan Pylon is constructed in the vicinity of continental shelf on seabed near bank by 350m or so on a caisson with depth of 12m, around the pylon an artificial island is constructed for protecting the impact from ships (Fig.4). This project decides the central span of 1 377m suspension and the side span on Mawan of 355.5m.

On the side of Tsing Yi, the topography is so precipitous as to seriously limit the grade separated interchange of newly constructed express highway No.3. Because the water near bank is deep, the project of highway line requires the approach road to separate with the main line started from the pylon.

The water depth near Tsing Yi bank requires the pylon to be constructed on bank near water. The alignment of highway grade separate interchange of preventing the adoption of suspended span project. On Tsing Yi, between anchorage abutment structure and the main pylon, there are 3 piers, on Mawan, there 2. The pier stems were constructed by the jump form method. The reinforced steel bars in the foundation are coated with epoxy to give additional protection in the marine environment. Finally completed is not only a highway and railway bi-purpose suspension bridge with longest clear span in the world[①], but also one of most unsymmetrical worldwide suspension bridge.

The reinforced concrete pylons with height of 206m were constructed with slide form, the width of every pylon column is 6m along the transverse, and along the longitudinal direction it is decreased from 18m to 9m by entasis method. The vertical slope of inclination of pylon columns is 1/100 and the columns are connected with PC portal deep beams to resist lateral wind forces. In order to guarantee the stability of pylon columns in the possible strong wind during construction, in the construction process with portal beams, which were finally cast in the permanent concrete beams. The

图2 青马大桥（1997年编者自拍摄）(b)
Fig.2 Tsing Ma Bridge (taken by the Editor in 1997)(b)

准规定各个塔柱间的不均匀沉降允许最大值为10mm。

重力锚碇对沿周围岩石的抗滑移和剪切的设计最小安全系数为2，它们同时也当桥面台座。青衣锚碇桥台大大地低于地面，岩石开挖达290 000m³；而马湾锚碇大部分被埋置，桥台则在地面以上。

主索用36m的间距，采用平行钢绞线，每股由127根φ5.12mm的镀锌钢丝组成，使用应力限制为破坏强度的44%。然而，承包者采用较为传统的空中绕丝技术，这样较便宜，但在施工中遭台风影响的危险性增大。主跨缆索的绕丝在1995年3月15日顺利完成，较大边跨的绕丝在两个星期后完成。缆索最终直径约为1.1m（图5），由φ5.38mm总长160 000km的钢丝绕成。缆索用三重防护螺旋钢绞线与锚碇相连。

桥面吊杆通过沟纹带固定到缆索。吊索间间距为18m，这些索通过铸钢锚头和桥面连接。

自从20世纪40年代美国的Tacoma峡谷桥塌毁以来，空气动力学的研究已经清楚指出，允许悬吊桥面的加劲桁架行车道间中央通风的益处，这种形式的通风曾体现在苏格兰Forth公路桥中[②]。然而其他的研究证明封闭箱形截面的有效性和阻力系数低。紧接在Forth桥之后设计的英格兰Severn桥具有相似的主跨，桥面采用了箱形截面[③]。

由于恶劣的大风气候，青马桥桥面需要最优的空气动力效率，因此开始研究组合Forth桥面和Severn桥面主要性能的潜在益处。青马桥最后的截面采用桁架加劲的双层箱形结构，并设有非结构边缘流线型外观的桥面，提供上下层的纵向通风设施，可增大稳定性（图6）。

主梁构造工程照片示于图7。

对桥面模型进行空气动力试验以监测不同布置通风设施的尺寸、位置和导向边缘细部时桥面的性能。对改变上部和下部通风设施的效果分开研究，发现当上部通风口宽度从9.4m减小到2m时，保持满意的临界风速，同时涡流发散振幅减小。当下部通风宽度改变时，发现涡流发散振幅减小，需要在铁轨两边有一段短的封闭长度。在两种情况下，得出完全封闭的通风可以导致临界风速的急剧下降。

4

5

② 1964年建造，主跨为1 006m的悬索桥，采用加劲桁架，除美国外是世界其他同类桥中第一座超过1km的悬索桥（参看G. Roberts. Design of the Forth Road Bridge. Proc. Inst. Civ. Engrs. Nov.1965）

③ 它是世界上第一座采用流线形箱形截面的悬索桥，箱高3.05m，主跨988m，采用的高跨比为1/423（参看N. J. Gimsing. Cable Supported Bridges, Concept and Design. New York: John Wiley & Sons, 1983: 400）

② It was constructed with stiffening trusses in 1964 and is a suspension bridge with main span of 1 006m, excepting USA, this bridge is the first worldwide suspension bridge exceeding 1km (see G. Roberts, Design of the Forth Road Bridge. Proc. Inst. Civ. Engrs. Nov. 1965).

③ It is suspension bridge firstly in the world used streamlined box section with box depth of 3.05, main span of 988m, the adopted depth-span ratio is 1/423 (see N. J. Gimsing. Cable Supported Bridges. Concept and Design. New York: John Wiley & Sons, 1983: 400)

图4 马湾塔人工岛（承Bd&e，1995）
Fig.4 Artificial island of Mawan (courtesy of Bd&e in 1995)

图5 足尺寸钢索模型照片（编者自拍摄）
Fig.5 Photo of full-size model of cable (taken by the Editor)

Standard controlling pylon foundation design stipulates the largest allowable unequal settlement between columns is 10mm.

The design minimum safety factors against slide and shear of the rock around gravity anchorage structure is 2. These anchorage are also the deck abutments. Tsing Yi anchorage abutment is enormously lower than ground surface, the cut rock reached 290 000m^3, but the most part of Mawan anchorage structure was buried and the abutment is on ground.

The spacing of 2 main cables is 36m, constituted of parallel strands, every one of which is made of 127 galvanizing wires ϕ5.12mm, the limitation of their serviceable stress was 44% ultimate strength. However, the contractor adopted the more traditional air-spinning technique, it was cheaper, but the danger of sustaining typhoon during construction was increased. The spinning of main cables was finished smooth on March 15, 1995, that of larger side span was done after 2 weeks. The final diameter cables is about 1.1m (Fig.5), constituted of wires of ϕ5.38mm with total length 160 000km. The cable is connected to anchorage by using of spiral strands with triple protection.

Deck hangers are fixed to cables through grooved bands. The spacings between hanging cables are 18m, these cables are connected with deck through cast steel anchorages.

Since the Tacoma Narrow Bridge in America collapsed in the 1940s, the research on air dynamics has clearly pointed out, the benefits to allow central ventilation between lanes of the stiffening truss in suspension bridge. The ventilation of this type has appeared in Scotland Forth Road Bridge[②]. However the other studies show the effectiveness and resistance coefficient of close box section are low. In the England Severn Bridge with similar main span design following closely Forth Bridge, the deck adopts box section[③].

Owing to adverse atmosphere climate, the deck of Tsing Ma Bridge requires the optimum air dynamical effect, so the relative experts start to study the potential benefits of combining the main behaviour of Forth Bridge deck and Severn Bridge deck. The final section of Tsing Ma Bridge adopts double-deck box structure stiffened with trusses, and there is set non-structural edge streamlined appearance, the upper and lower decks provide longitudinal ventilation facilities and increase the stability (Fig.6).

The engineering photos of the construction of main girder is showed in Fig.7.

The air dynamical tests conducted for the deck model monitor the deck behaviour under different arrangements of ventilation facilities, through their dimensions, places and the guiding edge detans. The separate studies of effects to change the upper and lower ventilation facilities show it can keep satisfactory critical wind velocity and the diverging amplitude of vortex decreases when the upper ventilation with decreases to 2m from 9.4m. When the lower ventilation width changes, it requires that there is a segment of close length beside both sides of rails. In 2 cases, all close ventilation will result in the critical wind velocity to have a sudden drop.

最初设计中，只有公路和铁路通往机场，而在大屿山的集装箱泊位也将经过青马桥，后来这条通道也被保留下来，以应付恶劣的气候。这种全天候的能力通过下层由空气动力性能好的不锈钢壳包住的铁路和两条公路行车道来达到。

最后的主梁截面（图6，图7）包括2榀6.3m高的纵向桁架，间距30m，它们与支承行车道的正交各向异性桥面板共同作用提供抗弯刚度。空腹横向框架支承在纵向斜撑式桁架之上，与加劲板行车道构件共同作用。非结构的1.5mm厚不锈钢挡板构成了边缘外壳面层，上层桥面两条车道之间采用3.5m宽纵向通风口分隔开，铁路主要在箱内，位于12m宽中央纵向通风口上，两边是两条隐蔽的公路线。

截面的空气动力试验证明没有发散的振荡并检测了涡流发散振荡。这些是在低风速时发生，振幅大小和频率都是可接受的。由于比较缺少实际的台风中心附近空气流动形式的知识，因此对桥位处可能遭受的风，桥面性能是在水平倾斜±7.5°之间测定的。但是，应强调仅是为了了解截面在风作用下的行为而包括了较大的角度，而不是反映预计的现场条件。

现青马大桥在当时世界悬索桥中占第7位，但在公铁两用悬索桥中却占第一位，因它较原世界纪录的日本本州—四国连接中线的南备讃濑户悬索桥主跨为1 100m大很多。

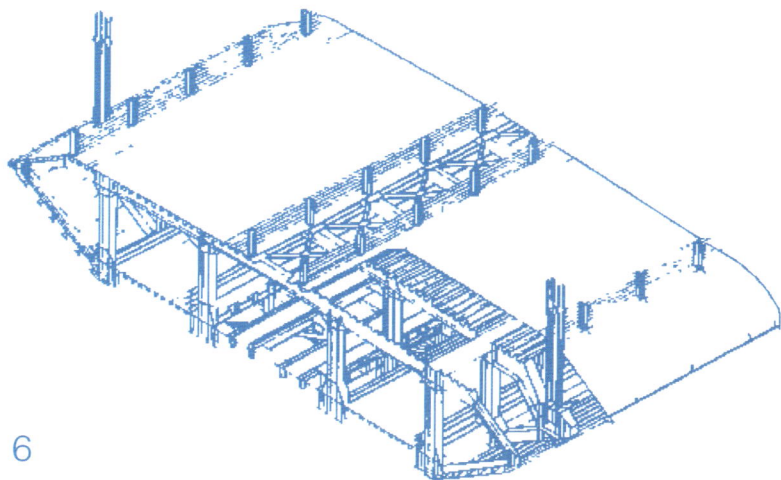

6

图6 主梁立体构造示意
Fig.6 Stereoscopic construction sketch of main girder

图7 主梁构造工程照片（承冯铭硕教授惠赠）
Fig.7 Engineering photo of construction of main girder open to traffic (courtesy of Prof. Feng Mingshuo)

7

In preliminary design, there are only road and railway to go to the airport, the berth of containers at Dayushan (Shan means mountain) will also pass through Tsing Ma Bridge, later this passage was also kept to meet the adverse weather. This all-water capacity can achieve through railway and 2 road lanes on lower deck encased in stainless steel shell with good air-dynamical behavouir.

Finally the section of main girder (Figs.6, 7) includes two 6.3m-depth longitudinal trusses with spacing of 30m, these trusses provide the flexural stiffness through the integral action with the orthotropic deck supporting the lanes. The transverse open-web trusses are supported on the longitudinal diagonal-bracing trussed and both of them institute integral action with the stiffening lane deck. The non-structural 1.5mm thick stainless sheetings form external shell cover on edges and the uppers deck between 2 lanes is separated by using 3.5m-wide vent, the railway is in the box and is located over the longitudinal 12m-wide central vent, there are 2 concealed road lines.

The air-dynamical tests of section show there is no diverging oscillation and the diverging oscillations of vortex is monitored. These occur under low wind velocity, the amplitude and vibration frequency are acceptable. Owing to lack of the knowledge of airflow form near practical typhoon center, hence for the wind possibly sustained at the bridge site, the behavior of bridge deck was measured under horizontal inclination between $\pm7.5°$. But it should be emphasized that including larger angles was only to understand the section behavior under wind action.

Now, Tsing Ma Bridge occupies the 7th place in the worldwide suspension bridges, but does the 1st in the bi-purposed highway-railway bridges, because its main span is greatly larger than 1 100m in Minamibisan Sets Bridge which is located on the line to connect Honsha & Shikoku and was the original worldwide record.

参考文献

2.安琳，丁大钧. 香港青马大桥简介. 桥梁建设，1997（3）：22-26

3.香港民政事务总署. 青马大桥中英文资料. 6页. 冯铭硕教授惠赠

REFERENCES

1.The Tsing Ma Bridge. Bd&e. 1995: 52-61

2.An Lin, Ding Dajun. Simple Introduction of Hong Kong Tsing Ma Bridge. Bridge Construction. 1997(3): 22-26

3.Home Affairs Department. Tsing Ma Bridge, 6pp. courtesy of Prof. Feng Mingshuo.

江阴长江大桥

1. 引言

江阴长江悬索大桥（图1）位于江苏省发达的长江三角洲，它与上海、浙江、山东、安徽诸省邻接，水陆交通十分繁忙。由于长江的天然阻隔，给两岸的交通和交易造成困难，因此，苏北仍处于不发达境地。1968年，一座公路和铁路双层大桥建于南京，在上游距江阴长江大桥约180km。但是它们仍不能消除江苏400km长的江面阻隔。在此后的年代里，有10多座为渡行人和车辆的渡口被投入营运，但这些仍不能满足渡江增长的需要。1986年，开始一项建桥和隧道跨过长江的规划研究。经过对经济、交通流和自然条件的仔细分析，十二个有利位置被鉴定建桥或隧道。但是缺乏资金和专门知识，使当时在长江上建造任一种通道成为不可能。直到20世纪90年代初，情况改变，在中国一些大跨桥被建成或在建设中。从这些大桥的建设中，广泛的建造超长跨桥的经验已曾获得，江阴长江大桥，当时中国最长跨度悬索桥于1994年11月开始建设，在1999年9月建成开放。

2. 总述

江阴长江大桥位于江苏省中部，它由两条国有高速公路分享，在东海岸的同江—三亚高速公路和在西边的北京—上海高速公路。江阴长江大桥有6条车道，每面3条，通航净空为50m。大桥位于江最狭窄的截面上。悬索桥选择一跨过江而不干扰泄洪和通航，其主跨为1 385m（图2）。桥的布置和形状为一美学设计，这使桥获得"鲁班奖"和2002年国际桥协颁发的"尤金·菲戈桥梁奖章"。人们说大桥看来像一条飞越长江的美玉装饰带。主桥做成流线形钢箱梁，用有相同高度、两边跨的引跨预应力混凝土连续梁连接。相反，塔和锚碇却不可摧毁地刚劲而坚固地屹立着。因此全桥证明是协调和动人的。

3. 锚碇

锚碇是悬索桥主要的锚定结构。南塔为一座建于岩床上的重力式结构。北塔有一层在岩床上超过80m的土壤覆盖。

1b 1a

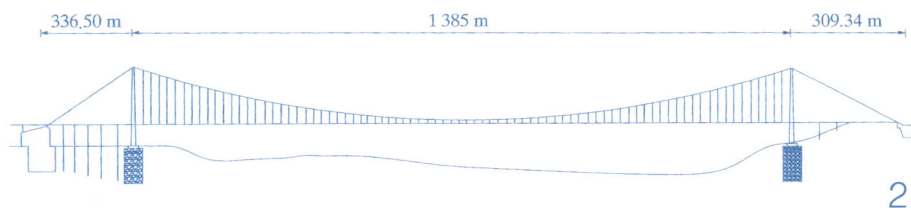

336.50 m　　　　　1 385 m　　　　　309.34 m

2

Jiangyin Yangtze River Bridge

1. Introduction

The Jiangyin Yangtze River suspension bridge(Fig.1) is located in Jiangsu Province at the developed Yangtze River Delta, it borders in the Shanghai, Zhejiang, Shandong and Anhui Provinces. Both land and water transportation is very busy. Owing to the natural barrier of the Yangtze River, communication and exchange between the two sides have been made difficult, as a result, the northern part of Jiangsu remains underdeveloped. In 1968, a double deck bridge for both highway and railway was built in Nanjing, about 180km upstream from the Jiangyin Yangtze Bridge. Nevertheless, it could not remove the 400km long barrier of the river in Jiangsu Province. In the years followed, more than 10 ferries for pedestrians and vehicles have been put into operation, but they still can not meet the increased demands of the river crossing. In 1986, a planning study was initiated for building bridges and tunnels across the Yangtze River. Twelve favorable sites were identified for bridges or tunnels after careful analysis of the economy, traffic flow and physical conditions.

However, a lack of funds and expertise made it impossible to build any of the crossings on the Yangtze River at the time. Up to the beginning of the 90's, the situation changed, some large bridges were completed or under constructed in China. From these bridges, extensive experience has been gained for the construction of super long span bridges. Combining local and overseas expertise, the Jiangyin Yangtze Bridge, China's current longest span suspension bridge at that time was brought into construction in November 1994 and completed and open to traffic in September 1999.

2. General Description

The Jiangyin Yangtze River Bridge is located in the center of the Jiangsu Province, it is shared by two national truck expressways: the Tongjiang-Sanya Expressway on the east coast and the Beijing-Shanghai Expressway on the west. The Jiangyin Yangtze Bridge has 6 traffic lanes, 3 in each direction. The height clearance for navigation is 50m. The bridge is located at the narrowest section of the river. The suspension bridge with one span crossing the river was selected for not interfering with flood discharge and navigation, its main span is 1 385m long (Fig.2). The layout and shape of the bridge is an aesthetic design, which contributed to the bridge winning the "Luban Prize" and the "Eugene C. Figg Jr. Medal for Signature Bridge" issued by IABSE in 2002. The bridge is said to look like a jade-studded belt flying over the river. The main bridge is made of flat streamlined steel box girders joined by prestressed continuous concrete girders of the same depth in approach spans of the two side spans. In contrast, the pylons and anchors stand unconquerably rigid and strong. Thus the whole bridge turns out to be harmonious and appealing.

3. Anchorage

The anchorage blocks are the main anchoring structures of the

1c

1d

图1 江阴大桥（承教授级高工周世忠惠赠）(a)~(d)
Fig.1 Jiangyin Bridge (courtesy of Senior Engr. Prof. Zhou Shizhong) (a)~(d)

图2 桥的布置
Fig.2 Bridge layout

为了锚定，选择和深埋沉箱一起的重力式结构。地面下有一层50m中砂和砾石密实的承力层。用钢筋混凝土做成的沉箱长69.51m，深58m（图3，图4）.

由于大尺寸和施工深度，锚碇是一项非常困难的下部结构工作。为了减小沉箱在施工期间的不均匀沉降，锚碇后5m宽的大体积混凝土直到加劲梁架设完成后才浇筑。在锚碇顶上的散索鞍沿江的方向在索缆架设后第1年移动48mm，第2年仅2mm。大部分位移在钢箱梁截面焊接前发生。对结构的承载力将没有很大影响。位移也小于设计中规定的容许值。

4. 主缆施工

主缆由平行高强钢丝制成，钢丝是镀锌的和焊接的。平行钢丝绞线法是用于架设主索（图5）。由于缆在架设过程中的严格控制，主缆的空隙比为16.6%。主悬缆和吊索架设同时连续进行。虽然主缆是在桥面架设前旋制的，它仍满足设计中对高程的要求。

5. 加劲梁的施工

加劲梁做成矩形钢箱（图6）。截面根据截面模型风洞试验选定。箱宽32.5m，截面高度3.02m，包括两个悬臂的总宽度为36.9m。

加劲梁是用固定在主缆上的起重机架设。架设梁的起重机是在工厂组装的而用船运至跨度位置。起重机固定在主缆上并沿主缆行驶而自提升，这样大大推动了架设过程。

6. 结束语

随着中国经济的快速发展，上海城市圈正在长江三角洲形成。沿江苏省长江工业区的快速发展确实促进江苏经济发展达到在中国的领先地位，并将对连接长江南北有着重要意义。

5

6

4

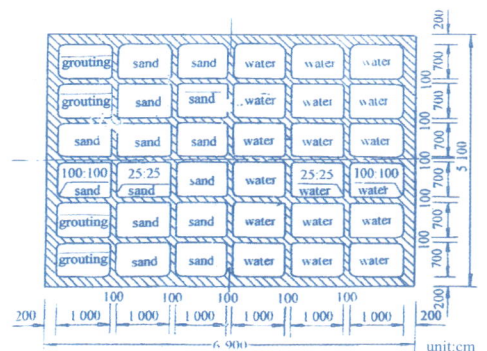

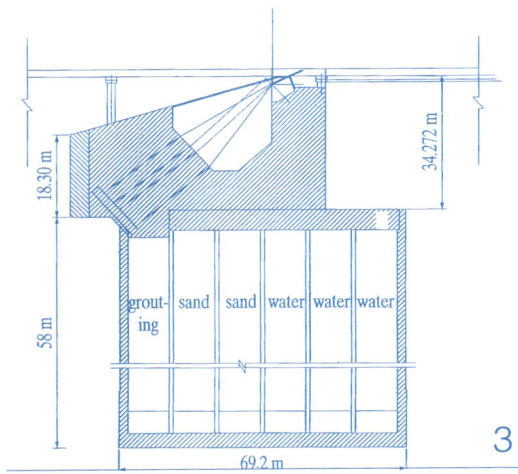

Labels in figure: 18.30 m, 34.272 m, 58 m, grout-ing, sand, sand, water, water, water, 69.2 m, 3

suspension bridge. The south pylons is a gravity structure built on bedrock. As the north bank has a soil covering of over 80m on bedrock, a gravity structure for the anchor was selected together with a deep embedded caisson. There is a dense bearing layer of medium-sized sand with gravel 50m below the ground. The caisson, made of reinforced concrete, is 69.51m in length and 58m in depth (Figs.3 and 4).

Owing to the great size and construction depth, the anchor was an extremely difficult substructure work. In order to reduce the uneven settlements of the caisson during construction, the 5m wide concrete mass behind the anchorage was not poured until the erection of the stiffening girders was completed. The splay saddle on the top of the anchor was displaced 48mm in the first year after the erection of the cables, and only 2mm in the second year, in the direction of the river. Most of the displacement happened before the sectional welding of steel box girders which will not have much impact on the loading capacity of the structure. The displacement is also less than the allowances specified in the design.

4. Construction of the Main Cables

The main cables are made of parallel high-strength wires, which are galvanized and welded. The parallel wire strand method is used for erection of the main cables (Fig.5). Owing to the strict control in the process of cable erection, the void ratio of the main cables is 16.6%. The erection of the main suspension cables and the hanged ropes continued simultaneously. Though the main cable was spun before the erection of the deck, it still met the elevation required in the design.

5. Construction of Stiffening Girder

The stiffening girders are made of rectangular steel boxes (Fig.6). The cross section was selected based on wind tunnel tests on the section model, the box girder is 32.5m wide and 3.02m in depth, with a total girder width of 36.9m including the two cantilevers.

The stiffening girders were erected from cranes fixed on the main cables. The cranes for the girder erection were assembled in the factory and transported to the span location by using boat. The crane is fixed on the main cables and self-hoisted to ride along the main cables, thus the progress of the erection was greatly pushed.

6. Conclusions

With the rapid economic development in China, the Shanghai metropolitan circle is taking shape in the Yangtze River Delta. Speedy development of industrial zones along the Yangtze River in Jiangsu Province will certainly promote the economic development of Jiangsu to a leading position in China and will have important signification to link the north and south of the Yangtze River.

图3 北锚碇截面
Fig.3 Section of north anchorage

图4 埋入的北锚碇沉箱（承周世忠教授级高工惠赠）
Fig.4 Embedded caisson of north anchorage (courtesy of Senior Engr. Prof. Zhou Shizhong)

图5 主缆施工（承周世忠教授级高工惠赠）
Fig.5 Construction of main cable (courtesy of Senior Engr. Prof. Zhou Shizhong)

图6 加劲梁施工（承周世忠教授级高工惠赠）
Fig.6 Construction of stiffening girder (courtesy of Senior Engr. Prof. Zhou Shizhong)

REFERENCES

1.Shizhong Zhou. Construction of the Jiangyin Yangtze Suspension Bridge. Structural Engineering International (IABSE Journal). 2004(1): 30-31

润扬长江公路大桥

润扬长江公路大桥北起扬州南绕城公路八字桥东约2.1km处，跨经长江世业洲，南迄于沪宁高速公路丹徒互通，全长35.66km，南汊桥采用主跨为1 490m的单孔双铰钢箱梁悬索桥，边跨为470m，北汊桥采用176m+406m+176m三跨双塔双索面钢箱梁斜拉桥（图1）。大桥通航净空：悬索桥为50m，可通行5万吨级巴拿马散装货轮，斜拉桥为18m。因镇江古称润州，故名润扬大桥。润扬大桥在江阴大桥上游约70km处。

润扬大桥建设工期为5年，于2000年9月开工，2005年5月正式通车。图2示悬索桥日出时全景，图3示悬索大桥夜景，图4示斜拉桥夜景。

图5示悬索桥北塔塔顶施工。图6示塔身一般构造，图7示南、北塔基一般构造，基础采用2.8m大直径钻孔群桩基，系梁为单箱双室空心截面。图8示塔基施工。

悬索桥钢箱梁（图9）采用扁平流线形全焊接结构，全宽38.1m，截面高3.0m。

图10示钢箱梁吊装合龙。

悬索桥南锚碇基础尺寸为70m×52.5m×29.1m（长×宽×深），采用冻融排桩法施工。图11示锚体施工，北锚碇位于长江世业洲的南侧，基础尺寸为69m×50m×44.5m，采用地下连续墙方案，碇体长64.27m×宽53.7m×高42.6m。

润扬大桥悬索桥的建成在我国建桥史上具有十分重要的意义。

1a

1b

Runyang Yangtze River Highway Bridge

The Runyang Yangtze River Highway Bridge starts from Yangzhou in the north at a place with 2.1km or so from Bazi Bridge in the east of the highway around city in the south, and crosses Shiye Islet in Yangtze River, the ends in the south at the interchange in Dantu on Shanghai-Nanjing express highway, the total length is 35.66km, for the bridge over south branch, a single-span and double-hinge suspension bridge of steel box girder with main span of 1490m and each side span of 470m is adopted, for the bridge over north branch, a cable-stayed bridge with spans of 176m+406m+176m and double-pylon and double-cable-plane is used (Fig.1). The navigable clearances are 50m for suspension bridge, it can pass over the Panama freighter for bulk cargoes of 5×10^4t and 18m for cable-stayed bridge. Because Zhenjiang was called Runzhou in ancient time, so this bridge is called Runyang Bridge. Runyang Bridge located at 70km or so in the upper reaches of Jiangyin Bridge.

The construction period of Runyang Bridge was 5 years, i.e., it started in Sept. 2000 and has been opened to traffic in May 2005. Fig.2 shows the full scene of suspension bridge as sun rises, Fig.3 shows the night scene of suspension bridge, Fig.4 shows the night scene of cable-stayed bridge.

Fig.5 shows the construction of north pylon top of suspension bridge, Fig.6 shows the general construction of pylon, Fig.7 shows the general construction of foundation of north and south pylons, for the foundation, a group of bored piles with large diameter of 2.8m is adopted, the tie beam has hollow section with single box and double cells. Fig.8 shows the full-welded the construction of pylon foundation.

The steel box girder (Fig.9) adopts shallow streamlined structure welded fully, the total width is 38.1m and section depth 3.0m.

Fig.10 shows the hoisting closure of steel box girder.

The dimensions of the foundation of south anchorage pier is 70m×52.5m×29.1m (length×width×height), was constructed by using the freezing method for the row of pile. Fig.11 shown the construction anchorage pier. North anchorage pier is located at the south side of the Shiye Islet in Yangtze River, with the foundation dimensions of 69m×50m×44.5m, the pier dimensions are length 64.27m×width 53.7m×height 42.6m was constructed by adopting the project of continuous wall under ground.

The completion of Runyang Suspension Bridge has a very important significance in the history of constructing bridges in China.

图1 润扬大桥（承欧庆保教授级高工惠赠）(a)，(b)
Fig.1 Runyang Bridge (courtesy of Senior Engr. Prof. Ou Qingbao)
(a), (b)

图2 日出时悬索大桥全景（承欧庆保教授级高工惠赠）
Fig.2 Full scene of suspension bridge as sun rises (courtesy of Senior Engr. Prof. Ou Qingbao)

图3 悬索桥夜景（承欧庆保教授级高工惠赠）
Fig.3 Night scene of suspension bridge (courtesy of Senior Engr. Prof. Ou Qingbao)

图4 斜拉桥夜景（承欧庆保教授级高工惠赠）
Fig.4 Night scene of cable-stayed bridge (courtesy of Senior Engr. Prof. Ou Qingbao)

图5 悬索桥北塔塔顶施工（承欧庆保教授级高工惠赠）
Fig.5 Construction of north pylon top (courtesy of Senior Engr. Prof. Ou Qingbao)

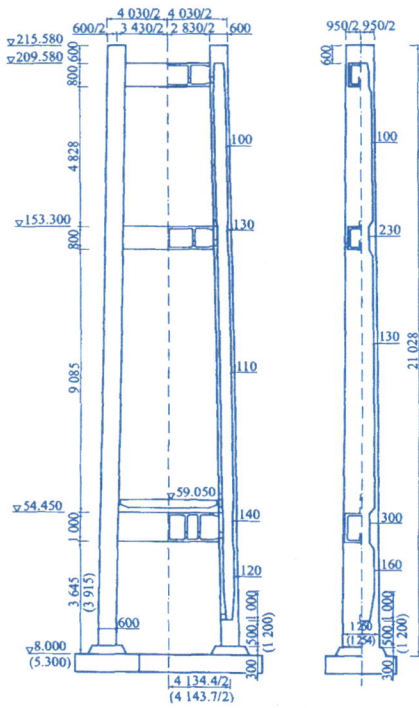

6

unit: cm

图6 塔身一般构造
Fig.6 General construction of pylon

图6 塔身一般构造
Fig.6 General construction of pylon

图7 南、北塔基一般构造（单位：cm，但标高按m）
Fig.7 General construction of foundations of north,
and south pylons (unit: cm, but the elevation in m)

图8 塔基施工（承欧庆保教授级高工惠赠）
Fig.8 Construction of pylon foundation
(courtesy of Senior Engr. Prof. Ou Qingbao)

图9 标准钢箱梁截面
Fig.9 Section of standard steel box girder

图10 钢箱梁吊装合龙（承欧庆保教授级高工惠赠）
Fig.10 Hoisting closure of steel box girder (courtesy
of Senior Engr. Prof. Ou Qingbao)

图11 锚体施工（承欧庆保教授级高工惠赠）
Fig.11 Construction of anchorage pier (courtesy of
Senior Engr. Prof. Ou Qingbao)

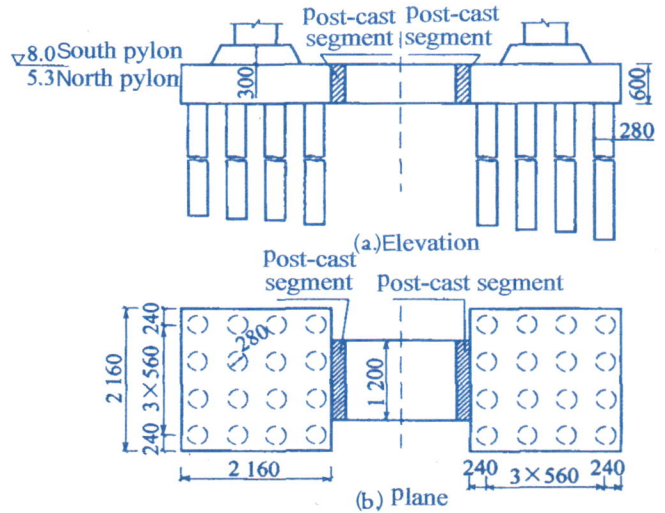

∇8.0 South pylon
5.3 North pylon

Post-cast segment   Post-cast segment

(a.) Elevation

Post-cast segment   Post-cast segment

(b) Plane

unit: cm

7

9

Center line of main cables   Center line of main cables

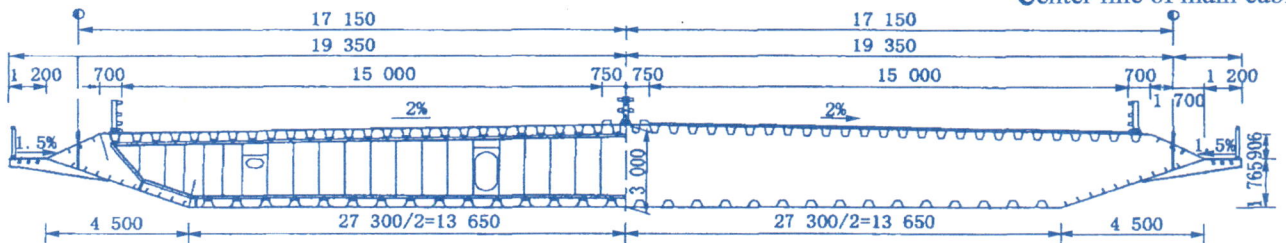

17 150   17 150
19 350   19 350
1 200   700   15 000   750 750   15 000   700   1 200
2%   2%
1.5%   1.5%
4 500   27 300/2=13 650   27 300/2=13 650   4 500

unit: mm

参考文献

1. 江苏省交通厅. 润扬大桥(画册), 2005: 107

2. 韦世国, 等5人. 润扬大桥悬索桥钢箱梁吊装技术. 桥梁建设, 2004 (4): 40-46

3. 王立新, 周欣, 华新. 润扬长江公路大桥南汊悬索桥桥墩的设计特色. 铁道建筑技术, 2004 (1): 13-16

REFERENCES

1. *Communication Department of Jiangsu Province. Runyang Bridge (Album), 2005: 107*

2. *Wei Shiguo, et al 5 persons. Lifting and installing techniques for steel box girder of Runyang suspension bridge. Bridge Construction. 2004(4): 40-46*

3. *Wang Lixin, Zhou Xin, Hua Xin. Design character of the suspension bridge in south branch of Runyang highway bridge over Yangtze River. Railway Construction Technology. 2004(1):13-16*

广东汕头海湾悬索桥

汕头海湾大桥设计经过比较、筛选，最后以混凝土加劲箱梁悬索桥和斜拉桥为竞标对象。针对哪种桥型更适应本地区强台风、海水腐蚀等自然条件，又经济合理、因地制宜，几经论证，认为采用混凝土加劲箱梁悬索桥主跨452m方案在技术上更为有利。

国内第一次修建这样大跨径悬索桥，特别是大桥采用预应力混凝土加劲梁，在世界同类悬索桥中跃居首座，已知加拿大于1965年建造的哈得孙·何扑预应力悬索大桥，桥的跨径仅207m[①]。

汕头海湾大桥建设完全依靠我国自己的力量，它的成功是建设者们智慧和汗水的结晶，是桥梁建设的一项重大成就，中国建桥人为此伟大成就而自豪。

汕头海湾大桥于1992年3月28日正式动工兴建，于1995年12月28日建成通车。大桥全长2 437m。主桥长760m，分为154m+452m+154m，北引桥在副通航道处设2孔50mT构，其余南北引桥为25m预应力混凝土简支T梁（图1），下部结构采用双柱式桥墩。

主桥主要由塔、锚碇、缆系统、钢筋混凝土预制箱梁以及桥面组成。南北主塔基础采用2组各6根直径2.2m的灌注桩和7m×11m单钢壳套现浇混凝土结构，塔身为钢筋混凝土框架结构，塔高95m（图2）。

海湾大桥全桥基础为钻孔桩或明挖基础，南北主塔基础均为直径2.2m的钻孔桩，钻孔桩穿越淤泥粉沙层和不同程度的风化花岗岩，最后支承于微风化的花岗岩内。主塔上下游基础各6根钻孔桩，桩群外侧各设由一个单壁钢壳套井，钢壳套井内的钢筋混凝土将桩身上部连为一体，钢壳套井上方为承台。

图3示北主塔基础结构。

图4示单壁钢壳套井钻孔桩钢护筒。

大桥每根主缆由10 010根φ5mm镀锌高强钢丝组成，设计面积为0.1 965m²。10 010根钢丝分成110股钢丝束，每束91根钢丝。架设时先将110股预制平行钢丝束编排成六角形截面，再挤成圆形。截面挤紧的空隙率一般部位按20%

Guangdong Shantou Bay Suspension Bridge

The design of Bay Bridge was through comparison and sifting, finally, a suspension bridge with concrete stiffening box girder and the other cable-stayed bridge were selected as competitive bids. Considering which is more suitable to the strong typhoon and corrosion of sea water, etc. natural conditions in this area, and it is also economic and reasonable, and suits to local conditions, through demonstration for several times, considering to adopt the suspension bridge with concrete stiffening box girder is more favorable on technique, the main span is 452m.

In this country, the first constructing suspension bridge with so large span, specially it adopts prestressed concrete stiffening girder to leap to the first place of the same type of suspension bridge in the world. It is know, that the Hudson Hope prestressed suspension bridge with span of 207m was built in 1965 in Canada[1].

Shantou Bay Bridge responds fully our own strength to construct, its success is the crystals of wisdom and sweat of constructors, the Chinese people of building Bridge are proud of the great achievements.

Shantou Bay Bridge started formally to construct on March 28, 1992 and has been completed and opened on Dec.28, 1995. The entire length of Bridge is 2 437m, the length of main bridge 760m, divided into 154m+452m+154m, in north approach, over the auxiliary navigable opening, there are 2-span, T-frame, each of 50m, the other north and south approaches are simply supported PC T-girders with span of 25m (Fig.1), the substructures are double-column piers.

The main bridge is basically constituted of pylons, anchors, cable system, precast reinforced concrete box girders and bridge surface. Two groups of 2.2m filling piles, each with 6 piles and 7m×11m single steel shell sleeve and cast-in-site concrete structure are adopted as the foundation of north and south pylons. The pylon body is reinforced concrete frame structure, its height is 95m (Fig.2).

In Bay Bridge, all the foundations are bored piles or foundation by open excavation. Both the foundations of north and south pylons are bored piles with diameter of 2.2m, these piles pass through silt, rock flour, sand rock and granite weathered in different degree, finally are supported in slightly weathered granite. 6 bored piles are adopted as each foundation of main pylon on upper or lower reaches. On the external side of each pile group, there is set a single-wall steel shell sleeve well, in which the reinforced concrete joins the upper part of pile body into an integral, the upper part of steel shell sleeve well is the bearing platform.

Fig.3 shows the foundation structure of north main pylon.

Fig.4 shows the steel protective tube of bored piles with single-wall steel shell sleeve well.

The main cable of this Bridge is constituted of 10 010 ϕ 5mm galvanized high-strength steel wires, the design section area is 0.1 965m². The 10 010 steel wires are divided into 110 parallel wire bundles, in each of which, there are 91 wires. As being erected, the 110 prefabricated

① 哈得孙·何扑大桥跨过和平江，两车道桥具有混凝土门式框架桥塔，而混凝土桥面没有加劲桁架，跨度分布为58m+207m+63m。

① Hudson Hope Bridge crosses the Peace River, 2-lane bridge has a concrete portal frame pylons and a concrete deck with no stiffening truss, the spans distribute as 58m+207m+63m.

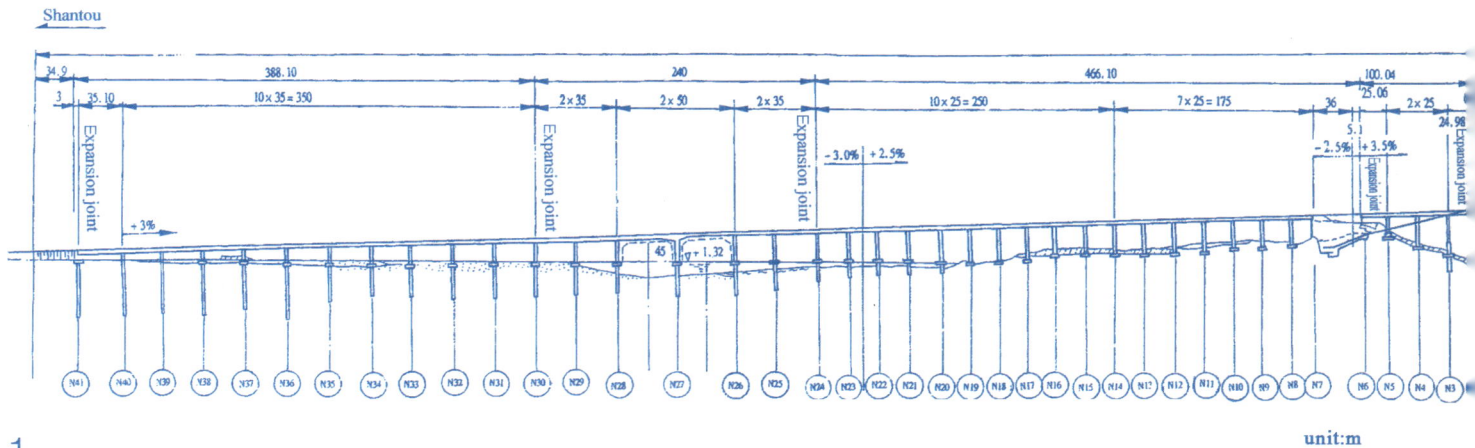

Shantou

1

unit:m

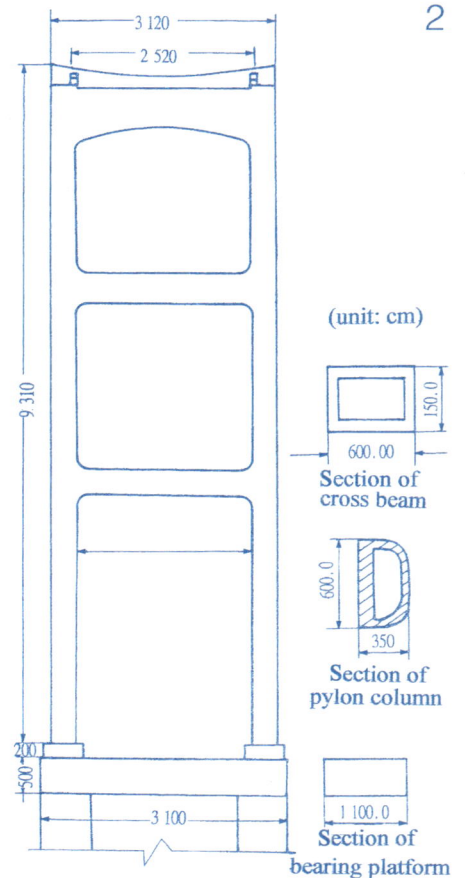

2

(unit: cm)

Section of cross beam

Section of pylon column

Section of bearing platform

2500

761.72

452   100.04   364.60   44.50

154   0.86   2×25   25.06   31.44   5×25=125   3×25=75   4×25=100   25.06   3

▽ +98.600   ▽ +99.600   +52.600   ▽ +99.600   ▽ +98.600   Central line of support 24.98   +3.5%   -2.5%

▽ +44.20

Expansion joint

Expansion joint

▽ +4.50   211.52   Center of main navigable pass   + 1.32 (average high tide level)

N1   S1   S2 S3 S4 S5 S6 S7 S8 S9 S10 S11 S12 S13 S14 S15 S16 S17 S18 S19 S20

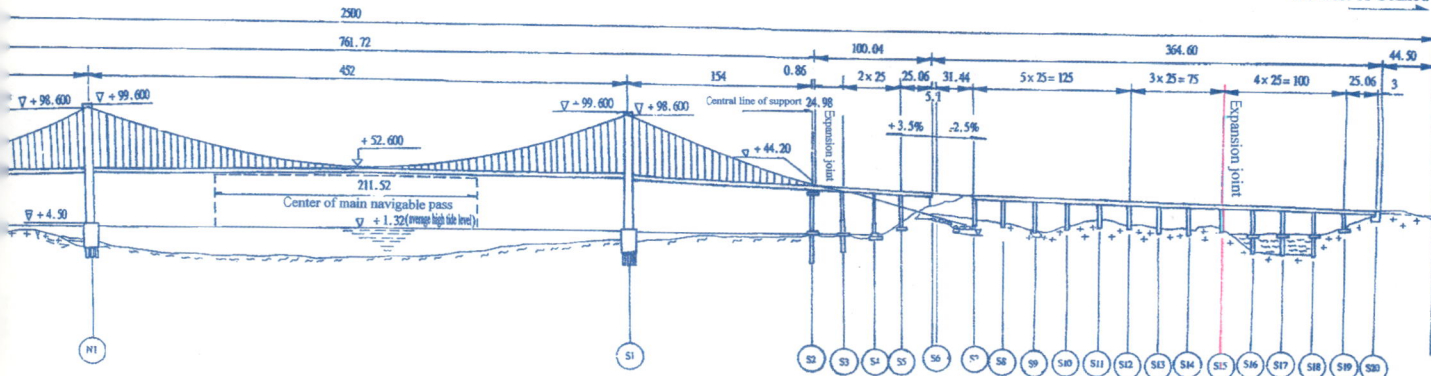

图1 汕头海湾大桥
Fig.1 Shantou Bridge over bay

图2 桥塔结构
Fig.2 Structure of bridge pylon

图3 北主塔基础结构
Fig.3 Foundation structure of north main pylon

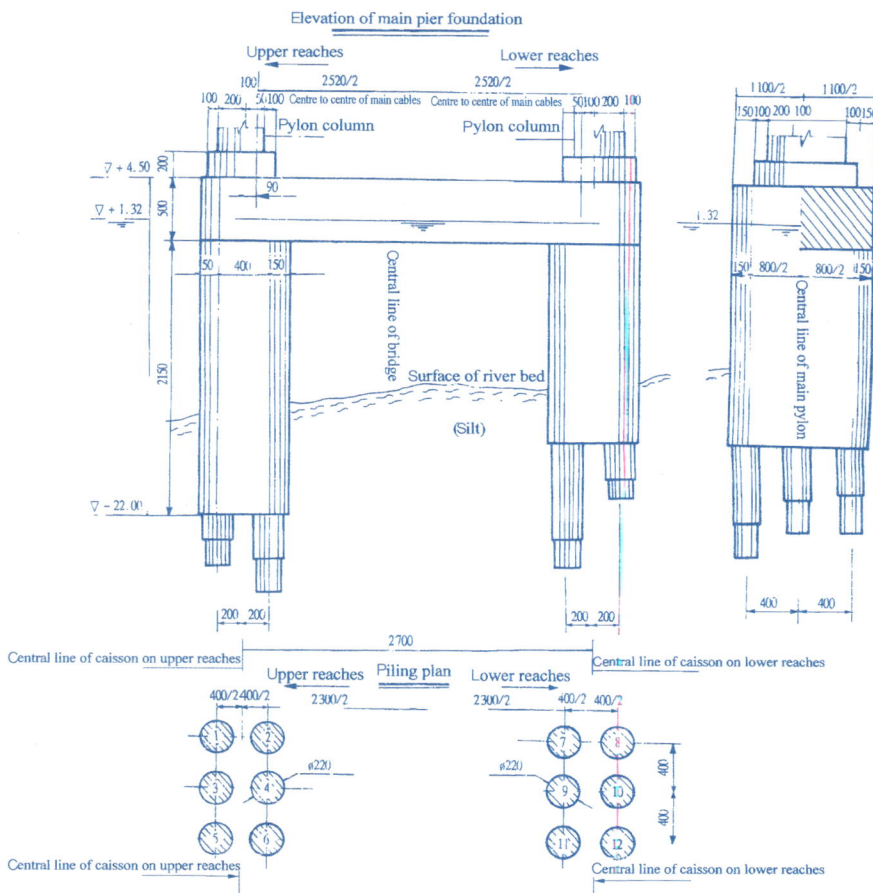

Elevation of main pier foundation

Upper reaches   Lower reaches

100   2520/2   2520/2   1100/2   1100/2

100 200   50 100   Centre to centre of main cables   Centre to centre of main cables   50 100 200 100   150 100 200 100   100 150

Pylon column   Pylon column

▽ +4.50   200

▽ +1.32   500   1.32

90   150   800/2   800/2   150

50   400   150   Central line of bridge   Central line of main pylon

2150   Surface of river bed

(Silt)

▽ −22.00

▽ −22.00   200 200   200 200   400 400

200 200   2700   200 200

Central line of caisson on upper reaches   Piling plan   Central line of caisson on lower reaches

Upper reaches   Lower reaches

400/2 400/2   2300/2   2300/2   400/2 400/2

1 2   7 8

φ220   φ220   400

3 4   9 10   400

5 6   11 12

Central line of caisson on upper reaches   Central line of caisson on lower reaches

unit: dimension in cm, elevation in m

3

4

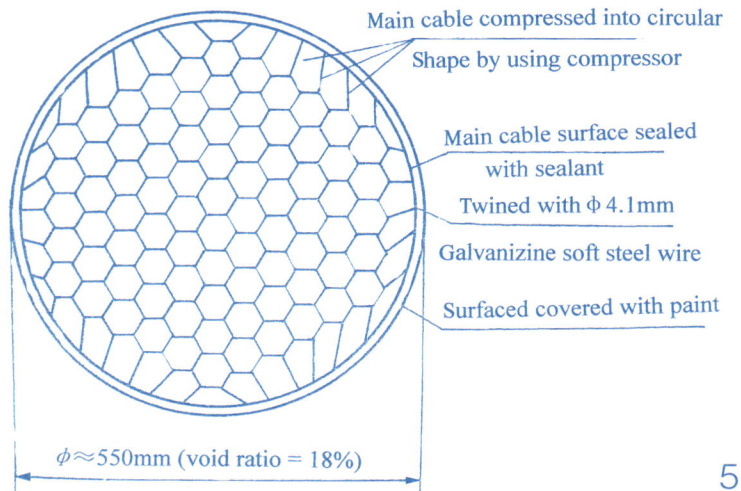

Main cable compressed into circular

Shape by using compressor

Main cable surface sealed with sealant

Twined with Φ4.1mm

Galvanizine soft steel wire

Surfaced covered with paint

$\phi \approx 550mm$ (void ratio = 18%)

5

图4 单壁钢壳套井钻孔桩钢护筒（承石国彬教授级高工惠赠）
Fig.4 Protective tube of bored piles with single wall steel shell sleeve well (courtesy of Senior Engr. Prof. Shi Guobin)

图5 挤紧后主缆截面
Fig.5 Section of main cable after being compressed

图6 主缆挤紧（承石国彬教授级高工惠赠）
Fig.6 Compression of main cable (courtesy of Senior Engr. Prof. Shi Guobin)

图7 加劲梁截面
Fig.7 Section of stiffening girder

6

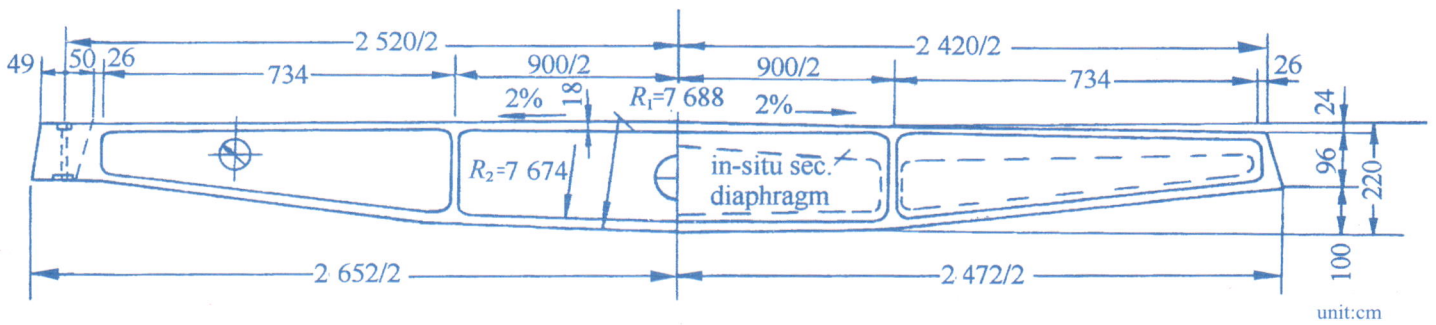

7

unit:cm

考虑，其相应的外径为570mm左右，在安装索夹的部位由于索夹的紧箍作用，空隙率将压缩至18%左右，此处主缆外径约为550mm（图5）。

图6示主缆挤紧。

加劲梁为单箱三室预应力混凝土薄壁箱形结构全流线形截面（图7），加劲梁是在现场分节段预制的，全桥共有121段预制节段，每个节段长5.7m，每节段箱梁之间用300mm钢筋混凝土湿接头连接，再进行纵向预应力张拉形成加劲梁。为避免梁段上桥过大的收缩徐变对结构产生过大的不利影响，预制梁需存放4个月以上。图8示加劲梁的吊装。

主缆锚碇不仅是悬索桥的重要组成部分，还是悬索的关键受力结构。本桥锚碇采用重力式嵌岩锚，它由锚体、锚固架及锚室等部分组成。每根主缆110束平行钢丝分别锚固于锚杆前端。巨大的主缆拉力通过锚杆及后背梁均匀地传递到锚体混凝土。

图9示锚碇设计时，充分利用了两岸锚区均为花岗岩山头这一有利条件，用混凝土锚体兜住石质山体，锚区顶部由砌石路基压重，从而大大减小了锚体体积。

锚碇施工顺序为：开挖基坑，清理基岩岩石，埋设预埋件，浇灌锚体混凝土。为了防止水化热引起混凝土开裂，除采用水化热较小的矿渣水泥外，还埋设了冷却环流带。

大桥地处南海湾海水及海洋大气侵蚀环境中，为了防止盐侵蚀，主桥的缆、索、紧固件、塔柱、主梁以及塔基等部位都做了防腐处理 —— 涂装防腐层。图10示吊索防腐。

建成后的汕头海湾大桥如图11~图14所示。

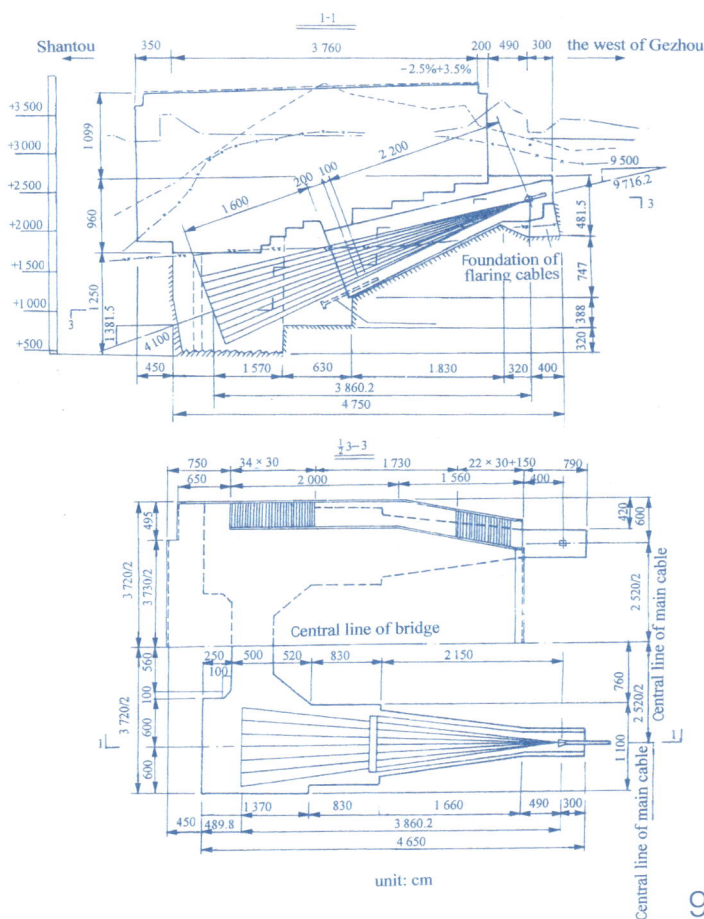

parallel wire bundles are firstly composed into a hexagonal section, which is compressed into circular shape. The void ratio after the section is compressed is 20% at general part, the corresponding external diameter is 570mm or so, at the place where the cable clamps are set, the void ratio is decreased to 18% or so due to the tightening effect of clamps, the external diameter of main cable is decreased to 550mm or so (Fig.5).

Fig.6 shows the compression of main cable.

The stiffening girder is a single-box and 3-cell prestressed concrete thin-wall box structure with fully streamlined section (Fig.7), this girder is precast by segmentation in-situ, in entire bridge, there are 121 precast segments, the length of every segment is 5.7m, the segment to segment is connected by using of 300mm reinforced concrete wet joint, then the tensioning of longitudinal prestressing is conducted to form the stiffening girder. In order to avoid too large unfavorable influence produced due to shrinkage and creep after the girder was erected on bridge, the precast girder (segment) is necessary to be kept for more than 4 months. Fig.8 shows the segments of stiffening girder to be hoisted.

The anchor of main cable is not only the important constitutive part of suspension bridge, but also the key stressed structure of suspension cable. In this Bridge, the gravity inserting rock anchor is adopted, it is constituted of anchorage body, anchorage frame and anchorage room, etc. 110 bundles of parallel wires are anchored respectively in the front end of anchorage rod. The huge tension from main cable is uniformly transferred in concrete of anchorage body through anchorage rod and rear beam.

Fig.9 shows when the anchor is designed, the favorable condition that the anchored areas of 2 banks are granite hills is fully utilized, using concrete anchorage body to bind the stony hill, the weight due to the road base of building stone on the top of anchored area, to decrease greatly the anchor volume.

The sequence of anchor construction is: excavating foundation pit, clearing the stone on base rock, embedding preformed parts, pouring the concrete of anchor. For the sake of avoiding the cracking of concrete due to hydration heat, excepting adopting the slag cement with smaller hydration heat, the ring belt for cooling is also set.

The Bridge is located in the corrosive circumstances of Southsea seawater and marine, for avoiding salt corrosion, to the cables, ropes, compression parts, pylon columns, main girders and pylon foundations, etc, the corrosion proof measures are all conducted—painting layers. Fig.10 shows the anti-corrosion of hanging ropes.

The completed Shantou Bay Bridge is shown in Fig.11~14.

图8 加劲梁的吊装（承石国彬教授级高工惠赠）
Fig.8 Hoisting of stiffening girders (courtesy of Senior Engr. Prof. Shi Guobin)

图9 锚碇结构（单位：cm）
Fig.9 Structure of anchor pier (unit: cm)

图10 吊索防腐（承石国彬教授级高工惠赠）
Fig.10 Preservation of hanging ropes (courtesy of Senior Engr. Prof. Shi Guobin)

图11 建成后的汕头海湾大桥（承石国彬教授级高工惠赠）
Fig.11 Completed Shantou Bay Bridge (courtesy of Senior Engr. Prof. Shi Guobin)

汕头海湾大桥
Shan Tou Gulf Bridge
全长
Length 2500 m

12

13

14

参考文献

1.广东汕头海湾大桥公司，铁道部大桥工程局，
广东省交通科学研究所.广东汕头海湾大桥工程
总结.北京：科学出版社，1988：364
2.广东汕头海湾大桥公司，铁道部大桥工程局，
广东省交通科学研究所.广东汕头海湾大桥·工
程画册，1998：54

REFERENCES

*1.Guangdong Shantou Bay Bridge Co., Bridge
Engineering Bureau of Railway Ministry,
Communication Research Institute of Guangdong
Province. Engineering Summation of Guangdong
Shantou Bay Bridge. Beijing: Science Press,
1998: 364*
*2.Guangdong Shantou Bay Bridge Co.,
Bridge Engineering Bureau of Railway
Ministry, Communication Research Institute of
Guangdong Province. Guangdong Shantou Bay
Bridge•Engineering Album, 1998: 54*

西堠门悬索桥

　　在中国上海之南的舟山群岛，2004—2008年一座大悬索桥已经建造，在2008年建成。西堠门大桥主跨1 650m，是世界第二长桥，较跨长1 624m丹麦大带东桥长20m。

1. 引言：舟山群岛大桥

　　西堠门大桥（图1a~e）位于浙江省舟山群岛。它是群岛与中国大陆连接的第4座桥，桥的走向是从北向南的，北端连接册子岛，南端连接金塘岛，全部连岛包括5座大桥，西堠门大桥是其中跨度最大的一座。这5座大桥是：

　　岑钢大桥（建设期为1999—2001年）连接舟山本岛与里钓岛：8×30m连续梁+3×50m连续T形梁+9×30m连续梁。

　　响胶门大桥（1999—2002年）连接里钓岛与富翅岛：多跨50m简支T形梁+（80+150+80）m连续梁+11×50m连续T形梁。

　　桃天门岛（2001—2003年）连接富翅岛与册子岛：（48+48+50）m+580m+（50+48+48）m双塔双索面组合斜拉桥。

　　西堠门大桥（2004—2008年）连接册子岛与金塘岛：578m+1 650m+485m悬索桥（北侧跨与中跨具有不同的索）。西堠门大桥按高速公路4车道，车速80km/h及路宽24.5m设计。该桥跨越西北-东南走向的西堠门水道，平均长7.7km，宽2.5km，最窄处1.9km，特征是水深达80~95m，急流2.7~3.7m/s，在水道中存在暴露的和孤立的土丘、暗礁、陡坡和强涡流。

　　金塘桥（2004—2008年）连接金塘岛和中国大陆宁波市：东通航跨122m+216m+122m预应力混凝土连续刚架桥；主通航跨（77+218）m+620m+（218+77）m双塔双索面钢箱加劲梁斜拉桥；西通航跨87m+156m+77m预应力混凝土连续梁；非通航跨，60m预应力混凝土连续梁，全长21km。

2. 总概念：西堠门大桥

2.1 桥址选择

　　根据桥址处的水文资料，采用长跨索支桥是合适的，以避免建造深水下基础。桥应定位在最窄处的水道以减小海上跨长。通航要求竖向净空49.5m，因此必须选择两岸有小山的处所，而后随着桥的纵向坡度以选择合适的连接等高线以减小引桥长度。

1a

1b

Xihoumen Suspension Bridge

In China, a great suspension bridge has been constructed during 2004–2008 in Zhoushan Islands, south of Shanghai. At completion in 2008 the 1 650m main span of the Xihoumen Bridge is the 2nd longest bridge in the world, more than 20m longer than the 1 624m span of the Great Belt East Bridge in Denmark.

1. Introduction: The Zhoushan Islands Bridges

The Xihoumen Bridge (Fig.1a~e) is located in Zhoushan Islands, Zhejiang Province. It is the 4th bridge linking these Islands with Mainland China, the trend of this bridge is from the north towards the south, its north end is connected to Cezi Island and its south end joined to Jintang Island, the whole connection includes 5 great bridges, and the Xihoumen Bridge is the one with the longest main span. These 5 bridges are as follows:

Cengang Bridge (construction period 1999–2001) links the main Zhoushan Island with Lidiao Island: 8×30m continuous girder + 3×50m continuous T-girders + 9×30m continuous girders.

XiangJiaomen Bridge (1999–2002) links Lidiao Island with Fuchi Island: many 50m simply supported T-girders + (80+150+80)m continuous girders + 11×50m continuous T-girders.

Taoyaomen Bridge (2001–2003) links Fuchi Island with Cezi Island: (48+48+50)m+580m+ (50+48+48)m composite cable-stayed bridge with bi-pylon and double cable planes.

Xihoumen Bridge (2004–2008) links Cezi Island with Jintang Island: 578m+1 650m+485m (with different cables in the north side span and in the middle span). Xihoumen Bridge is designed according to the Standard of 4-lane express highway with speed of 80km/h and the width of road of 24.5m. Xihoumen Bridge spans over Xihoumen Waterway which is one with northwest-southeast trend and has 7.7km long and 2.5km wide on an average as well as 1.9km the most narrow with characteristics: water depth reaches 80~90m, rapid flow 2.7~3.7m/s, and in the waterway there exist exposed and isolated hillocks, submerged reefs, steep slopes and strong vortexes;

Jintang Bridge (2004–2008) links Jintang Island with Ningbo City on Mainland China: the east navigable span 122m+216m+122m PC (prestressed concrete) continuous frame bridge; main navigable span (77+218)m+620m+(218+77)m cable-stayed bridge of steel box stiffening girder with bi-pylon and double-planes; west navigable span 87m+156m+77m PC continuous girders; un-navigable spans 60m PC continuous girders, total length 21km.

2. General Conception: Xihoumen Bridge

2.1 Selection of bridge site

Following the hydrological data at bridge site, it is appropriate to adopt a cable-supported bridge with a long span to avoid the construction of foundation under deep water. The bridge should be located over the waterway at most narrow place to decrease the span length over the sea. The navigable requirement demands a vertical

1c

1d

图1 西堠门大桥（承宋晖高工惠赠）
(a)~(d)远景
Fig.1 Xihoumen Bridge (courtesy of Senior Engr.
Song Hui)
(a)~(d) distant view

图1 西堠门大桥（承宋晖高工惠赠）(e)近景
Fig.1 Xihoumen Bridge (courtesy of Senior Engr. Song Hui)
(e) close view

根据上述要求选择3个桥址，其中从东岸靠近水中老虎山的门头山到上雄鹅嘴的距离可大大减小桥的主跨长，并还以老虎山作为桥塔的位置。这样规模与工程技术的困难大大小于其余2个桥址。

2.2 桥型

对西堠门大桥，一个桥塔设于老虎山。要求跨越南水道的全跨大于1 500m，因此采用悬索桥。

2.3 桥的主跨

主跨应由水文地质条件控制。也因为没有覆盖层，在水中基础施工是困难的，甚至在建筑临时设施后，固定基础亦较困难，甚至在建筑临时设施后，固定基础亦较困难。研究3个方案，即以1 650m、1 520m和1 312m作为主跨，分析表明这3个方案费用很接近，但对南桥塔位置，基础建设的困难、总的工程费用及建设周期的风险，1650m跨是最小的。这一方案有着设置南桥塔于岸上的条件，可降低施工困难，并使工程费用和周期较确定。

2.4 结构体系

北边跨跨越册子岛和老虎山之间的水道，因此采用一道由悬索支承的加劲梁是合适的。南边跨全在岸上，因此可用下面的锚碇支承。

采用一道2跨连续钢箱加劲梁作为结构体系以增加结构的整体性。根据桥址在册子岛上的地形条件，北边跨的长度应不小于600m，而北边跨和主跨的总长度应小于2 250m。根据分析，采用在北桥塔一座2跨连续桥。

2.5 锚碇安排

（1）北锚碇

地形较明确设置北锚碇（图2）于岸上近北边处，否则将在水中。为了减小边跨加劲梁长度，北边跨长为578m。

（2）南锚碇

在南锚碇范围内，有A区和B区适合安排锚碇。在2区前面，有些隆起的山脊可利用抵抗巨大的主索拉力和降低小山的开挖量，因而是有利的。如果锚碇靠近，设置在A区靠近中跨，南边跨将是280m，边跨对中跨的比将是0.17。

3

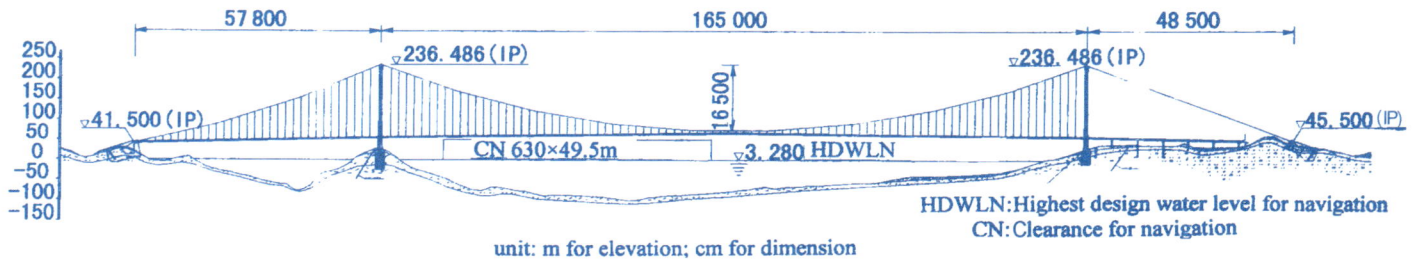

HDWLN: Highest design water level for navigation
CN: Clearance for navigation

unit: m for elevation; cm for dimension

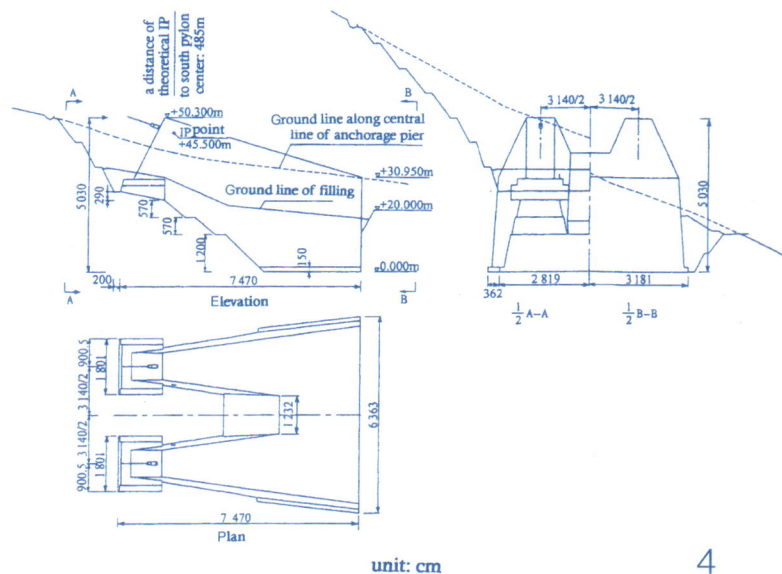

a distance of theoretical IP to south pylon center: 485m

unit: cm

4

clearance of 49.5m, thus it is necessary to select the place where there are hills on both banks, then follow the longitudinal slope of the bridge to select appropriate contour for linking to decrease the length of approach.

For the above requirements 3 bridge sites are selected, among which the distance over sea from Mentou Hill on east bank near Laohu (tiger) Hill in water to Shangxiongezui can decrease greatly the main span length of the bridge, and also using Laohu Hill as pylon location. Thus the scale and technical difficulty of engineering are greatly smaller than the other 2 bridge sites.

2.2 Bridge types

For the Xihoumen Bridge, one pylon is set on Laohu Hill. The demanded main span over the south waterway is larger than 1 500m, so suspension bridge is to be adopted.

2.3 Main span of bridge

The main span should be controlled with hydrological and geological conditions. Also, because there is no cover layer, the foundation construction in water is difficult, and even if after building temporary facilities, fixing the foundation is rather difficult. Studying 3 alternatives of 1 650m, 1 520m and 1 312m as main span, analysis shows the costs of 3 alternatives are very near, but for the location of south pylon, the construction difficulty of foundation, total engineering cost and the risk of construction period of 1 650m span are the smallest. This project has the condition to set south pylon on bank, enabling to decrease the construction difficulty and make the cost and period of engineering to be more definite.

2.4 Structural system

North side span is over the waterway between Cezi Island and Laohu Hill, so it is appropriate to adopt a stiffening girder supported with suspended cables. The south side span is all on land, so it be supported by underneath piers.

A 2-span continuous steel box stiffening girder is used as a structural system to increase the integrity of structure. Following the topographical condition of bridge cite on Cezi Island, the length of north side span should be shorter than 600m and the total length of north side and main span should be shorter than 2 250m. According to analysis, a 2-span continuous bridge is adopted at the north pylon.

2.5 Arrangement of anchorage piers

(1) north anchorage pier

The topography is more definite to set north anchorage pier (Fig.2) on the bank side near north to the north, otherwise, it would be in water. To decrease the length of the stiffening girder in the side span, the length of the north side span is 578m.

(2) south anchorage pier

In this field of south anchorage pier, there are areas A and B appropriate to arrange anchorage pier. In the fronts of 2 areas there are swelling ridges which can be utilized to resist against the huge tension forces from main cables, and to decrease the excavated amounts of hills, hence it is favorable. If the pier is set in area A closed to middle span, the length of south side span would be

2

图2 北锚碇施工（承宋晖高工惠赠）
Fig.2 Construction of the north anchorage pier (courtesy of Senior Engr. Song Hui)

图3 悬索桥跨度分布
Fig.3 Span distribution of Xihoumen Bridge

图4 南锚碇的实施方案
Fig.4 Practical project of the south anchorage pier

为了技术和经济理由，采用B区，可采用边跨长度为485m，则这时边跨对中跨之比为0.29。这样悬索桥跨度分布为578m+1 650m+485m（图3）。

根据桥址的纵剖面，当比较大基础的锚，嵌入岩中的重力锚和隧道锚，采用嵌入岩中的重力锚墩（图4）。

2.6 索塔

索塔高度（211.3m）略高于已建成的南京长江二桥的塔高（195.4m），为了比较，丹麦大带桥塔的高度为254m，我国苏通大桥桥塔的高度为300.4m。在这3座大桥中，都采用了混凝土桥塔，因此西堠门大桥也采用混凝土桥塔。

在悬索桥中，门式框架结构是经常采用的，在西堠门大桥中也采用这种结构。考虑桥塔稳定性和受力需要，在桥塔柱之间设置3道横向连接。南桥塔是主桥的边界，有一简支下部横梁支撑，并安排加劲梁的约束装置。加劲梁是在连续越过北桥塔，并不需设置下部横梁。从中间横梁到桩承台顶高度为133.7m，因此在承台与中间横梁之间设置横向拉结梁，也可形成2层框架（图5）。比较框架和下部横梁，下部桥塔柱中应力仅高7%，但降低施工困难和缩短建筑周期。

在每座桥塔下边设置12根嵌岩桩，直径为ϕ2.8m，根据埋入基岩深度桩长不同。

对矩形截面塔柱，根据空气动力学，用数值方法进行选型分析。分析几种情况：沿桥抗力最大达1.95而Stoloha数之比亦为最大。当不处理时，这易由涡流引起振动，因此该方案不予考虑；当直角和等边凹入0.7m和凸、凹2方案的抵抗系数相近似，但Stoloha数之比较小，因此采用这一方案（图6）。

2.7 索

（1）主索

对大跨度，大多采用1 670MPa平行钢丝。经过工程费用比较，本桥采用1 770MPa平行钢丝。

（2）吊索

对吊索，采用高质量钢芯钢丝绳，标准间距为18m。靠近北锚碇特殊间距为50m，靠近北塔48m，靠近南塔24m（图7）。

图5 索塔实施方案
Fig.5 Practical project of the cable pylon

图6 南桥塔的施工（承宋晖高工惠赠）
Fig.6 Construction of the south pylon (courtesy of Senior Engr. Song Hui)

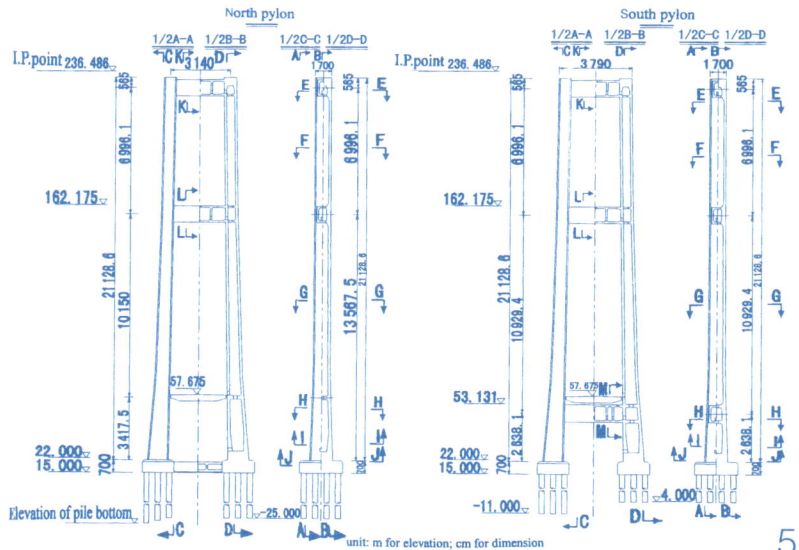

280m, and the ratio of side span to middle span would be 0.17. For technical and economical reasons area B was adopted, enabling to use a side span length of 485m, when the ratio of side span to middle span is 0.29. Thus span distribution of the suspension bridge is: 578m+1 650m+485m (Fig.3).

Following the longitudinal profile of the bridge site, as compared anchorage of enlarged foundation, inserted-in-rock gravity anchorage and tunnel anchorage, the insert-in-rock gravity anchorage pier was adopted (Fig.4).

2.6 Cable pylons

The height of cable pylons (211.3m) is slightly higher than that of the completed 2nd Nanjing Yangtze River Bridge (195.4m). For comparison, the height of pylons of the Great Belt Bridge in Denmark is 254m and that of the Sutong Bridge in China is 300.4m. In these 3 Bridges, concrete pylons are adopted. Thus it is feasible to adopt concrete pylons in Xihoumen Bridge.

In suspension bridges, portal-frame structure is generally adopted, and in the Xihoumen Bridge this structure is also used. From the consideration of the stability and stressed requirements of pylon, 3 transverse connections between pylon columns are set. South pylon is the boundary of main bridge and south side span, and there a lower transverse beam is set as simple support and to arrange the restraint installation of stiffening girder. The stiffening girder is continuous over north pylon, and it is unnecessary to set lower transverse beam. The height from the middle transverse beam to the top of pile cap reaches 133.7m, hence to set transverse tie beam between the cap and the middle transverse beam can also form a 2-story frame (Fig.5). Compared to the frame with lower transverse beam, the stress in lower pylon columns is higher only by 7%, but it decreases the construction difficulty and shortens the building period.

Under every cable pylon, there are set 12 insert-in piles with diameter of 2.8m and various length following the embedded depth of base rock.

For the rectangular section of pylon columns, following aerodynamics, the analysis for selecting type is conducted by numerical method. Analyzing several cases: the resistance is the max. reaching 1.95 along bridge and the Stoloha's number ratio is also the max. It is easy to produce vibration due vortex as being not disposed, so this project can not be considered; the resistance coefficient as right-angled and equilateral concave of 0.7m is approximate to those of 2 projects of convex and concave, but the Stoloha's number ratio is smaller, hence this project is adopted (Fig.6).

2.7 Cables

(1) main cables

For large-span, 1 670MPa parallel wires are mostly used. Through the comparison of engineering cost, in this Bridge, 1 770MPa parallel wires are adopted.

(2) hanging cables

For the hangers, high-quality steel core wire ropes are used, with standard spacing of 18m. Special spacings: near north anchorage

6

2.8 加劲梁

对双箱梁在5m、6m和6.5m中间洞口进行分析，并对风洞数系计算表明，当6m洞口时颤动临界风速达到峰值67.5m/s（对称振型）和69.9m/s（反对称振型）。因此在双箱方案中为了比较，采用6.0m洞口。此外对单箱截面，虽然在比例1：80的节段模型的试验中，量测的颤动临界风速为47.5m/s，小于从检验中得到的，因此必须采用量测的以控制振动。

为此目的，研究高度为1.16m、1.66m和2.16m的中心稳定板进行风动实验。结果表明，当风向角为-3°、0°和+3°时临界颤动风速全大于89.3m/s，检验的为78.7m/s，因此中心稳定板高度取作比较方案。另外的比较方案为空栅（在中国没有工程实例）。比较表明双箱截面方案综合指标是最好的（图8）。

2.9 桥面

根据国外和中国的经验，采用的桥面为一正交各向异性板。顶板厚14mm，底板厚10mm，采用U形加劲肋。

2.10 横向连接

根据抗风需要，对加劲梁，采用中间通风，因此必需建设一强的横向连接以保证加劲梁的横向整体性。在吊点处，箱结构横向连接设置和加劲梁相同高度3.5m，其宽度为3.6m，其腹板和封闭的单箱隔板的腹板连接。横向连接箱腹板也是带双边封闭的单箱隔板的腹板。在2横向连接箱之间也设置一I形梁以连接，其腹板也连接到另外封闭的横向隔板（图9）。

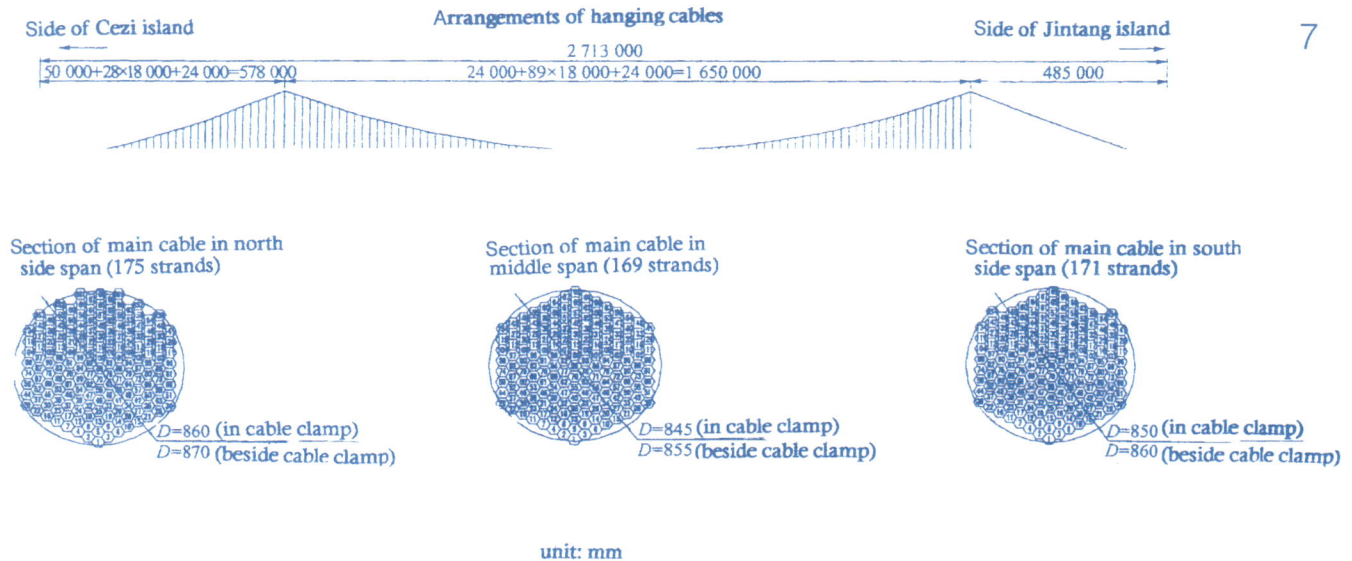

7

Side of Cezi island　　　Arrangements of hanging cables　　　Side of Jintang island

2 713 000

50 000+28×18 000+24 000=578 000　　24 000+89×18 000+24 000=1 650 000　　485 000

Section of main cable in north side span (175 strands)
D=860 (in cable clamp)
D=870 (beside cable clamp)

Section of main cable in middle span (169 strands)
D=845 (in cable clamp)
D=855 (beside cable clamp)

Section of main cable in south side span (171 strands)
D=850 (in cable clamp)
D=860 (beside cable clamp)

unit: mm

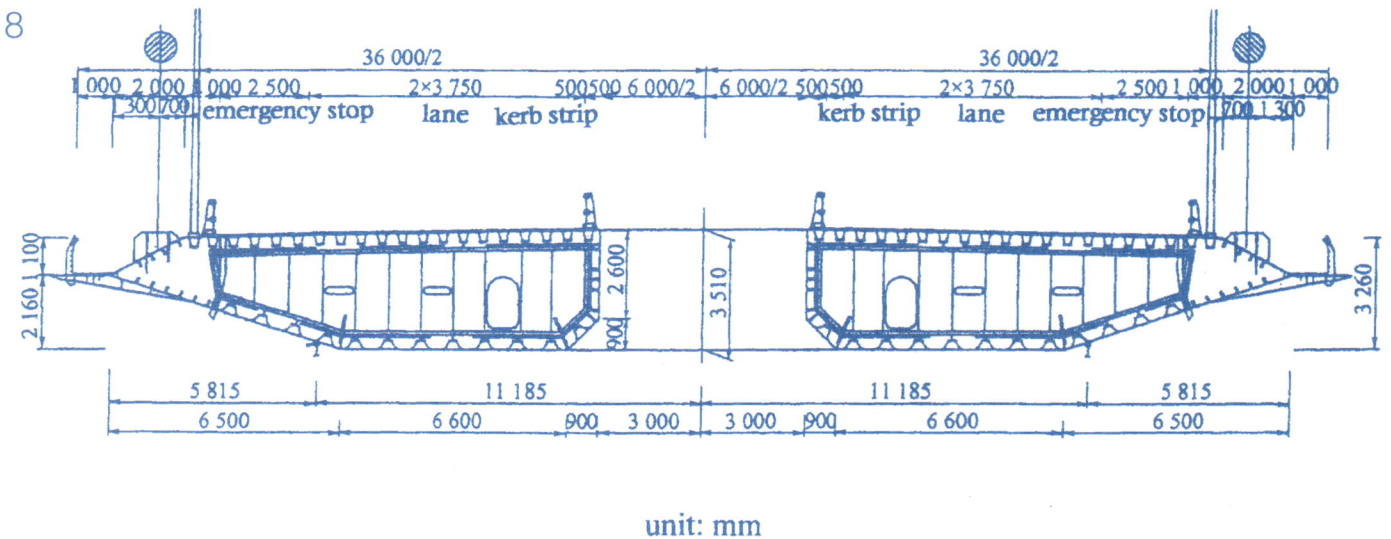

8

36 000/2　　　　36 000/2

1 000 2 000 000 2 500　　2×3 750　　500 500 6 000/2　6 000/2 500 500　　2×3 750　　2 500 1 000 2 000 1 000

300 700 emergency stop　lane　kerb strip　　kerb strip　lane　emergency stop 700 1 300

2 160 1 100　　2 600　　3 510　　900　　3 260

5 815　　11 185　　11 185　　5 815

6 500　　6 600　900　3 000　3 000　900　6 600　　6 500

unit: mm

图7 吊索体系实施方案
Fig.7 Practical project of the hanger system

图8 加劲梁体系实施方案
Fig.8 Practical project of stiffening girder

图9 一节标准梁段平面
Fig.9 Plan of a standard girder segment

参考文献

1.宋晖，陈卫国. 舟山群岛和大陆的连接工程
—— 西堠门大桥方案概念. 公路，2005（6）：
22-28；2005（7）：5-14

REFERENCES

1.Song Hui, Chen Weiguo. The connecting engineering of Zhoushan Islands and Mainland — The project conception of Xihoumen Bridge. Highway. 2005(6): 22-28; 2005(7): 5-14

2.Song Hui, Ding Dajun, Juhani Virola. The Xihoumen Bridge. RIA, 2005(6): 3-7

3.Song Hui, Chen Weiguo, Ding Dajun. Xihoumen: China's second longest. Bd&e, 2nd Quarter, 2006: 15

pier 50m, near north pylon 48m, and near south pylon 24m (Fig.7).

2.8 Stiffening girder

For double-box girder with middle opening of 5m, 6m and 6.5m, the analysis were conducted, and vthe numerical calculations on wind tunnel show: as the opening of 6m, the critical wind velocity of tremble vibration reaches a peak value of 67.5m/s (symmetric mode of vibration) and 69.9m/s (antisymmetric mode of vibration). So in the double-box project for comparison, the 6.0m opening was adopted. Besides, for single-box section, though the test on a segment model with scale of 1:80, the measured critical wind velocity of tremble vibration was 47.5m/s, smaller than that from examination, hence it is necessary to adopt the measured for controlling vibration.

For this aim, the study of central stabilizing board with heights of 1.16m, 1.66m and 2.16m was conducted in wind tunnel laboratory. The results show as wind direction angle of −3°, 0° and +3°, the critical wind velocities of tremble vibration are all larger than 89.3m/s, that examined is 78.7m/s, hence the height of central stabilizing board is taken as compared project. The other compared project was opening lattice (no engineering example in China). Comparison shows the comprehensive indexes of double-box section project are the best (Fig.8).

2.9 Deck

The adopted deck of bridge is an orthotropic plate, following the experience from foreign country and China, the thickness of top plate in 14mm and that of bottom plate is 10mm and the U-shaped stiffening rib are used.

2.10 Transverse connection

From the requirements against wind, for the stiffening girder the middle ventilation is adopted, hence it is necessary to establish powerful transverse connection to guarantee the transverse integrity of stiffening girder. At the hung point, the transverse connection of the box structure is set with the same depth of 3.5m as stiffening girder, its width is 3.6m and its web is connected with that of closed single-box diaphragm. The web of transverse connecting box is also that of the single-box diaphragm with both sides closed. Between 2 transverse connecting boxes, there is also set an I-shaped beam for connection, with its web also connected to that of the other closed transverse diaphragm (Fig.9).

9

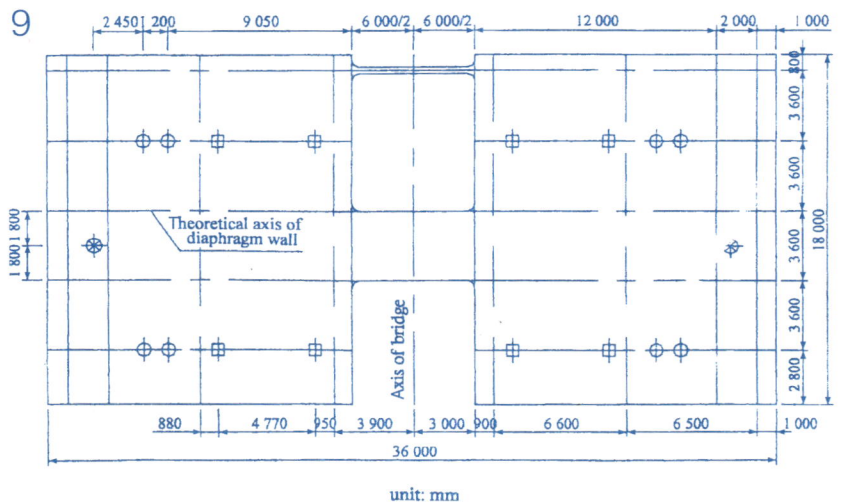

unit: mm

东海跨海大桥

　　东海大桥（图1）[1]是洋山深水港规划第一期重要组成部分，洋山深水港区服务于集装箱集中和运输、供水供电和交通等之用。它起始于西边芦潮港，向东南经小洋山和大洋山，再向东北和向东到浙江省嵊泗列岛中的嵊泗县。东海大桥线向呈曲线，总长约31km，分成三段：陆上段约长2.3km，从海墙到大乌龟岛的海上段约25.5km，在大乌龟岛和小洋山的港桥连接段约3.5km。在早期设计规划中，主通航道采用140m+200m+200m+140m连续梁。

　　在全桥中设置一5 000t通航跨，其能力为5 000总载重吨位(DWT)，通航净高40m，净宽400m，桥墩按抗冲击能力设计为10 000t，还设置副通航道，其能力为1 000DWT，净高为25m，净宽为140m，并设置两DWT的副通航道，净高17.5m，净宽为120m和160m。跨越主航道，建造一座双塔斜拉桥，主跨420m，塔高150m（图2）[1]。

　　在大乌龟岛和颗珠山岛之间约1.66km段上，主桥为双塔双索面斜拉桥，主跨为332m，100m高H形塔（图3）[1]。

　　跨越副通航孔的诸桥为4跨变高度预应力混凝土连续箱梁，用悬挂脚手架现场浇筑混凝土。

　　在海中桥墩总数达814座，重1 800~2 000t，60~70m长预制箱梁超过333跨，50m长连续T形梁用移动模架一跨接一跨地现浇。

　　ϕ2 500嵌岩钻孔桩和ϕ1 500钢管桩用于桥塔。

　　在东海大桥中，建设很多组成工程，例如大面积（达5 000m²）海上平台、海港、港区建设、地基加固、围护路堤、护坡工程、隧道等。可见建设规模是很大的。

1. 跨越主航道的斜拉桥

　　主要技术标准——①设计按高速公路标准控制双向6车道；②设计车速：80km/h；③车辆荷载等级：设计按超20并按拖车120和重集装箱，一个在前面，另一个的轴距为10m分布；④地震烈度：基本地震烈度为6度，但对该桥按7度。重要因素为1.7；⑤通航标准：对5 000t通航跨，对主桥上的抗冲击按10 000t，对副桥墩抗冲击按1 000t，而对边墩按

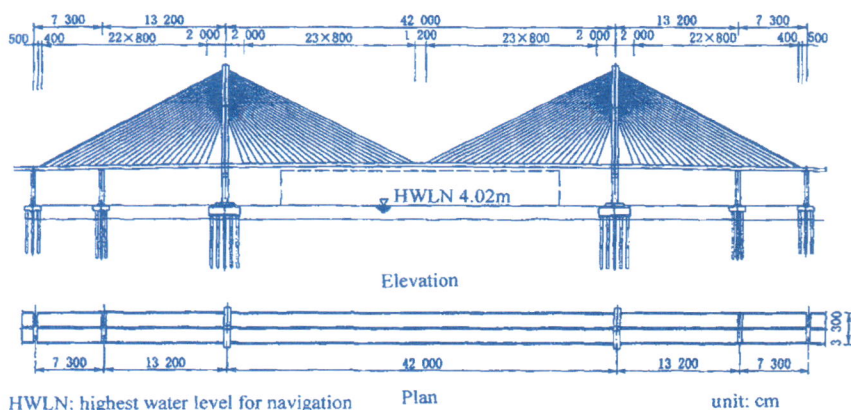

HWLN: highest water level for navigation　　　Plan　　　　　　　　unit: cm

Donghai Bridge over the Sea

Donghai Bridge(Fig.1)[1] is an important component part of the 1st phase of Yangshan (shan is Chinese pronunciation of mountain) Deep Water Port Project, for serving the Yangshan Deep Port Area on container collection and transportation, water supply power supply and communication etc. It starts in the west from Luchao Port towards southeast through Small- and Big-Yangshan, then towards northeast and towards east to Shengsi County in Shengsi Islands, Zhejiang Province. The alignment of Donghai Bridge appears curvilinear, with total length equal to 31km or so, dividing into 3 segments: the segment on land is about 2.3km, the segment over sea about 25.5km from sea wall to Big-Turtle Island and the port bridge connection segment about 3.5km between Big-Turtle Island and Small-Yangshan. In the earlier design project, for main navigable opening, a continuous girder with spans of 140m+200m+200m+140m was adopted.

In whole bridge, there are set a 5 000t main navigable span with capacity of 5 000 DWT, the navigable clear height is 40m and clear width 400m, the pier is designed to posses anti-impact capacity of 10 000t. Also an auxiliary navigable pass with capacity of 1 000DWT and clear height of 25m and clear width of 140m, and 2 auxiliary navigable spans of DWT are set, the clear height is 17.5m and the clear widths are 120m and 160m. Spanning the main navigable pass, a double-pylon cable-stayed bridge is constructed with main span of 420m and pylon height of 150m (Fig.2)[1].

The bridge structure on the segment about 1.66km between Big-Turtle Island and Kezhushan Island, the main bridge is cable-stayed one of double pylons and double cable-planes with main span of 332m and the height of H-shaped pylon of 100m (Fig.3)[1].

The bridges spanning auxiliary navigable passes are 4-span continuous PC box girders with variable depth, poured concrete in-site by using swinging scaffold.

Total number of piers in total in sea reaches 814, 60~70m long precast box-girder with weight of 1 800~2 000t over 333 spans, the 50m long continuous T-girder poured in-situ by using travelling model frame span by span.

ϕ2500 bored piles inserted into rock and ϕ1500 steel pipe piles are used for pylon.

In Donghai Bridge, there are constructed many component engineering, such as plateform over the sea with large area (reaching 5 000m^2), harbours, construction of port area, base strengthening, enclosing embankment and revetment engineering, tunnels, etc. It can see the construction scale is large.

1. Cable-Stayed Bridge Spanning Main Navigable Pass

Main technical standards — ① the design is controlled with two-way 6 lanes; following express highway standards; ② designed driving speed: 80km/h; ③ vehicle load grade: design following car-super 20 and check following tailer-120 and distributed heavy container cars with axis distance of 10m of a car after the other

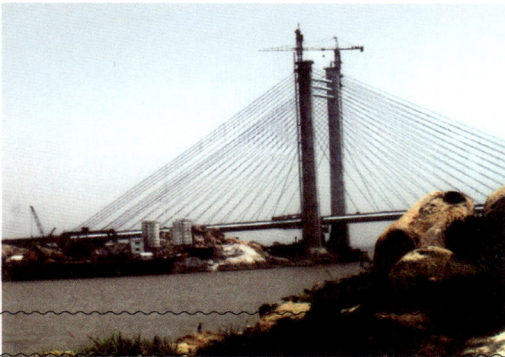

图2 主航道上斜拉桥
Fig.2 Cable-stayed bridge over main navigable pass

图3 主跨为332m的斜拉桥（承张健高工惠赠）
*Fig.3 Cable-stayed bridge with main span of 332m
(courtesy of Senior Engr. Zhang Jian)*

3

图1 东海大桥（承谢蔚鸿高工惠赠）
Fig.1 Donghai Bridge (courtesy of Senior Engr. Xie Weihong)

500t；⑥结构计算按50年一遇的水位和附加浪作用，50年一遇$H_1\%$，验算按100年一遇的水位和附加浪作用，100年一遇$H_1\%$；⑦风：设计风速按10m高度处、100年一遇的$v_{10}=42m/s$；⑧设计基准周期：100年。

2. 主通航跨度

对主通航道，通航安排在单跨内采用两向方案，净空不小于321m，考虑主墩基础和防冲击设施宽度的影响，主通航跨度不小于400m，最合适的桥的方案为斜拉桥；对这一方案，结合结构设计特点，例如主边跨合理比例和索的安排以及加劲梁的构造等，主通航决定采用420m。

3. 结构设计

（1）由于集装箱车辆是较重的，而结构体系的刚度将成为选择安排和边跨跨度的关键因素。根据研究，典型的主跨连续结构很难满足在集装箱车辆荷载作用下使用要求并且是不经济的，但采用5跨连续结构能满足要求和合理的受力。考虑力学性能和景观效应，最后跨度实施方案为73m+132m+420m+132m+73m，总长度为830m（参见图2）。

（2）支承体系：在主塔墩、辅助墩和边墩，全设置竖向和横向支承，在纵向，在主塔和加劲梁之间，采用液体阻尼器以约束加劲梁的纵向位移和改善驾车的舒适条件。在该桥中，为了解决边墩和副墩在自重和活荷载下的负反力，采用组合压重法（在加劲梁上设置铸铁块，从边墩分布到一定距离）以避免由自重引起的负反力，并采用体外预应力束（沿边墩钢绞线$4\times19\phi15$和沿辅助墩$4\times61\phi15$），以抵消由活荷载引起的负反力。

（3）加劲梁：加劲梁设计成3室单箱截面，高度4.0m和混凝土桥面宽33.0m，包括2悬臂板，各有4.5m宽，以及钢底板24.0m宽（图4）。采用混凝土C60和钢Q345qD。采用较大高度4.0m的理由是为了提供足够的刚度以抵抗扭转

4

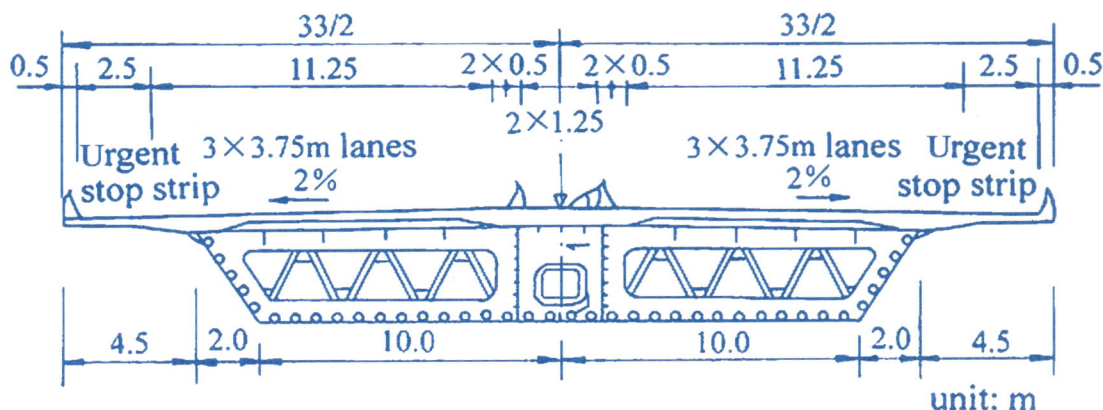

图4 主斜拉桥跨度分布
Fig.4 Span distribution of main cable-stayed bridge

front one; ④ seismic intensity: basic intensity is 6 degree, but the aseismic design for this bridge is conducted following 7 degree. The importance factor is 1.7; ⑤ navigable standard: for 5 000t navigable span, collision-proof to main pier following 10 000t; collision-proof to auxiliary pier following 1 000t and to edge pier following 500t; ⑥ structural calculation is conducted following the water level met once in 50 years and adding the wave action of $H_1\%$ met once in 50 years, checking following the water level met once in 100 year and adding the wave action of $H_1\%$ met once in 100 years; ⑦ wind: design wind velocity $v_{10}=42m/s$ at the height of 10m met once in 100 years; ⑧ design datum period: 100 years.

2. Span of main navigable pass

For main navigable pass, navigable arrangement adopts two-way project in single span with clearance not less than 321m, in consideration of the influences of foundation of main pier and the width of collision-proof facilities, the span of main navigable pass should not be less than 400m, the most suitable project of bridge is a cable-stayed one; for this project, combining structural design characteristics, such as the reasonable ratio of main and side spans and the arrangement of cable stays as well as the construction of stiffening girder, etc, the span of main navigable pass is decided to adopt 420m.

3. Structural design

(1) Owing to that the load of container car is heavier, the stiffness of structural system will become a key factor of selecting and arranging the span of side span. From study, the typical 3-span continuous structure is difficult to meet service requirements under the action of loads of container cars and is not economic, but to adopt 5-span continuous structure can meet the requirements and is reasonable to be stressed. Considering the mechanical behaviour and the landscape effect, finally the practical project of spans is 73m+132m+420m+132m+73m with total length of 830m (see Fig.2).

(2) Support system: At main pylon piers, auxiliary and edge piers, the vertical and transverse supports are all set, in the longitudinal direction between main pylons and stiffening girder, the hydraulic dampers are used to restrain the longitudinal displacement of stiffening girder and to improve the comfortable conditions of driving cars. In this bridge, for solving negative reaction at edge and auxiliary piers under the action of dead and live loads, combined method to adopt compressing weight (setting cast iron blocks on stiffening girder distributed from edge pier to a definite distance) for avoiding the negative reaction due to dead load and to use external prestress tendons (strands $4\times19\phi15$ along edge piers and $4\times61\phi15$ along auxiliary piers) for counteracting the negative reaction due to live load.

(3) Stiffening girder: Stiffening girder is designed into a 3-cell single box section with depth of 4.0m and the concrete deck width of 33.0m including 2 cantilever slabs, each possessing 4.5m wide and steel bottom plate of 24.0m wide (Fig.4). Concrete C60 and steel

而在中心索平面的斜拉桥中加劲梁满足抗风要求，同时使混凝土主梁深度与相邻非通航跨高墩区相匹配。

考虑诸多因素，采用8m作为标准段长度；对塔下No.0段总共采用8节5m长小段以减轻悬吊荷载，对2边跨，端段长度采用6.58m。在加劲梁中，除2×0.5m宽实施现浇混凝土端接头外，节段全截面是在预制厂制造的。在节段运至桥的现场和悬吊后，加劲梁的钢部件将被连接，而后混凝土桥面接头被浇灌。

加劲梁桥面一般厚28cm，靠近腹板顶部，加厚至55cm。底板及斜腹板钢结构截面一般厚16mm，竖向腹板和腹板顶翼缘厚24mm，靠近桥塔、辅助墩和边墩，加劲梁的钢板局部加厚。采用桁架形横隔是方便管线通过桥的安排。一般截面横隔厚度为16mm，截面顶部翼缘厚度为24mm。在钢结构和混凝土桥面之间，设置剪力钉以使它们相互作用。

在该桥抗风研究中，节段和整体模型试验曾分别进行过，结果表明在施工阶段和在成桥阶段，临界颤振风速当不采取气压措施时可达到80m/s，当采取一定的气压措施条件下，可超过100m/s。在该桥中，对加劲梁在斜腹下采取设置检修车轨道以保证施工和运营阶段抗风的稳定性。

（4）桥塔：桥塔为钢筋混凝土结构。桥塔上段采取倒Y形以适应中心索面安排，下段采用宽肩实体墩式，见图5，在承台上塔高150m，在桥面上高110m，桥塔中间柱为单室单箱截面，其余部分为双室单箱截面。纵向尺寸为8m，上柱横向7m，中间柱横向4.2m，下柱从37m逐渐变化到28m，桥塔用C50混凝土建造。

上塔柱中2/3斜拉索锚定于固接在桥塔的钢锚梁上，其余直接锚固于塔上。为了抵抗由斜拉索在塔中引起的拉力，或

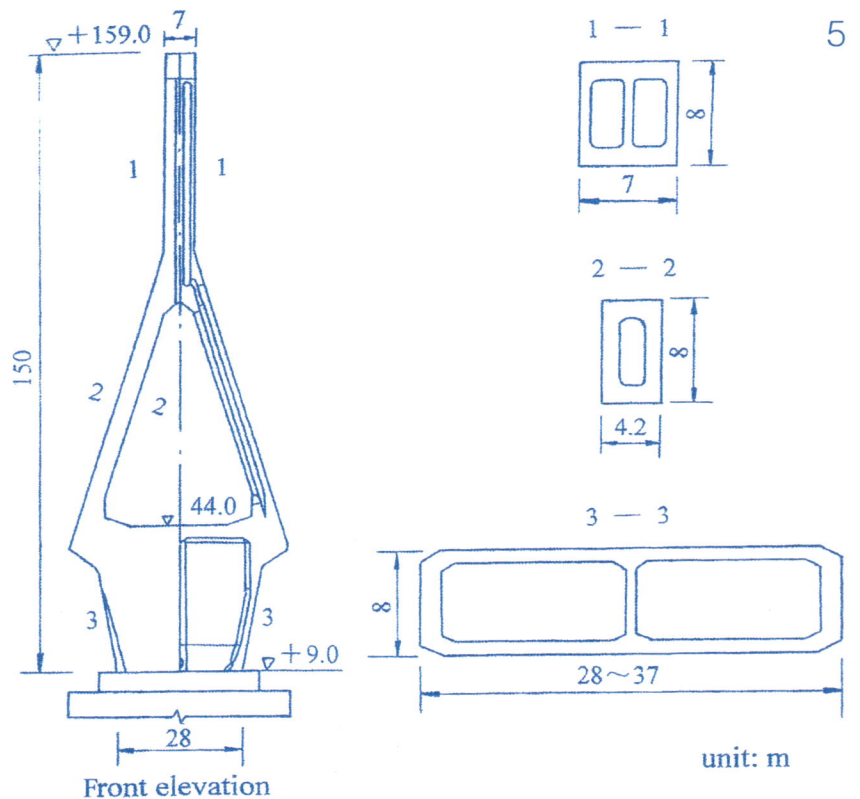

Front elevation

unit: m

Q345qD are used. The reason adopting greater depth of 4.0m is to provide sufficient stiffness against torsion to meet the requirements of wind-resistance of stiffening girder in cable-stayed bridge with central cable plane, at the same time to match with the depth of concrete main girders in the area of high piers of adjacent un-navigable spans.

Considering many factors, 8m is adopted as standard segment length; for No.0 segment under pylons, total 8 small segments of 5m long are adopted for decreasing hung load, for the 2 edge spans the end segments of 6.58m are used. In stiffening girder, except that 2×0.5m wide cast-in-situ concrete end joints preformed, overall section of segments were manufactured in the factory for prefabrication. After the segments were transported to bridge situ and hung, the steel components of stiffening girder would be spliced then the joints in concrete deck would be poured.

The deck of stiffening girder is generally 28cm thick, near the tops of web it is thickened to 55cm. The thickness sections of steel structure of bottom and inclined webs is generally 16mm, that of vertical webs and the top flanges of web is 24mm, near pylons, auxiliary and edge piers, the steel plate of stiffening girder is locally thickened. The truss type of diaphragm is adopted for the convenience of arrangement of pipe lines through bridge. The thickness of diaphragms at general sections of stiffening girder is 16mm, and that of their top flange is 24mm. Between the steel structure and concrete deck, there are set shearing nails so as to result in interaction of them.

In the wind-resistance study of this bridge, experiments of segment and integral model have been conducted respectively, the results show in construction stage and completed bridge stage, the fluttering critical wind velocity can reach 80m/s under the condition without adopting pneumatic measure and it can reach more than 100m/s under the condition to adopt definite pneumatic measure. In this bridge, it is to adopt the pneumatic measure to set the track of overhauling car for stiffening girder below the inclined web of the girder so as to guarantee the stability of wind resistance in the stages of construction and operation.

(4) Pylon: The pylons are reinforced concrete structures. The upper segment of pylons adopts inverted Y-shape type to suit the arrangement of central cable plane, the lower segment uses the pier type of solid-web wide shoulder, see Fig.5. The pylon is 150m high on pedestal and 110m over bridge deck. The mid column of pylon has single-cell and single-box section, the others possess double-cell and single box sections. The longitudinal dimension is 8m, the transverse 7m in upper column and 4.2m in mid columns, the lower columns are 37m gradually changing downwards to 28m. Pylon is constructed of concrete C50.

2/3 stays in upper pylon column are anchored on steel anchorage beam rigidly connected to pylon and the others are directly anchored on pylon. For counteracting the tension to produce in pylon due to stays or the horizontal component of unequalizing force in stays in edge span and central span, in overall pylon columns there are set

图5 加劲梁截面示意图
Fig.5 Section sketch of stiffening girder

在边跨中间跨索中不平衡力的水平分量，在全塔柱中设置环向预应力筋。

（5）斜拉索：对斜拉索，中心扇形平行索面在横桥向，在两索间采取2m间距，在塔的每个索面，有24对斜拉索，在梁上间距为8.0m，在塔上间距为2.2m，在全桥中，总共有192根斜拉索。ϕ7镀锌平行钢丝用作斜拉索，斜拉索9个规格，最小规格为121ϕ7mm，最大为283ϕ7mm。

（6）下部结构：对塔墩和辅助墩，采用钻孔桩基础，在每座塔墩下，设置38ϕ2.5m桩，长度110m；在辅助墩下，设置14ϕ2.5m钻孔桩，长度85m。为了增强桩底的承载力，在桩底设置砂浆圆板，在浇筑桩内混凝土后，通过探测管压注砂浆到桩底。对边墩，采用钢管桩基础，在每座墩，设置22ϕ1.5m管桩，长度60m。

对边墩和辅助墩，采用空心墩，在靠近桩帽处，设置混凝土锚梁以锚固受拉钢绞线索以抵抗向上的力，而在墩的下面部分设置部分预应力粗钢筋以延伸到桩帽内予以锚固。

除在沿桥轴向塔墩和辅助墩旁边，设置固定的防冲击体系以抵抗船舶的冲击。在桩帽桥轴旁，设置分离式防冲击墩，当塔墩和辅助墩承受较大船舶冲击时，防冲击设施的破坏将消耗能量以降低向桥墩的冲击力和减轻船舶的破坏，同时避免船舶前伸部分触及上部墩的结构和保护桩基础。

辅助通航斜拉桥的跨度实施方案为50m+139m+332m+139m+50m。

东海大桥工程开始于2002年6月26日正式建造，在2005年末，仅两年半时间即已完成。它的建成是中国建桥史上新的里程碑。

annular prestressed steel.

(5) Stayed cables: For stayed cables, a central fan-shaped parallel cable plane with spacing of 2m between these 2 planes transverse to bridge direction is adopted, in each cable plane of pylon, there are 24 pairs of stayed cables with spacing of 8.0m on girder and spacing of 2.2m on pylon, a total of 192 stayed cables in whole bridge. Galvanized parallel steel wires of $\phi 7$ are used as stayed cables, there are 9 standards of stayed cables, the min. standard is $121\phi 7$mm and the max. $283\phi 7$mm.

(6) Substructures: For pylon pier and auxiliary pier, the foundations of bored piles are adopted, under each of pylon pier, there are set $38\phi 2.5$m piles with length of 110m; under auxiliary piers, there are set $14\phi 2.5$m bored piles with length of 85m. For enhancing the load bearing capacity of pile bottom, under which there are set mortar disk, after casting concrete into pile, then injecting mortar to pile bottom is conducted through detecting pipe. For edge pier, the foundation of steel-pipe piles is adopted, under each pier, there are set $22\phi 1.5$m pipe pile with length of 60m.

For edge and auxiliary piers, hollow piers are adopted, near pile caps, there are set concrete anchorage beams for anchoring tension strand cables to counteract the uplift force, and in lower part of pier there are set partial prestressed thicker bars to extend into pile cap for anchoraging.

Beside pylon piers and auxiliary piers along bridge axis, there are set fixed collision-proof system to resist the collision force due to ship. Beside cap axis, there is set separate collision-proof piers, when pylon piers and auxiliary piers bear the collision due to bigger ship, the failure of collision-proof facilities will consume energy so as to reduce the collision force to piers and decrease the failure of ship, at the same time to avoid the front extending part of ship to touch the superstructure of piers and to protect pile foundation.

The practical project of the span of auxiliary navigable cable-stayed bridge is 50m+139m+332m+139m+50m.

Donghai Bridge engineering started to construct formally on 26th June, 2002, at the end of 2005, only for 2.5 years, has been finished. Its completion becomes a new milestone in Chinese history of bridge construction.

REFERENCES

1.Xie Weihong, Ding Dajun. Donghai Bridge —
The 1st worldwide longest bridge over sea will be
completed in China. Travaux International. n°829.
Apr, 2006: 77-81

杭州湾跨海大桥

杭州湾跨海大桥（图1a，b）北起浙江嘉兴市海盐郑家埭，跨越广阔的杭州湾海域后止于浙江宁波市慈溪水路湾，全长36km，其中大桥长35.673km，连续梁达33km，它已于2007年6月建成，于2008年3月8日提供游览一日，并于2008年5月通车，桥长超过2005年建成的长31km的东海大桥，而成为新的世界纪录。

杭州湾大桥的建成可以更充分地发挥上海的经济辐射和聚集功能，促进上海浦东的开发，进一步加强上海在长江三角洲的"龙头"地位，带动和促进浙江、江苏的经济快速持续发展。

大桥设有南北两个通航孔道，采用斜拉桥，跨越北通航孔为一座双塔双索面桥，全长908m，主跨448m，两侧跨每侧为70m和160m，钻石形钢筋混凝土桥塔在桥面上高130m，桥面由钢箱梁构成。南通航孔为A形独塔斜拉桥，单索面，主跨318m，背跨76m和160m（图2a，b）。

采用30~80m预应力混凝土连续箱梁桥作为其余非通航跨。统计表明混凝土总用量达2.45×10⁶m³，用钢量8×10⁵t预制50m箱梁404段、70m箱梁552段，630座桥墩和总的桩基础具有桩8 544根，其中3 400根钻孔桩、5 144根钢管桩。

杭州湾大桥的建成不仅能发展海上交通，而且能发展旅游。图3示高10 000m²观景平台，用作施工期间在36km跨度中道的基地。该平台不仅作为旅游者目的地，也可作为加油地和船只停靠点。

连接两座斜拉桥为一中心连续梁桥，向着南北引桥，包含多座60m跨桥。大桥总的形状在平面内为S形，不仅为了美学，也防止由于驾驶员长距离在直线中行驶发生意外。这种形状也保证桥结构垂直于大潮和低潮流方向，降低它们对大桥的冲击。

Hangzhou Bay Bridge over the Sea

Hangzhou Bay Bridge over the sea (Fig.1 a,b) starts from Haiyan Zhengjiadai, Jiaxing City in the north, Zhejiang Province, to span the vast see area of Hangzhou Bay, then ends at Cixi Shuiluwan of Ningbo City in the south, Zhejiang Province, with total length of 36km, among which, the bridge length is 35.673km, continuous bridges 33km. This bridge had been completed in June, 2007, it was opened to accept tourists to go sight-seeing on Mar.8, 2008, and has been formally opened in May 2008. It exceeds the length 31km of Donghai Bridge over the sea completed in 2005 and becomes new worldwide record.

The completion of Hangzhou Bay Bridge can develop fully the function of radiation and collection of Shanghai economics, promote the development of Shanghai Pudong strength further the leading position of Shanghai in Yangtze River delta, bring along the promote the fast and sustained developments of economics in Zhejiang Province and Jiangsu Province.

Along this Bridge, there are set navigable pass in the north and in the south. A cable-stayed bridge of double pylons and double cable planes is adopted to span the north pass with total length of 908m and the main span of 448m, each side span of 70m and 160m, diamond-shaped RC pylon with height of 130m over deck which is constituted of steel box girder. A cable-stayed bridge of A-shaped single pylon and single cable plane is adopted to span the south pass with main span of 318m and back span of 76m and 160m(Fig.2 a,b).

30~80m PC continuous box girder bridges are adopted as the other non-navigable spans. Statistics shows that the total consumption of concrete reached $2.45 \times 10^6 m^3$, that of steel $8 \times 10^5 t$ prefabricated 50m box girders 404 pieces, 70m box girders 552 pieces, 630 piers and total pile foundations with piles 8 544, among which there are 3 400 boring piles, 5 144 steel tube piles.

The completion of Hangzhou Bay Bridge can not only be able to develop the communication over the sea, but also can develop the tourism. Fig.3 shows go-seeing platform of $10\,000m^2$, used as a base during construction located midway along the 36km crossing. This platform acts not only a tourist destination, but also a refueling area as well as docking point of boats.

Connecting the two cable-stayed bridges is a central continuous beam bridge, which along with the northern and southern approaches, comprises 60m spans. The overall form of the bridge is S-shaped in plan, not only for aesthetic reasons but to help prevent accidents caused by motorists driving in a straight line for long distances. This shape also ensures that the bridge structure is perpendicular to the direction of spring and neap tidal currents, decreasing their impact on the bridge.

In elevation, the profile of the bridge rises towards the cable-stayed sections, resembling a swimming dragon. The central viaduct and southern approach over water will be built in deep water areas

1b

图1 杭州湾大桥（承支世平高工惠赠）(a)，(b)
Fig.1 Hangzhou Bay Bridge (courtesy of Senior Engr. Zhi Shiping) (a), (b)

图2 杭州湾大桥南通航孔上的斜拉桥（承支世平高工惠赠）(a)
Fig.2 Cable-stay bridge on south navigable pass of Hangzhou
Bay Bridge (courtesy of Senior Engr. Zhi Shiping) (a)

在立面中，桥朝向斜拉截面抬高，宛若一条游龙。水上中心高架桥和南引桥建在海湾深水域 —— 总延伸约16km。这些截面将建造在超过4 000根钢桩上，典型桩长超过70m。

沿6车道的桥长每1km定位1台监控设备以核对台风情况，或按需要自动关闭交通车道。在中国，杭州湾大桥被描写成"数字桥"。

北通航道斜拉桥在桥塔处并未纵向约束，在辅助墩处也未横向约束。对由温度变化引起内力提出分析，最好的解决是将桥塔及过渡墩横向一边约束。

SAP 2 000非线性有限元软件用于进行对结构的时程分析，采用带空间框架元模型和将桥面、桥塔和桥墩模拟作框架单元。垂直刚度、横向刚度、抗扭刚度、移动质量、旋转质量将积集在中心接点和桥面及索之间连以刚臂。斜拉索模拟为桁架单元，索的刚度考虑由自重的下垂高度应和几何刚度的冲击而折减。土与结构相互作用也予考虑，这用地面地震加速度在百年一遇中超过3%的概率来设计。用以设计的水平地震加速度的峰值为100gal，而竖向为95gal。考虑两个方向，首先纵向输入加一半竖向输入，其次是横向输入加一半竖向输入。因为北通航跨是用钢、桥塔用混凝土建造，在实践中桥的阻尼比可能是混凝土结构和钢结构间某值，因此为了计算取3%。

分析指出，在纵向地震作用下地震内力在上部塔腿底部为最大。这可能是控制设计的标准，但同时桥塔和桥面的纵向位移也是大的：在横向地震下，过渡墩的内力和风支承和桥塔一边内力明显较大。因此主要结构设计目的之一是为减小这些截面内力和位移。

在桥塔处无纵向约束，黏性阻尼器可安装在板面靠近桥塔并和塔连接，这将显著地减小纵向地震作用下的位移和由桥面与桥塔承受的力，也使在强震区对桥需要的膨胀缝尺寸变成最小。

2b

of the bay — a total stretch of nearly 16km. These sections will be founded on more than 4 000 steel piles, typically more than 70m in length.

Monitoring equipment will be located every 1km along the bridge, which will cany six lanes of traffic, to check for typhoon conditions or automatically close traffic lanes as required. In China, it is being described as a digital bridge.

The cable-stay bridge over north navigable pass is not restrained longitudinally at the pylons, and not in the transverse direction at the auxiliary piers. As analysis of the internal forces arising from temperature change suggested that the best solution would be for the pylons and the transition piers to be restrained on one side in the transverse direction.

SAP 2 000 non-linear finite element software was used to carry out the time-history analysis for this structure, with a spatial frame element model being adopted and the deck, pylons and piers being simulated as frame units. The vertical stiffness, transverse stiffness, torsional stiffness and the translation mass, rotation mass were focused on the centre of joints and the joints between the deck and the cables were connected together with rigid arms. The stayed cable were simulated as truss units, and the stiffness of cables was discounted to take account of the effect of sag and the impact of geometric rigidity caused by dead load. Soil-structure interaction was also considered. It was designed by using the seismic acceleration of ground surface with a 3% probability of exceedance in a period of 100 years. The peak value of horizontal seismic acceleration for which it was designed was 100gal and the vertical was 95gal. Two seismic directions were considered, the first being the longitudinal input plus half the vertical input; the second being transverse input plus half the vertical input. Because the deck of the north navigable span is made of steel and the pylons are made of concrete, the damping ratio of the bridge is likely in practice to be somewhere between that of a concrete structure and that of a steel structure; hence it has been set at 3% for the calculations.

Analysis indicated that the internal seismic force under longitudinal seismic action is largest at the base of the upper pylon leg. This may be the dominating criteria for the design, but at the same time, the longitudinal displacement of the pylon and deck are also large; under transverse seismic action, the internal forces of transition piers on the side with wind bearing and pylons are both significantly large. Therefore, one of our main structure design goals is to reduce these internal sectional forces and displacements.

Why no longitudinal restraint at the pylon, viscous dampers can be installed on the deck near the pylon and connected to it. This will drastically reduce the displacements and the forces suffered by the deck and pylons under longitudinal seismic action and also minimizes the size of expansion joints required for bridges in highly seismic regions.

If the cable-stayed bridge is very large or the seismic intensity is very high, the size of viscous dampers needs to be correspondingly

图2 南通航孔上的斜拉桥（承支世平高工惠赠）(b)
Fig.2 Cable-stay bridge on south navigable pass (courtesy of Senior Engr. Zhi Shiping) (b)

如果斜拉桥很大或地震烈度很高，黏性阻尼器规格需相应地大。但仅在桥面与桥塔之间安装黏性阻尼器也可安装在辅助墩和过渡墩上。

对北水道桥的支承体系包括两对纵向黏性阻尼器，共4对，安装在桥面靠近桥塔并和它对称连接。优化设计结果，桥墩纵向内力和位移显著减小，最后是内力低于风和温度变化引起的。在这种情况下由地震作用引起的内力和位移不再是控制因素，纵向黏性阻尼器所需的阻尼力不仅为1 100kN，节点设计是不困难的。因此不需要在辅助墩和过渡墩上同时安装黏性阻尼器。

对斜拉桥减振横向结构体系正常地包括在过渡墩上和在选择的辅助墩上的减振装置。如果横向阻尼器安装在辅助墩上，桥面横向水平地震力可转移到桥塔和桥墩。因此过渡墩和桥塔中的力将减小，以及在不同部件之间将较均匀分布，因而结构的整体抗震能力将增大，而所有部件承载力可适当发挥。

如果减振设置的参数合理设计，辅助墩上的力还可减小。因此如果结构承载力还可支承附加荷载，常规横向约束可不设置在辅助墩上，而减振装置不仅作为横向约束作用，而且还不增加结构刚度，在北水道跨，一座墩是自由的，另一座是约束的以抵抗风力。

有两种方法设置黏性阻尼器：如果风支承设计在任何状态下不失效，横向黏性阻尼器仅在过渡墩向内边上设置。但是，如果横向约束按在预定地震烈度下剪力设计，减振装置应安装在过渡墩两边。

对杭州湾大桥，提出建议的方案，即在斜拉桥中黏性阻尼器设置在纵向及横向时，如果阻尼器设计成合理构造，则粘性阻尼器可独立工作。

在减振分析中，结构振动优化分析可借调整阻尼系数和速度指数进行，以达到较好结果。虽然北边桥为纵向对称结

3

larger. But the installation of viscous dampers between deck and pylon only, may lead to more difficult design for some local structural parts. Hence longitudinal viscous dampers may also be installed on the auxiliary piers and the transition piers.

The longitudinal support system for the north channel bridge consists of two pairs of longitudinal viscous dampers, a total of four, installed on the deck near the pylon and connected to it symmetrically. This optimum design results is the longitudinal internal forces and displacements of the pylons being drastically reduced, with the end result that the internal forces are lower than those caused by wind and temperature change. In this case the internal forces and displacements caused by seismic action are no longer the controlling factor, the damping force required for the longitudinal viscous damper is only 1 100kN, and nodal design is not difficult. Therefore there is no need for viscous dampers to be installed on auxiliary piers and on transition piers at the same time.

The transverse structural system of vibration reduction for cable-stayed bridges normally consists of vibration reduction devices on transition piers and on selected auxiliary piers. If transverse viscous dampers are installed on the auxiliary piers, the transverse horizontal seismic forces of the deck can be transferred to the pylon and piers. As a result, the forces in the transition piers and pylons will be reduced, and will be more evenly distributed between the different components, hence the integral seismic capacity of the structure will be increased, and the bearing capacity of all components can be developed adequately.

If the parameters of vibration reduction devices are designed rationally, the forces on the auxiliary piers may also be reduced. Therefore, if the bearing capacity of the structure can also support additional loadings, conventional transverse restraint may not be set on auxiliary pier, and vibration reduction devices not only act as transverse restraint but also do not increase the stiffness of structure. On the north channel span one pier is free and the other is restrained to resist wind forces.

There are two methods to set viscous dampers: if the wind bearing is designed not to fail in any way, transverse viscous dampers are installed only on the free side of the transition pier. However, if the transverse restraint is designed to shear under the predicted seismic intensity, the vibration reduction devices should be installed on both sides of transition pier.

For the Hangzhou Bay Bridge, the proposed scheme suggests the viscous dampers that are set both longitudinally and transversely in a cable-stayed bridge can work independently, if a reasonable construction of dampers is designed.

During the analysis of vibration reduction, the optimal analysis of the vibration of the structure can be conducted by adjusting the damping coefficient and velocity index so as to achieve a better result. Though the northern bridge is a longitudinally-symmetrical structure, the level of the continental shelf varies, hence the seismic responses also vary. Internal forces in the pylons and transition piers on the symmetrical position have larger spatial difference; this part of

图3 杭州湾大桥海上观光平台（承支世平高工惠赠）
Fig.3 Sight-seeing platform on the sea along Hangzhou Bay Bridge (courtesy of Senior Engr. Zhi Shiping)

构，大陆架标高是变化的，因此地震反应也是变化的。桥塔和过渡墩对称位置处的内力有着较大的空间差：北桥部分也是横向对称的，但为了限制主梁在膨胀缝处的侧向位移，并防止剪切破坏，一项横向风支承设置在过渡墩一边，而另一边使自由。这时过渡墩对称位置的内力差别将较大。北边跨特征意味着当分析减振时，聚焦在使相同形式组分截面以使其内力尽可能地小和均匀分布，优化黏性阻尼器系数以充分发挥组成承载力，同时减小所需阻尼力至最小。因为一个减振的合理结构体系被利用和一项科学优化被设定在北边跨，一个有效减振方案可以获得。

选择黏性阻尼器的速度愈快，吸收能量愈多，而获得的减振愈有效。但在本方案中，横向风支承设置在桥塔和过渡墩的一边，以保证在正常条件下膨胀缝的安全。因此在主梁和另一边横向墩以及主梁和辅助墩之间速度差异为最小。速度微小差别将制约横向黏性阻尼器减振效率。北通航跨纵向速度较大，因此减振效率将较横向为好。

视斜拉桥结构体系，减振体系可以在纵向或者横向以及同时在两向择一工作。

对采用纵向漂浮体系的斜拉桥，纵向减振设置应安装在桥面上，靠近和连接于桥塔。这样将能显著降低在纵向地震力下梁的内力和位移。斜拉桥横向减振体系一般由在过渡墩上和北边辅助墩减振设置组成。分析指出，随着减振，主要构件连接内力显著减低，构件内力变成较均匀，这会改进结构抵抗地震力的能力而充分发挥构件的承载力。

减振设计的主要目的是为了控制构件内力，降低它们和使它们均匀分布，或减小节点位移。工程师应保证单元阻尼力足够低而有效。

对该大桥曾进行过耐久性设计。此外还正在进行桥的健康监测，东南大学土木工程学院也参加了这一工作。

the north bridge is also symmetric transversely, but in order to limit the main girder's lateral displacement at the expansion joint and prevent its shearing failure, a transverse wind bearing is set on one side of the transition piers, with the other side being left free. At this time, the difference of internal forces in two transition piers on symmetric position will be larger. This characteristic of the northern span means that when the analysis of vibration reduction is undertaken, it focuses on making the component sections of the same type in order to make the internal forces as small as evenly-distributed as possible, to optimize the coefficients of the viscous dampers in order to fully develop the bearing capacity of components and at the same time to minimize the required damping force. Because a reasonable structural system of vibration reduction is employed and a scientific optimal goal is set, an effective vibration reduction scheme can be obtained on the northern span.

The faster the speed selected for the viscous damper, the more energy will be absorbed, and the more effective the vibration reduction that is obtained. In this project however, transverse wind bearings are set on one side of the pylon and the transition pier to ensure the safety of the expansion joint under normal conditions. Therefore the difference of speed between the main girder and the transverse pier on the other side, as well as the main girder and auxiliary pier is minimal. This slight difference of speed will restrict the effect of the vibration reduction of the transverse viscous dampers. The longitudinal speed of the north navigable span is larger, so the effect of longitudinal vibration reduction will be better than that of the transverse.

Depending on the structural system of cable-stayed bridge, vibration reduction systems can work either longitudinally or transversely, as well as in both directions at the same time.

For cable-stayed bridges adopting the longitudinal floating system, longitudinal vibration reduction devices should be installed on the deck, near to, and connected to, the pylon. This can significantly decrease the internal forces and displacements in the girder and pylon under longitudinal seismic forces. The transverse vibration reduction system of the cable-stayed bridge is generally composed of vibration reduction devices on transition piers and on partial auxiliary piers. Analysis indicates that with vibration reduction the controlling forces of the main members decrease significantly, and the internal forces in all members will become more even which improves the ability of the structure to resist seismic forces, an develops fully the carrying capacities of all members.

The main purpose of vibration reduction design is to control the internal forces of the members, reducing them and making them more evenly distributed, or reducing the displacement of joints. Engineers should ensure that the damping force of the units is low enough to be effective.

For this bridge, the durable design was carried out. Besides, a health monitoring is being also conducted. The Civil Engineering college of Southeast University takes part in this task.

参考文献

2.方明山. 杭州湾跨海大桥工程新型实用施工技术研发与运用. 第十七届全国桥梁学术会议论文集（上册）. 重庆，2006：411-420

REFERENCES

1.Ding Dajun. Construction starts on China's 'bay bridge'. Bd&e. 3ʳᵈ Quarter, 2004: 10

2.Fang Mingshan. Research and development of New-Type practical technique of construction of Hangzhou Bay Bridge. Proceedings of the 17ᵗʰ National Symposium on Bridge, the 1ˢᵗ vol. of 2. Chongqing, 2006: 411-420

3.Xiuli Xu, et al 5 persons. A matter of restraint, the risk of seismie activity in one of China's major bay areas has affected the design of the major crossing being built. Bd&e, 1ˢᵗ Quarter, 2005: 28-29

图书在版编目（C I P）数据

中国桥梁建设新进展：1991~：汉英对照 / 丁大钧编著.
一南京：东南大学出版社，2009.10
ISBN 978-7-5641-1817-4

Ⅰ.中… Ⅱ.丁… Ⅲ.桥梁工程—中国—汉、英 Ⅳ.U44

中国版本图书馆CIP数据核字（2009）第151483号

中国桥梁建设新进展（1991— ）（中英文双解）

编　　著：丁大钧
出版发行：东南大学出版社
社　　址：南京四牌楼 2 号 邮编：210096
出 版 人：江汉
网　　址：http://press.seu.edu.cn
电子邮箱：press@seu.edu.cn
责任编辑：丁丁
责任印制：张文礼
书籍设计：瀚清堂 · 赵清 + 周伟伟

经销：全国各地新华书店经销
印刷：恒美印务（广州）有限公司
开本：789mm × 1092mm　1/16
印张：21
字数：670千字
版次：2009年10月第1版
印次：2009年10月第 1 次印刷
书号：ISBN 978-7-5641-1817-4
定价：298.00元

本社图书若有印装质量问题，请直接与读者服务部联系。
电话（传真）：025-83792328

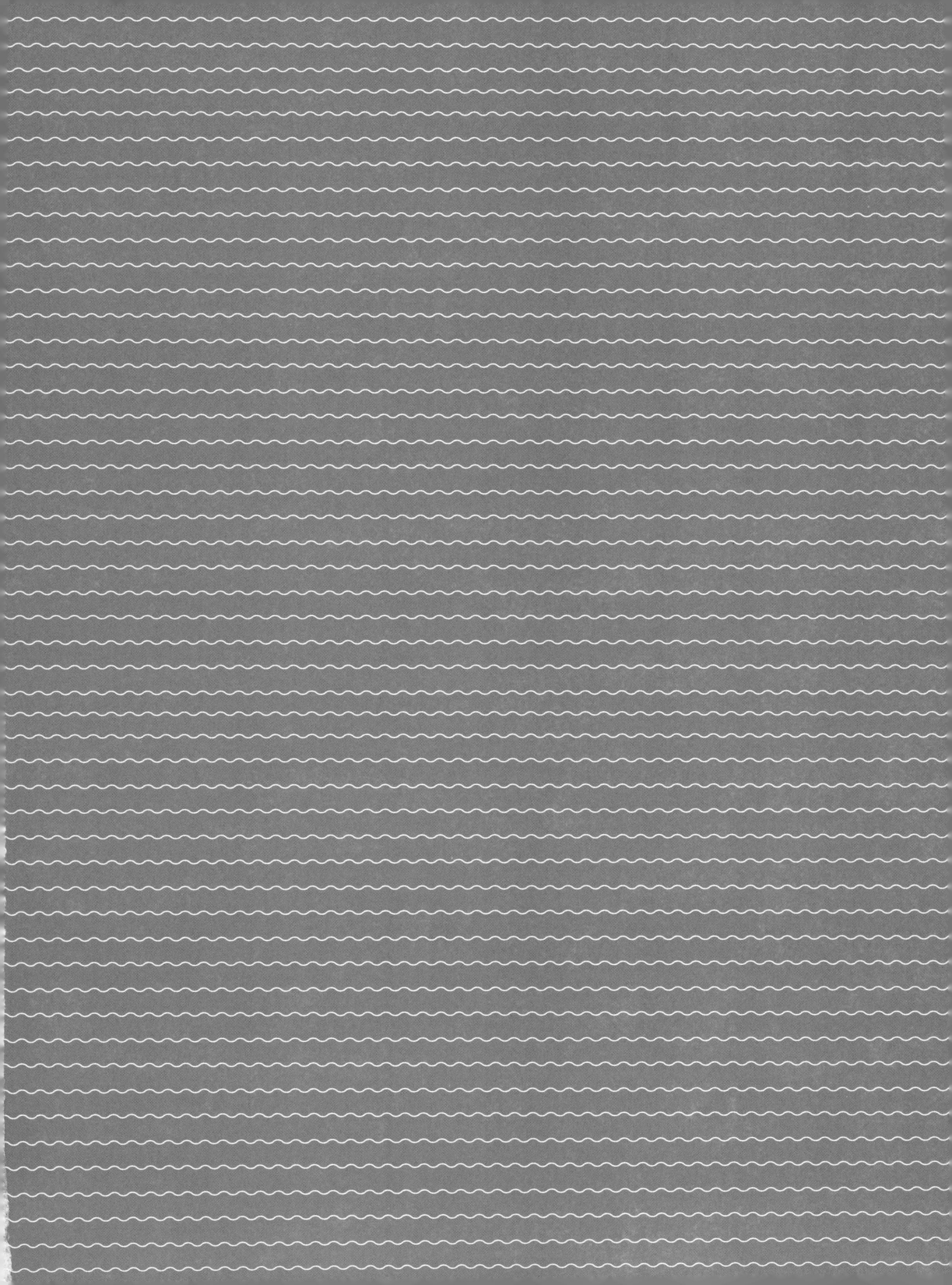